Sustainable Fashion: *Why Now?*

Sustainable Fashion

Why Now?

A conversation about issues, practices, and possibilities

Janet Hethorn
UNIVERSITY OF DELAWARE

Connie Ulasewicz
SAN FRANCISCO STATE UNIVERSITY

FAIRCHILD BOOKS, INC.
NEW YORK

Director of Sales and Acquisitions: Dana Meltzer-Berkowitz

Executive Editor: Olga T. Kontzias

Acquisitions Editor: Jacqueline Bergeron

Senior Development Editor: Jennifer Crane

Development Editor: Rob Phelps

Art Director: Adam B. Bohannon

Production Manager: Ginger Hillman

Senior Production Editor: Elizabeth Marotta

Photo Researcher: Erin Fitzsimmons

Copyeditor: Joanne Slike

Cover and text design: Adam B. Bohannon

Page composition and typography: Susan Ramundo

Library of Congress Catalog Card Number: 2007932769

ISBN: 978-1-56367-534-8

GST R 133004424

Printed in the United States of America

TP09

CONTENTS

FOREWORD

Known for his unconventional wisdom and gutsy yet visionary business strate-
gies, environmentalist and entrepreneur Yvon Chouinard is the founder and
owner of the 35-year-young, California-based technical outdoor apparel and
gear company Patagonia, Inc.

A few years ago at Patagonia we banned the use of the word "sustainable." It's a soft ban, so I'm sure you'll see the word every once in a while on our Web site or in a catalog or press release. But not too often. Once we switched from virgin to recycled polyester (about 15 years ago) and from chemically grown to organic cotton (about a dozen years ago) and set about becoming a more sustainable business, we began to realize what a high bar we had set for ourselves.

To be sustainable means that you take out of a system the same amount of energy as you put in, with no pollution or waste. A sustainable process is one you can do forever without exhausting resources or fouling the environment, which is scary. There has never yet been, nor is there now, a sustainable business or a sustainable fashion on this planet. And no one should ever pretend—in setting out for a place— that you've actually gotten there.

I don't mean to discourage the reader of this book who wants to create something like sustainable fashion or work toward it. We all need to do everything we possibly can to reduce the harm we do to the environment in our work lives as well as in our personal lives. It's even more important at work because the decisions we make play out on an industrial scale.

Friends sometimes ask me why I haven't sold out and retired with my surfboard and fly rod to the South Pacific. The answer is the challenge that our current mess presents. What keeps me in business is the opportunity to change the way business can be done, to reduce environmental harm, and inspire other business people to do the same.

Whether you're fresh out of school or have been at the trade for a while, whether you're a CAD designer, a salesperson, a colorist, or a CEO, what you learn in this book can help change the way you do your work. To figure out how to harm the planet less makes our lives—as well as our work—more interesting and satisfying. Read this book and be inspired. And bring your inspiration to work.

—YVON CHOUINARD
Founder and Owner, Patagonia, Inc.

PREFACE

Our Invitation to You
to Join the Conversation Now

As you prepare for, or engage in, some aspect of the fashion industry, do you consider how your actions impact fashion's ecological footprint? Do you think about how fashion can hinder or enhance people's sense of self and their relationships with others? Have you pondered innovative processes and alternative materials that might lend improvements, and are you reluctant to resign yourself to fashion's status quo of unsustainable ways?

If you answered yes to these questions, then you are concerned about fashion and sustainability and this book is for you. Within these pages, a conversation begins that needs to happen now. The ideas behind it started through conversation. We then invited many writers to join us, and we now invite you to participate.

Addressed within this book are the issues and consequences that consumers, marketers, designers, and product developers engage in as they move toward sustainability. It features an exploration of systems that facilitate the least burden on the environment with the most benefit to people. Yes, this is complex and involves all aspects of the fashion industry. To begin the conversation, we have chosen to primarily focus on issues and practices of concern within design and product development processes. Anyone involved in any dimension of fashion will benefit from reading, discussing, and putting these ideas into action. The time is now for taking action toward sustainability through fashion. Join in the conversation and together we will take action.

The format of this book is an anthology, divided into three sections, each focused on an in-depth exploration of sustainable opportunities that we have identified as people, processes, and environment. This innovative model is explained in the introduction and then expanded upon throughout the book. Our model provides an interconnected and circular way to explore these issues that is not possible through old linear models of understanding the fashion industry. A new and different approach is needed now.

We begin each section by introducing the overall concepts, issues, and practices that arise within each section's five chapters. Each chapter stands alone, yet together they form the conversation. They may be read in any order. You may come back to some often and skip over others, depending on your current concerns and interests. Included at the end of each section is an interview with a business or individual actively engaged in sustainable practices in order to show application of the issues raised within that section. Throughout your reading, please formulate your own challenges and responses to the question "Why now?"

We have invited fashion academics and practitioners, each with their own unique knowledge and expertise, to write the chapters that contribute to this dialogue. These contributing writers provide many diverse voices and writing styles, making for lively conversation. The writing is in varying levels of depth and perspectives. And, as with any important conversation, there are conflicts and agreements. Because of the variety in both content and viewpoint, this book is appropriate for graduate and undergraduate students, as well as for people working to bring about change within the fashion industry. It is also important reading for consumers of fashion. We are all in this together. So, thank you for picking up this book. Welcome to the conversation.

INTRODUCTION

"Eco chic," "environmentally conscious," "ethical consumerism," and "clothing with a conscience." Terms such as these abound. But what do they mean for the people who design and develop clothing? What do they mean for the people who buy and wear clothing? Most want to wear clothes that are made in "responsible" ways and that do not harm the planet, but how do we factor this in along with other considerations as we shop for and put together what we wear each day?

Is it okay to use the word "sustainable" alongside the word "fashion"? Most would agree that sustainable fashion is somewhat of an oxymoron. After all, sustainability is about longevity, and fashion is about change. Other areas of design activity are quite comfortable with sustainability, yet "sustainable" is a concept not fully embraced by fashion. How do we resolve this? How do we design, develop, and wear fashion in sustainable ways and still participate with fashion as we know it?

Green design, an approach familiar in many design endeavors, is a contemporary beacon for designers of products, interiors, and architecture. But when green design is discussed in terms of clothing, some may hold the narrow assumption that the focus is on outdated designs for aging hippies. What does it mean to be "green" in the fashion world where there is a desire for a much wider color choice and the name of the game is change and staying ahead of the next great thing?

Generally, "sustainable" is thought of as having to do with environmental concerns. Unique to this book, we expand the definition, and thus emerges the opportunity to make broad sustainable impact through fashion. We explore "green," but in addition to environmental concerns, we also embrace the wide-ranging complexities of sustainability that fashion can address. By asking the question "sustaining what?" within the context of fashion, we have identified three venues within which to explore sustainability: people, processes, and environment.

People

People consume clothing. They have basic needs that fashion can address. Sustainability works both ways here; as people can sustain the environment by addressing their clothing choices, fashion can also sustain people in various ways.

Processes

Processes, both production and economic, have a large impact on the directions that sustainability takes. The way we approach the making of fashion guides the resulting ecological footprint and well-being of society. In this book, we will also consider the ways that processes can be changed and sustained in relation to new ways of approaching fashion.

Environment

Environmental concerns and opportunities are closely tied to fashion. Since garments are made of materials (e.g., fibers, fabrics, notions), there are direct physical environmental impacts connected to the use, reuse, resilience, and sustainable actions that surround fashion.

Approaching a Model of Interconnectivity

These segments are interrelated; they do not operate independently, yet each has its own topical focus. By purchasing and wearing cloth-

A model for sustainable fashion: Interconnecting people, processes, and environment. The potential to have a large impact on sustainable issues *through fashion* can be realized when we explore how fashion interacts within all three interconnected areas. Since fashion is more than the materials that garments are made of, we have broader opportunities to explore. The possibilities are much greater when this concept is core to our thinking. (Concept developed by Janet Hethorn and Connie Ulasewicz; illustrated by Joseph M. Sipia and David Brown.)

ing, people express choices about their own ecological footprint. Production processes have a major impact on the planet. Clothing has the potential, when designed thoughtfully, to better sustain people as they go about their everyday lives.

The materials available from which to produce fashion items may be unfamiliar to consumers; thus, choices may not be well informed. How do these connections work? We need new ways of thinking about our next steps; understanding the expanded and interconnected model is a beginning. How can we, as designers and producers of clothing, impact the many possibilities for sustainable outcomes? How do we take responsibility for informed choices and actions?

This book addresses the issues and consequences that consumers, marketers, designers, and product developers engage in as they move toward and develop sustainable products. It features an exploration of systems that facilitate the least burden on the environment with the most benefit to people. As discussed, this book is an anthology, divided into three sections, each an in-depth exploration of one of the three segments of sustainable opportunity that we have identified. We have invited both academics and practitioners, each with his or her own unique knowledge and expertise, to write the chapters that contribute to this dialogue. Each chapter, through its own voice, participates in this important conversation.

We begin each section by introducing the overall concepts, issues, and practices that arise in its five chapters. Included at the end of each section is an interview with a business or individual that is actively engaged in sustainable practices, in order to show application of the issues raised within the section.

Engaging in the "Conversation"

The chapters, interviews, and introductory segments collectively form a conversation. Your reading of these ideas draws you into the conversation too. Through the diverse voices that come together in this book, we investigate, in a broad and meaningful way, what sustainability means alongside fashion. We examine ways of understanding the concepts, as we explore the issues that designers and product developers confront as they go about their business of creating clothing and fashion. We examine practices in all stages of the development process from design through production, retail distribution, consumption, and beyond. Our intention in creating this conversation is to develop a sense of possibility and provide new directions that will allow designers and product developers to work in sustainable ways for sustainable fashion futures.

Understanding "Sustainable Fashion"

As we contemplate the complexities involved in sustainable fashion, several questions seem to underlie our exploration. The following are a few of these questions, followed by our responses. We feel this will help provide the background to our thinking and approach.

What Is Meant by "Sustainability"?

This question comes up in relation to our book for two reasons. First, it seems that there is some confusion around the term, as it is used so differently in different contexts, and second, it isn't usually a term that is followed by the word "fashion." So let's take a moment to look at where it came from and how we are using it here.

Sustainability, or *the ability to sustain*, is used in conjunction with other terms in order to craft the commonly referred-to definitions. For example, "Our Common Future" (World Commission on Development and Environment, 1987), frequently referred to as the "Brundtland Report," defines sustainable development as "development that meets the needs of the present without compromising the ability of future generations to meet their own needs." It is recognized, as reported in the United Nations World Summit Outcome document (2005), that sustainable development has impact and action possibility within the connected contexts of the social, economic, and environmental. Policies developed must take into account these "interdependent and mutually reinforcing pillars." This concept is also behind the "three Ps" (i.e., people, planet, and profit) that compose the descriptive model of sustainability within social entrepreneurship as expressed by a Dutch Social-Economic Planning Council report in 2000.

Many descriptions of sustainability express a holistic approach and encourage the need to address the issues that are core to creating sustainable futures. As expressed in the UN World Summit report, any action plan must take into consideration the social, economic, and environmental factors that work together to drive solutions. For this reason, our book has identified the three aligned areas of sustainable action, which is shown in our model on page xv as people, processes, and environment.

Fashion has a perhaps surprising, yet quite powerful, role to play in sustainability. Fashion is a process, is expressed and worn by people, and as a material object, has a direct link to the environment. It is embedded in everyday life. Thus, fashion is ripe for sustainable action on all fronts. So, basically for us, taking into account broad definitions of sustainability and the unique potential of fashion, sustainability within fashion means that through the development and use of a thing or a process, there is no harm done to people or the planet, and that thing or process, once put into action, can enhance the well-being of the people who interact with it and the environment it is developed and used within.

Most importantly, what does sustainability mean to you? Really think about this and how you might take action related to your answer. It is up to each of us to sort out our own unique course, given our individual passions and possibilities. Through individual introspection, followed by collective action, we will create sustainable futures together.

What Is Unique about Fashion That Allows Us
to Look at Sustainability in Innovative Ways?

Everyone wears clothing; thus, people have a link to possible improvements toward sustainable fashion and a resilient future. Certainly the people who design, produce, market, and consume fashion must be informed and be a part of the larger conversation on sustainable issues and practices. The solution is as close as the clothes on their backs! Fashion provides a major opportunity to broaden sustainable concepts. Fashion provides an opportunity of awareness for sustainability. It is embedded in a system of communication, and it is everywhere.

Fashion is so deep and goes directly to who we are and how we connect to one another. Some may think of fashion as frivolous, but it is at the root of the conversation that guides people to respond to the changing world around them. Just consider how massive change could be once the potential of sustainable fashion is realized. Many sustainable practices and movements are gaining momentum and moving toward mainstream. Green buildings, interiors, home products, and even green weddings and events are flourishing, yet fashion, when embraced in sustainable ways, holds even greater impact potential.

What is also unique to fashion, more so than other sustainable pathways, is that it is a large vehicle. There are many opportunities to purchase and wear clothing, and at many price points and product classifications. People have opportunities to behave in sustainable ways every day when they get dressed, and fashion, when created within a broad understanding of sustainability, can sustain people, as well as the environment. People have a desire to make socially responsible choices regarding the fashions they purchase. As designers and product developers of fashion, we are challenged to provide responsible choices. We need to stretch the perception of fashion to remain open to the many layers and complexities that exist. The people, processes, and environments that embody fashion are also calling for new sustainable directions. What a fabulous opportunity that awaits.

What Is It about Fashion that Makes Sustainability Difficult?
The concept of fashion is one of change, and the process of change generally produces waste. You may feel fashionable one day, and the next week you desire a change, a new color or silhouette, something to replace what you wore. Little thought is given to what happens to the old. Fashion includes the generation and consumption of products that come in and out of style. As consumers of fashion goods, many people have moved toward overconsumption and desire to pay the least possible price for the most products. Many closets are full of

choices that go beyond what is actually needed or even desired. This, coupled with a lack of understanding or interest about where the clothes come from, who makes them, and at what price, has led to a somewhat hopeless view of fashion in relationship to sustainability.

Inherent in fashion is change; thus, fashion is not an area that has a built-in or obvious connection to sustainability and longevity. In other industries like automobiles and architecture, products are designed and produced with a longer life span in mind. They do not turn around as quickly as clothing. A house may be certified green with bamboo floors, but those floors are not changing every week.

The fashion industry is complex, with many venues of sustainable opportunity, yet people mostly consider sustainability on the material, or environmental, level. Consumers are looking for organic clothing now in addition to organic food. The connection to the environment is now highlighted in advertising campaigns, and people are becoming more aware of recycled materials and options. If the fashion industry addresses sustainability only in the use of organic or recycled materials, we are missing major opportunities. There is much more to sustainable fashion than the materials component. New concepts are needed that embrace a rethinking of the process of garment creation, use, and disposal, re-creation, or reuse with the focus on extending the life span of products and the meaning they bring. Are you up to the challenge?

Why Now for Sustainable Fashion?
Sustainability is a contemporary, meaningful term and approach to looking at processes. It allows that fashion, as a medium or tool, can communicate. Fashion, as a nonverbal form of communication responding to what is going on in the world, offers us a tangible tool for communicating ideas and concepts. People of all ages and walks of life wear clothing; clothing provides a forum to participate in and think about sustainability.

Globalization has opened channels of international communication and allowed us the opportunity to question how design and clothing production decisions affect the people and the planet we all share. The manufacturing of clothing has moved to areas of our world where the lowest wages are paid and where little concern exists for the air and water pollution created by textile fiber, yarn, and fabric production. Sustainable fashion permits us to think more creatively about our current fiber and garment production practices and to acknowledge that what we have created in the name of fashion is not okay and needs to change. Preserving the environment is only part of the puzzle. Sustainability is about seeking solutions while maintaining healthy economies and solving social inequities. Fashion connects to all of this. The idea is that creating and consuming fashion uses resources, some renewable and some not. We should use these resources to meet our own needs today while ensuring that future generations will also be able to meet their needs. That's what "sustainable" means.

Designers, product developers, and retailers must model best practices and contribute to the vision of sustainable fashion. Now is the time to rethink the process, to generate new ideas to produce garments with a sense of ethics, using organic or renewable resources and manufacturing them in humane conditions that together sustain the planet and the people that design, produce, retail, and purchase them. The new interconnected model of people, processes, and environment that guides this book represents a necessary way of thinking.

Why now? Because if sustainability is our goal, we need to move beyond the old, linear models that no longer work (e.g., the fiber-to-consumer textile pipeline). Start now by joining the conversation.

Fashion is relevant and pleasurable. Everyone participates. Together let's realize the sustainable power that can be harnessed by taking the necessary steps toward even more exciting fashion futures.

References

Dutch Ministry for the Environment document. (2001, February). *People, profit, planet: Policy issues and options around triple bottom line reporting.*

United Nations General Assembly (2005, September 15). 2005 United Nations World Summit Outcome, Item 48, p. 12. Retrieved July 18, 2006 from http://www.who.int/hiv/universalaccess2010/worldsummit.pdf

World Commission on Environment and Development. (1987). *Our common future.* Oxford: Oxford University Press.

ACKNOWLEDGMENTS

The two of us have truly enjoyed developing this project together. We each have deep connections to sustainable pursuits over time and materials. Janet was influenced as a young designer by the social activism of the sixties, and Connie was raised with the idea that "recreating" clothing was the norm.

Our connections to sustainability began on separate paths but our efforts and commitment quickly aligned. We were working with students in product development, merchandising, and design classes on different coasts yet exploring similar issues. These early interactions with our students via projects and discussions were pivotal to the development of our thinking, and we are thankful for them. It was the energy from these conversations—united with our own passion and encouragement from friends—that spawned this project. We thank the contributors for their willingness to join in these growing conversations and craft the vision of sustainability together with us. This book is vibrant due to their diligence and expertise.

To the many people at Fairchild who worked to bring this project to you, we are very appreciative. Special thanks to Olga Kontzias, executive editor. Her vision regarding the importance of embracing sustainability within fashion was crucial in getting this book off the ground. We thank Rob Phelps, development editor, for his timely and professional guidance. His continued joy at times of uncertainty clearly kept us moving forward, not to mention his technical competence, which is extraordinary. Blake Royer, assistant development editor, we thank for his work managing the reviewers and summarizing their comments. We found these especially helpful early on in setting the course. And we are appreciative of Jennifer Crane, senior development editor, for her encouragement with the entire process. We thank the talented production team of Elizabeth Marotta, production editor; Adam Bohannon, art director; and Erin Fitzsimmons, photo editor. And we thank the following reviewers, selected by the publisher: Melody LeHew, Kansas State University; Minjeong Kim, Oregon State University; Karen Steen, Cazenovia College.

We cherish the continued encouragement we receive from our families and friends. Connie values her many conversations with Katrina, Adam, and Mike, exploring the contradictions and possibilities within sustainability. Janet gives special thanks to Rachel and Caden who have always been a source of creative support.

SECTION 1

Connecting with People
on Sustainable Practices

INTRODUCTION

Looking at sustainability through the lens of fashion provides unique opportunities. Since fashion is both a verb and a noun (i.e., something that is created, expressed, and worn by people), fashion offers myriad opportunities for people to take sustainable actions. By focusing on *people,* their behaviors, their uniqueness, and their interests, this section uncovers exciting possibilities that aren't often considered in contexts of sustainability. These new insights provide an exciting potential for positive change.

People are the driving force behind sustainable practices. Usually when we think about sustainable fashion, our thinking gravitates toward environmental issues and green design. The issues involved in sustainable fashion include, but go beyond, environmental ones. They are actually quite broad. It is really the people, working as designers, retailers, manufacturers, and consumers, living in countries throughout the world who have power to act in ways to create the most impact, both positive and negative. People are intimately connected to fashion, so we must think about how they behave, what they want, and what might improve their lives and well-being. People are the stakeholders; we are in the unique position to maintain, improve, or destroy our environment through the choices we make. By being smart about these choices and including this knowledge of how to improve the lives and well-being of people through design, product development, and retail decision making, we have interesting opportunities for sustainable outcomes.

We begin this segment with an overview of how sustainability as a concept has evolved throughout history and how people have either advanced it or restricted it through their actions and desires. Linda Welters, in Chapter 1, tells this story, beginning in the sixteenth century when clothing was very precious and continuing to the era of over-consumption that we live in today. She weaves together movements and trends in textile and fashion, laying a beautiful foundation for understanding the history of sustainability in the garment industry and why we need to make changes now.

Recognizing that people are interested in personal and social change, Connie Ulasewicz writes in Chapter 2 about how eco-savvy consumers look to retailers and manufacturers to integrate more sustainable practices in the products they market, promote, and sell. She explains how people can respond like social entrepreneurs and invest in the transformation of the apparel industry through their purchases and monetary contributions to sustainable causes. She lays out simple choices that individuals can make in altering their lifestyles toward sustainability.

Furthering our knowledge about the connection between sustainability and people, in Chapter 3 Janet Hethorn embraces the notion that it is possible to actually sustain people through the vehicle of fashion, as both process and product. Clothing and its expression can figure into providing for and meeting basic needs, including the physical, social, and aesthetic. Toward this end, she shares insights into ways of designing to meet consumer desire and to ultimately enhance individual well-being.

Rebecca Luke, in Chapter 4, explores ethical contrasts and ways of marketing correct ethical messages. Using her own nonprofit foundation as a source of examples, Luke has developed an approach to encourage and enable consumers to nourish the seeds of sustainability. She outlines how people, as stylemakers, can use multimedia, entertainment, fashion, and design as ways to inspire others to make ethical and sustainable choices.

Chapter 5 completes this section by looking at how technology is implemented as a tool in creating sustainable products and environments for people. Technology can change the ways we design and shop for clothing. Suzanne Loker identifies and discusses the technology that allows fashion to enhance, protect, and sustain people as we embark on a new fashion frontier.

Why Now?

- The overconsumption of clothing is based on an old model and is not fashionable.
- People have the power to support with their purchases the growth of sustainable practices of retailers and manufacturers.
- Sustainable fashion can enhance the physical, emotional, and psychological well-being of people.
- People are the driving force behind sustainable choices in the fashion industry.

LINDA WELTERS, PH.D., is professor and chair of the Textiles, Fashion
Merchandising, and Design Department at the University of Rhode
Island. She has published on European folk dress, archaeological tex-
tiles, American quilts, and American fashion. Her most recent publication
is *A Fashion Reader* (Berg 2007), which she coedited with Abby Lillethun.
With Patricia Cunningham, she coedited *Twentieth-Century American
Fashion* (Berg 2005). She is coauthoring *Fashioning America* (under
contract with Greenwood), again with Cunningham.

CHAPTER I

The Fashion
of Sustainability

Linda Welters

To answer the question "why now?" for sustainable fashion, we
must first look to the past. How has sustainability come and gone
throughout the history of modern fashion, from 1600 until today?
This chapter revisits various movements and trends in fashion history
as they relate to sustainability. Where did these movements and trends
originate? What inspired them? What is currently moving them forward? An exploration of these questions will lead to an understanding
of why the time for sustainable fashion is indeed now.

Sustainability: From Necessity to Choice

Sustainability is not a new concept in the history of fashion. It has
been part of the fashion repertoire, albeit in various guises, since the
1960s, when the counterculture rejected mainstream styles. Yet long

before the overabundance of goods available to consumers today, economical use of resources was a way of life.

In the preindustrial era, it took a long time to produce fabrics; thus, only the elite could afford to participate fully in fashion. Even the wealthy saved fabrics, remodeled clothes, and sold unwanted items in the secondhand market. Sustainability was a way of life. Over the course of four centuries, the concept of sustainability has gone from the given of preindustrial days to a choice in our contemporary era of plenty.

This chapter provides a history of sustainability related to fashion since early modern times. It is divided into three time periods–preindustrial, industrial, and postmodern–which together trace the history of fashion from 1600 to the saturated market we are experiencing today.

Preindustrial Era to Early Industrialization: 1600–1860

Prior to the Industrial Revolution, conserving resources was habitual for the vast majority of humanity simply because of the cost and labor it took to produce the basic necessities of life. Fibers, the raw materials for textiles, came only from nature and were processed into fabrics through laborious, time-consuming processes. For example, flax, the world's oldest fiber, required many steps to go from the mature plant to a fine linen fabric suitable for a gentleman's white shirt. The plant was pulled from the ground and retted to loosen the fibers from the stalk. The sequential processes of braking, scutching, and hackling extracted the strands, which were then combed to straighten them out and to separate long fibers termed *line* from short fibers called *tow* (Coons, 1980). The line was then spun into yarns, woven into *linen* fabric, and finished by bleaching the yardage white. For fine linen fabrics, a finishing process called beetling (i.e., pounding with a wooden malletlike device) imparted a luster to the fabric. If the fabric was to be dyed, additional steps occurred. The short tow fibers did not go unused. They were processed into coarse fabrics for sacks, mattress covers, and rough workwear. The other major natural fibers besides flax (e.g., wool, silk, and cotton) underwent similar labor-intensive processes to become fabrics.

The Preindustrial World

Textile production was not evenly distributed around the world, resulting in limited fabric choices for consumers despite trade between distant markets. For example, northern Europe's climate was ideal for flax cultivation, but the growing season was too short for cotton cultivation. As a result, Europeans did not wear cotton before the English and Dutch commenced trade with cotton-producing India around the year 1600. Cotton was indigenous to India, where skilled artisans had been painting and printing fine cotton cloth for centuries (Harris, 2004). When the colorful cottons first appeared in Europe, they became the rage among those who could afford them. Their popularity threatened the domestic wool industry in England and the silk industry in France, resulting in legislation against the importation and wearing of Indian painted cottons until the mid 1700s.

Luxurious Apparel for the Wealthy

As a result of the labor involved in production, textiles had high monetary value. Specialized techniques for making luxurious fabrics (e.g., embroidery, lace, brocade, and velvet) further increased prices. Costly raw materials such as silk or gilded thread added additional expense. Conversely, the labor needed to cut and sew fabric into garments was cheap. Thus, the quality of the fabrics in wearing apparel marked a person's status more than its style. Only the aristocracy and the gentry could afford beautiful fabrics and trimmings. They had their clothes made by specialists, who took inspiration from the leading courts of Europe. Portraits that survive from the seventeenth and eighteenth centuries show how elaborate and colorful fashion became in this period. Aristocratic men followed fashion just as closely as women, embellishing themselves in ribbons, bows, and lace. By the eighteenth century, merchants and others of the "middling sort" also sought fashionable clothing as a conduit to higher social standing.

Precious Few Clothes for the Common Folk

Less often depicted in paintings are farmers and laborers, who donned dull-colored clothes of coarse, plain fabrics. Some of these wearers had made both the fabric and the clothing themselves. Sometimes neighbors in farming communities bartered rather than paid cash for both raw materials and services, such as spinning, weaving, cutting, and sewing.

Most people in Europe and North America owned just a few sets of clothes; thus, they had no need for closets. They hung their everyday apparel on hooks and stored seldom-used clothing in trunks. Women altered their best dresses to reflect changes in fashion. People repaired clothes repeatedly to extend wear. A pair of handwoven cotton work trousers in the Historic Textile and Costume Collection at the University of Rhode Island has been patched 24 times on the knees and seat (Figure 1.1).

Old but still usable clothes were sold at local markets and through traveling peddlers. Even rags had value, as evidenced by the *ragpicker* of nineteenth-century literature. Clothes were so precious that they were often stolen from laundry baskets or off the backs of drunks leaving taverns and pawned for cash (Lemire, 1990). People named specific clothing items in their wills, as evidenced in the probate documents of the widow Ellinor Quayle Bridson, who died on the Isle of Man in England on April 19, 1764. Bridson carefully enumerated who should receive her unused fabrics as well as specific items of clothing. She bequeathed "unto her eldest son William as much medley [*woolen fabric*] as will make him a coat and britches," "unto her daughter Jane her red dominey [*cloak*], a shag hat, best bodys [*corset*] & stomanger [i.e., *stomacher*] & her blue calamankey [i.e., *calimanco*, a shiny worsted wool fabric] gown," "unto her daughter Catherine a blue camlet gown & nine yards of poplin for a gown," "unto her two daughters all the check for aprons & all her shaped linen," "unto her mother a new bed gown . . . , a drugget petticoat, a pledden [probably *plaid*] petticoat, and a blanket," "unto her maidservant a drugget stripped quilted petticoat," and "unto Jane Bridson Gibdle all the worsted that she had for a gown, the warp double, and the weft single." The remainder of her clothes she bequeathed to her four children "for them to wear" (Will–Ellinor Quayle [als Brid-

FIGURE 1.1. All but one of the numerous striped and checked fabrics used to repair these cotton work trousers was handwoven. A total of 24 patches were used to repair these circa 1830–1840 pants from New England. (Photo by Linda Welters. Trousers courtesy of Historic Textile and Costume Collection, University of Rhode Island.)

son], 1764). It is worth noting that the fabrics described are mostly wool or linen, which would have been locally available in towns throughout the United Kingdom.

Early Industrialization

During the second half of the eighteenth century, creative minds in Great Britain, France, and America invented devices to mechanize the processing of fiber into fabric (Wilson, 1979). First, John Kay invented the flying shuttle in 1733, which sped up the weaving of cloth. Next, attention turned to the spinning of yarn. In 1767 James Hargreaves developed the spinning jenny, and in 1769 Richard Arkwright invented the water-powered spinning frame. In the 1780s Edmund Cartwright developed a power loom that could weave cloth by water-powered mill wheels, and in the 1790s Eli Whitney built a machine that ginned cotton. About that same time, Thomas Bell patented the first engraved cylinders to print cloth; previously, printers had stamped the patterns on the cloth with flat copper plates or wooden blocks. This sequence of inventions set the stage for the industrial production of textiles. The Industrial Revolution itself began with innovations in the textiles sector; indeed, Richard Arkwright is remembered as the "father of the Industrial Revolution" (Wilson, 1979, p. 200).

Emergence of Factory-Made Cloth

By the 1820s, factories on both sides of the Atlantic began producing cloth mechanically, which increased supply and reduced price. Farmers stopped cultivating flax for linen and raising sheep for wool. The abundance of inexpensive, factory-made cloth allowed more people to dress well than at any previous period in history.

Introduction of the Fashion Periodical

The same engraved cylinders that printed coloring agents onto textiles could also rapidly print paper; soon the inexpensive fashion periodical appeared. Interested women no longer had to rely on letters and word-of-mouth to learn the latest styles in Europe's fashion capitals. They could subscribe to magazines such as the long-running American periodical *Godey's Lady's Book* (1830–1898). Men could peruse the latest trends in publications such as *The Gentleman's Magazine of Fashion* at their favorite tailors. The rate of fashion change accelerated. Local dressmakers and tailors quickly translated printed illustrations into fashionable clothing for clients. Wardrobes, not surprisingly, increased in size, necessitating the inclusion of closets in the building of homes. Textiles for the home also proliferated.

Early Industrialization, the Environment, and Social Responsibility
Early textile manufacturers did not consider the effects of pollution. Textile wet finishing processes used chemicals that were discharged into nearby rivers and streams. Often, neighbors could tell what colors were going onto the cloth because of the residual dye emptied out into the stream adjacent to the local dyehouse or printworks. Also of concern should have been the mordants used to bind coloring agents to the cloth, namely iron, tin, chrome, and copper. Today mills remove dyes, pigments, and mordants before discharging the spent dyebath into the environment.

The textile industry was not much concerned with fair labor practices either. Manufacturers looked for the cheapest labor, just as they do now. They employed children, young women, and immigrants, sometimes exploiting their lack of recourse over unfair labor practices. Long hours and fluctuating pay scales characterized the industry in the early years. Conditions in the mills were also problematic. Lung diseases such as tuberculosis spread easily in the moist, lint-laden air. Additionally, the machinery, powered by a system of belts and pulleys, did not stop immediately when turned off. Thus, when clothing or a limb got caught up in the works, serious injuries often resulted. Not all textile manufacturers maintained such inhumane working conditions, however. Some mill owners constructed housing, schools, libraries, and local meeting halls for their employees.

Components of the Mechanized Apparel Factory in Place
Although textile production was mechanized in the first half of the nineteenth century, apparel production was, for the most part, not. Until the invention of the sewing machine in 1846, all sewing was

done by hand. Small apparel factories did exist, however, and ready-made clothing was sometimes sold in retail stores and through mail-order catalogs. In the eighteenth century, for example, workers in English factories produced ready-to-wear quilted petticoats for export to the American colonies (Lemire, 1994). Tailors in American seaside towns stitched jackets and trousers and sold them to sailors on shore leave for just a day or two; the clothes were called *slops* and the stores *slop shops*. Prior to the Civil War, mills in Rhode Island and Massachusetts produced rough fabric known as "negro cloth," which was sewn into crude trousers by local women, then shipped to the South for use by slaves on cotton plantations. However, most apparel was still custom-made in the 1850s. The development of the full-fledged apparel factory depended on the mechanization of textile production. By 1860, all the components were in place.

Industrialization: 1860–1960

In this section, the technological and social developments that affected both the production and consumption of fashion are explored. These include the birth of the couture system, changes in the social system, and the growth of the ready-to-wear industry. These developments paved the way to proliferation of fashionable goods and set the stage for the problem of overabundance that we currently face.

Couture and the Fashion Plate

The couture system developed in Paris when Charles Frederick Worth, a transplanted Englishman, opened a dressmaking establishment in 1857 that featured a predesigned collection from which clients ordered custom-made copies. This shifted the design function to the dressmaker, whose label now appeared in the garment. It also solidified Paris as the fashion capital of the world for women's dress. For men's dress, England led the way. London's Savile Row gained prominence in establishing trends among the elite for both town and country clothes. The wealth created through the Industrial Revolution ensured a healthy client base for both Paris couturiers and London tailors.

While those at the top of the social strata displayed their status through acquisition of prestigious clothing labels made in the world's style capitals, the rising middle class wanted to be in fashion too. They aspired to move up the social ladder with the help of a respectable appearance. Fashion plates in the proliferating number of women's magazines and tailoring guides allowed everyone to follow the latest fashions from Europe, close facsimiles of which could be obtained through local dressmakers, tailors, or retail stores. The development of the paper pattern industry in the 1860s gave those with sewing skills the opportunity to assemble fashionable garments at home. Ebenezer Butterick of Sterling, Massachusetts, began selling tissue paper patterns for boy's and men's wear in 1863. His business expanded rapidly to include patterns for women's fashions. Soon women's magazines included paper patterns too. *Harper's Bazaar*, founded in 1867, published trends for clothes, accessories, and hairdos as well as pattern supplements so that enterprising subscribers could re-create the fashions for themselves.

Technology, Manufacturing, and Retail in the Late Nineteenth Century

Technological developments continued to occur in textile manufacturing. By this time all types of textiles, including the laces, velvets, and patterned silks that previously constituted the most expensive fabrics, were made by machine. Synthetic dyes were introduced after William Perkin discovered mauve in 1856, ushering in a period of bright purples, pinks, blues, and oranges in fashion fabrics.

The second half of the nineteenth century also saw the development of the apparel factory, where multiples of prevailing styles were made in a range of sizes. Several factors contributed to America's rapid leap forward as a producer of manufactured clothing. These factors included the lower cost and greater availability of textiles; the invention of the sewing machine; the standardization of sizing for menswear due to advances in the production of military uniforms during the Civil War; and immigration, both as a source of skilled labor and as a market for ready-to-wear apparel. Jewish immigrants from Europe often came with experience in the garment industry as tailors, peddlers, and shop owners (Yeshiva University Museum, 2005). They played an important part in developing the apparel and the retail industries in North America.

Technological advances (e.g., vertical knives to cut multiple layers of fabric, electricity to power equipment, and steam pressers) improved production (Kidwell & Christman, 1974). The new ready-made clothes were distributed through a novel retail venue, the department store. These emporiums brought manufactured goods to the middle classes in stylish settings, first in major cities like London, Paris, New York, Boston, and Chicago, and then in smaller cities. The development of department stores occurred in the second half of the nineteenth century at the same time that the Industrial Revolution produced increasing amounts of manufactured products. Distribution to areas far from urban centers expanded with the railroad. Mail-order catalogs made fashionable ready-to-wear clothing available to farmers and ranchers who had settled in the Midwest and western territories of the United States and Canada.

A significant textile and apparel production complex developed in America and Great Britain after the sewing machine sped up clothing and shoe assembly (Kidwell & Christman, 1974). As the nineteenth century drew to a close, factories produced all manner of menswear and children's wear as well as certain women's garments that did not require a customized fit. Women's dresses, because of the close-fitting bodices that dominated fashion, continued to be made to order until styles changed in the first quarter of the twentieth century.

FIGURE 1.2. In this March 1921 illustration, "Along Fifth Avenue," from *Harper's Bazaar*, a maid is removing a hat from a hatbox as her mistress, dressed in a negligee, looks on. The woman's negligee is from Bonwit Teller, an exclusive New York City department store. Three dresses hang in the closet, suggesting greater choice than in the past, thanks to less expensive, mass-manufactured clothing for women. (Photo courtesy of Historic Textile and Costume Collection, University of Rhode Island.)

Women's ready-to-wear apparel expanded rapidly after French designer Paul Poiret introduced new, loose-fitting tunic dresses in the late Edwardian period (circa 1908). Copies of his simplified styles could be successfully sized for a range of body types and manufactured as ready-to-wear garments. Dressmakers decreased in number, while women's designers proliferated.

Paris labels were much desired. Coco Chanel, Madeleine Vionnet, and Jean Patou were just some of the designer labels to cherish in the years between World Wars I and II. American apparel manufacturers both legally and illegally copied designs from Paris couturiers and manufactured them in the United States for sale at a fraction of the price of the originals. Companies scattered throughout the country created attractive, wearable fashions for style-conscious Americans.

New York City was known for women's dresses and coats. California, with its casual lifestyles, excelled at manufacturing sportswear. Chicago and Kansas City were home to menswear companies, while a cluster of cities north of Boston, Massachusetts, made shoes.

World War II and Fashion

World War II cut off Paris from the rest of the fashionable world. British and American firms began to highlight their own designers, which strengthened the identities of non-Parisian labels. Leading department stores promoted home-grown designers in window displays, advertising campaigns, and award ceremonies. Consumers balanced personal style with patriotism and the practical need to send scarce resources to the front lines. Nylon, for example, went into parachutes, not stockings. Some women, early social entrepreneurs, drew seams down their bare legs to simulate fashionable stockings. Sustainability may not have been the goal, but as with the movements to come in the 1960s, social consciousness demonstrated the ability to control consumption, ergo production.

After the war, Paris once again rose to dominance with the opening of Christian Dior's couture house in 1947. Dior's New Look influenced women's fashion for more than a decade and reinstated France to its former position as fashion's world leader. Fashion once again followed the decrees of French designers. Americans, Europeans, Australians, South Africans, and many other nationalities wore Parisian-inspired styles, discarding the old and donning the new as fashion changed.

Introduction of Manufactured Fibers

From the late nineteenth century through the mid-twentieth century, numerous types of manufactured fibers appeared in the marketplace. Artificial silk, first produced commercially by Count Hilaire de Chardonnet in 1891, was renamed rayon in 1924 and took off in the marketplace for women's hosiery and silk-like dresses. Rayon's close relative, acetate, soon followed. Nylon made its debut in 1939, just before World War II began. Fiber research accelerated in the postwar era when attention turned away from military needs and toward developing consumer products. Acrylic and polyester were introduced for use in a variety of apparel products. While rayon and acetate came from regenerated cellulose, or *wood pulp*, which is a renewable resource, the new synthetic fibers (e.g., nylon, acrylic, and polyester) came from fossil fuels (e.g., oil, gas, and coal), which are nonrenewable resources. This disparity would become an issue for the environmental movement later in the twentieth century.

Glimmerings of an Anti-Fashion Movement

As the nuclear age dawned, rumblings of dissatisfaction surfaced in America and Europe. Many people feared the atomic bomb. Some young people began to resent the social conformity expected during the postwar era and formed subcultures. In the 1950s, a subculture known as the Teddy Boys and a group of playwrights and writers dubbed the Angry Young Men appeared in Great Britain. In the United States, the Beat Generation grew from a handful of writers and poets into a full-blown youth phenomenon by 1959. Subcultural heroes appeared on the silver screen (e.g., Marlon Brando in 1953's *The Wild One* and James Dean in 1955's *Rebel Without a Cause*), foreshadowing the youth revolution of the 1960s. The clothing choices of these groups revealed a tendency to reject fashion in favor of blue-collar workers' clothing, specifically blue jeans, T-shirts, and workboots. Old army jackets and secondhand clothes were also featured in their wardrobes. The glimmerings of an anti-fashion movement had appeared on the horizon, a movement that would profoundly influence the direction of fashion in the following decade. This was a pivotal moment for the rejection of the old ways of producing and consuming fashion, ushering in an era of exploration for a more sustainable future.

Postmodern Times: 1960 to Early Twenty-First Century
This section explores how fashion production and consumption changed in the postmodern era. During the 1960s, England and Italy joined France as fashion centers. As the first of the babies born after World War II grew up, youthful fashions took center stage. Novelty in fashion was much desired to mirror rapid social changes. Department stores, which experienced a three- to six-month lag time from placing orders until the merchandise arrived in stores, faded in popularity. Instead, boutiques with new styles appearing daily became the retail darlings. Throwaway fashion, cheap and disposable, replaced the classic styling of the 1950s and early 1960s. This was epitomized in the paper dress. New fibers and fabrics appeared with rapidity. Spandex, vinyl, saran, polyethylene, and polypropylene emerged from the chemists' laboratories. Couture designers soon incorporated these new materials into mini dresses, jumpsuits, coats, shoes, boots, and hats. Paco Rabanne, for example, made dresses out of linked plastic or aluminum disks (Lehnert, 2000). The decade itself was characterized by swift change influenced by political unrest and social protest. Civil rights and the antiwar movement caused liberals to rethink the status quo. It was also the era of urban renewal, during which developers razed old neighborhoods and downtowns in the name of progress.

The space race contributed to an aura of futurism that pervaded the 1960s. In 1968, the crew of the Apollo 8 command module took the first photograph of the earth as seen from space. Space exploration inspired fashion designers. André Courrèges, with his otherworldly styles, was dubbed the "space age" designer.

Emergence of the Counterculture
In 1962, Rachel Carson's *Silent Spring* raised awareness of the damage done to the environment as a result of increased use of chemicals. The culprits included cotton growers, who used large amounts of pesticides and fertilizers to achieve greater crop yields, as well as textile

manufacturers, who discharged chemical-laden water from their mills into local rivers and streams. Leather tanners were especially oblivious to the problems they created using old-fashioned production methods. The 1998 motion picture *A Civil Action* tells the story of one such company in Woburn, Massachusetts, where an unusually high number of children developed cancer as a result of toxic waste dumped in a pond near the factory. Those concerned with the environment began the ecology movement, the forerunner of today's efforts toward creating a sustainable future for our planet. Over the years, the issues have ranged from pesticides to nuclear power, acid rain to ozone depletion, and deforestation to global warming.

At the end of the sixties, a counterculture developed among youth in a number of Western countries that rejected the values of their parents' generation, including the way their elders followed fashion. The sixties youth wore jeans, workshirts, personalized tie-dyed T-shirts, love beads, and old-fashioned items acquired in secondhand stores. Women wore their hair long and gave up make-up, in effect rejecting the beauty industry. Men stopped cutting their hair and shaving, which introduced the word "unisex" to the lexicon, as both sexes looked alike in their long hair and jeans. A group of art students at Pratt Institute in Brooklyn, New York, embraced fiber as an art form (Dale, 1986). They crocheted yarns of natural fibers into textured, organic garments that could just as easily be displayed on a wall as worn on the body. The art-to-wear movement had begun.

By 1970 the counterculture had profoundly influenced fashion. Old rules of etiquette that dictated correct attire for specific occasions broke down. People did not need to dress up anymore; consequently, they rapidly adopted casual attire for everyday wear. Jeans made their way into everyone's wardrobe. Consumers developed an aversion to synthetics, preferring the *natural* look. The back-to-the-earth movement was born. Color palettes showed a preference for tan, brown, gold, and avocado green. Even footwear got into the act. While handcrafted leather sandals had been a favorite of the hippies in the 1960s,

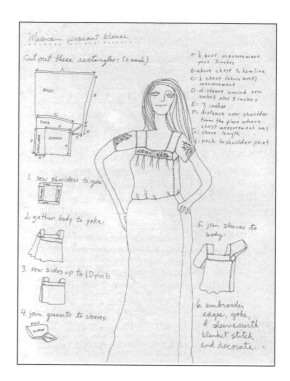

FIGURE 1.3. This drawing, "Directions for Making a Mexican Peasant Blouse," appeared in Alicia Bay Laurel's Living on the Earth, which was published in 1971. Laurel lived on Wheeler Ranch in Sonoma County, California, in the 1970s. She wrote and illustrated the book for others living on communes. *Living on Earth* sold 350,000 copies and appeared on the *New York Times* Bestseller List. (Illustration copyright Alicia Bay Laurel.)

hiking boots became the footwear of choice for the back-to-the-land crowd. In Denmark, Anne Kalso developed the Earth Shoe™, based on negative heel technology. Advertisements claimed that it was like walking on the beach, leaving footprints in the sand (Earth, 2006).

The Link between Consumption and Conservation

Ecology was the buzzword, and natural fibers rebounded. The link was drawn between consumption and conservation. Debates about which fibers and fabrics depleted resources took place—to wit, while cotton, a natural fiber, was renewable, it was not as durable as polyester, meaning that it would require replacement more quickly. It also took longer to

dry in the clothes dryer, using up more energy than quick-drying synthetics. Additionally, it needed ironing. Double-knitted polyester, on the
other hand, a favorite of the early 1970s, earned a reputation for being
too "plastic" as the decade progressed. Synthetic fiber manufacturers
responded to these debates with modifications to make their products
more wearable and more environmentally friendly. Fiber producers
built grooves into the fibers to improve wicking of moisture away from
the skin. In the United Kingdom, researchers looked for more environmentally friendly methods to produce rayon, which resulted in the new
fiber Lyocell in the 1990s. This regenerated cellulose fiber is marketed
under the trade name Tencel®. Although chemically identical to rayon,
the solvent that is used in Lyocell production is more benign and more
easily recovered than the solvents involved in the production of rayon.
Research into improving synthetic fibers continued in the 1980s, and in
1990 the high-denier microfiber was introduced to the marketplace.
"High-tech" fabric developments occurred regularly in the 1990s, inspir-
ing fashion designers to create new styles using these fabrics.

Emergence of Environmentalism and Social Consciousness

In the meantime, production of fashion items slowly began moving
out of countries with mature economies to developing nations in the
Caribbean and in Asian countries. Low labor costs reduced the price
of apparel to the point where the average family could buy clothes
more often than in the past. Shopping became a national pastime.
Malls proliferated. Outlet stores and off-price retailers appeared as a
venue for manufacturers to get rid of overstock.

Consumers themselves began to consider how to dispose of
unused clothes. They purged their closets to get rid of clothes and
shoes no longer worn yet still in good shape. Church rummage sales
and yard sales were one method of finding a second life for apparel
and other goods. But these venues were not enough. Soon Goodwill,
The Salvation Army, and other purveyors of secondhand clothes were

inundated and no longer disposed of their stock domestically. They started shipping bales of used clothing to third-world countries, particularly in Africa. In those countries, indigenous textile and apparel industries sometimes suffered the consequences of decreased demand in the face of cheap used clothing from America and Europe sold in local markets. Karen Hansen (2000) has studied this phenomenon in Zambia, while Pietra Rivoli (2005) investigated the used clothing markets of Tanzania.

The 1980s saw an increase in the acceptability of wearing "used" clothing by fashionable young people in developed countries, although for the most part as a fashion choice and not with an eye toward conservation. Movies, such as 1985's *Desperately Seeking Susan,* showed how stars like Madonna borrowed old items to create new looks. The punk movement, a subculture that first appeared in Great Britain and rapidly spread internationally, endorsed the mixing of old clothes with new, edgy garments. "Vintage" entered the fashion scene, and used clothing found a new market. Upscale used clothing stores opened across the United States with names like Second Time Around and Elite Repeat. By the 1990s, actresses began donning vintage designer gowns on the red carpet in an effort to distinguish themselves from the competition.

Some brands incorporated socially conscious advertising to promote their products, although critics argued that the companies were just capitalizing on these issues. Still, these advertising campaigns once again proved how social consciousness can affect consumer behavior. Leading the way was Benetton, an Italian firm that produced knitwear. During the 1980s and 1990s, their controversial ads took on numerous controversial issues such as racism, religion, and gender. The company has continued its commitment to social causes by focusing on world hunger and human rights.

In the 1990s the consumer's consciousness was raised again, this time under the banner of *environmentalism*. Organic cotton and Sally Fox's naturally colored cottons (e.g., FoxFibre®) drew attention, as did hemp, which can be grown without fertilizers.

FIGURE 1.4. Label for a 1994 organic cotton T-shirt by O Wear. The twill tape around the neck is printed with the phrases "change your clothes" and "conserve and recycle." (Photograph by Linda Welters.)

A new link had been made between conservation and the environment, but organic cotton did not fare well with consumers at the time, who were more concerned about price than the environment Still, Wellman Inc., a New Jersey company, began recycling PET polyester soda bottles for fiber. Some of this fiber, labeled Fortrel® EcoSpun™, appeared in the new fleece fabrics. Other companies began researching renewable raw materials, such as soybeans and corn, for fiber.

The Conscientious Lifestyle and Its Challenges

Environmentalists and those sympathetic to environmental issues developed a conscientious lifestyle. Healthy eating, regular exercise, and fuel-efficient cars characterized this segment of the population. They also signified their values through their appearance. They wore comfortable "classic" styles and socially conscious brands. Companies associated with outdoor clothing such as Patagonia and L.L.Bean became favorites of environmentalists. Small companies offering hemp clothing emerged. As handcrafted sandals and Earth Shoes had before them, a new brand of footwear from the German company Birkenstock gained cache within the environmental movement.

Meanwhile, the drive to lower prices for apparel resulted in labor abuses in apparel factories both in the United States and abroad. Illegal immigrants to the United States sometimes found work as operators in apparel factories, where long hours and unsafe conditions were standard operating procedures. Low-wage countries in the Caribbean Basin and the Far East expanded their production. The National Labor Committee exposed conditions in sweatshops that manufactured clothing lines by television talk-show host Kathie Lee Gifford in the 1990s. Consumer pressure on big-name companies connected to sweatshops such as Nike affected sales; the companies responded with programs that certified fair labor practices in their factories. Yet the consumer still wanted the cheapest price, and labor problems persisted in the global apparel business. Labor abuses spring up in new places every year in the apparel industry. In 2006, factory managers in Jordan were accused of enslaving guest workers from Bangladesh, making them work 20-hour shifts, withholding wages, and physically abusing those who complained (Greenhouse & Barbara, 2006).

The textile industry also began moving offshore. High labor costs were one reason, but the increased expense of meeting environmental legislation was another. Developing countries with lower wages and less stringent environmental regulations took up the slack. In effect, industrialized countries exported their environmental problems to countries eager to develop the manufacturing sector of their economies.

Now Is the Time for Sustainable Fashion

The early twenty-first century is an era of overabundance. Well-designed clothes are available at all price levels, including mass merchandise chains such as Target, H&M, and Zara. New styles are presented so frequently that the industry has labeled this sector *fast fashion*. Everyone can afford to be fashionable and to change his or her wardrobe regularly. Fashion is again disposable. And consumers want variety in their wardrobes. Ours is an era when women have different handbags and shoes for each outfit. Space is needed to store all the clothes and accessories necessary to maintain a fashionable appearance. This means that large walk-in closets are standard features in new homes. For the consumer goods that do not fit in our homes, storage units are available.

Interest in fashion is at an all-time high. Cities in all corners of the globe, from Tokyo, Seoul, and Shanghai to Sydney, Dubai, and Sao Paulo, join the ranks of world fashion capitals. Educational institutions are expanding to serve students from throughout the world who seek to pursue careers in fashion. Fashion, with its propensity for change, is not going away anytime soon. How future generations deal with overabundance, fair labor practices, and environmental concerns is of paramount importance to the well-being of the planet.

The time is right for the fashion industry and consumers to embrace sustainability. The many advances being made in the technology sector are ripe for development. Increased awareness of the damage caused by greenhouse gases calls for stricter environmental controls for industry, particularly in developing countries. In an era of fast, disposable fashion, designers must consider the problem of post-consumer waste. Consumers themselves have a growing awareness of practices that lead to sustainable living. The interest in and potential for sustainability in the production and consumption of textile and apparel products is unique to our times.

Conclusion

This chapter explored the development of fashion from 1600 to the present in terms of sustainability. Textiles were scarce in the beginning of the period, requiring laborious processes to produce usable cloth; consequently, people had few clothes. Both clothes and fabrics had value and were passed on to heirs. People practiced sustainability without realizing it. The Industrial Revolution ushered in an era of abundant fabrics, followed by the mechanized production of apparel. Fashionable apparel became available to all classes of people in industrialized countries, sometimes at the expense of the environment and through unfair labor practices. Over the past few decades, however, a growing awareness of environmental issues in the production of textiles and apparel has resulted in some improvements.

We still have a long way to go. The solution lies with researchers, designers, regulators, and consumers who conceive of and choose to wear safer, healthier, and more environmentally sound fashion in the future.

References

Coons, M. (1980). *All sorts of good sufficient cloth: Linen-making in New England, 1640–1860*. North Andover, MA: Merrimack Valley Textile Museum.

Dale, J. S. (1986). *Art to wear*. New York: Abbeville Press.

Earth. (2006). Company Web site. Retrieved December 31, 2006, from http://www.earth.us/

Greenhouse, S. & Barbara, G. (2006, May 3). An ugly side of free trade: Sweatshops in Jordan. *New York Times*.

Hansen, K. T. (2000). *Salaula: The world of secondhand clothing and Zambia*. Chicago: University of Chicago Press.

Harris, J. (Ed.) (2004). *5,000 years of textiles*. Washington D.C.: Smithsonian Books.

Humphries, M. (2004). *Fabric reference* (3rd ed.). Upper Saddle River, NJ: Prentice Hall.

Kidwell, C. B. & Christman, M. C. (1974). *Suiting everyone: The democratization of clothing in America*. Washington, DC: Smithsonian Institution Press.

Lehnert, G. (2000). *A history of fashion in the twentieth century*. Cologne, Germany: Könemann.

Lemire, B. (1990). The theft of clothes and popular consumerism in early modern England. *Journal of Social History, 24*(2), 255–276.

Lemire, B. (1994). Redressing the history of the clothing trade in England: Ready-made clothing, guilds, and women workers, 1650–1800. *Dress*, 21, 61–74.

Rivoli, P. (2005). *The travels of a t-shirt in the global economy*. Hoboken, NJ: John Wiley & Sons.

Will–Ellinor Quayle (als Bridson) (1764). Retrieved January 21, 2007, from http://www.isle-of-man.com/manxnotebook/famhist/wills/1764_eq.htm

Wilson, K. (1979). *A history of textiles*. Boulder, CO: Westview Press.

Yeshiva University Museum. (2005). *A perfect fit: The garment industry and American Jewry*. New York: Yeshiva University.

CONNIE ULASEWICZ, PH.D., is an international consultant focusing on issues of sustainable design, product development, and social entrepreneurship. She engages with students as an assistant professor at San Francisco State University and with industry professionals through GarmentoSpeak (www.garmentopspeak.com). "Fashion is about change," she says. "If sustainable design and development are our goals, then let us engage thoughtfully and intelligently as we participate in changing what is considered fashionable."

CHAPTER 2

Fashion, Social Marketing, and the Eco-Savvy Shopper

Connie Ulasewicz

Eco-savvy consumers look to retailers to offer more "responsible" clothing manufactured with environmentally sound methods that enable them to tread lightly on the Earth. Pairing their passion for style with a passion for positive change, some consumers purchase based on the social or monetary contribution a retailer or manufacturer makes to a sustainable cause or foundation. Through such innovative approaches, consumers are increasingly becoming agents of change—social entrepreneurs who invest not only in a transformation of the fashion industry but in the welfare of society and the planet that we all share.

> "It's got to be fashion and not what people perceive as 'organic fashion'—those hippie, oatmeal type of clothing—they have to be gorgeous clothes. Otherwise, no one would buy them."
>
> —Katharine Hamnet, *DNR,* August 8, 2005

Eco-Fashion: Trend or Movement?

The ongoing overexploitation of natural resources and the destruction of the environment have pushed many consumers of fashionable products to question their purchases. We read that the clothing, footwear, and textile industries are second only to agriculture in consuming the most water and contaminating waterways with chemicals for bleaching, dyeing, and finishing fashion products (Stockinger, 2006). We hear the terms "sustainable design," "eco chic," "eco-fashion," and "ecologically friendly couture" and wonder, are these terms a trendy response to this environmental degradation or a new movement within our industry?

Looking at the organic food industry, one can find an interesting parallel. Environmental journalist Michael Pollan, author of *The Omnivore's Dilemma* (2006), writes that consumers voting with their dollars created the $30 billion organic-food industry. He explains that normally a sharp distinction is made between people's actions as citizens, in which they are expected to consider the well-being of society, and their actions as consumers, which are assumed to be more selfish.

The eco-savvy fashion shopper appears to be struggling and pushing to reconcile the roles of being a conscientious consumer and a conscientious citizen. We are actively looking for clothes that we consider "responsible," that make us feel like we are treading lightly on the Earth by practicing consumerism with a conscience. Business professor Arthur Carroll (1999) developed a definition of corporate social responsibility in 1970 that included an ethical component relating to a firm's responsiveness to the expectations of society. Some of us push our expectations for positive change and our passion for style by searching for garments made from fibers whose production respects the environment, sold by retailers with a strong ethical component. We question the sustainability of natural fibers (e.g., cotton or wool) and synthetic fibers (e.g., nylon or polyester) as we learn about new fibers and fabrics like Eco-Spun, a sheepskin-like fabric made from recycled soda bottles; Lenpur, a cashmere-like fabric made from wood pulp of white pine trees; soya, a silky and soft cottonlike fabric made from soybeans; and sasawashi, a cotton- or linen-like naturally absorbent fabric made from a mixture of kumazasa bamboo with washi, a type of rice paper. Some of us also look beyond the brand or designer label and seek substance with our style, purchasing products that give a percentage of sales or profits back to the environment or support social causes such as breast cancer or heart disease. Social responsibility then relates to the raw materials, design, production, merchandising, retailing, consumption, and disposal of textile and apparel products (Dickson & Eckerman, 2007).

This chapter focuses on the needs and desires of the consumer. Each of us has the option to make sustainable choices when we spend our money on a particular line of clothing, style of T-shirt, or branded product from the Web, a catalog, or a department or specialty retail store. More and more, we are acting like socially responsible agents who desire personal change and respond as social entrepreneurs by investing in the transformation of our industry, society, and planet. At the same time, retailers are increasingly embracing this movement of social entrepreneurialism by launching cause marketing campaigns that promote products through philanthropic activities that *give back* to the community in order to align themselves with our desires to be good citizens. Exemplary retailers and manufacturers are highlighted throughout the following pages. The chapter closes with some suggested guidelines to follow as we act as conscientious citizens and consumers making honest evaluations of new products, processes, and the myriad of issues that surround sustainable choices in our textile and apparel industries.

Consumers as Social Entrepreneurs and the Power of New Ideas

I like to think of consumers, you and I, as agents of change; we push fashion corporations and businesses to make the right decisions that reflect the needs of the time. My theory is based on the idea that textile and apparel businesses are launched by people who are inspired with design ideas and impassioned to see their ideas become reality. The U.S. domestic textile industry, fueled by the entrepreneurial visions of New England mill owners such as Samuel Slater and Francis Lowell, pushed the Industrial Revolution forward in the eighteenth century. These entrepreneurs pioneered the domestic textile industry with their cloth-producing factories and mill systems (Dunwell, 1978). Apparel design and production followed a different path. In the mid-nineteenth century, Charles Fredrick Worth, an English-born fashion designer, made his mark in Paris by creating what has been termed *haute couture*. He turned his dressmaking practice into a seasonal line of dresses from which his patronesses would choose a design for him to custom fit. It was not until many years later in the twentieth century that French designers no longer dominated fashion and an international industry was launched (Cosgrave, 2000). In 1938, *Vogue* published its first annual American issue, highlighting the creations of Claire McCardell, Norman Norell, Mainbocher, and others who birthed another revolutionary concept by designing American sportswear. These individuals, self-motivated by their design-based product ideas, envisioned themselves and their products as engines of change as they launched new textile and apparel industries.

Social Entrepreneurialism in the Twenty-First Century

A new entrepreneurial revolution growing in the twenty-first century is pushing sustainable fashion forward. Green industries, ranging from those that provide products and services made in eco-friendly manners to those that supply renewable energy, have grown into a multi-billion-dollar market, according to the Center for Small Business and the Environment (CSBE) in Washington, DC (CSBE, n.d.). CSBE's contention is that it is the entrepreneurs who can solve most of the environmental crises affecting the globe. Jacob Singer, program director of the Green MBA program at New College of California in San

Francisco, finds that market demand dictates entrepreneurial success. According to Singer, this is equally true for products that offer obvious environmental benefits as well as plans that integrate green practices into business (Spaeder, 2006).

The spirit of entrepreneurialism that fuels change in our industry is different today than in the days of Samuel Slater, Charles Worth, or American sportswear designer Claire McCardell because the challenges are different. Today, we purchase fashion products, including fabrics, trims, and accessories, that may inflict damage upon our planet and our people, thereby creating significant social problems. The new entrepreneurs in our industry must have the ability to solve social problems on a large scale. Called "social entrepreneurs," they must be able to persuade, enlighten, touch hearts, shift perceptions, articulate new meanings, and move new concepts through the fashion system. Social entrepreneurship scholar and author David Bornstein (2004) describes contemporary social entrepreneurs as transformative forces. These are people who are relentless in pursuit of their visions, who will not take no for an answer, and who will not give up until they have created the change they believe that needs to happen. Social entrepreneurialism is one of the most current terms in the nonprofit sector. The term is now more broadly used as applied to individuals as well as companies. Dr. Paul C. Light, political scientist and founding director for the Brookings Center for Public Service, suggests in a *Stanford Social Innovation Review* article (2006) the following basic goals and strategies of the social entrepreneur or the socially entrepreneurial organization:

- Social entrepreneurship can start with individuals, groups, teams, companies, or communities that band together to create pattern-breaking change in what or how governments, nonprofits, and for-profit businesses address significant social problems.
- Social entrepreneurship involves a desire to not just get something done but to be involved in the process of how it gets done.

- Social entrepreneurs face serious barriers to success and sometimes can fail because it is hard to break patterns.

Dr. J. Gregory Dees (2001), author and leading educator in social entrepreneurship, writes that social entrepreneurs play the role of change agent in the social sector. Change agents are people or companies who recognize and pursue opportunities that will sustain a new social mission; they tend to act boldly while continually adapting and learning. Social entrepreneurs have a heightened sense of accountability to the social mission and the outcomes they seek to create.

In the twenty-first century, social entrepreneurs are looking for new strategies to benefit society. These strategies might involve using both charitable contributions and private investment capital. One example of such a strategy, the men's and women's eco-fashion line Edun (or *nude* spelled backward), was launched in 2005 by Paul David Hewson, or Bono, the activist and Irish singer in the post-punk band U2; his wife, Ali Hewson; designer Rogan Gregory; and their partner, Scott Hahn. The main objective behind Edun is to produce garments in family-run factories in Africa and South America. Instead of bringing charity to Africa by donating money, Edun brings manufacturing jobs that pay living wages to people in villages. Another part of Edun's commitment is the donation of 25 percent or $10 from each Edun-designed T-shirt sold with the ONE logo, which promotes the ONE Campaign. The ONE Campaign is an effort to rally people, one by one, to fight the emergency of global AIDS and extreme poverty (Edun, n.d.). Edun donates funds from T-shirt sales to the Apparel Lesotho Alliance to Fight AIDS fund, which provides education and medicine to factory workers and their families in the African country of Lesotho, where the shirts are manufactured. Equally, Edun acts as a voice to encourage the fashion community to do business in Africa as a means to bring the continent out of extreme poverty. The company's mission is to increase trade and to create sustainable employment for developing areas of the world.

FIGURE 2.1. A portion of the sales of each EDUN ONE tee goes dIrectly back to the Apparel Lesotho Alliance to Fight AIDS, which provides lifesaving care to factory workers and their families. (Photo courtesy of One.)

As we begin to recognize and acknowledge that fiber, fabric, and design innovations are required by our industry to design, manufacture, and retail sustainable products, we begin to better appreciate the work of the social entrepreneurs who have the passion to move us forward. Social entrepreneurs in our industry are required to shift behavior patterns and perceptions. Some question who initiates the change, the manufacturers and retailers or the consumers, and who responds to the change, again, the manufacturers and retailers or the consumers. I see the process as a symbiotic relationship; consumers and apparel companies hold each other accountable for their actions. This pushes the sustainable momentum forward. The rise of social entrepreneurship can be seen as a development that has occurred across the world over the past three decades with the emergence of millions of new citizen organizations (Bornstein, 2004). Organizations inspired by individuals who create new models to promote social well-being restore the environment and create wealth, thereby continuing the cycle of promoting social well-being.

Planet Aid is an example of an organization with a vision toward

FIGURE 2.2. Clothes collection bins placed in convenient locations that people can remember make it easy for citizens to recycle. The average American consumes 70 pounds of textiles a year. More than 85 percent of this is discarded with the trash. (Photo by Adam M. Lee.)

social well-being. A nonprofit organization, Planet Aid is dedicated to improving the lives of people in developing countries. The primary method developed to achieve its goals is its clothing collection and recycling program. Clothing collection bins are placed in major U.S., Canadian, and UK cities. Consumers deposit their unwanted clothes into these bins for recycling. The objective is to establish an efficient, locally based reuse system for secondhand clothing that benefits community development projects in Africa and Asia (Planet Aid, n.d.). After collection, the clothing is sorted, packaged, and resold in U.S., UK, and Canadian thrift shops. The proceeds from the sale of the clothing are used for community development projects. Clothing is also exported in bulk overseas to developing countries through Planet Aid's membership with the Humana People to People Movement (International Humana People to People Movement, n.d.). The Humana People to People Movement started in Denmark in 1977 and consists of development organizations such as Planet Aid. It supports sustainable programs that concentrate on creating development through projects in a wide range of areas such as education, child aid, relief aid, community development, and agricultural training. Also included are income-generating activities such as collection, distribution, and sale of secondhand clothes.

The New Ethical Dilemmas of Social-Conscious Businesses

The new standard of corporate performance envisioned by the social entrepreneurs encompasses both financial and ethical dimensions, regardless of the size of the company. A consideration of a textile and apparel company's ethical attributes includes investigating its environmental and social practices. An example of what may be considered an ethical dilemma encountered in our industry revolves around the definition of what makes a fiber eco-friendly. In 2003, Paris hosted the first Ethical Fashion Show®. Founded by Paris designer Isabelle Quéhé, the European event is centered on ethical fashion, promoting designers using fibers and dye processes that support the environment (Turkish Daily News, 2006). The fashion presented at the Ethical Fashion Show® aims for a fair balance between creativity, quality, and price. Products are manufactured with raw materials and dyes that are not harmful to the environment (Ethical Fashion Show, n.d.).

Of all the interesting new fibers, from sweet potatoes to pineapple bark, at the 2006 show, bamboo seemed to get the most favorable response from designers. Bamboo fiber has a smooth hand; it drapes well, feels soft to the touch, and combines well with other fibers like cotton, Lycra®, and silk. Bamboo usually requires no pesticides due to its incredibly quick growth and does not need to be replanted because it is a perennial species. There is, however, a hard outer core on bamboo that must be broken down to make the fiber usable for spinning into yarn. Caustic chemicals are often used in this process. It is this chemical processing that has been questioned. Summer Rayne Oakes, consultant in socio-environmental sustainability, writes in the industry newsletter *S4trends* that before marketing bamboo as organic or eco-friendly, manufacturers, retailers, and consumers must understand the processes by which the fiber is produced. If bamboo is to be considered truly sustainable, the problem of chemicals required in this fiber's processing must first be worked out.

Another ethical fiber dilemma concerns the choice of cotton because it is considered natural and biodegradable yet is environmentally a challenging fiber to produce. In 2004, Goede Warr & Company, a Dutch business that represents the interests of socially and environmentally conscious consumers, funded a study investigating the sustainability of cotton. Scientists from Wageningen University in the Netherlands, reported in their findings that

- More than 90 percent of cotton production involves the use of synthetic chemicals.
- Genetically modified organism (GMO) cotton is grown on an estimated 20 percent of acres worldwide, and an estimated 80 percent of U.S. cotton is GMO.
- Certified organic cotton currently represents an estimated 1 percent of the cotton grown in the world (Kooistra, Pyburn, et al., 2006)

All cotton production practices have environmental, social, and economic impacts that can and should be measured. The current conventional cotton production system is heavily dependent upon pesticides and fertilizers. Current data from the USDA indicates that almost 6 pounds of pesticides are applied per acre. Pesticides used on cotton can cause a number of heath risks as they impact the soil, water, and air that we all share.

As earlier stated, social entrepreneurial companies consider the new standard for corporate performance one that encompasses financial and ethical dimensions for all companies, no matter their size. The Los Angeles designer Linda Loudermilk, considered a pioneer in the ecologically friendly couture design arena, aims to hit people at a gut level by capturing the soul and raw beauty of people and nature in her designs. The garments in her collections inherently bring up our universal connectedness and our responsibility to take care of each other and the Earth (Loudermilk, n.d.). Each season, Loudermilk creates a theme that she features on T-shirts. For Spring 2006 her theme was "Water is a human right," with 100 percent of the profits going to Global Green's water initiative. English designer Katherine Hamnett took a three-year hiatus from fashion as she put together her 2006 E line for men. "E" stands for "ethically and environmentally made." She believes the effect of change in the clothing industry will have more impact on climate change "than if the entire world signed the Kyoto agreement" (Epiro, 2005). On a larger scale, Marks and Spencer (M&S), the British retailer with more than 500 stores located throughout the United Kingdom and 150 stores worldwide, is recognized for their progressive approach to sustainable business practices (Marks and Spencer, n.d.). In 2007 they initiated Plan A, a five-year commitment to work with their customers to reduce their carbon (CO_2) emissions. A part of this plan, M&S launched a new care label campaign to encourage consumers to reduce their impact on the environment by lowering their clothes washing water temperature. The reminder "Think climate–Wash at 30C" will be imprinted on the clothing labels of all M&S products. Under the A plan, "By 2012 M&S aims to become carbon neutral, send no waste to landfill, extend sustainable sourcing, improve ethical trading, and help customers and employees lead healthier lifestyles (Marks and Spencer, 2007).

Linda Loudermilk, Katherine Hamnett, and Marks and Spencer provide us with just three examples of small and large companies acting and responding as social entrepreneurs as they choose to support and promote the use of sustainability in their products.

Is Marketing Believable? Social Marketing and Good Citizenship
The basic tenet of sustainable design requires that the needs of the current generation must be met without compromising the needs of

future generations (World Commission on Environment and Development, 1987). I like to think that most of us want to be socially and environmentally conscious but find it difficult to identify the important issues. Not having a framework to assess and analyze the sustainable issues and choices we face in our industry can be daunting. It is challenging to make informed decisions and move forward.

Fashion for Good is a professional nonprofit association of men and women who practice and promote ethical values in the fashion business. In its marketing plan, Fashion for Good professes that successful companies are those that hold corporate social responsibility as an attitude that starts with the company's vision and mission (Fashion for Good, n.d.). As consumers change their perceptions of brands because of new respect or diminishing respect for a company's culture or business practices, they force companies to reassess and understand that corporate social responsibility must be a part of a business's corporate culture. According to 2007 findings from the U.S. National Marketing Institute, 52 percent of consumers said they feel more loyal to companies that are socially responsible and 38 percent said they would be willing to pay extra for products manufactured by socially responsible companies (Hein, 2007).

It follows then that many consumers would make purchases based on ethical value or emotional commitment they feel toward a brand or a company. In 2006, the San Francisco retailer Gap, Inc. rolled out an entire collection of men's and women's apparel and accessories labeled (Gap) RED, with one vintage style T-shirt manufactured in Lesotho, Africa, and pledged to donate half of the profits from it to the Global Fund to fight AIDS, tuberculosis, and malaria (Russell, 2006). A number of companies, including Motorola, American Express, Apple, Emporio Armani, and Converse, joined the RED campaign by donating a percentage of their profits from particular products, and they too tapped into consumers' growing desire to do good deeds with their purchasing dollars.

The high-profile (PRODUCT)[RED] campaign came under attack in March 2007 when the U.S. Marketing Trade magazine *Marketing Age*

FIGURE 2.3. As a global partner of (PROD-UCT)^{RED}, the Gap contributes half the profits from sales of its Gap (PRODUCT)^{RED}, such as this T-shirt, to the Global Fund to help women and children affected by HIV/AIDS in Africa. (Photo courtesy of Gap, Inc.)

reported that the campaign raised $18 million despite a marketing outlay by Gap, Apple, and Motorola estimated as high as $100 million. How much has RED raised to fight AIDS? As reported by the UK *Independent,* $25 million was raised during the first six months of the (PRODUCT)^{RED} campaign.

Whether or not a company profits from such a campaign, and even when a campaign raises funds to benefit a cause, the question remains: Is it ethical to use causes to promote brands?

In 2005, retail companies gave away 1.7 percent of their profits before paying taxes, compared with 0.9 percent for companies in other industries, according to the Committee to Encourage Philanthropy, a nonprofit group in New York (Barbaro, 2006). Increasingly, corporations are tying their brands to nonprofit causes, while nonprofits are basically competing with corporations for consumer attention and consumer dollars. Clearly, causes sell; they touch human emotions and create deep allegiances to experiences and quite possibly to products. In fact, nonprofit organizations are spending big dollars on media, public relations, advertising, and communications, according to exclusive research by Changing Our World, Inc., the parent company to onPhilanthropy (Watson, 2006). In many cases, it's the nonprof-

FIGURE 2.4. Awareness ribbons are folded into loops and are used by the wearer to make a subtle statement of support for a cause or an issue. The meaning behind the awareness ribbon depends on its color.

its that are driving the message recognition by branding philanthropic causes, and they are spending billions doing it.

But with all of the new campaigns and products, it can often be very confusing to choose the right cause to support. It's difficult to be sure that marketing tools and advertising campaigns designed to make us aware of the choices are truthful and honest. Does the money collected go to the correct cause, and do the products promoting that cause actually have any relationship to it? The practice of linking specific products to charitable donations, or *cause marketing*, has become an increasingly popular method for corporations to possibly clean up their image while contributing to charity. The abundance of ribbon campaigns (e.g., pink for breast cancer awareness, red for AIDS awareness, mint for abuse awareness, and dark red for Mothers Against Drunk Driving) are intended to raise the conscientious consumer's awareness, and yet sometimes the abundance of the products produced in the color or carrying the ribbon logo just confuse and irritate potential consumers.

The commitment of the women's apparel company Carlisle to its cause is quite real. Its "Our Fabric of Hope" program grew out of asking its Carlisle Consultants which philanthropic agency they most wanted the Carlisle Collection to support. The company chose to join the fight against breast cancer because so many of its target customers were affected by that disease. Each year, the company designs a Fabric of Hope scarf bearing the pink ribbon symbolic of breast cancer awareness, and all proceeds from sales of the scarf go directly to the Susan G. Komen Breast Cancer Foundation. Since 1998, the Carlisle Collection has donated more than $1.3 million (Carlisle, n.d.).

Brand Names and Cause Marketing

As the model for entrepreneurship evolved from business-for-profit to business-for-social-change, the retail marketing sector has kept in step. In the 1990s, retailers resisted developing and selling products that would link a brand name to a potentially controversial cause (Barbaro, 2006). In the twenty-first century, there is little hesitancy to link brand names with a cause because the response from the consumer to pioneering companies that tried to do so has been so great. The trend can be traced back to 2004, when millions of people bought $1 Livestrong bracelets to benefit the Lance Armstrong Foundation (Barbaro, 2006). Consumers not only wanted to support a charity but also wanted to broadcast their philanthropy to the world with a yellow plastic bracelet worn on their wrist.

Cause marketing is created when a for-profit business and nonprofit business join to create a marketing partnership to support a social cause. At its best, cause marketing is a win-win-win proposition: The cause wins by being both promoted and funded, the consumer wins by feeling good about making a positive choice, and the retailer wins by making the sale and presumably feeling good about being an agent of positive change (Linial, 2003). As retailers engage in cause marketing, they put philanthropy at the center of their products and campaigns and develop yearlong sustainable models.

Cause marketing is a term that can be used to describe the idea behind the Gap (PRODUCT)[RED] campaign previously described. Gap, Inc. continues to design products that are projected to be sold for five years until 2011; this is a sustained way for them to get into and stay involved in philanthropy.

For the past 10 years, Cone, Inc., a Boston-based strategy and communications agency, has researched American attitudes toward corporate support of social issues and has found that more than ever before, companies must get involved with social issues in order to protect and enhance their reputations. As reported in its 2004 Cone Corporate Citizenship Study (http://www.coneinc.com):

- 8 in 10 Americans say that corporate support of causes wins their trust in that company, a 21 percent increase since 1993.
- 86 percent of Americans say they are likely to switch to a brand that supports a cause when price and quality are equal, a 20 percent increase since 1993.
- 80 percent of Americans can name a company that stands out in their mind as a strong corporate citizen, a 54 percent increase from 1993.

Go Red for Women, the American Heart Association's first national awareness campaign, is an example of a Cone-created social marketing campaign. The campaign began in February 2004 to raise awareness that heart disease is women's number one killer. In 2005, 8,600 U.S. companies participated in National Wear Red Day, and more than $40 million dollars was projected to have been raised for women and heart disease. February 4 is National Wear Red Day, and in 2007 an entire Web site was devoted to providing consumers with products to purchase to support the cause (Shop Go Red, n.d.). Macy's is a corporate sponsor of the National Wear Red Campaign and supports and promotes this cause throughout the year.

Expectations are that the trend for causal retailing will continue. In 2006, the Cone Millennial Cause, the first in-depth study of its kind, shows that 61 percent of the 78 million-strong Millennials, born between 1979 and 2001, feel personally responsible for making a difference in the world. Cone found that

- 74 percent are more likely to pay attention to a company's message when they see that the company has a deep commitment to a cause.

- 69 percent consider a company's social and environmental commitment when deciding where to shop.
- 83 percent will trust a company more if it is socially and environmentally responsible.

Causal Campaigns Can Help a Business and Its Product

Causal marketing campaigns that can build trust with consumers will be more sustainable for businesses. Gaining consumer confidence will be imperative. Marketers know that appealing to sustainability values will not overcome a fundamental weakness in a product, but sometimes a weakness is also a strength.

The bast fiber hemp is a perfect example of a valuable and environmentally friendly crop that has yet to overcome some unfortunate weaknesses. With a relatively short growth cycle of 120 days, industrial hemp is an efficient and economical crop for farmers to grow, as it has moderate water and fertilizer requirements. However, because of its association with marijuana and the psychoactive ingredient THC, its acceptance in the consumer market has been very limited. A good-cause marketing campaign could help the hemp industry.

Terrific campaigns exist, but consumers may not know about them. In 2006, Timberland, a global leader in the design, engineering, and marketing of premium quality footwear, launched a causal marketing campaign: a three-section "nutritional label" on each box intended to educate consumers about the products they purchase. The manufactured section gives the name and location of the factory where the product was made. The environmental impact section reports how much energy is needed to produce the footwear and how much of Timberland's energy is generated from renewable resources such as the sun, wind, and water. The community impact section reports on issues of social responsibility. Timberland is enhancing its brand image with the intent that it will see an increase in sales as its demonstrates its respect for the environment through socially responsible business practices. Its CEO, Jeff Swart, is, "re-imagining every aspect of its business practices so our children will not be confronted with irreversible damage" (Michelson, 2006).

In 2001, Yvon Chouinard, founder of Patagonia, Inc., and Craig Mathews, owner of Blue Ribbon Flies (which sells fly-fishing equipment), launched One Percent for the Planet, an alliance of more than 370 companies from the United States, Canada, Europe, Japan, the South Pacific, and South America. The alliance recognizes the true cost of doing business and donates 1 percent of its sales to environmental organizations worldwide. This environmental alliance is designed to help members become sustainable businesses.

In 2007, Nau, a Portland, Oregon, company with a new message, emerged. Hailed in the press as a "transformational" clothing company, Nau will meld social responsibility and good outdoor clothing and gear. Nau states that it is "committed to radically altering the landscape of corporate philanthropy, so much so that we'd like to change that ungainly phrase. We prefer community partnership" (Nau, n.d.). Customers are able to direct 5 percent of every sale to an environmental, social, or humanitarian charitable organization of their choice. By inviting the customer to determine where the company donations are directed, the consumer will in essence be able to participate in choosing where they would effect change.

Where Do We Go from Here?
I would like to include you, the reader, as a participant in this movement of social good. I would like for us to together decide how we can be eco-savvy fashion consumers. The ideas of fashion sustainability and eco chic need to move from the fringe to the mainstream, and to do that, they must be skillfully marketed before they will shift people's perceptions and behaviors. We need to collectively find a common voice and respond by (1) purchasing products that come from renewable resources, (2) actively supporting the reuse or recycling of prod-

ucts, and (3) ensuring that manufacturing processes are safe for human ecological health in all phases of the product life cycle. The path to engage in these three activities is challenging because a new business model is needed, one that demands that manufacturers, retailers, and consumers act together in making sustainable choices. If we act as both good citizens and good consumers, we will send a consistent message all the way back up the design supply chain asking for new processes to be followed.

The U.S. Federal Trade Commission (FTC) has developed guides for the use of environmental marketing claims. As stated on its Web site (Federal Trade Commission, n.d.):

> These guides apply to environmental claims included in labeling, advertising, promotional materials, and all other forms of marketing, whether asserted directly or by implication, through words, symbols, emblems, logos, depictions, product brand names, or through any other means, including marketing through digital or electronic means, such as the Internet or electronic mail. The guides apply to any claim about the environmental attributes of a product, package, or service in connection with the sale, offering for sale, or marketing of such product, package or service for personal, family, or household use, or for commercial, institutional, or industrial use.

The guidelines are not legislative rules and are therefore unenforceable, yet they are still very helpful and informative as guiding principles for eco-savvy companies to promote and market their products. Over time, as more clothing companies engage in environmental practices, the labeling will become clearer so we can make informed consumer choices.

The 2006 University of Cambridge study "Well Dressed" sets out a different type of model than the FTC and a vision of a sustainable clothing industry that would also offer new opportunities to retailers and manufacturers. "The key to change is to ensure that the government, industry, and consumers work together to achieve a more sustainable clothes and textiles industry" (Allwood, Laursen et al., 2006). The research supports the concepts of conscientious consumerism and puts forth the idea that to reduce environmental impact and promote social equity within our industry, the consumer will need to demand more choices. Its suggestions include the following:

- Buy secondhand clothing when possible.
- Buy fewer and more durable products.
- Lease or rent clothing that would otherwise not be worn to the end of the garment's natural life.
- Wash clothes less often at lower temperatures, using eco-detergents, hang dry, and do not iron.

At first these findings may seem challenging for the fashionable consumer to support, but fashion is about change. Design entrepreneurs can turn these possibilities into fashionable realities. The designer is the central connection between the manufacturers that produce the goods and the consumers who buy them.

Tierra Del Forte, the designer behind Del Forte Denim (www.delforte.com), has integrated a model for new consumerism within her business model. It's called Project Rejeaneration. Consumers send their used jeans back to the company after they have tired of them, and the company refreshes and produces a second generation of new products from them. As a reward for recycling, it also takes 10 percent off the next purchase of Del Forte Denim, or donates 10 percent to the Sustainable Cotton Project, of which they are a supporting member.

Conclusion: What Can You Do?
If sustainable design and sustainable development is our goal, then we must engage thoughtfully and with knowledge as we participate in

the socially responsible consumption of fashion. With the awareness that there is a pro and a con to all decisions, consider the following five actions for the eco-savvy shopper, and remember that every act of consumption is a vote for the type of world in which you wish to be a part:

- Do question marketing campaigns, but do not dismiss a product because of the campaign.
- Do read clothing labels and try new fibers.
- Do fix, mend, or alter clothing to extend the natural life.
- Do think twice before you purchase, and do buy fewer and more durable products.
- Do dispose of used garments through recycling.

Start to look beyond the surface appearance, and consider the total life span of the fashionable products you purchase. Remember, it is a symbiotic relationship between the consumer and the manufacturers and retailers from which we purchase, and what seems like radical or unusual fashion today may well be considered acceptable and main-stream tomorrow.

References

Barbaro, M. (2006, November 13). Candles, jeans, lipsticks: products with ulterior motives. *New York Times*, p. 33.

Bornstein, D. (2006). *How to Change the World*. New York: Oxford Press.

Carlisle. (n.d.). Retrieved from http://www.carlislecollection.com/fabric_of_hope

Carroll, A. (1999). Corporate social responsibility. *Business & Society, 38*(3), 268–295.

Center for Small Business and the Environment. (n.d.). Retrieved July 27, 2007, from http://www.geocities.com/aboutcsbe/index.html

Cosgrave, B. (2000). The Complete History of Costume and Fashion.

Dees, J. G. (2001). The meaning of social entrepreneurship. Retrieved January 5, 2007, from http://www.fuqua.duke.edu/centers/case/documents/Dees_SEdef.pdf

Dickson, M., & Eckman, M. (2006, July). Social responsibility: The concept as defined by apparel and textile scholars. *Clothing and Textiles Research Journal*, 24(3), 178–191.

Dunwell, S. (1978). The run of the mill, Boston, Massachusetts: David R. Godine.

Edun Web site. (n.d.). Retrieved from http://www.edun.ie/one.asp

Epiro, S. (2005, August 8). Woman on a mission. *DNR*.

Ethical Fashion Show. (n.d.). Retrieved from http://www.ethicalfashionshow.com/efs_va.htm

Fashion for Good Web site. (n.d.). Retrieved from http://www.fashionforgood.com

Hein, K. (2007, March 19). Research: Good things come to brands that give [Electronic version]. *BrandWeek*. Retrieved March 19, 2007, from http://www.brandweek.com/bw/magazine/current/afticle display.js

Federal Trade Commission Guide for the Use of Environmental Marketing Claims. (n.d.). Retrieved July 27, 2007, from the Federal Trade Commission Web site: http://www.ftc.gov/bcp/grnrule/guides980427.htm#260.7

The International Humana People to People Movement. (n.d.). Retrieved from http://www.humana.org

Kooistra, K., Pyburn, R., & Termorshuizen, A. (2006). The sustainability of cotton: Consequences for man and environment. Report Number 23. Science Shop, Wageningen, UR. Retrieved September 1, 2006, from Wageningen University and Research Center Web site: http://library.wur.nl/wasp/bestanden/LUWPUBRD_00345417_A502_001.pdf

Light, P. (2006). Reshaping social entrepreneurship [Electronic version]. *Stanford Social Innovation Review*. Retrieved November 30, 2006, from http://ssireview.org/site/printer/reshaping_social_entrepreneruship

Linial, P. (2003). *Marketing from the heart*. Scottsdale, Arizona: Morpheus Publications.

Loudermilk Web site. (n.d.). Retrieved from http://www.lindaloudermilk.com

Marks and Spencer appoints eco champions to promote its £200m environmental programme. (2007, June 18). *Personnel Today*. Retrieved June 20, 2007, from http://www.personneltoday.com/Articles/2007/06/18/41132/marks-and-spencer-appoints-eco-champions-to-promote-its-200m-environmental-programme.html

Marks & Spencer Web site (n.d.). Retrieved from http://www.lindaloudermilk.com

Michelson, M. (2007, April). Project green all-stars [Electronic version]. *Outside,* 76.

Nau Web site (n.d.). Retrieved from http://www.nau.com

Potatoes, pineapples to dress environmentally minded fashionistas [Electronic version]. (2006, October 17). *Turkish Daily News,* Retrieved from http://www.turkishdailynews.com.tr/article.php?enewsid=56890

Pollan, M. (2006). The omnivore's dilemma: A natural history of four meals. New York: Penguin Press.

Planet Aid Web site. (n.d.) Retrieved from http://www.planetaid.org

Russell, S. (2006, Oct. 12). Businesses start 'red' campaign to help Africa. *San Francisco Chronicle,* B1, B3.

Shop Go Red. (n.d.). Retrieved from http://www.shopgored.org

Spaeder, K. E. (2006). Think green [Electronic version]. *Entrepreneur Magazine.* Retrieved September 15, 2006 from http://www.entrepreneur.com/magazine/entrepreneur/2006/March/

Stockinger, B. (2006, May/June) The fairest of them all. *Sportswear International.* Retrieved August 30, 2006, from http://katharinehamnett.com/Editorial/00s/Sportswear+International

Summer Rayne Oakes Web site (n.d.) Retrieved from http://www.summerrayneoakes.com

Wexler, R. (2006). Social enterprise a legal constraint. *The Exempt Organization Tax Review 54*(3), 233–243.

Watson, T. (2006, December 13). Consumer philanthropy: Nonprofits spend billions to reach consumers [Electronic version]. *onPhilanthropy.* Retrieved 12/30/06 from http://www.onphilanthropy.com/site/News2?page=NewsArticle&id=6863

Valley, P. (2007, March 23). The big question: Does the red campaign help big western brands more than Africa? [Electronic version]. *The Independent.* Retrieved March 23, 2007, from http://news.independent.co.uk/world/politics/article2341310.ece

World commission on environment and development. (1987). *Our common future.* Oxford: Oxford University Press.

JANET HETHORN, PH.D., is a designer
and writer, focusing on aesthetic
response and contextual understanding of style and appearance.
Current research projects examine
how viewers respond to expressions
of visual style in everyday situations
and the issues that emerge from
these responses. Her studio work
integrates these findings with
an exploration of performance,
movement, and garment fit. Janet
is a professor at the University
of Delaware.

CHAPTER 3

Consideration of Consumer Desire

Janet Hethorn

Sustainable fashion begs the question, "sustaining what?" While most might answer "environment," a less obvious but just as important answer is "people." This chapter explores the myriad ways that designers and product developers can access and tap into consumer desire as a way to positively meet people's needs through fashion. When a designer focuses on the needs of the individual, the individual's sense of self and sustained well-being significantly improves. This significance emerges as we look at examples that include the relationship between clothing and the body, and the power of fashion to express meaning and identity. Sustaining people through clothing is not a new concept. Most will agree that clothing is a basic need, much like food and shelter. What is suggested here are ways to place these ideas as central components within the design process.

The Power of Design

This chapter is about ideas and opportunities. It's about thinking of the consumer in ways slightly different from what traditional design practices dictate. To create sustainable outcomes, we must start by critiquing the way we design and how our practices best serve consumers and meet their desires. Design has the power to change our perception, action, and mind-set. It is our responsibility as designers to shift our thinking and put our ideas into action in order to tap into this power.

People as a Focus in the Design Process

The first shift that needs to be made is to simply visualize the end result in a new way. Instead of considering the object, the *garment*, as the focus of your design activity, visualize someone wearing and moving and enjoying his or her life in the garment that you design. Move your focus away from the object to the *person*. In that way, the shift toward sustainability can begin. The opportunity exists to create fashion that sustains people and creates a sense of well-being for the wearer as an individual.

Our traditional design process runs counter to this way of thinking. We think abstractly about people from the get-go. We follow trends and directions that are derived from abstractions of target markets, and from reports of what they purchased in the past along with projections of future buying. Then we generalize these target markets, creating stereotypes of who they are. In pattern development, we use fit models that "represent" this market, thus building in problems with garment fit from the start. People are abstracted further as we design through sketches and illustrations that are drawn mostly as front views. Fashions are communicated through magazine images that are static abstractions of "ideal" people wearing your designs.

Even real garments, displayed on mannequins in stores, are pinned and tucked to form an ideal silhouette, and the clothing inevitably looks different when seen on moving, breathing people.

As we rethink fashion and turn away from modern industrial techniques, we should start visualizing people, individual people, interacting with their garments in ways that are healthy and meaningful. Truly sustainable fashion should address the emotional, expressive, and physical qualities that garments can provide for consumers. In addition to meeting needs and desires, the resulting satisfaction leads to greater use and a longer functioning cycle. Think about your favorite garment, maybe a T-shirt or an old sweater, that may be threadbare or faded but is still a part of your core wardrobe because of your emotional attachment to it, and think about how you feel when you wear it. Imagine a world where everyone is wearing clothes that fit well. The fabric is comfortable and enhances, not hinders, their performance. The ideas and identity the wearers express through their appearance feel just right to them. They can move through their days with no annoyance or uncertainty generated from their clothes. Furthermore, they look great. Together, these qualities generate a sense of overall well-being. We have done our job.

Getting There: Moving from Target Markets to Individual Consumers

As introduced above, designers and marketers traditionally think of consumers as "targets." In fact, it is critical for you, as a designer, to consider your target market. Who are you designing for, and how do you create garments that they will want to buy? Marketing firms and merchandisers focus on creating profiles and lifestyle analyses as guidelines for product development. I am not suggesting that we drop this perspective entirely, but merely that we consider a more fruitful path for sustainability. If we are to sustain people, we need to look more closely at individuals—who they are, what they want to wear, and what they need. By thinking about people as a group, the opportunities for sustainable design narrow. In fact, I would argue that a goal for hitting the center of a target market breeds waste. It means that there are many people on the fringes whose needs are not met, perpetuating many fashion items that are unacceptable, flawed, or left for discounted secondary choices.

Consumers reflect this narrow target market approach by finding flaws in themselves because they constantly compare themselves to the ideal and come up short. If something doesn't fit, it is their fault. "My seat is too flat," "my legs are too long," or "if the waist fits, my hips are too big"; these are comments that reflect a self-critique instead of something that is wrong with the garment (e.g., a sizing problem or other flaw). No wonder body images are tattered and self-concept diminished when people see themselves different from the idealized target markets that are the goal of fashion design. What are they comparing themselves against, and who is taking the responsibility for creating this dynamic? To move in new sustainable directions, we must address these questions.

A downside of a generalized target market is the possibility of being so focused as to create a stereotype, perhaps missing other nuances that a focus on the individual would possess. We think of people in groups, we label these groups, and these groups are categorized as departments in stores. As consumers, we are accustomed to this; we shop based on categories. It helps us find things and keep an organized system. But the balance has gone too far. I am simply suggesting that we add back in the focus on individual people who wear clothes and have desires related to those clothes and their total appearance.

As part of the design process, it is critical to get inside the consumers' individual heads and not their collective heads. What would happen if we designed for individuals with individual needs and desires? Now you might say we are already doing that. Then I would say if that is the case, then design has failed. We aren't designing for individuals if over 60 percent of people report that they can't find clothes that fit and consumers often complain that they have a hard time finding styles that they feel and look great in.

What if we turn this around? Instead of targeting the consumer, how about *listening* to them? We could find out what they want in order to best represent their aesthetic preferences. We could discover the full range of performance needs they will encounter and how their clothing might address them. What makes for comfortable clothing? How are these concepts different for different individuals? How are they the same? Consider undertaking methods and observations that can uncover the issues that present themselves in what people are currently wearing and what they might wear instead to better meet their needs. As we move further into this chapter, issues and strategies will be identified to help us move in this direction. Let's get started.

Well-Being: A Basic Concept of Sustainability

Whether within the realms of the social, the economic, or the environmental, sustainability is based on the concept of well-being. We diminish environmental well-being through waste and pollution, and we can improve it through lowering carbon emissions and improving bio-friendly practices. This is easy to grasp and generally acceptable. Not so clear, but still important, is the potential to diminish or enhance the well-being of people through the garments and fashion we create for them. And, when we consider people as the focus of our sustainability efforts, the idea of well-being allows us to open our creativity to embrace meaningful problem solving within the fashion process. Think about a time when you felt absolutely fabulous in what you were wearing. What were the characteristics and features of the clothing, the situation? Then, recall the opposite, a situation when you were at odds with your clothes. Once again, what were the elements that were the culprits? By doing this brief exercise, you can rather simply notice the garment qualities that can be manipulated to impact the relationship between successful design and a sense of well-being. There are many levels of potential success or failure in clothing design. For a garment to fully realize success, and thus enhance the feeling of well-being of the person who is wearing it, the design must meet his or her total needs. Put simply, this means that it should be aesthetically and functionally appropriate for the person and the situation of use. Often designers focus on one or the other of these qualities, functionality *or* aesthetics, but I would argue that both dimensions are addressed and integrated in all successful designs. Let's take a look at what this means for design potential:

- *Aesthetic* refers to all of the visual and expressive elements of a garment, and more inclusively, the total look.
- *Function* is all about what the garment needs to do, how it performs for and with the body to meet various activities and movements.

When aesthetic and functional concerns are fully addressed within the design process, the possibility for fashion to sustain people comes into focus. In addition, fashion is embedded within social and cultural contexts, and people are constantly searching for and providing meaning within these contexts through what they wear and the resulting visual communication. So, if we are to take full advantage of the opportunity to create fashion that sustains people, we must expand our thinking of how to meet consumer desire. We must go beyond general notions of markets and focus instead on designing for individual well-being.

Approaches to Discovering Design Opportunities
To create meaningful and desirable designs, a successful strategy for inspiration is to go right to the source. Find out what people need and then use what you learn as a basis for your design strategies. Watch them in action, walking down the street, sitting on a subway car, engaging in a sports activity, or any place at all. Instead of just focusing on fashion magazines, trend reports, and shopping the market for what everyone else is designing, simply open your eyes to *how* people are wearing what they currently put together in everyday situations,

and analyze what is working and what is not. Take photographs, write notes, talk with them. Here are some specific strategies.

Observations

Position yourself in a location that allows you to watch people and what they wear. Go to public spaces, parks, shopping malls, street cafés, and pay attention to how individuals have put together their looks. See how they arrange items in combinations and how they present themselves through movement and expression. Notice the entire experience and how the context that you are viewing it impacts how you see and interpret the visual information. Also, be sure to question how you select what to view. The richest information comes from going past what you like or see as the next trend. Look carefully at what blends in, as well as what stands out. Then, document your observations by writing notes, drawing pictures, and taking photographs. In this activity, you must remember that you are the "outsider." You are seeing what is present in the visual field and making your own meaning out of it. This may be different from what the wearer, or the "insider," is thinking they are expressing; their sense of what their clothing means to them is not always obvious. By developing a combination of approaches, you can better assess consumer desire and needs.

Participant Observations

Involve yourself in the activities of what the people for whom you are designing are doing. Firsthand experience is a great teacher. I often have my students do fieldwork related to their design goals. If they are designing for people who need clothes for strenuous outdoor activities, I have them wear their best guess at the appropriate outfits and go for a hike in the woods. They go in teams and discuss their findings as they are engaged. What may seem simple, such as the need for clothing that doesn't catch on branches, is immediately obvious, while other findings, such as the need for garments that keep the wearer warm while at the same time allow for changes to cool as the body warms from exercise, really hits home when they experience it directly. With the mind-set of discovery, the ideas for solutions come quickly. I have also sent students to bowling alleys, taken group yoga classes, and even gone to shooting ranges. The "Walk a mile in my shoes . . ." perspective can go a long way.

Interviews

There are two basic kinds of interview strategies that work well in gaining design insight: individual and group. People love to talk about their clothes and what they would like to see developed differently, so a structured interview can be a beneficial tool. Develop a series of questions, and take along a tape recorder. The key to a successful interview is to really listen to the issues that are raised. Be open to allowing the interviewee to express his or her opinions. You may find that the most informative interviews do not answer all of the questions on your list, but the details revealed through conversation uncover findings that your plan didn't anticipate. Ask questions that do not lead to a "yes" or "no" response. Then follow up with additional questions to dig deeper into what you are finding. You could do a series of short interviews, two to five minutes, but also consider conducting longer interviews lasting up to a half an hour or more. If you can gain access to a group of people who share similar interests or needs, a focus group interview may be helpful. It's best to limit the group to less than eight members in order to allow everyone to feel comfortable and be able to bounce ideas off of each other easily. You can even ask them to bring examples of clothing, perhaps their favorite as well as their least favorite, in order to have real items that will spawn discussion. Or, select a range of photos or images from magazines as a visual starting point for generating reactions. A group of students I worked with were charged with designing wrestling sin-glets for a client. They invited the university wrestling team to our stu-dio and had a lively discussion, complete with demonstrations. The wrestlers brought their current garments and couldn't stop talking about the problems they were experiencing. As a result, the complet-ed informed designs went beyond the client's expectations. *The Sage Handbook of Qualitative Research* (Denzin and Lincoln, 2005) is a good source for information on interviews, participant observation, as well as other helpful methods.

Data Management and Electronic Assessment

Beyond the basic observations and interviews, consider how you are going to manage all the photographs you have taken and then how you might further analyze them for useful design inspiration. Remember, the focus of this data collection is to gather the consumer perspective and visual support of their preferences. Searching for visu-al patterns is a useful strategy. Consider the complete image of the body, the clothing, and the interaction among the contexts (e.g., gar-ment to body, body to surround) as you analyze your images. Look for visual structure, both layout and surface, as well as how the visual definers such as line, shape, color, and texture are interacting. A good reference for this process is *The Way We Look* (DeLong, 1998). If you develop an image database or image management system, you will be able to track the evolution of visual information as well as combine it with other text-based responses, either from your own analysis or from interview transcriptions. FileMaker Pro and Aperture are two software offerings that provide useful tools for these tasks.

Beyond your own image collections, there are many sources you could explore to gather visual knowledge from particular individuals and groups. Flickr.com and blogs that focus on fashion topics are great resources of images and descriptions. You could also set up your own chat topic to post questions and gather responses. A class of mine that

was designing warm-weather gear for female hunters used this strategy and found access to women they had difficulty finding otherwise.
A lively dialogue pursued that included images posted and detailed
descriptions of consumer need.

For a more advanced approach to visual analysis, utilize complex
data management systems that allow for image search by image content. Query by image content (QBIC) (http://wwwqbic.almaden.
ibm.com/) and content-based image retrieval (CBIR) are two
approaches that do not rely on people for assigning meaning and textual descriptors. Instead, they search and sort by similar image content
and features, making for innovative analysis. I utilized QBIC in a study
of skiwear and was able to find visual information not possible otherwise. For example, during interviews with skiers, whom I also pho-
tographed, I asked what they liked about what they were wearing. A
common response was "it's comfortable." When I followed up with a
question about what made it comfortable, they found if difficult to
articulate further. But by using QBIC and pulling up all the images of
people who used the word "comfortable" to describe their clothing, I
was able to have a visual reference of what comfortable meant and
could analyze the images for visual and functional factors that might
support the concept of "comfort" (Hethorn, 2005; see Figure 3.1).

Then, further visual search within the database, beginning with
these images, could find similar visual information based on qualities
of the image such as color, location, and texture (Holt, Hethorn, et al.,
1995). There are exciting possibilities for aesthetic analysis and design
research studies when you are utilizing image content searches. The
ability to search hundreds and thousands of images, locate specific
image properties, and view images with meanings common to particular consumer groups and individuals will allow for new ways of
understanding aesthetic perception (Hethorn, 2005). Just think of the
possibilities for sustainable design when qualities and visual directions
can be identified in meaningful ways and can inform the design
process to better meet consumer desire.

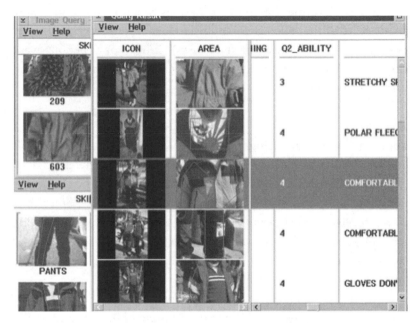

FIGURE 3.1. Query by image content (QBIC) is a tool created by IBM, Almaden Research Lab to search images by their visual content without the need for text. This screen shot is part of a study of skiwear preferences. (Photograph and content by Janet Hethorn.)

Creating Well-Being through Design

So far, I have introduced the need to focus on individuals and I have described ways to identify their needs and desires, aesthetic and functional, as a basis for creating a sense of well-being through design. Next, I will highlight various ways to hone in on specific elements that, when combined, address consumer desire through fashion. As mentioned earlier, clothing and fashion looks have aesthetic, or visually expressive, qualities and functional qualities that allow for movement and performance. The pieces that come together that embody these qualities are fabric and bodies. Obviously the combinations are almost limitless. So, design development along with consumer choice narrow down the selection for what is possible to wear.

Going back to the notion of discovering what people want, think about what all that encompasses. What does clothing do for people? How does fashion work in their lives? Simply put, people want clothes that help them look good, feel good, and work for them in various situations.

Looking Good: Expressing Visual Style

You are familiar with the saying "beauty is in the eye of the beholder." It is also in the eye of the expresser. Certainly the person wearing and projecting a look is actively expressing a visual presence, and this is connected to a direct sense of self and beauty. Seeing and making sense of a fashion form is a two-way street in which the designer plays an important role. The clothed body is a visual expression that can generate a range of responses that are not the same for every viewer. Also, what looks good to, or on, one person may be less than ideal for another. The designer is not the *giver* of taste and the consumer simply a receiver. This is not a sustainable model. Instead, think about being the *interpreter* of visual desire for the person (and people) for whom you are designing. This concept is often at odds with design philosophy. Many designers see themselves as the "all knowing" when it comes to what is considered beautiful. In fact, some designers actually feel that their work is put out there for people to buy, like it or not, with little consideration of what the consumer might actually desire as beautiful. In order to design with sustainability in mind, you must develop a relationship between interpreting visual desire and professional visual creativity. Once this mind-set is put into place, it becomes possible to develop fashion that holds meaning for consumers, projects a sense of identity, and connects them to a larger cultural community within which visual relationships are developed. The result of this effort can provide the wearer with improved self-esteem, sense of identity, and respect of place within cultural meaning.

There is no shortage of reading on this topic. Many books have emerged recently that focus on understanding perception and the senses, as well as on recognizing the importance of visual knowledge and design as a holistic process, taking into account objects, users, and contexts of use (Caplan, 2005; Nelson, 2003). Consumers are astute in their awareness of the importance of style and sensory response to their buying decisions. "The twenty-first century has become the age of aesthetics, and whether we realize it or not, this influence has taken over the marketplace" (Postrel, 2003). The importance of understanding aesthetic preference has never been greater.

What makes this difficult to respond to is that most design training does not cover methods of discovering aesthetic preference, opting instead for creating "good" design based on elements and principles leading to beauty as determined by the designer. But the question of "who gets to decide?" is an important one. Many would end this conversation by stating that the consumer decides with their purchase. However, consumers are limited to choosing from what is presented, and the visual selection is becoming more of the same as the "look" across brands narrows due to marketing and lifestyle analysis advising careful development of products for "known" targets. The opportunities to instead create fashion that represents visual meaning and cultural connection for consumers are wide open. As stated by George Nelson (2003), "The pursuit of design is not about the way things appear, but rather about the way things give meaning and relevance to the human experience."

A clear understanding of aesthetic preference is formed in part by observations in the world on a daily basis. Consumers are constantly creating visual references, changing preferences, and creating new ways of expressing their fashion outlook. Fashion is a powerful form of communication and a meaningful way for individuals to connect to groups, together constructing cultural meaning. In addition to the design research methods described earlier, it may be helpful to look at the process of seeing, to capture and describe references being viewed and to analyze them in relationship with already accepted aesthetic preferences, articulated both visually and verbally (Hethorn, 2005).

It is not easy to capture and interpret aesthetic preference for indi-

FIGURE 3.2. This group of young individuals share an aesthetic preference. Note the similar way of wearing the pants, the careful details of the fit of the shirts, and shape of shoes and laces. Hairstyles and even posture contribute to the details of viewing and communicating through appearance. Noting the details of a "look" as expressed in the context of wearing (here, on the street) is a design strategy that can lead to more meaningful product development. (Photograph by Janet Hethorn.)

viduals and groups, but it is certainly a worthy pursuit if the goal is to develop products that advance the creation of meaningful cultural connections and that celebrate diversity among individuals. Tap into this understanding, and the resulting design process will aid in supporting sustainability through individual and cultural well-being.

Feeling Good: Comfort and Fit

Certainly looking good contributes to a sense of feeling good. However, when talking about feeling good, we can expand our understanding with a concrete exploration of the actual physical relationship between fabric and the body. Many people equate feeling good with comfort. If it feels good, it's comfortable. So, what does that mean? The sensory experience of fabric against the body is part of it, as is how the fabric responds to movement and performance. The body is certainly not static. Even when still, the body breathes and functions physiologically in ways that fabric can both impede and enhance. This is only emphasized with movement. Design possibilities are expansive when an understanding of fabric characteristics and body functions are combined.

There are many innovations in fabric technology that make comfort more achievable. Whether it is stretch for mobility, moisture management, stain resistance, or antimicrobial characteristics. And, on a nano-level, even more exciting fabric developments are in the works. Do explore the options here and focus on achieving garment designs that are comfortable. Not only will people feel better about themselves and be able to move more freely, but the environment benefits also. Comfortable clothing gets worn more often and is kept longer. Future possibilities in design efforts toward developing comfortable environments will require a strong understanding of both textile (i.e., fiber and fabric) properties as well as the anatomy and physiology of the body. The design process for fashion needs to become more complex and holistic in order for sustainability to be realized. The usual way of developing products must change.

Nothing needs to undergo more change than the way we address garment fit. Fit underlies comfort, and the apparel industry has a long way to go in order to actualize satisfactory fit for a range of bodies. Bodies are not standard, and standard sizing is a myth. The sizes assigned to particular ranges of patterns and garments are not at all standard across apparel companies. Our current system of sizing is based on an inconsistent interpretation of body measurements and proportions. Fortunately, there are many design scholars and industry efforts working toward solutions. This, along with advances in technology, provides promise.

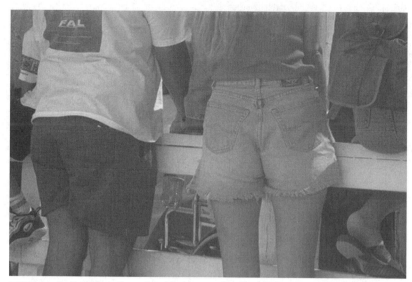

FIGURE 3.3. Personal fit preference and fashion can direct how tight or loose a garment fits, yet the real problems in fit are generated from the differences in how real body shapes vary from the "ideal" for which patterns are generated. Recognizing fit and misfit with a knowledge of how to make the technical pattern corrections remain a challenge. (Photograph by Janet Hethorn.)

Again, start with the individual and consideration of his or her desires. The majority of consumers are unhappy with the selection of fit options in the marketplace. They would be more than thrilled if solutions were implemented that allowed them to consistently find clothing to fit their bodies. There are several reasons that explain how we got here, but now we should focus on finding solutions. Advances in understanding body shape and dimension are being realized through body scanning and new exploration of categorizing data to represent real bodies (Ashdown, Loker, et al., 2004). Technical advances in 3-D visualization and computerized pattern development will provide designers with a new approach for creating the shapes necessary for real bodies. Efforts such as these are leading the way toward exciting and hopeful technical solutions.

FIGURE 3.4. Through design details such as embedded lacing and dimension flexibility, the wearer's clothes can follow her size as it expands and contracts; this is a mark of "size sustainability." (Design by Meagan Edmond.)

Design solutions also can be developed that address fit from a different angle. Think about designing garments that are adjustable for comfort and variations in wearing. Creating garments that expand and contract as the body changes is another sustainable solution, reducing the need for separate garments or sets of clothing so as to cover fluctuations in body size dimensions. Meagan Edmond addressed this through her collection, which marks size sustainability (see Figure 3.4). Through adjustments in structural design details, the garments can cover a range of sizes.

There is still the issue of recognizing and correcting fit during sample development. Garments should be tested on bodies in motion as opposed to static dress forms, and more training is needed in the visual identification of misfit, in order for designers and product developers to make appropriate decisions and corrections. I have often explained to my students that providing people with clothing that fits well is a step toward world peace. When they look amazed, I go on to remind them that when they are wearing something that doesn't fit like they would prefer, is slightly off and bothersome, they go through the day knowing something isn't quite right. If we could get rid of that annoyance, if people wore clothes they felt fabulous in, perhaps they would be nicer to one another. Think about it. Fit and comfort are basic.

Working Well: Meeting Wearing Requirements

Beyond looking good and feeling good, consumers also desire their clothing and fashion expressions to do what they are intended to do, such as keep them warm and safe, allow them to move more easily, and perform at their best. These qualities represent the most basic level of sustaining people (i.e., life) through fashion by protecting and enhancing body functions. Some of the best design ideas here can be found in the technical areas of sports design and military wear. Looking to these designs for inspiration can be a place to start when thinking of improving everyday clothing for consumers. For example, the sleeve designs in mountaineering jackets can be adapted for casual wear to allow for the arm to move more smoothly and not disturb the hang of the torso covering. Advances in protection and ballistic impact strategies may find their way into urban outerwear and children's sportswear.

In today's world, protection can take on many meanings. Clothing can also aid in protecting us from harmful biological and chemical agents, and can carry needed tools for survival. The surface colors and patterns of a garment can reflect, stand out, or blend into various environments. It can be a creative challenge to think about sustaining people through innovative protective design strategies, and not just for extreme situations. You only need to consider all the possibilities of where people might find themselves and the various needs that surface when considering the demands we put our bodies through. The Nomad Coat (see Figure 3.5) was designed for survival and is the one

Nomad Coat #1   Worn with or without protective hooded vest. Layered wool with couched trim embellishment and vintage metallic piping on edges. Interior pockets hold tools for survival.

FIGURE 3.5. The Nomad Coat is an outer garment that can be layered for weather variation. Inside pockets are strategically placed and contain everything needed for urban survival. (Photograph by Kathy Atkinson of a design by Janet Hethorn.)

coat that would be grabbed on the way out the door if there were only a few minutes to pack up and leave, not knowing when, or if, return would be possible. The situation might be a natural disaster or other emergency, where the coat would need to provide the shelter and tools to assist basic survival and travel. At the same time, the wearer would need to blend in and feel comfortable in a variety of possible environments, both social and physical. The exterior of the coat was designed with inspiration from nomadic folk cultures, and the interior is fully lined with pockets to carry matches, tools, flashlight, whistle, and an assortment of other survival necessities. There is enough ease between the body and the garment to allow for wearing a camelback water pack or a bulletproof vest.

Once you begin to think about how clothing can work for people, beyond the expressive and comfort qualities, many possibilities open

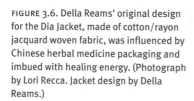

FIGURE 3.6. Della Reams' original design for the Dia Jacket, made of cotton/rayon jacquard woven fabric, was influenced by Chinese herbal medicine packaging and imbued with healing energy. (Photograph by Lori Recca. Jacket design by Della Reams.)

up for sustaining people through clothing. As a near environment, clothing is a shelter, a protective layer next to the skin, and also a vehicle for holding and transporting necessities. Clothing can enhance health and wellness, through carrying needed items, or through actual bio-delivery systems on the fiber level. Energetic symbols, amulets, and charms also provide many people with a sense of protection and well-being. Historically, there are many examples of warriors going into battle wearing a shirt that they designed from dream information or spiritual guidance, and you don't need to go far for contemporary examples of people wearing their lucky shirt in their favorite color embellished with a meaningful motif, when they think they need to be brave or to bolster self-confidence.

So, yes, opportunities abound for innovative design strategies to help clothing work toward meeting consumer need and desire. Engineers and architects are looking to "biomimicry," the inspiration from nature and systems, to inform new approaches to building. There are many reasons why fashion could benefit from this kind of investigation and design application. The study of biological systems that have sustained life in nature certainly can provide inspiration for new ways of thinking how designs in clothing structures and systems can assist in sustaining life for people. We are designing for living, breathing organisms, individuals with particular needs. Through expanding our creative thinking, and embracing new ways of approaching design, we can better address our sustainable options.

We also must expand our notion of who we are designing for. Our design culture, from students to industry professionals, tends to prefer a focus on designs for the elite, or for people just like them. Yes, the exploration of design ideas for sophisticated applications utilizing quality materials is important, and often lesser expensive ideas are generated from these developments. But who is designing for underserved segments? Search for ways to provide quality at low cost. There are many people who don't have the money to purchase the clothing that designers may have a preference to work on, yet their needs are greater. Through better and more thoughtful design, we can lead real change and stop the wasteful production of junk. An exhibition at the Cooper-Hewitt museum in New York, "Design for the other 90%" highlights an awareness of design for social change and focuses on innovations of products and environments that are developed as solutions for people who don't usually receive design attention. Natalia Allen, in her review of the exhibition (2007), noted that there was no fashion on exhibition. "Perhaps fashion designers are not best known for catering to social causes," she states, but many are becoming aware of the need. A quote from Paul Polack, founder of International Development Enterprises, that was noted at the exhibit, truly identifies the opportunities we have ahead of us: "The majority of the world's designers focus all their efforts on developing products and services for the richest 10 percent of the world's customers."

Beyond Development and into Use

Really good companies know what consumers want and are willing to change to meet their needs (Tisch and Weber, 2007). This chapter has provided suggestions and potential directions for shifting the design and development process in order to embrace consumer desire as a sustainable practice. Clearly garments have the potential to sustain people, but the way they are used can also have an effect on environmental sustainability, specifically through how they are cared for and in the length of time they are in use. Therefore, as a person designing and developing a product (e.g., clothing, fashion), you have the responsibility to think about the life of this product as it is being used.

How Will It Be Cleaned?

You can select materials and garment labeling practices that will lessen the environmental impact of water use and pollutants. As the producer of the garments, you are the expert, and the consumer is the novice. You know all about what has gone into the finished product and how it can best be maintained. It is your responsibility to communicate these ideas clearly to the consumer.

What Might Extend the Garment's Time of Use?

By engaging in a design process that addresses consumer desire, as this chapter has focused on, the design professional will create garments that will be kept and used longer. That is already a step toward lessening environmental impact, but think about the opportunities to take this further. How about setting up a system where consumers can return items for repair? This is common in some outerwear companies, but what's to stop us from expanding this practice to fashion items also? In addition to extended garment life and happier consumers, knowing what and where things break is a first step toward avoiding future problems.

Feedback as Helpful Codesign

Many consumer products have stringent quality control and testing labs in-house at the production level. Think about automobiles and appliances. Clothing, as a product, often relies on the feedback from consumers for much of the information about quality and use problems. When a garment has a problem, people either return it, discard it, or don't purchase it in the first place. The manufacturer receives the information about problems through an indirect communication channel. Why not set up a system of direct feedback from the consumer? Put contact information on labels and obviously placed on Web sites. Invite feedback and use this information to continually improve the products you develop. The people who use your designs have intimate knowledge of fit, feel, sizing, and performance. This is useful. Tap it. A sustainable fashion process requires open communication.

Conclusion

Everyone knows that clothing should fit comfortably, that people would be happier if they felt good about how they looked, and that garments that perform well are better than those that don't. Connecting these ideas to sustainability also makes sense. But what are we doing about this? Has the real-world fashion practice met these goals? The textile pipeline fiber-to-consumer model has not invited action toward embracing the sustainability options regarding people. When consumers are at the end of a linear process, they are left to choose from what is pumped out, including garments that fall short of their desires. I have suggested that consciously putting the consumer in the center of the conversation in order to meet the consumer's needs and provide well-being is a more sustainable model. This focus through the design and production process should be just as essential as choosing the correct fabric for a garment. Fashion innovation is a powerful process when we expand our thinking about what is possible.

Yes, fashion does provide pleasure, and it can provide even more if we get it right. This is a good thing. I keep imagining a world where people are leading happy and meaningful lives. They are wearing clothes that support this direction. They are wearing clothes that represent who they are. Instead of creating stereotypes and generalized looks, we are creating a clothing environment that supports and sustains individual well-being. Knowing that people have needs and designing toward those needs is core to sustainability.

References

Allen, N. (n.d.). Design for the other 90 percent: A review of the Cooper-Hewitt exhibition. *Core 77 Industrial Design Supersite*. Retrieved May 8, 2007, from http://www. core77.com/reactor/05.07_90percent.asp

Ashdown, S., Loker, S., Schoenfelder, K., & Lyman-Clarke, L. (2004, Summer). Using 3d scans for fit analysis. *Journal of Textile and Apparel, Technology and Management* 4(1).

Branson, D., and Sweeney, M. (1991). "Conceptualization and measurement of clothing comfort: Toward a metatheory." *Critical Linkages in Textiles and Clothing Subject Matter: Theory, Method, and Practice*. Susan B. Kaiser & Mary Lynn Damhorst (Eds.). ITAA Special Publication. #4, part 2, p. 94.

Caplan, R. (2005). *By design* (2nd ed). New York: Fairchild Publications.

DeLong, M. R. (1998). *The way we look: Dress and aesthetics*. New York: Fairchild Publications.

Denzin, N, & Lincoln, Y. (2005). *The sage handbook of qualitative research* (3rd ed.). Thousand Oaks, CA: Sage Publications, Inc.

Hethorn, J. (2005, Spring). Understanding aesthetic preference: Approaches toward improved product development. *Journal of Textile and Apparel Technology and Management* 4(3).

Holt, B., Hethorn, J., Petkovic, D., Niblack, W., Tung, P., & Treat, H. (1995, August). Applications of query by image content (QBIC) at UC Davis. Proceedings of the 2nd IASTED/ISMM Conference on Distributed Multimedia Systems and Applications. Stanford, CA.

Nelson, G. (2003). *How to see*. Oakland, CA: Design Within Reach.

Postrel, V. (2003). *The substance of style*. New York: HarperCollins Publishers.

Tisch, J. and Weber, K. (2007). *Chocolates on the pillow aren't enough: Reinventing the customer experience*. Hoboken, NJ: John Wiley & Sons, Inc.

REBECCA LUKE founded les Egoistes, a creative services company with a focus on fashion, in 2000 with 15 years experience in fashion and event production. Rebecca's skills run the gamut from production, public relations, and marketing services to art direction, styling, costume design, choreography, and visual display. Her expertise has been honed by working with clients both locally and nationally in nonprofit, retail, clothing manufacturing, television, film, theater, and other arts industries. As cofounder of the Sustainable Style Foundation (www.sustainablestyle.org), Rebecca continues to merge her passion for giving back with her style industry experience. Rebecca holds a BA in marketing with an emphasis in clothing and textiles.

CHAPTER 4

Popular Culture, Marketing, and the Ethical Consumer

Rebecca Luke

Consumers play a role in promoting peace and sustaining life through the choices they make when they purchase apparel and other goods. To inspire consumers to make stylish and sustainable choices, a nonprofit organization called the Sustainable Style Foundation (SSF) was developed. In this chapter, co-founder and senior stylist Rebecca Luke explains how SSF is a Web portal where stylemakers can showcase their sustainable products. She reviews how the popular culture movement of ethical consumerism can combat the philosophy that consumerism must lead to global environmental and socioeconomic crises.

Sustainability as a Common Value

Starting a dialogue about ethics and marketing must begin with a definition of *ethics*. The classic and most commonly understood definition of ethics is a "system of moral principals." Generally, most groups or movements revert to their own ethics, or "that branch of philosophy dealing with values relating to human conduct, with respect to the rightness and wrongness of certain actions and to the goodness and badness of the motives and ends of such actions" (*Random House Unabridged Dictionary*, 2006).

Morality, or the personal beliefs regarding right and wrong that one holds to be true, is a grey area for us all. Each of us develops our own set of ethics based on the influences in our life (e.g., family, education, religion, and culture). For example, for many of us in the garment industry, short skirts and revealing clothing on women often mean nothing but a trend. However, to another group, they can symbolize the degradation of women. Dr. Tim Jackson, professor of sustainable development at the Center for Environmental Study at the University of Surrey, United Kingdom, in his report on "Motivating Sustainable Consumption," references social psychologist and professor at the Hebrew School of Jerusalem Dr. Shalom Schwartz's concept of the norm-activation theory; in this theory, Schwartz "suggests that moral behaviors are the result of a personal norm to act in a particular way. These norms arise, according to Schwartz, from an awareness of the consequences of one's actions and the ability and willingness to assume responsibility for those consequences" (Jackson, 2004). Jackson goes on to cite more studies on the value-belief-norm theory that focus on the "moral dimensions of pro-environmental behaviors." Jackson states that one of the most well-known studies is that of Dr. Paul Stern, environmental psychologist and president of the Social and Environmental Research Institute (SERI) and his colleagues. "Their value-belief-norm theory," Jackson writes, "attempts to elucidate a chain of influence from people's value sets and beliefs to the emergence of a personal norm to act in a given way. The importance of this work is its insight into the value basis of different behaviors and behavioral intentions." Jackson goes on to cite social psychologist Dr. Robert Cialdini's "focus theory of normative behavior, which also offers key factors for understanding consumer behavior. "Cialdini suggests that people are continually influenced in their behaviors by social norms which prescribe or proscribe certain behavioral options." Jackson concludes that "the existence of such social norms can be a powerful force both in inhibiting and in encouraging pro-environmental behavior. At one level, pro-environmental behavioral change can be thought of as a transition in social norms" (Jackson, 2004).

These theories make it clear that it is complicated to determine whose ethics are correct and how to market the "correct" messages to consumers. However, a message that focuses on sustainability can be a common ground upon which to build because sustainability, broadly defined as the creation of a better world for us all, is a platform few would find debatable.

Using Popular Culture

Our world is in a crisis. Popular culture has become aware of this fact, as evidenced by the success of global impact movies, green issues of fashion and design magazines, and television programs that touch on the topic. Further evidence of this awareness is the significant change in corporate culture to include departments of social responsibility.

Marketing to the ever-growing demographic of "ethical" or "ethically minded" consumers concerned about sustainability should include developing initiatives to "promote behavior change" that "are often most effective when they are carried out at the community level and involve direct contact with people" (McKenzie-Mohr & Smith 1999).

As stylemakers, we can use multimedia, entertainment, fashion, and design as a way to *inspire* consumers to make ethical choices. Our messages would be based on our consideration of sustainable choices such as a garment's environmental performance, which includes the impact of its construction and production, the extension of its product life, and the energy requirements for its care and disposal. Much energy has been spent on the "doom and gloom" approach as to the impact that our choices, both as consumers and producers, make. Why not consider a positive approach so that consumers will feel like their choices really make a difference? Why not nourish the seeds of sustainability?

In the business of fashion, we are included in the group of the trendsetters involved in the creation of pop culture. We take our inspirations from the street, music, politics, and more. Many may argue that in the clothing industry, we have to stick to examples of what already works in the industry, but this does not necessarily mean we must repeat mistakes of the past. Part of our market research is to learn of the practices and innovations in other industries that might be applicable in their own craft (i.e., fashion designers and clothing manufacturers can learn from interior and consumer product designers who have been working in sustainability since the 1960s). We can learn from each other.

Armed with the knowledge that we are the trendsetters, and with the understanding of what others are doing out there, we can use modern culture to market ethical issues. Through Web sites (e.g., YouTube and MySpace), magazines, daily pings on our PDAs, and programming on entertainment shows such as MTV, unique marketing techniques can create fresh trends. For example, a sustainable dance club event thrown in Rotterdam, Netherlands, in 2006 called The Critical Mass was a sold-out event. Dance floors generated power from human feet. Toilets flushed with rainwater. Walls changed color with heat fluctuations. This group envisions a "network of eco-clubs where music and dance converge with 'culinary theater' and 'honest fashion.' With their throbbing sounds and pulsing lights, conventional dance clubs may be the SUVs of the underground, but an extreme green makeover that appeals to the young and hip is a smart way to lighten their impact. Many Millennials are already thinking green, so the concept isn't a hard sell" (SASS Magazine & The Critical Mass, 2006). This event hit the international news three to four months after

FIGURE 4.1. With the ad campaign featured in this image and her narration of many public service announcements, Stella McCartney advocates for People for the Ethical Treatment of Animals (PETA).

the fact and continues to be a prime example of how effective the pop culture approach to marketing can be.

Using popular culture to influence consumer choices as marketers, we can also showcase high-profile lifestyle role models to inspire consumers to make more sustainable personal lifestyle choices themselves. We have seen the effect that celebrities such as Cameron Diaz, Angelina Jolie, Jay-Z, and Leonardo DiCaprio have had on consumer choices. When PETA advocate and celebrity Pamela Anderson came out against wearing no animal products, a trend was started. Since then, many designers, such as Stella McCartney, have chosen to highlight their choice to use no animal products.

We can also team up. Fashion and music are logical teammates with a proven track record. Successful examples include Sarah McLachlan's 2005 "World on Fire" video, Bono's Red Campaign, and CD compilations sold at Urban Outfitters retail stores to raise funds for tsunami victims. The film, television, and gaming entertainment industry is another great member to have on your marketing team. The popularity of "issue" movies, such as 2006's *An Inconvenient Truth*,

2005's *Syriana,* and 2006's *Blood Diamond* and sustainability programming for popular reality shows, such as *Extreme Makeover: Home Improvement*, prove that television and film is an important multimedia partner. We can also well imagine a future where sustainability messages can be designed into Nintendo Wii and Sony PlayStation games.

In the fashion industry, we know that sustainability is here to stay. Since 2003, sustainable designs and initiatives have been highlighted at the various fashion weeks across the world, with Armani and Zegna leading the way and including design houses such as Linda Loudermilk, Edun, and Loomstate.

Impact of Individual Choice

As consumers, we have a choice. We may ask what impact our choice can make. But if we consider all of our lifestyle choices, from the car we drive and the coffee we drink to the clothes we wear, we can see that we really do have the power to effect change. "The cornerstone to sustainability is delivering programs that are effective in changing peoples' behavior" (McKenzie-Mohr & Smith, 1999). This task may seem daunting, but given the demand in the current marketplace, the time is now. We can effect this change by accepting or rejecting products as they are developed and marketed.

The Style Factor

Even with the amount of information out there, we can still surprise consumers by highlighting the breadth of sustainability already underway across the many and diverse style and design industries. We can also surprise them by the selling style factor (i.e., appealing design along with pop culture fashion). "Aesthetics, or styling, has become an accepted unique selling point on a global business. In a crowded marketplace, aesthetics is often the only way to make a product stand out" (Postrel, 2003).

FIGURE 4.2. Reuse-a-Shoe is a key component of Nike's long-term commitment to waste elimination. Nike collects worn-out athletic shoes of any brand, not just Nike. Shoe materials are ground up to make sports surfacing products used in athletic fields. (Photo by Adam Lee.)

When it comes to sustainable and green products, the style factor must be amped up in order to get over the consumer's initial idea that the product may be a bit "too hippy" or "just not my thing." If we show that the product is stylish as well as trendy, more consumers may chose it.

Knowledge Is Power

For the consumer, knowledge has the ability to evoke emotion and action. For example, labor issues regarding insufficient pay for workers at shoe factories in Indonesia in the 1990s that involved manufacturers such as Nike and many others not only changed the actions of consumers, provoked a crying out for justice, but instilled paramount changes on the manufacturing end. Now, Nike is leading the way, having employed a "group of more than 70 people working solely on corporate responsibility issues around the world. The new Corporate Responsibility division is an integrated group that brings together the Nike departments of Labor Practices, Nike Environmental Action Team (NEAT), the Nike Foundation, and Global Community Affairs. The formation of the new Corporate Responsibility division was destined to ensure that Nike presents a consistent face of corporate responsibility to communities around the world" (Nike and Global Labor Practices, 2001). Environmentally, Nike continues to provide leadership by phasing out PVC and purchasing loads of organic cotton for their new apparel. The company also reuses the rubber from shoe outsoles and combines it with recycled manufacturing material to build baseball and soccer fields, as well as golf products, weight room flooring, and running tracks. Taking that ethos into its newly considered line of shoes, Nike will be using recycled rubber, reducing manufacturing waste, and building them without adhesives of any kind.

Making It Easy
Identifying barriers to the potential action you want the consumer to make and removing them so that it is easier to take action will help encourage the final result. For example, American Apparel, a clothing company and retailer, made the use and purchase of their organic cotton products very easy. Organic cotton is in all of their retail stores and is available to every mom-and-pop T-shirt maker around the world. One doesn't have to go to a special location or site, or take extra steps. American Apparel has made access so easy and affordable that local rock bands can use their sustainable products. When designers consider all aspects of sustainability before placing their products in the market and making them easy to identify, consumers are able to make choices easily.

Keeping It Out There

Ensure continuous forward progress to counteract the perception of sustainability as something that happens in fits and starts (e.g., a green building goes up here, a fashion designer uses organic cotton there). Jackson (2004) writes, "cognitive psychology suggests that habits, routines, and automaticity play a vital role in the cognitive effort required to function effectively." By keeping it out there, we can see that an "ability for efficient cognitive processing" becomes necessary in a "message-dense environment, such as the modern society in which we live" (Jackson, 2004). If we can make sustainable choices part of routine daily behavior, these choices could become habitual. "Habit is one of the key challenges for behavioral change policy since many environmentally significant behaviors have this routine character" (Jackson, 2004). Consider that sustainability could no longer be the "trend of the year," but the standard expectation of all. Perhaps we can create a society where we don't give it a second thought; sustainability would become second nature.

The Sustainable Style Foundation

As cofounder and senior stylist of SSF (http://www.sustainablestyle.org), I wanted to create an online place where stylemakers all over the world could showcase their design work and save the world at the same time. While I was a layperson in the area of sustainability, I did come from the fashion industry and already had a long history of giving back. To bring forth the education component of the organization, I partnered with Sean Schmidt, who had a strong sustainability/corporate social responsibility background.

SSF is a nonprofit member-based charitable organization with a mission to educate, support, and inspire people from all walks of life to make more sustainable personal lifestyle choices at work, at home, and at play. From fashion, food, and film to interior design, travel, and music, SSF had designs on making sustainability the next big thing, as well as a timeless trend by using the power of popular culture to influence consumer choices.

By connecting Hollywood and fashion with organizations and issues, SSF has worked with several environmental organizations such as Global Green, Earth Communication Office, and Lifestyles of Health and Sustainability to build relationships and increase media exposure for celebrities who make positive lifestyle choices. SSF has also collaborated with online green retailers such as Tree-Hugger.com to provide resources and sponsor international sustainability events. The agency sponsored Umbrella Inside Out, a design competition, and EPIC, an exposition of sustainable products that was the first to feature everything from fashion and technology to transport and food in Vancouver, BC. SSF has used its online presence to highlight new magazines such as *Sublime* and *Plenty* and been on hand to provide resources for the producers of the Sundance Channel's Green Series.

As a nonprofit, SSF is in a unique position to support new initiatives, products, and concepts in the area of sustainability and be the neutral ground for business, nongovernment organizations (NGOs), and nonprofits. SSF is often called upon by media all over the world to discuss sustainability.

As the premier resource on sustainable lifestyles and design, SSF provides useful and up-to-date information and resources to both design professionals and consumers so that they can more easily incorporate sustainability into their work and personal lives. Since its start in 2002, SSF is currently the largest nonretail, nonprofit portal for sustainable lifestyle choices that have style, with close to 2,000 listed resources, as of January 2007, based in North America.

Triple Target Sustainability™

As marketers, we can encourage sustainable behavior in businesses and their consumers by considering Triple Target Sustainability™, an initiative of SSF. Triple Target Sustainability is an SSF concept devel-

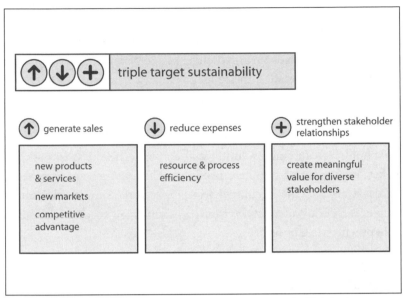

FIGURE 4.3. This chart reviews three simple steps to encourage sustainable behavior. (Courtesy of Sustainable Style Foundation.)

oped to help businesses understand the ease of introducing sustainability into their offerings. The concept was inspired by the business model, triple bottom line.

Through Triple Target Sustainability™ businesses aim to achieve three simple tenets as shown in Figure 4.3.

Case in Point
Each day at Nordstrom, new clothing was arriving packaged in plastic. A few stakeholders, sales associates who had a vested interest in the sustainable success of the company, were concerned about the waste involved with the plastic and took their concerns to corporate management. After some research, the management found a vendor that

would purchase all the plastic for recycling. This vendor determined that it could have the bundles of plastic go back on the trucks that were already going back to the distribution center and sell the plastic from there. So, (1) Nordstrom found a way to generate sales through a new product, the plastic; (2) it reduced expenses through resource and process efficiency by utilizing trucks that were already headed back to the distribution center and by not paying for disposing of the plastic; and (3) it increased the value of its relationship with its sales associate stakeholders by finding a solution to their concern. The sales associate is key to success of any new product or change in company standards—especially in a retail scenario. These three simple concepts of Triple Target Sustainability™ can help ensure the success of sustainable practices in a business.

Sustainability and Style

Combining sustainability and style was a new concept in 2001. It became commonplace only a few years later, as seen with the emergence of organic garment trade shows in Las Vegas, retail designing of grocery stores, building development, celebrity causes, green fashion issues in all major fashion magazines, and design across the board. As style professionals in the early years, we were often challenged with the question of what sustainability has to do with style. A definition of *style* will help clarify this relationship. Style is defined as a way to act or be, or personal self-expression. Different from fashions or trends, style can be deeply personal. As founders of SSF, we understand that sustainability has everything to do with style because each one of us makes personal choices of self-expression every day.

As other chapters in this book consider the definition of sustainability, so must we think about marketing and its impact on the choices of an ethical consumer. At SSF we have developed buzz phrases for sustainability in order to market its meaning in various ways to various consumer groups. Our buzz phrases include "Seven generations";

FIGURE 4.4. Sustainable Style Foundation logo. The foundation advocates for sustainable lifestyle choices with style. (Courtesy of Sustainable Style Foundation.)

"Improving the quality of life for everyone"; "Living enterprises and economies"; "Family, friends, community"; "Equality"; "Sustainability is all this and more"; and "Most importantly, it's understanding that each of us has a role in making all of the above a reality" (SSF, 2002).

Identifying an Ethical Choice: SSF Total Awareness Guide (SSFtags)

As both the supply of and demand for sustainable products and services in the large and diverse style and design industries grow, one of the biggest challenges in our current marketplace is to make it easy to identify sustainable choices. "The main vehicles for the communication of ethical values associated with products are labels affixed to the commodities" (Howard & Allen, 2006).

The history-making White Label Campaign from the nineteenth century led by Florence Kelley, general secretary of the National Consumer League (NCL), is "an example of a market exchange-based activity that has its root in an established civil society organization" (Micheletti, 2000). The product was women's and children's machine-made white cotton underwear, a product purchased frequently by middle-class women. Qualifying for the label required manufacturers to meet standards for minimum wage and safe working conditions. Even though the market was competitive, there were a few manufacturers worthy of the label. With target groups of consumers and producers identified, Kelley began to mobilize support nationwide for the campaign and to establish local NCL chapters to participate in the labeling movement. Using a popular culture technique of the time, she launched a letter-writing campaign to keep in touch with the different chapters and the headquarters. The government's role was restricted to passing factory legislation, which formed one of the qualifications for labeling. For the first time in U.S. history, private manufacturers were not only required to label, but were forced to maintain standards because their consumer base of middle-class women was aware of what that label required. At stake for these manufacturers were their profits and standing in the community. "The code of conduct used by the campaign represented the concerns prevalent at the time (i.e., the values of industrial society). Manufacturers were encouraged to follow state ordinances and adopt more progressive personnel policies than required by law" (Micheletti, 2000).

A twentieth-century example of an internationally recognized symbol that allows consumers to not only understand what they were purchasing but also helped them identify how to discard or reuse the item, is the recycle symbol. From a graphic design point of view, this symbol is a prime example of how to easily communicate ethical values through a label.

In the twenty-first century, as green issues and the awareness of sustainability arise, so does the emergence of symbols or certifications. Labels are being created to help consumers identify products, from organic vegetables and free-range meats to clothing and sustainable buildings. Labeling campaigns often begin on a grassroots community level. Fashion High, a nonprofit network of fashion professionals based in British Columbia, is one example. It has created a symbol for identifying current issues relating to sustainability in the Vancouver area. It also encourages its citizens to dress and shop local-

FIGURE 4.5. Symbols that help consumers identify ethical choices: (a) the recycle symbol, (b) a sticker for Vancouver's Fashion High, and (c) an SSFtag. (Courtesy of Sustainable Style Foundation.)

ly by buying clothing created by local designers in locally owned businesses.

SSF developed the SSF Total Awareness Guide, or "SSFtag," in an effort to create an internationally recognized symbol for stylish sustainable choices. The SSFtag can be used as a certification mark for any service, product, event, or business, including governmental or nonprofit organizations, that meets the criteria. SSFtag guidelines are based on a diverse and varied list of sustainable business practices and achievements. There are three categories: Human Rights/Social Compliance, Environment, and Other Business Practices. Each product, business, event, organization, or other applicant is evaluated on its awareness of and commitment to sustainability. SSFtags encourage and enable consumers to make more sustainable purchasing choices across lifestyle categories, from fashion, food, and film to interior design, architecture, travel, and music. SSFtags also provide companies and nonprofit organizations with a clear signal to send consumers that their product, service, event, or project has incorporated sustainability in some way, raising the consumers' awareness about the good things that are happening in the marketplace, and raising the profile of sustainability in the world. SSFtags would also continue to work toward promoting cross-industry learning.

Beyond Consumption: Continued Complexity

In 2000, the world's consumers spent approximately $1 trillion on clothing (Well dressed?, 2006). As style professionals in an industry that exists because people consume, we have to challenge ourselves to look at choices beyond consumption. Examples of these can be seen in Chapter 2, with designers teaming up with celebrities, such as Edun's Rogan Gregory and Bono, who take sustainability beyond the fabrication of garments.

Brands that promote sustainability with no celebrity backing are also emerging. Moral Fervor, for example, is taking another step and partnering with a nonprofit to develop its brands so that the brand and the nonprofit reflect each other. Mainstream brands such as Polo, Aldo, and Ugg have become quite public about their campaigns in connection with the entertainment industry to highlight their community involvement and contributions.

As the science and practice of sustainability continue to evolve, so will the marketing of its concepts and products. In the garment industry, there are companies that may choose not to tout their great works for the fear of watchdog organizations pointing at other areas of their business that may not be sustainable. But a company doesn't need to brag about itself to promote sustainability. The smallest positive reinforcement from a marketing or consumer campaign can create a big change. By remaining out of the political arena and recognizing that "no one is perfect" (Sustainable Style Foundation, n.d.), we can nourish the seeds of sustainability.

I ask the following questions of designers and clothing manufacturers who have green brands and want to take the step toward sustainability in their businesses. How are you packaging your garments? What method are you using to ship across the country and/or overseas? What are your retailers doing? Their answers initiate the next steps toward increasing the level of sustainability for their brands.

Flipping through the channels on my television, I land on MTV's THINK campaign of the month, where they're giving daily tips on

"Shopping Smarter." While a lot of the tips are non-apparel-related, what I do see reminds the viewers that we don't have to always buy "stuff" but can make choices about our purchases. However, what really impacts is that this campaign is *on* MTV.

As professionals in the fashion industry, we have to recognize that one of our biggest marketing challenges within popular culture is to make sure that consumers receive these messages daily. We must consider how to develop and identify our products in preparation for the demand that is ultimately going to be there. It can and will get confusing, especially in the age of the Internet, with many online sites and blogs that may or may not present the correct information.

According to Michele Micheletti (2000, p. 4):

Consumers are active agents, and shopping is not only a necessary activity for survival but the dominant mode of social interaction and primary way for people to participate in social and public life. Shopping gives individuals knowledge about themselves as individuals and about their own society as well as education about product choice. Shopping choices also help individuals manage and express their complex identities in a fragmented society. This is the meaning of *lifestyle politics*. What we buy influences how we construct our everyday lives. Conflicts over what to consume are, therefore, central to understanding the functioning of affluent western societies. Sociologists even view the refusal to consume as a form of resistance. Shopping is, therefore, potentially empowering. Conscious consumerism can, thus, change the world.

Given our affluent society and the satisfaction that consumers feel when they participate in the fashion industry, it seems unrealistic to advocate stopping consumption. Ethical marketing campaigns can educate us so that we can make daily choices to promote sustainability;

we can save the world in style. We can make these sustainable style choices count.

References

Allen, P., & Philip, H. (2006, September). Beyond organic: Consumer interest in new labeling schemes in the central coast of California. *International Journal of Consumer Studies 30*(5), 439–451.

Critical Mass. (n.d.). Retrieved January 1, 2006, from http://www.enviu.org/cm/cm_index_site.html

McKenzie-Mohr, D., & Smith, W. (1999). *Fostering sustainable behavior.* Vancouver, BC: New Society Publishers.

Jackson, T. (2004, August). *Motivating sustainable consumption: A review of evidence on consumer behavior and behavioral change.* Center for Environmental Strategy, University of Surrey. Retrieved June 25, 2007, from

http://admin.sd-research.org.uk/wp-content/uploads/2007/04/motivatingscfinal_000.pdf

Mathew, D., & Murphy, D. F. (2001, January). Nike and global labour practices. Case study prepared for the New Academy of Business Innovation Network for Socially Responsible Business.

Random House unabridged dictionary. (2006). New York: Random House.

SASS Magazine: The music issue. (2006). Retrieved November 15, 2006, from http://www.sustainablestyle.org/blog/2006/10/sass-magazine-sneak-peek-ssfs-inter

Micheletti, M. (2000). *Shopping and the re-invention of a democracy.* Stockholm: Stockholm and City University.

Postrel, V. (2003). *The substance of style.* New York: HarperCollins.

Sustainable Style Foundation. (n.d.). Retrieved November 15, 2006, from http://www.sustainablestyle.org

Sustainable Style Foundation Sourcebook (n.d.). Retrieved from http://www.sustainablestyle.org

Well dressed? The present and future sustainability of clothing and textiles in the United Kingdom. (2006). Cambridge, UK: University of Cambridge Institute for Manufacturing, Mill Lane.

SUZANNE LOKER, PH.D., is a J. Thomas Clark Professor of Entrepreneurship and Personal Enterprise in the Department of Fiber Science and Apparel Design at Cornell University. She has published widely on the apparel industry, international apparel production and marketing, and home-based work. Her current research program focuses on innovative business strategies in the apparel industry, specifically those involving body scanners and mass-customization technologies, and socially responsible practices.

CHAPTER 5

A Technology-Enabled Sustainable Fashion System: Fashion's Future

Suzanne Loker

Smart fabrics, seamless knitting, digital textile printing, wearable technology, made-to-order clothing, fiber-to-fiber recycling. These technology-enabled apparel applications evoke a future of design and product development that is rich with possibilities for developing sustainable solutions. This chapter explores ways that fashion can participate in adding benefits through innovative fibers, fabrics, processes, and consumer-use choices while increasing efficiencies and reducing product waste. With this technology-enabled sustainable fashion system, we embark on a new frontier.

Opening Up to the Possibilities
Technology can change the ways we design and shop for clothing so that we can embrace sustainability and create a sustainable fashion

system. It can provide the technical capacity for developing innovative materials with added benefits that will extend the product life span of the material and the apparel products designed with it. Technology can facilitate consumer involvement in clothing design, use, and disposal methods that decrease the amounts and flow of apparel garments in our fashion system. It can help us manage and reduce our excess inventory by improving apparel fit, design, production, and distribution to make the right amount of the right product and deliver it to the right customer. Wearable technology and smart fabrics connect consumers with technology to address personal needs, such as biological monitoring; adjustments to temperature, moisture, and activity; sound; and continuous communication anywhere at any time. Smart technologies can add sensing and communication functions to fashion to extend a product's life span, add meaning, and sustain life itself by monitoring biological health.

A Sustainable Fashion System

> *Sustainable development is development that meets the needs of the person without compromising the ability of future generations to meet their own needs.*
> —Brundtland Commission, 1987

When analyzing technology in the context of sustainability, a business often uses a linear analysis of the fashion system organized by functional area in an apparel manufacturing business (see Figure 5.1).

In this linear model, the functional areas work separately and often begin their work only when the previous department has completed its work. So a garment is designed and the patterns are developed for a style. When it is approved and the volume established, materials are ordered. Assembly begins when materials arrive, and then the sales department writes orders. The completed product is distributed to fill orders or sent as inventory to warehouses.

FIGURE 5.1. Apparel manufacturing departments.

A model of a sustainable fashion system is enhanced by integrating sustainable concepts and technological enablers; that is, technology is used to facilitate sustainable fashion concepts. The technology-enabled sustainable fashion system (see Figure 5.2) operates similarly to an ecosystem where there is a conscious evaluation of the impacts of both inputs and outputs, how they depend upon and influence one another, and the environmental as well as economic cost of each decision. A design team makes choices that affect the inputs, outputs, and waste at each stage in the fashion system: materials, design, and assembly into apparel; distribution and transport; consumer use; and disposal, refurbishment, and recycling. Considering the entire system instead of each stage separately strengthens the opportunities to infuse sustainability into the fashion system.

Let's consider two approaches to sustainability:

1. Increasing the efficiencies of the system to reduce inputs and unwanted products
2. Decreasing the amount or flow of material and garments in the system to reduce waste (Well-dressed, 2005)

Technology can help us with both. It can increase the efficiencies of

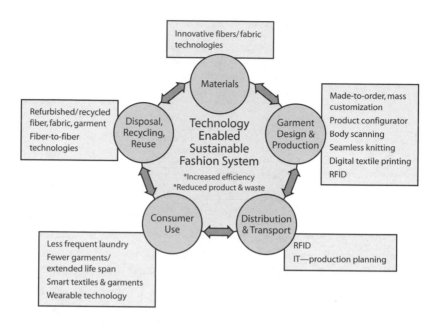

FIGURE 5.2. Model for a technology-enabled sustainable fashion system. (Illustration by Jenny Green from a model by Suzanne Loker.)

the system by developing new materials, production processes, and reuses in order to help us spend our resources wisely and extend the life span and functional characteristics of our clothing. It can also help us reduce the flow of material and garments in our system by matching production to consumption through better design, forecasting and production planning, and disposal strategies such as refurbishment and recycling.

Figure 5.2 illustrates opportunities for sustainable choices in each stage in the fashion system as well as specific technologies that are discussed in this chapter. It is the organizing scheme for our discussion and will be referred to throughout the chapter.

Increasing System Efficiencies

[Resilience is] the capacity of a system to absorb and utilize or even benefit from per-turbations and changes that attain it, and so to persist without a qualitative change in the system's structure.

—C. S. Holling (van der Leeuw & Aschan-Leygonie, 2000)

Just as a natural ecosystem sustains itself through systemic resources, processes, and restorative reuse, fashion can be viewed and built as a long-term sustainable system by extending product life through design choices. Ann Thorpe (2005), senior lecturer at Surrey Institute of Art and Design, United Kingdom, applied *resilience* to a sustainable fashion system by focusing on strategic use of time and dimension. She argued that designers could incorporate time and dimension into their design philosophy and process through "cathedral thinking," or designing resilient clothing to last beyond their lifetime to generations in the future; this would involve adjusting their designs to changing needs and external environments. Resilient designers would consider both the short-term material and style variations that are usually described as fashion as well as the longer-term material and style variations that make up the history of our clothing over many generations.

Applying the ideas of Thorp by thinking systemically and designing systemically, we can begin to create a fashion system that extends the product life span by investing in the resilience of our inputs and outputs, technologies, and behavior changes that adjust to the individual, environmental, and civilization turbulence of our everyday lives and across generations. This sustainable fashion system extends the product life span by means of enabling technologies that increase the efficiencies of our material choices and processing, our business strategies, consumer involvement, and our reuse and recycling approaches.

We can also view a sustainable fashion system from a production-consumption perspective. A balanced system consumes as much as it produces, with methods for forecasting and producing garments that match the rate of use and then manage the waste through reuse, recycling, and biodegradable approaches. Our current fashion system in the United States is out of kilter, as it produces much more than our population consumes and contributes excessive fabric and garment wastes to our landfill. Currently we have almost infinite choices of clothing to select from a variety of retail outlets, such as malls, stores, Internet businesses, and thrift stores. Merchandise that is not sold quickly is marked down from full price and sold to outlet stores when it has been on the floor too long.

Much unsold, first-hand clothing finally ends up in third-world countries and in the second-hand clothing system (Hawley, 2006). Clothing often lasts longer than the first owner has interest in wearing it, and a second-hand clothing system has developed. Secondhand, thrift, and vintage clothing stores have developed business models that depend on donations of expensive, still fashionable clothing or sturdy, reminiscent styles from the past. There is waste in the unsold inventory at every level of our system because production does not match consumption in volume or in personal preference.

Information technology (IT) that tracks and manages individual items or orders could help us take advantage of opportunities to decrease this product flow by matching the production volume and product designs to the consumption needs of the system. Extending the life span of products can also help us balance production and consumption through increased durability, expansion of functional or emotional value, and refurbishment to create another life for a product.

Technologies in a Sustainable Fashion System

With the conceptual model in Figure 5.2, it is clear that a selection of technologies are being used or are in development throughout the fashion system to advance sustainability. Each of the following examples represents one stage in the sustainable fashion system and presents and evaluates technologies and strategies for increased system efficiencies, reduced product and waste flow, or a combination of the two.

Innovative Fibers and Fabric Technologies

Sustainability in materials can be viewed in two ways. First, we can conceptualize smart or intelligent textiles and clothing as an extension of the product life span. By definition, these include a sensor, a processor, and an actuator. Information such as body temperature is read by the *sensor*, sent to the *processor* to decide what to do to raise or lower the temperature, and then sent to the *actuator* to do it (Matilla, 2006). By adding smart functions to the product, consumers may keep the product longer than a typical fashion product. Second, enhanced smart textiles and clothing are implements to facilitate or extend human life, either in providing a service directly to individual wearers or by improving the environment in which they live. Selected research endeavors using innovative fiber and fabric technologies are pioneering the paths to a sustainable fashion system through added functions. The following examples are just a few of the interesting projects that one can find in this exciting area of research.

Sport materials currently on the market provide functions desirable during aerobic movement, physical contact, and focused strength. Flexibility, moisture management, and heat and injury resistance have been integrated into the fiber, fabric, and garment structures to maximize an individual's physical performance. Although fashionable colors and styles change seasonally and could potentially shorten the life span of a garment, the added functional benefits can extend its life span well past the months of one fashion season.

For example, in smart fibers and fabrics where electronics are incorporated, their life span may be more similar in length to that of electronics than of fashion clothing. Extending the life span achieves a higher level of sustainability. In some advanced technical fibers and fabrics where color, thermal function, moisture, protective functions such as impact and sun protection, or style can change on demand during wear or across different wearing sessions, consumers would need fewer clothing articles to achieve both physical and psychological comfort.

Working at the Nanolevel to Create Conductivity

Professor Juan Hinestroza and his Cornell University textiles nanotechnology research group (http://www.people.cornell.edu/pages/jh433) have been exploring a new avenue for the development of flexible electronic and smart textiles by attaching metallic nanoparticles (e.g., silver, platinum, gold, and copper) to nylon and natural materials. Hinestroza says that "for a clothing designer, clothing is an expression of an idea. For a scientist, clothing is a collection of molecules that don't do anything. I want the molecules to work, have function. That is my goal." His research focuses on the links that are missing between the three functions of conductivity in smart textiles: sensing, processing information, and reacting to information.

Dr. Hinestroza works at the nanolevel of fibers to take advantage of the mechanical and electrical properties of nanofibers. Because of increased surface area at the nanolevel, his group has been able to add 10 to 15 percent more metal into the fiber than with larger fibers. Fewer fibers can affect performance, so there is decreased consumption of fiber. At the nanolevel, all the work can be accomplished in water-based solutions because the fibers are so small that they are soluble in water, another sustainable characteristic of his approach.

Hinestroza's group's early work has attached metal to single fibers successfully and, as a result, has achieved conductivity. They will use the same methods for threads in the future. An unexpected outcome was the ability to manipulate color by rearranging the metallic particles. For example, gold can create a blue or black color. This process does not use dyes, just signals to change metallic particles, and will be an exciting contribution to a sustainable fashion system.

Other contributions that Hinestroza hopes to make to the sustainable fashion system focus on sustaining a quality human life by adding function to fibers and fabrics used in clothing. He foresees research that finds a way to load lotions into fabric that slowly release to help people with dry-skin conditions. He also sees clothing fabric as a means to deliver medicines over an extended time period. In both cases, the friction of fabric to skin or a chemical reaction of the lotion or medicine with the skin will effect the movement out of the fabric and into the skin (Hinestroza, 2007).

Preventing Disease through Detection and Absorption

Taking advantage of the greater surface area nanofibers, Cornell University Professor Margaret Frey electrospins fibers about 0.1 to 1 micron in diameter to make nonwoven fabrics that can control the absorption and release of chemicals. These advanced fiber technologies add functions through the nanofiber characteristics that can be applied to control and systematically release liquids that include chemicals. Frey worked with biological and environmental engineering Professor Antje Baeumner to test the application of these nanofiber membranes to capture and detect biohazards. This application focused on testing for *E. coli* bacteria that often causes food poisoning when eaten by humans. Frey's nanofiber membranes are being formed into swabs similar to Q-tips and into wipes that can be easily used by food technicians to test for bacteria (Frey, 2007).

Fabric Level Technology Innovations

Other researchers have integrated electronics at the thread or fabric levels. Led by Professor Sundaresan Jayraman, Georgia Tech researchers developed the SmartShirt technology system that was eventually commercialized by Sensatex (http://www.sensatex.com). The SmartShirt system technology can be incorporated into any fabric without looking or feeling like electronic devices. Its first applications monitor heart and respiratory rate, body temperature, caloric burn, and other body functions by using convenient read-out devices such as wristwatches. SmartShirt technology is being sold to first responders to evaluate the health of casualties, to health providers to monitor patient health, and to athletes to maximize training and performance.

Phase change materials adjust to temperature change to keep a person warm or cool based on environmental changes (McCullough & Shim, 2006). The technology is based on the science of storing and releasing thermal energy through the melting and crystallization of different types of paraffins. These paraffins are attached to the fabric in a series of layers that react to a person's body heat. Functional applications for phase change materials include workers who are exposed to very high or very low temperatures for a short period of time. Phase change materials can offset the heat or cold by cooling or warming the person at the end of exposure. Race car drivers and arctic explorers are two extreme examples, but it is easy to recognize applications for outdoor winter activities such as skiing and snowshoeing and everyday aerobic activities.

Shape memory materials are another example of electronically controlled materials using either temperature, stress, magnetic or electronic fields, light, or water (Honkala, 2006) to cause transformations or deformations and recovery. One exciting fashion experiment by international designer Hussein Chalayan (http://www.husseinchalayan. com) suggests possible fashion applications of this and related technologies (Sixth Annual Year in Ideas, 2006). Chalayan uses mechanization rather than electronics to create dresses that transform or morph into multiple silhouettes that represent the styles across decades. For example, "the slats of a 1940s A-line silhouette opened outward, umbrella-style, to become the full, New Look silhouette of the 1950s;

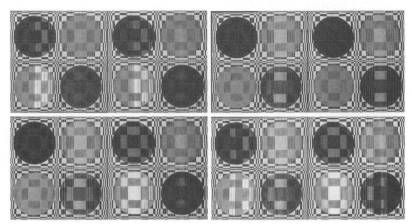

FIGURE 5.3. Dynamic double weave is a handwoven color-change fabric, electronically controllable textile printed with thermochromic ink. (Photo by Maggie Orth.)

the skirt then released and rose to mod mini-dress proportions while decorative metal plates dropped from hidden pockets in the bodices. [Then] a gauzy sheath retracted into a model's wide-brimmed hat leaving her naked" (p. 78). Combined with shape memory materials, the creative fashion opportunities are almost unimaginable.

Maggie Orth, an artist and technologist and founder of International Fashion Machines (http://www.ifmachines.com), combines sensing electronics with product design using electronics in fabrics. Her electric plaid and running plaid designs were created as exhibition pieces that showcase color-change technology (see Figure 5.3). Its plaids can continuously change colors or create waves of color using fuzzy sensors and proprietary software. Future applications in clothing design (e.g., dresses that change color with your mood, setting, or to match accessories) are not hard to imagine.

Orth is working toward computer software that has a definable and colorful form as well as function. She calls it "de-neutralizing technology to make it more a reflection of our aesthetic selves" (Galloway, 2007).

Garment Design and Production

Making the right product is one of the most important parts of a sustainable fashion system. This means both designing the right product and producing the right amount of the product. In the nineteenth century, the fashion system was mostly custom, where people either personally sewed their own clothing at home or contracted with tailors to sew for them. A custom fashion system is very effective at making the right amount of the right product. However, as the ready-to-wear system evolved in the twentieth century with the implementation of mass production, the system became less balanced and less sustainable.

Technology offers a number of opportunities to involve the consumer so that the right product is designed and produced. Apparel can be customized for style, size, or function with the help of technology. The business strategy for producing and delivering the right product at the right time to the right place is *mass customization* (Pine, 1993). With the help of enabling technologies, mass customization combines the production efficiencies of mass production and the individualization of custom production. Clothing can be made on demand so that product will only be produced when there is an ultimate consumer to buy it. These technologies facilitate a sustainable fashion system by decreasing the flow of product and therefore waste in the system.

Involving Consumers in Design

Product configurators have been available since the early twenty-first century in the clothing industry. Using interactive computer software that is often easily found on the Internet, consumers can customize their own clothing by selecting from color, style, fabric, or size options. Specifically, as consumers enter an interactive site for jackets and pants at Web sites such as Beyondclothing.com, they are asked to select style, color, front opening, hood options, pocket types, and fas-

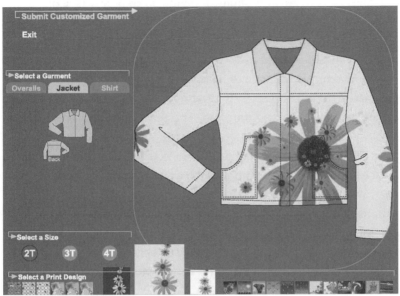

FIGURE 5.4. DigiKids Product Configuration is a research Web site that investigates and illustrates the interaction between the user and the design process. This screen shot shows one segment of the site found at www.digikids.cornell.edu.

teners, and they will see a sketch of the product change as they make their selections. Size is determined by entering into the program a set of measurements and description of the fit, such as *standard, technical,* and *built for layering.* On other sites, there are more style and fabric choices to create a unique product. The Digikids product configurator in Figure 5.4 was developed by Iowa State and Cornell University professors for research purposes. It facilitates codesign by giving choices to the customer in the design of digitally printed children's clothing (http://www.digikids.cornell.edu).

Product configurators involve consumers in the design process so that the resulting product is exactly what consumers want. There is no leftover inventory on the shelves for markdown and eventual disposal because the process shifts away from selecting from multitudes of finished products to creating single, individualized products. Consumers will like the product because they had choices in building its design and fabrication. Their enjoyment in the process should increase the product's meaning to them as well.

One major disadvantage to involving customers in online design is the change in the shopping paradigm. We are used to having multiple apparel selections, trying them on, and returning them if we decide later we do not want them. When using a product configurator for mass customization, consumers are restricted to a virtual view of the finished product design, cannot touch or try on garments and see it on their own bodies, and must pay in advance for the product, sometimes without chance of return. Virtual visualization technologies are in development to push past these barriers of tactility and exact size and style try-on. In addition, design takes some skill and patience, and consumers may not have interest in design participation, particularly when too many options are offered (Kamali & Loker, 2004).

Businesses offering codesign options through product configurators or less technical custom approaches must overcome another challenge. They must be able to deliver one-of-a-kind products at a competitive price within a two- to three-week delivery date. This requires either (1) huge stocks of material, which would defeat the inventory advantage provided by making the right product, or (2) very good relationships with textile vendors and apparel factories. For fashion apparel with constantly changing styles and colors, this is an especially challenging process to accomplish without much excess material and finished product inventory. Some businesses have applied digital textile printing and garment dyeing (e.g., Benetton) to move the selection and production of fabric color and print closer to the consumer. In both approaches, building good relationships with vendors is vital. A third sustainable approach is to order and produce small quantities in a short time to reduce the flow of products, also dependent on strong relationships across the sustainable fashion system.

Body Scans for Improved Fit

There has long been a consumer outcry for better-fitting clothing. The dilemma is that ready-to-wear producers cannot profitably make the infinite number of sizes necessary for a good fit for every person. Their solution is to develop a sizing system with a limited number of sizes that fit many people in their target market. Unfortunately, the remaining people in the population are left without proper-fitting clothing options. The 3-D body scanning technology can address this problem by:

- Producing custom made clothing from an individual's body scan
- Conducting large-scale anthropometric studies to provide accurate body measurements of the population
- Developing statistically representative body measurements of specific target markets (e.g., women between 18 and 30 years old or men between 40 and 60 years old)
- Applying measurements to sizing strategies for pattern development (Loker & Ashdown, 2005)

In all four ways, body scan technology can reduce the flow of unsold and returned apparel due to poor fit and assist in building a more sustainable fashion system. Given that the return rate of clothing in mail order averages between 30 and 50 percent, this is an enormous contribution.

Custom-sized clothing by definition means that consumers are involved in the design and production processes to make garments uniquely for them, based on their individual measurements, usually with one or more fittings, and sometimes with decisions about fabric and style. Focusing on individual sizing, the body scanner makes the measuring process quicker, taking only about 12 seconds, less invasive by eliminating physical touching, and more reliable by reducing variability in measuring (Ashdown & Loker, 2004). The scanner captures a set of measurements that, in a perfect translation, can be applied to computer-assisted design (CAD) pattern-making software to create a one-of-a-kind pattern for producing the custom garment. The chance for misfit is reduced, thus ensuring few returns and no excess inventory.

The body scanner has also been used in large-scale anthropometric studies of whole populations, such as the U.S. National Size Survey (http://www.sizeusa.com) and the UK National Sizing Survey (http://www.size.org), to develop databases of body measurements that are representative of the population. Then, these databases are sorted by gender, age, weight, ethnicity, and other demographic variables that were recorded for each scan. The subsets can be analyzed to describe specific target markets of individual apparel firms.

The resulting data can be statistically organized into a reasonable number of size categories, thereby developing a sizing system particular to each target market. Another approach is to use the data to adjust existing apparel firm sizing systems to fit more people in their target market (Ashdown, Loker, & Schoenfelder, 2005). The objective in both approaches is to reduce flow in the sustainable fashion system by eliminating the production of garments that are not sold due to fitting problems.

Digital Textile Printing

Digital textile printing offers two paths to a sustainable fashion system: (1) lowering the use of harmful dyes in the printing process and (2) matching the production to consumption by printing with less ink or dye and water, reducing fabric waste, and producing only to order. Inkjet printers, similar to those used for paper, can print fabric from digital files. A colorant is chosen that works with the type of fabric. For example, for best results acid dyes are used with silk, wool, and polyamide; resist dyes are used with cotton, silk, linen, and wool; and disperse dyes are used with polyester. Pigments can be used with any textile fiber. Digital textile printing requires the use of pre- and post-treatments to fix color, and a variety of methods are still being developed for acceptable color, sharpness, and durability (May-Plumley & Bau, 2005).

FIGURE 5.5. "Transformation Overload" is a coat/work of art made of digitally printed cotton duck. It transforms to several wearing possibilities. See the movie demonstrating the transformation at www.jrcampbell.net. The digital printing process uses very little ink/dye and requires much less water for processing, compared to more traditional print processes. (Designed by J.R. Campbell and Jean Parsons.)

Digital printing is a mass-customization technology that has the potential for reducing the flow of garments in a sustainable fashion system. Digital printing can occur at the end of the production cycle, close to final product assembly, so that individualization occurs near consumer purchase. Printing can be on cut pattern pieces, thus restricting the total dye or ink to the final garment pieces and allowing fabric waste to be reclaimed for reuse in its uncolored state.

Digital technology can be integrated with CAD design and production manufacturing technology to produce one or several pieces of apparel quickly and efficiently and with creativity. J. R. Campbell, research fellow at the Centre for Advanced Textiles at the Glasgow School of Art, and Jean Parsons (http://www.jrcampbell.net), professor at Iowa State University, have experimented with digital printing as a tool for apparel design. They explored the relationships between 2-D and 3-D design possibilities when adding digital printed surface design. Their resulting designs are printed in 2-D but created to display in 3-D, as shown in Figure 5.5. Using digital printing for execution also reduces the amount of colorant, water, and total fabric needed, all sustainable approaches to design.

Challenges to sustainability are present throughout digital textile printing. Planning designs can be very complex so that they can be printed on two-dimensional fabrics that will be matched in the final three-dimensional clothing. The pre- and post-treatment of fabric adds steps in the printing process and sometimes counteracts some of the efficiency and continuous manufacturing process from cut through assembly (I. T. Strategies, 2006).

Even with these technical challenges, digital textile printing is increasingly used in tests, samples, and commercially sold garments, as it offers efficiency gains and flow reductions that will help realize a sustainable apparel system.

Seamless Knitting

Seamless knitting was commercialized in the mid-1990s (Choi & Powell, 2005) as the knitting technology became commercially available. This process uses one yarn to complete an entire apparel garment, without cut-and-sew assembly. Little yarn waste and no waste from cutting makes the process more efficient in materials use and waste (see Figure 5.6). It also reduces the amount of garment flow in a fashion system by its mass-customization characteristics because it can be used to make one garment at a time, allowing individual attention to a customer's design needs with quick-response production. Seamless knitting provides another technology-enabled option to the sustainable fashion system: Production process costs are lowered with decreased required time and labor. Machine costs are less because machines can knit multiple-gauge sizes so fewer machines need to be purchased. Finally, due to the reduction in the number of production steps, costly defects and damages during production are minimized (Choi & Powell, 2005).

Manufacturers of knitting equipment Shima Seiki (http://www.shimaseiki.co.jp/) and Stoll (http://www.stoll.de) both offer five machines that integrate seamless knitting technology with CAD systems for design development, as do other companies, such as San-

FIGURE 5.6. Example of a seamless knit.

toni (http://www.santoni.com). The machines vary in gauge size, single or multiple gauges, and other characteristics to produce a variety of knit weights and designs appropriate for products such as underwear, gloves, hats, socks, and sweaters. Notice the intricate stitch designs that produce unusual garment silhouettes as well as surface interest.

Distribution and Transport

The logistics of getting the right product to the right person involves materials acquisition, forecasting, production management, and distribution. Technology has become useful in creating successful logistic strategies such as information collectors, processors, and analytical tools. The following are a few examples that fit into an effective fashion system.

Radio Frequency Identification

Radio frequency identification (RFID) is a tagging system that holds unique identifying information in a microchip that can be read using an antenna system. RFID is currently being used in the fashion system to identify cartons of product that make up an order. Most notably, Wal-Mart required its largest business customers to use RFID tags starting in January 2005. At this time, RFID tags cost considerably more than bar code tags, although the prices are dropping as the technology adoption increases. In addition, there is a large financial investment to install RFID readers, the large equipment, often resembling a doorway, that reads the tags as the cartons are moved past it. RFID tags can be read anywhere within 10 to 20 feet of the reader in typical installations.

Bar codes have long been used in textile and apparel production and sales to identify the producer, product lot number, production location and date, and other information that provides tracking information for the producer and buyer. Scanners at the point of purchase send information back to the producer as well as provide data for retailers to track inventory and analyze sales. RFID can replace bar codes in these functions and also expand the information coded and used for shoplifting prevention, authenticity to combat counterfeiting, and even presentation of product information and displays for consumers at retail stores. The use of RFID tags in a sustainable fashion system can both increase efficiencies of production and distribution and reduce the total product flow in the system.

The power of RFID tags to carry information grows dramatically at the item level. RFID tags identify each unique item, providing a tracking record vital to efficient inventory management, forecasting, restocking, and preventing stock from running out. It increases the efficiency of both production and distribution, getting the right product in the right volume to the person who will buy it. When apparel products are tagged with RFID, inventory can be identified electronically rather than by counting each item on each shelf. The system can be programmed to identify fast-selling products for reorder and slow-selling items for cancellation of future orders. In this way, RFID can be used to manage purchasing plans and inventory levels to prevent excess production.

International Organization of Standards (ISO) and Electronic Product Code standards (EPC) have been developed for RFID use in the United States and Europe. However, some criticism and concern about use of this information, particularly of recording consumer purchasing practices, has been expressed by consumer advocacy groups such as Consumers Against Supermarket Privacy Invasion and Numbering (CASPIAN; http://www.spychips.com). Even though using RFID-collected information about past customer purchases to provide consumer services based on them is not widespread, current business practice is to request permission from customers when doing so.

Information Technology and Production Planning

Production planning can be enabled by technology to build a more sustainable supply chain and fashion system. Offshore production of apparel has become the norm in the past decade, closing down many U.S. apparel assembly factories. During the early twentieth century, a similar offshore exodus occurred in the textile industry. At the same time, several vertical textile and apparel firms, such as Inditex (http://www.inditex.com), that design and produce both textiles and apparel in their companies and trading companies, such as Li & Fung (http://www.lifung.com), have been heralded for their ability to quickly and effectively produce the right amount of the right product. These companies use information technology to identify trends, gather orders, and then spread production across extensive factory networks either owned by vertical firms or contracted out to partnering factories.

IT software applies data about the raw material availability and production capacity of network factories, along with order data and real-time sales. In this way, the technology can identify open capacity that matches production needs as well as make quick decisions about adding or canceling production of styles that are selling briskly or not at all. Technology can help us make decisions that effectively reduce inventory, a primary goal of a sustainable fashion system.

Specifically, three approaches have been successfully used with information technology to increase efficiencies and decrease product waste:

1. Viewing all production as part of a fashion system in order to make the right amount of the right products while maximizing the use of production capacity and minimizing costs, including energy for transportation.
2. Using networks of local production facilities whenever possible to reduce transportation costs and use of nonrenewable energy. Quick turnaround of production orders is also more easily accommodated.
3. Contracting offshore production for large, basic product orders that will sell through and can be ordered far in advance without risk of poor sales that result in excess inventory.

IT is an enabling technology to a sustainable fashion system that increases efficiencies of production planning and distribution. It can bring the production and consumption in a sustainable fashion system into balance using available information inputs.

Consumer Use

Consumer selection, purchase, use, and disposal patterns have a significant impact on a sustainable fashion system. When their actions are informed by sustainable principles, consumers can contribute by applying technology or analyzing its impacts on reducing energy inputs to care, purchasing fewer garments and wearing them longer, and replacing many quickly disposed garments for adaptive smart clothing that add functional and aesthetically adaptive characteristics.

Laundering: Reducing Energy Inputs

Often we forget the impacts of product use on a sustainable fashion system, while focusing on eco-friendly materials that are organic, have low impacts on the soil, and pass on low toxicity and air emissions during processing. For example, the greatest effects on the environment of organic cotton are in its use stage, through laundering and ironing of the products ("Well-dressed," 2005). Kate Fletcher, a graduate student, and researchers Emma Dewberry and Phillipp Goggin from Chelsea College of Art and Design (2001) analyze the entire laundry process, including equipment costs and impacts, water and water temperature, and ironing. They propose a variety of consumer-involved alternatives that provide system efficiency gains but require some modification in cultural norms. For example, consumers could actively reduce their environmental footprints by:

- Lowering water temperatures
- Laundering less frequently and redefining "clean"
- Sharing equipment through community laundries
- Bypassing ironing

While these suggestions promote a sustainable fashion system, they require a shift in consumer behavior norms that will take time to gain broad consumer acceptance.

Fewer Garments, Longer Use

Other obvious ways to reduce product and waste are to purchase and use fewer garments and to use them longer. The two issues here are to use garments for more activities or in different ways and to modify consumer norms to lengthen a garment's life span beyond short fashion cycles.

Transformable garments have great potential to broaden the use of a single garment. Familiar examples of "transformables" are jackets that transform into skirts and raincoats that also serve as tents. The objective is to be functional in more than one setting. Velcro, zippers, and structural detailing facilitate a successful design process that is both functional and aesthetically pleasing.

Issey Miyake (2001) exhibited designs at the Vitra Design Museum in Berlin in 2001 that allowed the consumer to transform the garment after purchase. Named APOC for A Piece of Cloth, examples of his design group's presentations were:

- *The Baguette.* Stretch knits that could be cut any place to create a garment
- *Frame Work.* Garments with the same frame but different warp and weft to create color and texture variations
- *Spider.* Teeny sweaters that stretch to any size

Miyake used technology in his choices of fiber, fabric, and assembly to involve consumers in the design of garments after purchase. These technologies transformed fabric and garments into new designs, providing longer and varied use for potentially fewer garments to reduce the product volume and waste stream in the fashion system.

Changing consumer norms may be more problematic than coming up with designs that can be used in a variety of settings. Consumers are used to rapidly changing styles, colors, and fabrics, as well as established norms of wearing different outfits every day of the week and for not more than one or two years. This is a challenge for a technology-enabled sustainable fashion system that smart clothing and wearable technologies may address.

Smart Clothing and Wearable Technology

Smart or "intelligent" clothing possess additional functionality beyond its usual structures at the fiber, fabric, or garment levels. In wearable technology, or *smart technology combined with clothing*, electronic devices are incorporated into apparel systems often as add-ons with hard shapes and heavy weights. Electronic devices such as cell phones, BlackBerries, iPods, and portable computers are familiar examples of technology that is accommodated by pockets and clips on clothing to make them wearable technology. In addition to adding communication capacity, smart clothing and wearable technology can monitor body functions such as heart rate, breathing, and heat level.

Smart clothing and wearable technology can address sustainable design by extending the product use and life span and thereby reducing the product flow in a sustainable fashion system. The added functions that address the communication and monitoring needs of one's daily life may outweigh the short-term style changes now dominating our fashion system. However, researchers Lucy Dunne and Barry Smyth of the Computer Science and Informatics School at University College of Dublin, Ireland (2007) argue that wearability is an important consideration to functional apparel design. Wearability criteria include thermal and moisture management, flexibility, mobility, durability, and size and fit. Technology developers and functional apparel designers must work together to fully integrate wearability needs with technology requirements to make smart clothing sustainable through its expanded functions and adaptable or dynamic design that extends its life span. One smart clothing item that is versatile could replace many disposable pieces. Designing wearable technology systems with adaptability of style that matches longevity of the electronic devices is a step in a sustainable direction. As electronics are built to last even longer, so too will the life span of the garment be extended.

Lucy Dunne is a pioneer on the apparel side of wearable technolo-

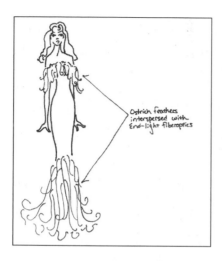

Ostrich feathers interspersed with End-light fiberoptics

FIGURE 5.7. The top and lower edges of this dress are embellished with ostrich feathers interspersed with end-light fiber optics. The motion of the feathers and light tips respond to rapid movement of the abdomen, or giggling. This dress is part of a series of garments designed by Dunne that combine the glamour of 1930s Hollywood with the technologies of the future to express emotion. (Designed and illustrated by Lucy Dunne.)

gy. Initially a functional apparel designer, she has explored the frontiers of wearable technology through the eyes and systems of a designer while studying and collaborating with technology experts. Her research program evaluates apparel design along with sensor position, body functions, movement, and expression. She "breaks it down into three categories of capability imparted to clothing by technology: device interface (e.g., communications capability, information storage/retrieval), apparel functionality (e.g., temperature, visibility, protection, medical monitoring), and dynamic expression (i.e., versatile aesthetics in shape/color/pattern) (Dunne, 2007)." For example, Dunne designed a set of evening gowns that were aesthetically pleasing as well as expressing alertness, speeding pulse, or giggling (see Figure 5.7).

Another leader in apparel design for wearables, designer Natalia Allen (http://www.nataliaallen.com) has a strong passion for technology and eco-fashion. She argues that wearable technology should be created through a partnership between engineers and designers because neither alone could address the form, fit, function, and fabric characteristics within the context of computer-enabled technologies.

Her designs and consulting projects usually incorporate "innovative (e.g., waterproof, organic, breathable) textiles and new methods of construction (laser cutting, seam bonding, CAD)" (The future of eco-fashion, 2007).

Disposal versus Reusing, Refurbishing, and Recycling

Reuse, refurbishment, and recycling of fibers, fabrics, and garments can be a profitable as well as a sustainable business practice. This section describes several examples of businesses using advanced technology to develop new strategies for reducing the amount of waste in the fashion system by recycling, refurbishment, and reuse.

Business Take-Back Programs and Fiber-to-Fiber Recycling

Recovery of materials and reuse in new products instead of disposal in the landfill is a sustainable victory. New process technologies make fiber-to-fiber recycling possible but there are still challenges of product development and logistics to make the opportunity profitable.

Patagonia and Malden Mills

An early success story is the use of soda pop bottles for polyester fleece production. A Malden Mills and Patagonia collaboration lead the technological breakthrough in the early 1980s, and now the technology has diffused throughout the apparel fleece industry. Essentially, the soda pop bottles are melted down to a basic polymer, extruded into fiber, and knit into fleece. The availability of massive amounts of used soda pop bottles combined with the fashion and functional warmth of the fleece product for active sports and everyday apparel made this recycled material profitable. Available used product and desirable fabric characteristics were both needed to make the product the runaway success that it is.

Patagonia and Teijin Group

With the introduction of William McDonough and Michael Braun-gart's 2002 book *Cradle to Cradle* and its concept of waste = food, fiber manufacturers became interested in other potential recycling oppor-tunities. Patagonia has been a leader in following and promoting other environmentally sound business practices and material choices such as the use of 100 percent organic cotton in its products. Its newest ini-tiative is ECO CIRCLE®, a closed-loop fiber-to-fiber recycling system developed by Japan's Teijin Group in 1999 where used fabric is returned to the fiber state and reused. Patagonia partnered with Teijin in 2005 to initiate the Common Threads Recycling program, where customers voluntarily return worn-out Capilene® garments to Patag-onia by mail or to their retail stores to be returned to the fiber state using the ECO CIRCLE process and then fashioned into new gar-ments (Patagonia, n.d.).

The Teijin Group recycles any polyester product (e.g., bottles, fibers, films, and used garments) into virgin-quality polyester. For the Common Threads program, buttons and zippers and other hard-ware are removed and the garments are shredded. The chemical process granulates the fibers into small pellets, purifies and decol-orizes the pellets to form polyester raw material, polymerizes this raw material into polymer chips, and spins the virgin-quality fibers. This technology-enabled process has great potential for strengthen-ing the sustainable fashion system at the disposal stage through materials recovery.

Nike

Nike (http://www.nikebiz.com/reuseashoe) uses recycled materials from its athletic shoes to create a variety of sports playing surfaces. The recycling program serves as an integral part of its NikeGO Places program to increase physical activity in children in low-income com-munities. The program depends upon community and business col-lection drives and individual consumer contributions by mail.

Chaco

Chaco (http://www.chaco.com) embraces sustainability throughout its company, including a performance sandal product that can be re-soled to increase its life span. The design of Chaco products allows them to be re-soled and re-webbed for a small fee by sending sandals to Chaco. As styles and designs are upgraded, older styles of sandals can be repaired with components of newer styles, a modular approach aided by CAD design technology as well as production technology. Chaco has also developed an in-store shoe recycling program where customers can exchange used, clean pairs of shoes at its participating dealers for a 20 percent discount on a Chaco product. The used shoes are then donated to the dZi Foundation, an organization dedicated to promoting education, health, and awareness of indigenous cultures of the Himalayas. In both programs, Chaco reduces the flow of product into landfills by refurbishing or by sending to secondhand markets.

Consumer Awareness

The success of these initiatives for recycling that returns waste to fibers and take-back products when consumers are done with them will ultimately depend on consumer and business environmental awareness, consumer assistance to ensure the availability of used products, effective business logistics systems, and profitable recycling economic structures. However, more fashion industry-wide programs are needed that capture large amounts of used materials and reuse them as food for the next cycle of products through fiber-to-fiber technology similar to ECO CIRCLE.

Conclusion

Advancing technology has added a new opportunity to design and improved a sustainable fashion system by increasing material and production efficiencies and reducing the total amount of textile materials and garments through the fashion system. Viable approaches to sustainability include the adoption of innovative materials; mass-customized garment design, production planning, and distribution; smart textiles and wearable technology; and refurbished and fiber-to-fiber reuses of used clothing. These technologies are one step on the path to a positive future for a sustainable fashion system.

Consumers need to become activists in articulating their needs. Technology is facilitating consumer involvement both through easier and more powerful communication tools and through accessible information. Thoughtful debate, increasing knowledge about the relationships between sustainability and fashion, and technologies to enable our progress make our future bright.

Technology is crucial, as it can enable a sustainable fashion system by making the right product, getting the right product to the right person, and adding beneficial functions to the product for the owner.

References

Allen, N. (2005, September 14–16). The discontents of wearable technology: Improving transition from concept to market. Presented at Wearable Futures conference, University of Wales, UK.

Ashdown, S., & Loker, S. (2004). Use of body scan data to design sizing systems based on target markets. National Textile Center Annual Report 2004. Retrieved September 12, 2006, from http://www.NTCresearch.org

Caulfield, B., Dunne, L. E., & Walsh, P. (2007, March). Proceedings of the Fourth International Workshop on Wearable and Implantable Body Sensor Networks in Aachen, Germany.

Choi, W., & Powell, N. (2005). Three dimensional seamless garment knitting on v-bed flat knitting machines. *Journal of Textiles and Apparel, Technology and Management*, 4(3). Retrieved September 12, 2006, from http://www.tx.ncsu.edu/jtatm/volume4issue3/vo4_issue3_abstracts.htm

Dunne, L. (2007). Personal interview.

Dunne, L., & Smyth, B. (2007, April). Psychophysical elements of wearability. Proceedings of Computer-Human Interaction, San Jose, CA.

Dunne, L., Walsh, P., Smyth, B., & Caulfield, B.(2007, March). A system for wearable monitoring of seated posture in computer users. Proceedings of the Fourth International Workshop on Wearable and Implantable Body Sensor Networks, Aachen, Germany.

Fletcher, K., Dewberry, E., & Goggin, P. (2001). Sustainable consumption by design. In Cohen, M. J., & Murphy, J. (Eds.), *Exploring Sustainable Consumption: Environmental Policy and the Social Sciences* (pp. 213–224). Amsterdam: Pergamon.

Frey, M. (2007). Personal interview.

Galloway, A. (2007). Fashion sensing/Fashioning sense. Retrieved March 28, 2007, from http://www.horizonzero.ca/textsite.wear

Hawley, J. (2006). Digging for diamonds: A conceptual framework for understanding reclaimed textiles. *Clothing and Textiles Research Journal* 24(3), 262–275.

Hinestroza, J. (2007). Personal interview.

I.T. Strategies. (2006).

Honkala, M. (2006.) Introduction to shape memory materials. In Mattila, H. R. (Ed.) *Intelligent textiles and clothing* (pp.85–90). New York: The Textile Institute.

Kamali, N. N. & Loker, S. (2002). Mass customization: On-line consumer involvement in product design. *Journal of Computer Mediated Communication, 7*(4). Retrieved September 12, 2006, from http://jcmc.indiana.edu//vol7/issue4/loker.html

Loker, S. & Ashdown, S. P. (2005, September 18–21). The body scanner: Mass customization technology applied to ready-to-wear. Proceedings from the 2005 World Congress on Mass Customization and Personalization, Hong Kong University of Science and Technology.

Loker, S., Ashdown, S. P., & Schoenfelder, K. A. (2005). Size specific analysis for body scan data to improve apparel fit. *Journal of Textiles and Apparel, Management and Technology, 4*(3). Retrieved September 12, 2006, from http://www.tx.ncsu.edu/jtatm/

McCullough, E. A., & Shim, H. (2006). The use of phase change materials in outdoor clothing. In Mattila, H.R. (Ed.), *Intelligent textiles and clothing,* pp.63-83. New York: The Textile Institute.

McDonough, W. & Braungart, M. (2002). *Cradle to cradle.* New York: North Point Press.

Mattila, H. R. (2006). Intelligent textiles and clothing (pp. 1–4). New York: The Textile Institute.

May-Plumley, T. & Bau (2005). Behavior of Prepared-For-Print Fabrics in Digital Printing. *Journal of Textiles and Apparel, Technology and Management, 4*(3). http://www.tx.ncsu.edu/jtatm/volume4issue3/vo4_issue3_abstracts.htm

Miyake, I. (2001). *Clothing For the future: Captured by imagination and technology.* Berlin, Germany: Vitra Design Museum.

Patagonia. (n.d.). Retrieved from http://www.patagonia.com/pdf/common_threads_whitepaper.pdf

Pine, J. III. (1993). *Mass customization.* Boston: Harvard Business School Press.

Sixth annual year in ideas. (2006). *The New York Times Magazine,* December 10, 77–78.

"The future of eco-fashion: Natalia Allen." (2007). Retrieved March 28, 2007, from http://groovygreen.com/groove/?p=1154

Thorpe, A. (2004). *Time & design.* Rotterdam: 010 Publishers.

Van der Leeuw, S. E., & Aschan-Leygonie, C. (2000). A long-term perspective to resilience in socio-natural systems. Presented at workshop on system shocks–system resilience in Abisko, Sweden, May 22–26.

Well-dressed: The present and future sustainability of clothing and textiles in the United Kingdom. (2006). Cambridge, UK: University of Cambridge.

BEST PRACTICES

Look Again™
Interview by Connie Ulasewicz, May 2007

As we've seen in this section, people are the driving force behind sustainable practices. When we think about sustainable fashion, we often gravitate toward environmental issues, but it is the people who have the power to act in ways to create the most impact. People are intimately connected to fashion, so we must think about how they behave, what they want, and what might improve their lives and well-being. Look Again™ is a line of one-of-a-kind garments recycled, transformed, or reborn from previously produced clothing. The line is created by people who have the opportunity to be the driving force in the sustainable fashion movement: students at Cazenovia College in Cazenovia, New York.

Their concept of a "4-way win" for purchasing a Look Again™ product is as follows:

- Customers enjoy a new look while consuming less, supporting students, small businesses, and charities.
- Students learn, creative, and sustainable solutions to fashion and small-business operations.

- Community receives well-priced designer fashions, and 25 percent of the purchase price goes to local charities.
- Environment sustains less impact in supply production.

The following interview provides a closer examination of the practices of this project. I am grateful for the time and information shared with me from Karen Steen, associate professor, fashion design program, and department director; Laura Pirkl, lecturer in fashion design; and Joanne Gilbert, lecturer in fashion design.

How Are You and This Project Involved in Sustainable Business Practices?
"We offer students current industry skills while demonstrating socially responsible business practices," explains Gilbert. "We do this by designing, producing, and merchandising unique apparel through a partnership with a popular local thrift shop. Our students maintain a sales rack and display area plus a highly visible store window display. We contribute to our community economically, socially, and environmentally. Also, by recycling apparel from the thrift store into one-of-a-kind designs, we are not only teaching design and merchandising skills, we are demonstrating a green design process that offers a unique product to consumers, uses very few resources, and supports local charities with every sale."

"We decided to incorporate sustainability into our fashion program not just because it was morally a good thing to do, but because we are in the business of educating our students of current business practices within our industry," says Pirkl, who is responsible for teaching the classes where students produce the wearable garments and accessory items. "With many new brands focusing on solely sustainable products, or fair labor practices, we would not be doing our job if we were not incorporating this into our course material. Fortunately, the two fit like puzzle pieces. The more green is accepted as a valid and lucrative business framework, the more we all contribute to a healthy environment."

Students participate in the healthy environment of their local community as they interact with potential customers on a more personal level, creating garments that contribute to their well-being. Steen, as department chair and program director, fully supports the Look Again™ line as well as the service learning aspect (i.e., outreach in the community) and the unique integration or socially responsible fashion into the Fashion Studies Program at Cazenovia College. "The idea has developed into a social entrepreneurship project that enables both design and merchandising students to develop their academic and professional skills in a realistic small-business environment."

What Is the Most Innovative Aspect of Your Project?

"We are actually reinventing everyday small choices and reframing market attitudes toward recycling," says Gilbert, referring to how Look Again™ offers a more innovative approach to sustainability than simply the creation of products from recycled garments. An integral part of this stems from the integration of students and local community business working together. "We are appealing to the natural inclination to want new, special, and unique fashions without actually consuming new materials. We are replacing the image of recycled items from that which goes away in a bin to that which you bring home, embrace, and enjoy! Students can gain an understanding of what a 'sustainable' lifestyle means and what creativity and technology can do for the future of our industries."

Pirkl expresses the impact that this project has on the entire Cazenovia campus and the community. "The true innovative action with Look Again™ is not in the product, but rather the integration of sustainability into our course content, and transference of sustainable efforts campuswide. We are birthing more than the practice of recycling paper, cans, or textiles. We are introducing an awareness within our students that is essential to the growth of green product future, and global health." The student designer in the photo above is redesigning a dated pair of wool herringbone trousers into a tote bag.

What Is the Most Challenging Aspect of Your Project?

Laura Pirkl explains how Look Again™ is a real fashion line, created for a defined target market with real in-store delivery dates. Students, who have their own tastes, demands, and academic time schedule, create the line under the guidance of Pirkl, who explains the process. "When the consumer looks at the rack, they see the same top made from different fabrics for each size," she says. "The look is cohesive, but each piece is one of a kind. One of the challenges is pulling together old garments that work with the functional and aesthetic aspects of the new garment desired for the new line; this is a lengthy process. The students are learning to understand the beauty within the complexity of the design process. They have to learn to piece creatively and work with existing seams to create a pleasing design." For example, the image on page 131 is of an old sweater that was converted into a dress bodice; the skirt was created from leftover sample yardage that was headed for the trash.

The potential to expand the Look Again™ product line increases as the consumer awareness for sustainable products increases. However, the project faces the same challenges that most start-up businesses deal with: capital. "Being a nonprofit institution with an academic schedule, academic purpose, and no working capital limits our ability to respond and grow our ideas as a normal small business might," explains Gilbert. "As the project gains momentum and a wider audience, we are constantly stretched for time and re-

sources to reconcile the outreach requests for exhibits and production within the limitations of our academic function."

What Are the Possibilities for Sustainable Futures? New Directions?
The Look Again™ project received national attention when it was featured in the March/April 2007 *Sierra Club* magazine, increasing the possibilities for the capital support needed to fund its growth. I believe the Cazenovia college fashion design department has very successfully connected their students with their community and has created a model of social entrepreneurship that other fashion curriculum can follow as they venture into teaching fashion sustainability. Look Again™ is supported in the Fashion Studies Curriculum at Cazenovia through two courses. The fall semester explores working with recycled materials and surface technique while producing the fall grouping of merchandise. In the spring semester students use their creative

and technical skills to efficiently develop and produce garments that meet industry specifications, while preserving the Look Again™ one-of-a-kind philosophy. As students graduate with the business skills and experience of creating and retailing sustainable garments, the Look Again™ model has great potential to expand to other communities and countries as the public gains knowledge of its benefits.

SECTION 2

*Production and Economic Processes
in the Global Economy*

INTRODUCTION

There are many ways to think about how fashion is manufactured and the impact of production and economic processes on sustainability. Clearly a first step toward bringing about change would be to examine our thinking and actions. For example, fashion goods are consumable, thus waste is inevitable—or is it? Are there processes we can develop and implement that can reduce or eliminate the consequences of overconsumption? Our way of producing more to sell more in order to keep the economic engine behind fashion functioning is unsustainable and in need of a serious and thoughtful overhaul.

It is time to approach production and economic processes from a different perspective, adjusting not just the ways of doing but also our ways of thinking. The traditional linear concept of beginning to end leaves many issues unsolved. From beginning to beginning is a more sustainable model.

This section of our book starts with a provocative discussion in Chapter 6 of the disconnect between production and consumption. Using metaphors to help us understand the complexities, Susan Kaiser encourages us to think in new ways about processes of putting together more flexible supply chains for environmentally sensitive apparel production. Using Patagonia as a case study, and drawing on an interview with their director of environmental analysis, Susan submits that sustainable fashion requires a flexible mix of metaphors.

In Chapter 7, Paul Gill expands on flexibility by exploring the dynamics of decision making and questioning the possibilities of sustainable product development as we participate in global production and trade. Through his own experiences as an international trade executive working in China, he provides a context for understanding the origins of the quota system and how we are forging forward without it. His experiences are embedded in a changing world of mass production where lessons can be gleaned for future action.

Taking the stance that sustainable design action is possible on a production level, Timo Rissanen introduces an inventive jigsaw approach in Chapter 8. He explains methods to increase fabric yield and reduce fabric waste through the design process and innovative patternmaking. As things currently exist, however, we generate massive waste within our industry and consumption practices.

What is the process for reusing the waste that is created? Jana Hawley writes in Chapter 9 about the hidden industry of apparel and textile recycling. She asks, if most postconsumer waste is recyclable, then why is such a high percentage of textiles and clothing products dumped into the landfill? Jana reviews the economic impact of the textile recycling process and the global challenges faced throughout the world in addressing this challenge.

Van Dyk Lewis closes this section in Chapter 10 by questioning the design process and rethinking and reframing the fashion system into a sustainable system. He leaves us with a deeper sense of the complexities involved in processes to create fashion, yet a realization that they must interconnect and refurbish if we are to turn around what is not working and embrace sustainability as a possibility.

Why Now?
- Textiles are nearly 100 percent recyclable, and yet textile and apparel products are still sent to landfills.
- As our global population increases, so does the consumption of textile products.
- We understand the processes to design and develop garments with lower fabric consumption.

- The manufacturing of clothing has moved to areas of our world where the lowest wages are paid and where there is little concern for the air and water pollution created by the production of textile fiber, yarn, and fabric.
- Sustainable fashion permits us to think more creatively about our current fiber and garment production practices.

SUSAN B. KAISER, PH.D. is professor of textiles and clothing, as well as women and gender studies, at the University of California, Davis. She is a fellow and past president of the International Textile and Apparel Association and serves on the editorial board of *Fashion Theory*. Her research revolves around the interplay between fashion theory and feminist cultural studies, with a particular focus on the production-consumption interface in textile and apparel systems, and (re)constructions of masculinities through style and fashion.

CHAPTER 6

Mixing Metaphors in the Fiber, Textile, and Apparel Complex: Moving Toward a More Sustainable Fashion System

Susan Kaiser

Various metaphors are commonly used to interpret the fiber, textile, and apparel complex: pipeline, value chain, upstream versus downstream, and even bathtub. A sustainable fashion system, however, requires moving beyond comparisons based on binary and linear frameworks. Drawing on an interview with Jill Dumain, director of environmental analysis at Patagonia, and using Patagonia as a case study, this chapter introduces circular and weblike alternatives, submitting that sustainable fashion requires a flexible mix of metaphors.

(De)constructing Metaphors

The jeans are funky, patched with color and highly decorated. But who could believe that this hip denim is having a second recycled fashion life and that the fabric is ecologically and environmentally sound? The fashion industry, built on constant change and quick turnover, is taking a longer view. You no longer have to be an eco-warrior or a hippie to grasp the message. For the cool and stylish, green is the new black (Menkes, 2006).

When Suzy Menkes (2006), reporter for the *International Herald Tribune*, declares that "green is the new black," she is developing a metaphor for sustainable fashion. This metaphor creates a useful analogy between eco-friendliness and fashion, as well as a connection between short- and long-term goals. This metaphor helps us to assign meaning and value to cultural moods (e.g., caring about the environment), as well as to materiality (e.g., eco-friendly textiles and processes). Fashion, in fact, may be described as fostering flexible linkages among materiality, cultural moods, and metaphors (Kaiser and Ketchum, 2005). "Green is the new black" can be seen as a metaphor that has what cultural studies scholars would call a "structure of feeling," or a *cultural mood*, that becomes tangible as materials are processed and marketed for consumer acceptance.

Metaphors are good to express ideas. They provide words or images that represent abstract concepts; metaphors suggest analogies that enable us to visualize and understand concepts that might otherwise be difficult to grasp. In this chapter, we explore various metaphors that have been used to make sense of the fiber, textile, and apparel complex. We consider the extent to which these metaphors have enabled or hindered the possibility of sustainable fashion and propose some additional alternative metaphors.

As helpful as metaphors may be, they do have their limits. Even illuminating metaphors that help us make new connections eventually break down when we push or press them persistently. Feminist philosopher Marilyn Frye (1996) indicates that we can learn a lot by pressing helpful metaphors and by exploring their limits. By understanding where and why metaphors break down, we can realize where and why they may actually *limit* our ability to think critically and creatively, or to envision new possibilities. Frye (1996) argues that we need a variety of metaphors to understand complicated phenomena and to envision new ways of seeing and experiencing the world. She suggests that it is not only okay, but also instructive, to *mix* metaphors. The development of multiple metaphors requires diversity of thought, thereby affording us with multiple perspectives and possibilities for the future. Such diversity enables us to reap the benefits of any single metaphor while also gathering additional metaphors from which we can select when the limits of the first one have been reached:

> What we are about is re-metaphorizing the world. We need as many and various perceivers as possible to mix metaphors wildly enough so we will never be short of them, never have to push one beyond its limits, just for lack of another to take up where it left off (Frye, 1996, p. 42).

For example, let's examine the benefits and the limits of the "green is the new black" metaphor. The idea that green is the "new black" has more than one meaning. The use of black can be interpreted to mean that environmental responsibility can be profitable for a clothing business (i.e., "in the black," as compared to "in the red"). Another meaning of black is its classic or basic quality in one's wardrobe; it can be mixed and matched with a range of colors, across seasons and situations. We might say that black has "contextual flexibility" when it comes to appearance style (Kaiser, Freeman, and Chandler, 1993).

If we continue to press the metaphor of green as the "new black," however, we might begin to consider the limits of color as a metaphor for sustainability. First, the idea of a "new black" suggests that green is this season's *new* basic color, just as brown, gray, purple, or other colors have been in past seasons. If green is new this season, there is an implication that it may not be fashionable in future seasons. Second, if we push the metaphor of green to mean *environmental*, there is a danger that it can become little more than an advertising slogan, without the research or long-term commitment required to ensure that the materials, processes, and practices associated with fashion are sustainable in terms of the planet, people, and profitability.

The "green is the new black" metaphor is helpful to the extent that it enables us to envision possible connections among nature, profit, fashionability, sustainability, and contextual flexibility. The use of colors alone does not necessarily help us think through the complex flow and processing of materials associated with the fiber, textile, and apparel complex.

Exploring Metaphors for the Fiber, Textile, and Apparel Complex
In the textiles and apparel field, various metaphors have been used to describe the fiber, textile, and apparel complex and its material flows. These have primarily derived from the modern, Western ways of knowing associated with industrial capitalism. Often these metaphors have either referred to a *binary*, or either/or, opposition between production and consumption (i.e., the production versus consumption metaphor) or to a one-dimensional, or *linear*, flow of materials from production to consumption (i.e., the pipeline or value chain metaphors). The remainder of this chapter is organized around the binary and linear metaphors associated with the modern industrialization of the fiber, textile, and apparel complex, including some metaphors that grapple with the environmental issues associated with this complex. I then suggest some additional metaphors that move toward more circular or connective patterns for envisioning and enabling sustainable fashion.

In the development of this chapter, especially the more circular metaphors in the final section, I am indebted to Jill Dumain, director for environmental analysis at Patagonia. She graduated from the University of California at Davis in 1991 and has worked at Patagonia in various capacities, from an intern to a fabric development specialist to her current position. Over the years, and beginning with her time as a student at UC Davis, Dumain has influenced my thinking in many ways. Her ability to "connect the dots" in the fiber, textile, and apparel complex and her commitment to issues of sustainability are remarkable. This chapter draws heavily on a recent interview with her (Dumain, 2007), and on Patagonia (Chouinard, 2005) more generally as a case study for a company that has made the environment a central component of its mission.

Binary Metaphors

Binary metaphors (e.g., production *versus* consumption) contribute to binary thinking, or thinking in *twos* with an oppositional mind-set (see Figure 6.1). Binary or oppositional thinking emphasizes differences *between* two categories and minimizes differences *within* each category. Although binary metaphors provide a certain kind of clarity as they simplify reality, they ultimately limit our ability to envision new possibilities. Binary thinking restricts us from considering, for example, three or more categories; new ways of forging alliances; and relationships in general that are more flexible, multiple, overlapping, and complicated than binary metaphors can contain.

The following two sections consider two sets of binary metaphors, both of which have roots in modern industrial thinking and practice.

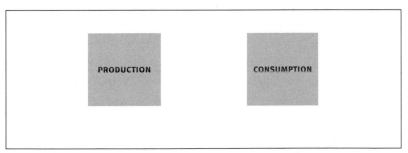

FIGURE 6.1. This drawing depicts the production/consumption binary metaphor.

Production and Consumption

Prior to the industrialization of the fiber, textile, and apparel complex that occurred between the late eighteenth and early twentieth centuries, production and consumption were basically connected through activities in the home or village. Only the wealthy could afford to have many clothes; materials were expensive. Working with natural fibers, individuals and families spun yarn, wove or knitted fabrics, and sewed them into garments. They either wore them to the point of threadbare materials or they passed them on to family members, friends, or servants. Once the garments were worn, they might be cut into scraps for rags to be used around the home for cleaning or occasionally worked into a quilt or a rug.

This connection between producing, or *making*, and consuming, or *using* (i.e., wearing), began to break down with processes of industrialization. Beginning in the latter part of the eighteenth century, textiles became the first industrialized product, with the development of the cotton gin and later with mechanized spinning, weaving, and knitting processes. With the advent of the sewing machine around the middle of the nineteenth century, clothes could be mass-produced as well, although garment production remained a labor-intensive process, as it still is today.

An oppositional system, or binary way of thinking, emerged between production and consumption. Production became conceptualized as an orderly, mechanized, and rational process of making goods for the purpose of profit. In contrast, consumption became understood as the opposite of productivity. Consumption involved "using up" products or goods. Cultural studies scholar Raymond Williams (1980) described how consumption is based upon the metaphor of the stomach and the digestive system; consumers take the goods created by producers and become the channels "along which the product flows and disappears" (p. 43). Because clothes are generally worn on the body rather than eaten, there are some limitations to the consumption metaphor. Yet the majority of people are seen as consumers rather than producers: "We are the market, which the system of industrial production has organized" (Williams, 1980, p. 43).

Part of the disconnect between production and consumption stems from the fact that consumers often buy more than they actually need. Advertising and cultural processes create what Williams (1980) described as a magical system through which clothing consumption becomes a process of human desires. These processes create a disconnect between the *material* side of production, resource use, and textile and clothing properties; and a *magical* world based on a sense of promise, pleasure, and power:

> You do not only buy an object: you buy social respect, discrimination, health, beauty, success, power to control your environment. The magic obscures its real sources of general satisfaction because their discovery would involve radical change in the whole common way of life (Williams, 1980, p. 47).

Because users tend to buy more than "an adequate supply of personal 'consumer goods,'" Williams argues that the larger needs of society are denied. He critiques the "consumer ideal" to the extent that "consumption tends always to materialize as an individual activity" (p. 43). In many ways, consumption, as a process, boils down to the purchase and use of products by sufficient numbers of individual consumers. How, in this context, can consumption be critiqued from a cultural point of view? If there is a philosophy of "to each his or her own," then how can the larger needs of society be understood, beyond a capitalist framework?

Since at least the late 1970s and early 1980s, the global restructuring of capitalism has further intensified the disconnect between production and consumption. In the 1990s, the media spotlighted the consequences of this disconnect through issues ranging from environmental degradation to sweatshops. By this time, some apparel companies were already exploring ways to enhance their social responsibility by addressing these issues directly in their own production practices and those that preceded theirs (i.e., fiber, yarn, and textile production). Among the many challenges associated with these explorations were those spawned by global capitalism: larger, multinational corporations; rapid change in apparel fashion; an increasing "speed to market" to meet consumer demand; a "race to the bottom" for lower labor costs; and lower prices for consumers in a highly competitive global marketplace. These factors spawned the idea of "fast fashion," or the buying of new, inexpensive clothes every couple of weeks. As one consumer cited in a *New York Times* article noted, "If it falls apart, you just toss it away!" (Rosenthal, 2007). These discarded clothes do not simply disappear, however. A recent report by Cambridge University described "fast clothes" as a large and worsening source of the carbon emissions contributing to global warming (Allwood et al., 2006). Ultimately, the limitations of understanding production and consumption as opposites of one another can be realized through the environmental and social issues associated with globalization.

Yet there are exceptions to the production-consumption disconnect. In the experience described below by Jill Dumain in the book *Let My People Go Surfing* by Yvon Chouinard (2005), founder and owner of Patagonia. Dumain, Patagonia's director for environmental analysis, is wearing a dress derived from a fiber that she sees being produced firsthand; she characterizes the connection in a compelling way (Jill Dumain, quoted in Chouinard, 2005, p. 116):

"How to seed a dress": We have been driving for several hours up winding roads high into the mountains of China's Shaanxi Province. I am here to visit the fields where our hemp is grown (see Figure 6.2). Hemp farming is complex and difficult to understand without seeing it firsthand. At the end of this long, isolated road I expect to see no more than one field with a farmer. I am surprised to find an entire village in a flurry of

FIGURE 6.2. A field of growing hemp, which will be harvested, delivered to a mill, and woven into fabric. (Photo courtesy of Patagonia.)

activity . . . Most of the villagers are busy getting the hemp ready to be delivered to the mill that weaves our [Patagonia's] fabric. Bundles of hemp stand in the field to dry. Seeds are being separated from the stalks, which are then carried to the river and submerged for retting (a process that loosens the fiber from the woody pulp) . . . Later in the seasons, when the retting is complete, the stable fibers will be separated from the stalks and delivered to the mill. I am amazed to witness an entire village working to produce the dress I am wearing today—from a seed.

Dumain's story reveals how, despite the disconnect between global production and consumption, it is possible to make connections, but it takes some effort. Her experience is relatively unique. Rarely do many of us have or take the opportunity to trace the clothes we wear back to the raw fibers from which they are made. Dumain's story is a helpful reminder that it is possible and important to make the connection.

Upstream and Downstream

Metaphors derived from nature have been used to describe how materials flow like water from production to consumption. "Downstream" is used to represent the movement of produced goods in the direction of the consumer, whereas "upstream" references earlier stages of production, back to the raw fiber or natural resource required. Like production and consumption, the upstream and downstream metaphors are based upon binary opposition, or thinking in "twos." The difference is that at least there is some sense of movement or flowing associated with upstream versus downstream, as compared to production versus consumption.

The focus of industrial capitalism was production for the sake of "downstream" profit, in the direction of the buyer, or consumer. By the end of the century, cultural critics such as Thorstein Veblen (1899) expressed concerns about a society producing "conspicuous consumption" and an ethos of wastefulness. Production and consumption became less connected as the processes of growing fibrous materials and making them into fashion moved from the home or local studio into factories.

When pushed to their limits, the downstream and upstream metaphors raise the question: Who gets to decide which way is up and which way is down? Are the dynamics about physical gravity, or cultural power, or both? Presumably, the consumption end of the equation has more gravitational pull, downward, but in many ways the oppositional metaphors prioritize production as being on a higher cultural plane. Indeed, the upstream/downstream metaphor seems to belie the ambivalence (i.e., the "both/and" rather than the "either/or" feelings) that underpin fashion and capitalism alike.

Pushing the metaphor a bit further, there is no feedback mechanism (i.e., some way for consumer issues to get back to those producing for them) for communication between downstream and upstream. From an environmental point of view, one can imagine waste materials (e.g., affluent dyes and other chemicals) floating downstream, possibly polluting rivers and streams. This kind of imagery brings to mind the need to delineate among the stages of production. What occurs at each stage, from the initial use of natural resources to their processing and fashioning for their ultimate consumers? And, what consequences do these stages have for the concept of sustainable fashion?

Linear Metaphors

Many of the metaphors used to visualize and understand the fiber, textile, and apparel complex are linear and one-way in terms of material flows. Linear thinking, like binary thinking, is a legacy of modern industrialization. Since the environmental movement of the late 1960s and early 1970s, the idea of linear industrial thinking has been critiqued (McDonough and Braungart, 2002, p. 26):

> Neither the health of natural systems, nor an awareness of their delicacy, complexity, and interconnectedness, have been part of the industrial design agenda. At its deepest foundation, the industrial infrastructure we have today is linear; it is focused on making a product and getting it to a customer quickly and cheaply without considering much else.

Pipeline

The pipeline metaphor is based upon the movement of gases or liquids (e.g., oil, natural gas, water) along a series of pipes that have become fused together so as to become seamless. The whole idea is one of movement: keeping the goods flowing (see Figure 6.3).

The pipeline does help to interpret how materials generally flow from one stage to another: fiber producer to yarn spinner to fabric maker to garment manufacturer, and then through the distribution process (i.e., marketing and retailing) to the ultimate consumer. However, when we press the metaphor, what do we find? To what extent does the pipeline metaphor bring to mind "dumping" out processed materials on consumers and anyone else who may be downstream?

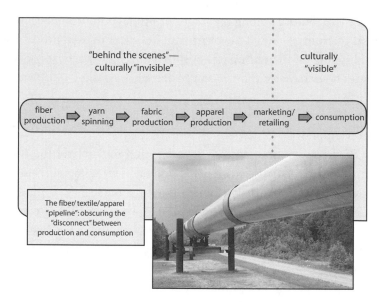

FIGURE 6.3. This drawing depicts the fiber/textile/apparel pipeline metaphor, which obscures the disconnect between production and consumption. (Illustration by Erin Fitzsimmons based on a drawing by Susan Kaiser.)

Where are the feedback loops from producer to consumer? And, perhaps most critically, which parts of the pipeline are visible and which are invisible? To what extent does this still create a disconnect between production and consumption? To what extent is it feasible for consumers (the downstream folks), to be aware of the conditions of production (i.e., the implications for the environment and for workers' economic situations and human rights)?

Value Chain

The value "chain" metaphor is also basically linear, but it is not seamless. Rather, it enables us to visualize the linkages from one stage of production to another, through production and to the consumer, "downstream." The value chain may also be called the "supply chain," referring, for example, to an apparel manufacturer's consideration of his or her suppliers. The chain metaphor acknowledges the series of exchanges required to process the materials at each stage in the process from fiber to consumer (see Figure 6.4). Each stage presumably adds further value to the materials, and there are buyers and sellers involved with each link in the chain (e.g., between the weaver or knitter and garment manufacturer). The chain metaphor reminds us of the relationships and negotiations involved in the flow of materials. The whole process is not simply about movement; it is about adding value, with consumption as the end goal.

So, what are the limitations of the value chain metaphor? In my interview with Dumain of Patagonia, she pointed out that according to this system, apparel manufacturers would only interact with their fabric suppliers and retailers and consumers. Hence, the materials, processes, and people involved in earlier stages along the chain (i.e., fiber and yarn production) are "out of sight and out of mind," as are the environmental consequences of these processes. The chain metaphor absolves apparel manufacturers from responsibility for the choices made in cotton production, for example.

As Patagonia made a commitment to research the environmental impacts all along the value chain, cotton became a key focus, Dumain explained. She realized the need to make direct linkages between sus-

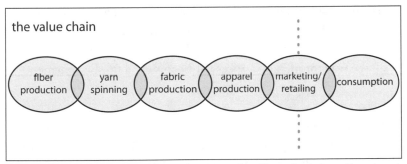

FIGURE 6.4. This drawing depicts the value chain metaphor. (Illustration by Jenny Green based on a drawing by Susan Kaiser.)

tainable agriculture and apparel production (i.e., to foster the fiber-fashion nexus). She discussed how Patagonia's research led to a policy, beginning in 1996, of using 100 percent organic cotton to avoid chemical pesticides and defoliants used in industrialized cotton production. She revealed that until about 1991, the value chain model had previously kept the agricultural fields "out of sight and out of mind." Up until this time, Patagonia had been interacting primarily with its fabric suppliers on the left, or "upstream," side of the production chain. They realized that if they wanted to fulfill their environmental goals, they needed to look back to the raw material; they felt the need to dig further. The more they learned, the more responsible they needed to become in putting together their own supply chains. Chouinard (2005) describes this process in his book (p. 215):

> Many of our existing fabric vendors refused to participate in our
> process of switching over to organic cotton, mostly because of a
> lack of alternative suppliers and their skepticism about the market potential. The staff at Patagonia had to go back all the way to
> the beginning of the supply chain. We searched out cotton brokers with access to bales of organic cotton. Of all the fabric mills
> we ended up using for our supply of organic cotton, only two
> had had prior experience working with it . . . Our organic cotton
> program has been a success, but not just because our customers
> are making the same choice we made—to pay more now for
> organics rather than pay the hidden environmental costs down
> the road—but because our designers and production people now
> have to begin their work with a bale of raw cotton and follow it
> all the way through the process of becoming a finished garment.

Bathtub: Stock and Flow

Nearly 40 years ago, clothing economist Geitel Winakor (1969) observed that the problem with the chain metaphor, which she described as marketing-based, was that the consumer can only be seen as a customer. In fact, there are three processes associated with consumption: acquisition, inventory, and discard. The first process, acquisition, may be described as a "flow" from retailer to consumer (e.g., as a purchase), or as a flow from one consumer to another (e.g., as a gift or a hand-me-down). The second process involves consumer *inventory,* or "stock" management. Inventory involves use or wear, care, and active storage. The third process is that of *discard* (e.g., the act of literally discarding, disposing, donating, or recycling). Discard refers to the stage at which the garment leaves the possession of the individual. Like acquisition, discard constitutes a kind of flow (out of the closet). Winakor used the economic metaphor of a bathtub to visualize her stock-and-flow model of clothing consumption. In this metaphor, water flows in through a faucet and then is stored for a period of time in the tub (i.e., the wardrobe). The tub can only become so full before it overflows (i.e., experiences wardrobe overload). The process of releasing the water down the drain is analogous to the process of discard. Usually, the flows in and out of the tub are intermittent rather than continuous. The flows depend on how often the consumer shops and discards.

Whereas marketing models of consumption generally prioritize the point of acquisition, Winakor (1969) emphasized that it is usually more challenging "to pinpoint the moment of discard" (p. 631). Why is this so? She outlined a number of reasons. First, the "moment of acquisition" is usually "more pleasurable and more memorable." Second, "the moment of discard" often involves some degree of doubt or uncertainty: Will I ever wear this again? What should I do with this?

Some kind of "feedback mechanism" presumably connects acquisition with inventory and discard in order to maintain some sense of equilibrium. Winakor (1969) called for more clarification of this feedback mechanism. She noted the complex and individualized nature of the overall process: Each consumer probably has her or his own equilibrium level. For example, consumers may have guidelines they use when they discard such as, "Have I worn it in the last year?" Some might have a "shirt in, shirt out" policy; if they buy something new, they get rid of something else. Other consumers just let the closet overflow until they clearly need to do something.

Winakor pointed out the uniqueness of clothing as compared to other basic human needs. Clothing is not as durable as a house, but it cannot be "consumed once and for all like food." Nearly 40 years after Winakor wrote this, Rebecca Calahan-Klein, president of Organic Exchange, comments: "The big joke in the organic advocacy world is that one day we will have a shirt we can eat" (Jana, 2006). Until this day comes, the issue of environmental waste is one that plagues environmentally conscious textile and apparel producers and consumers alike. The contemporary concept of "fast fashion" and the shorter life cycles of clothes in the inventory phase of Winakor's metaphor contribute to more waste for the discard phase, due to a dynamic and continuous, rather than an intermittent, flow in and out of the bathtub metaphor.

Winakor's bathtub metaphor is helpful, because (1) it expands our thinking about consumption, which becomes more than the end of a pipeline or chain, and (2) it includes the need for a feedback mechanism. Although it did not fully take environmental issues into account (not surprisingly, since it was developed nearly 40 years ago) and although it still basically follows a linear model, Winakor's model still enables us to conceptualize consumption in ways that enable us to imagine feedback mechanisms and the implications of consumer waste.

Cradle to Grave

The cradle-to-grave metaphor calls attention to the complete life cycle of a garment from an environmental point of view. It recognizes that materials come from the earth and ultimately return to the earth. They do not simply appear or disappear according to fashion cycles. Like Winakor's bathtub metaphor, the cradle-to-grave metaphor considers the life of the garment once it reaches the consumer, including how it is cared for, how it is disposed or recycled, and the like. Such a life cycle analysis is critical, because research generally indicates that the "post-sale care" of a clothing product causes as much as four times the amount of harm to the environment, primarily through water and energy use, as the entire manufacturing "pipeline" (Chouinard, 2005; Allwood et al., 2006).

With an awareness of environmental impacts along every stage of this linear process from birth to death, the negative environmental and social consequences of production, distribution, and consumption can be minimized, or in other words made "less bad." However, there are still major problems with a cradle-to-grave way of thinking: Earth's resources are finite; resources need to become more renewable. Secondly, Earth's ability to store waste (e.g., in landfills) is limited; waste needs to be minimized. Moreover, our thinking is still constrained by the linear, one-way metaphor.

Cradle to Cradle

The cradle-to-cradle metaphor builds upon an environmentally conscious cradle-to-grave metaphor, with a focus on design and product development: the creation of innovative and high-quality products that not only generate economic value but also enhance the well-being of nature and culture. A cradle-to-cradle approach conceptualizes products as contributing to what McDonough and Braungart (2002) call the "triple top line": the interplay among ecology, economy, and equity. A cradle-to-cradle approach involves a supply chain with a feedback loop. One product's life cycle becomes connected with a new product's life cycle. Making and consuming clothes becomes transformed into a "regenerative force." The grave of one garment's life cycle becomes the cradle of its own or another product's life cycle. Ultimately, this means producing clothes that will never become waste. Instead, they become the "food" or nutrients for

new, high-quality products. And here, quality includes vibrant contributions to nature, to individuals (consumers and workers alike), communities, and the economy. Industrial systems themselves help to
restore nature and culture.

To develop cradle-to-cradle cycles, McDonough and Braungart
(2002, pp. 103–104) say that we can take important cues from nature:

> If humans are truly going to prosper, we will have to learn to
> imitate nature's highly effective cradle-to-cradle system of nutri-
> ent flow and metabolism, in which the very concept of waste
> does not exist . . . It means that the valuable nutrients contained
> in the materials shape and determine the design: form follows
> evolution, not just function.

In the cradle-to-cradle metaphor, diversity in design becomes a key
idea as the end of life span of one product may be the beginning of a
new life span for that product. The concept of diversity refers both to
nature and to culture. Diversity in design includes "not only how a

FIGURE 6.5. Patagonia's Synchilla
jacket. (Photo courtesy of
Patagonia.)

product is made but how it is to be used, and by whom . . . [I]t may have many uses, and many users, over time and space" (McDonough and Braungart, 2002, p. 139).

As Patagonia began to explore ways of minimizing environmental waste, it analyzed its fleece jackets, manufactured with "virgin" polyester. Working with a company called Wellman, Patagonia developed a process that takes soda pop bottles, which are also made of polyester, and recycles them into raw material for jackets. The process of making a single jacket requires 25 bottles; between 1993 and 2003, Patagonia and Wellman diverted 86 million soda bottles from landfills: "For every 150 virgin polyester jackets that we replaced with post-consumer recycled (PCR), we saved 42 gallons of oil and prevented a half-ton of toxic air emissions" (Chouinard, 2005, p. 212). Adopting the cradle-to-cradle metaphor, Chouinard takes a self-reflexive look at Patagonia's environmental mission (pp. 114-115):

> But we can never be satisfied with our progress . . . Recycling some of our wastes and making Synchilla jackets (see Figure 6.5) out of recycled soda pop bottles are not enough. We have to take responsibility for what we make, from birth to death and then beyond death, back to rebirth, what the architect, designer, and author Bill McDonough calls "cradle to cradle." It means making a pair of pants out of infinitely recyclable polyester or a polymer like Nylon 6 and, when it is finally worn out, melting down the pants to a resin and creating another pair from the same resin—over and over again.

Thinking in Circles: Creating Connections, Closing Loops

In my recent conversation with Dumain, I asked her how she visualizes the fiber, textile, and apparel complex. She replied that she initially had thought of it as linear, but now she finds herself "thinking in circles." The issue, she said, is who needs to communicate with whom;

who needs to be connecting; where feedback is required (Dumain, 2007).

From Lines to Loops

As Dumain and I talked further, she clarified how lines begin to "loop over" in unexpected places. She noted how in her 16 years of problem-solving experience with Patagonia, she has come to envision the fiber, textile, and apparel complex in new ways (Dumain, 2007):

> When we embarked [on the organic cotton commitment], we were very linear. We traveled down the line . . . But the linear approach turned into circles. The [yarn] spinner asked "What's organic?" He had to come to us, and everybody had to be talking to each other for the success of the program. Everybody needed to have access to each other.

The need to make the necessary connections to achieve longer-term goals for the environment, and to build new relationships as required, demanded a lot of effort. It entailed moving beyond linear

FIGURE 6.6. This drawing depicts the concept "thinking in circles," crossing over and creating loops in the supply chain metaphor. (Illustration by Jenny Green based on a drawing by Susan Kaiser.)

thinking toward a process of collective learning, creating, and constructing new, more flexible ways of knowing.

The supply or "value" chain did not simply materialize for Dumain and Patagonia; rather, if they wanted to make a difference in the environment, they had to build their own and let it take its course in terms of the twists and turns necessary to foster communication and trust (see Figure 6.6). This was no longer a linear process.

So, let's push the metaphor of a linear chain that loops over a bit further. Let's imagine a necklace; it's basically linear, but if one wants to wear it around one's neck, some curving is required. If it is a small or fine chain-link necklace, it is not difficult for knots to appear. I must confess that I am often ambivalent when I unknot a necklace. On the one hand, the correction, which takes some effort, lines it up in an orderly manner. But on the other hand, it only seems "natural" and perhaps instructive for a necklace to double back on itself; as a result, there are some unexpected twists and maybe even some knots. Although these can be a hassle in everyday life, they remind us of the need to cross over . . . Twists and turns can point out challenges that need to be addressed.

Sustainability probably requires thinking more in circles than in a straight line. The supply chain needs to become less rigid, or more flexible, so that crossing over becomes a possibility in order to sustain multiple businesses as well as the environment. Crossing over and developing loops is even more important and possible than ever in the "flatter" world associated with globalization, wherein new technologies become coupled with local networks (Friedman, 2006). The process of putting together a supply chain for environmentally sensitive apparel production demands forging new connections and closing some loops.

Spiderwebs

Perhaps we can begin to imagine a metaphor that is three-dimensional. A spiderweb is an intriguing metaphor[1] (see Figure 6.7). It encour-

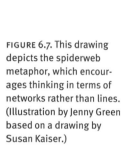

FIGURE 6.7. This drawing depicts the spiderweb metaphor, which encourages thinking in terms of networks rather than lines. (Illustration by Jenny Green based on a drawing by Susan Kaiser.)

ages us to think in terms of networks rather than lines. Spider silk is a highly flexible material, and spiders have a repertoire of at least five different silks. Spider silk is biocompatible and biodegradable; it is eight times more extensible than Kevlar fiber (i.e., the "active ingredient" used in bulletproof vests) and five times tougher. A spiderweb is a highly complex and yet elegantly simple construction. It is a "self-organized pattern formation" (Camazine et al., 2003). And it can be repaired or replaced flexibly as necessary.

What is at the center of the spiderweb metaphor for the fiber, textile, and apparel complex? Because a spiderweb is a flexible rather than a fixed structure, it makes sense to visualize different configurations. The center may change from one web to the next. For example, often it will be the consumer at the center, with the opportunity for numerous players, not only retailers, to interact directly with her or him. At times, however, a company may want to visualize itself in the center so that it can reimagine its relationship with other players beyond the linear format that keeps some players "out of sight and out of mind" (Dumain, 2007). When Patagonia did a lot of soul searching regarding its environmental mission in the late 1980s, it reenvisioned its "supply chain" and began to see the need to interact directly with cotton growers, for example (Chouinard, 2005).

Dumain explained in her interview how the center of Patagonia's "supply chain" can emerge in unexpected places. For example, a yarn spinner became central to the development of a production web in Bangkok, Thailand. The yarn spinner became the "center of the deal" or the "common denominator" who knew a lot of people. The spinner helped to make connections with the organic cotton growers and cotton brokers, as well as with weavers and knitters. Dumain put together the organic cotton web that Patagonia desired by working with the yarn spinner's contacts. As a result, she said, "we became much more effective in our R&D. Otherwise, it would have stopped along the line [or linear chain], at its weakest link." Initially, the fabric supplier would say, "I can't get that [organic cotton and polyester blend] yarn." Dumain asked, "Will you knit it if I can get the yarn?" (Dumain, 2007).

The yarn spinner, accustomed to working with conventional cotton, then set up a separate operation for Patagonia's organic cotton, blended in various percentages with polyester. This yarn spinner had set up his mill with an eye toward the flexibility to handle smaller specialty items. This enabled Patagonia to experiment with different ratios of organic cotton and polyester in small quantities. The spinner then coordinated his timing with weavers and knitters, in the spirit of experimenting through a small-scale R&D effort.

In its commitment to use only organic cotton in its clothing, Patagonia keeps a consistent supply web in place. The web is built on relationships, and enables Patagonia "to do a lot more R&D than would normally be possible for a company our size" (Dumain, 2007). Patagonia also uses organic cotton from California, Texas, New Mexico, Turkey, Africa, and Israel. Dumain stressed the importance of addressing both short- and long-term goals in building supply webs based on trust (Dumain, 2007):

We need both [short- and long-term goals]. One hundred years is very different than 100 days, but the latter is part of our daily world. In the short run, especially with new projects, we need some "wins" at the beginning. It is so hard to do something different. People can then get excited; they see the possibilities . . . You just need to start in—to start from scratch—and then short-term wins encourage people in the long term.

The spiderweb metaphor can be useful to imagine short- and long-term "wins" in diverse configurations. No two webs will be identical, just as there is biodiversity in nature. Rather, the web will depend upon the specific project or network required for a specific context or challenge. If we push the spiderweb metaphor to its limits, as always, we will find some limits. However, at least it, as do the other circular metaphors, breaks us out of a binary or linear mind-set and opens up new possibilities for understanding relationship building as a vital part of sustainable fashion.

Conclusion

As Frye (1996) argues, there are advantages to keeping multiple metaphors at hand, and to continuing to create them. Whether the metaphors used to visualize the fiber, textile, and apparel complex are based on binary, linear, circular, or other frameworks, they have all made some contributions to our ways of understanding this complex. I write this chapter in the spirit of breaking out of the binary and linear metaphors as the sole frameworks for understanding the possibilities for a more sustainable, and hopefully more equitable, fashion system.

At the same time, following Frye (1996), I want to conclude with a call to *mix* metaphors, including those that are binary and linear with those that are more circular. Metaphors come in all kinds of colors, shapes, and sizes; sustainable fashion requires a critical and creative mixing of metaphors. As various environmental and social challenges present themselves to producers and consumers alike, it is advantageous to have an array of metaphors available to mix, match, and juxtapose in our collective toolkits.

Endnote

1. I am most grateful to two graduate students, Ryan Looysen and Jennifer Norah Sorensen, for independently suggesting this metaphor, on different occasions, as I was working on this chapter and discussing it with them. Their suggestions really got me thinking "outside of the box," or the linear mode, actually, as did my interview with Jill Dumain. I sincerely appreciate all of their contributions and thought-provoking insights.

References

Allwood, J. M., Laursen, S. E., de Rodriguez, C. M., & Bocken, N. M. P. (2006). *Well dressed? The present and future of clothing and textiles in the United Kingdom*. Cambridge, UK: University of Cambridge Institute for Manufacturing.

Camazine, S. et al. (2003). *Self-organization in biological systems*. Princeton, NJ: Princeton University Press.

Chouinard, Y. (2005). *Let my people go surfing: The education of a reluctant businessman*. New York: The Penguin Press.

Dumain, J., director of environmental analysis, Patagonia. (2007, January 12). Personal interview.

Friedman, T. L. (2006). *The world is flat: A brief history of the twenty-first century* (2nd ed.). New York: Farrar, Straus and Giroux.

Frye, M. (1996). The possibility of feminist theory. In Ann Garry & Marilyn Pearsall (Eds.), *Women, knowledge, and reality: explorations in feminist philosophy*. New York/London: Routledge.

Jana, R. (2006). Green threads for the eco chic. *Business Week Online*, September 29.

Kaiser, S. B., Freeman, C. M., & Chandler, J. L. (1993). Favorite clothes and gendered subjectivities: Multiple readings. *Studies in Symbolic Interaction, 15*, 27–50.

Kaiser, S. B., & Ketchum, K. (2005). Consuming fashion as flexibility: Metaphor, cultural mood, and materiality. In Ratneshwar, S. & Mick, D. G. (Eds.), *Inside consumption: Consumer motives, goals, and desires*. London: Routledge.

McDonough, W., & Braungart, M. (2002). *Cradle to cradle: Remaking the way we make things*. New York: North Point Press.

Menkes, S. (2006, May 31). Eco-friendly: Why green is the new black. *International Herald Tribune.*

Rosenthal, E. (2007). Can polyester save the world? *New York Times,* January 25, p. G-1.

Veblen, T. (1899). *The theory of the leisure class.* New York/London: Macmillan.

Williams, R. (1980). The magic of advertising. In Williams, R. (Ed.), *Problems in materialism and culture* (pp. 170–195). London: Verso.

Winakor, G. (1969). The process of clothing consumption. *Journal of Home Economics, 61*(8), 629–634.

PAUL GILL is a garment industry executive with more than 25 years of experience specializing in areas of manufacturing, production, scouring, and factory relationships. He is renowned for his work to promote and resolve issues of fair trade with domestic and international manufacturing firms.

CHAPTER 7

Economy of Scale: A Global Context

Paul Gill

W hat can global manufacturing teach us about sustainability? In the early 1970s, a quota system was instituted to control the flow of goods manufactured in developing countries and sold to richer consuming regions like the United States and the European Union. In 2005, that system was removed. International trade executive Paul Gill experienced it all, and in this chapter he lends his personal experience to help us consider the rise and fall of the quota system, the emergence of China as a global trade leader, and what it all means for developing sustainable sourcing and manufacturing in the twenty-first century.

The Rise and Fall of the Quota System
The history of the textile and apparel industries' quota system provides a framework for an understanding of global manufacturing. For more than 30 years, this system served as a means to control and sus-

tain the flow of goods between countries that are developed (e.g., United States and Europe) and developing (e.g., China). Quotas were numerical limits on the number of products in specific categories, determined by the fiber type and garment style, that could be imported from particular countries. Quotas were intended to be a means to sustain and protect domestic manufacturers from "unfair" competition from other countries. This protectionist idea went down with the quota system with an eye to developing and sustaining a global textile and apparel manufacturing system.

Quotas

In 1973, the United States imposed a quota system for textiles and apparel on its predominantly Asian trading partners, which included Hong Kong, Korea, Indonesia, and Taiwan (Rivoli, 2005). Japan also had quota imposed on it because it was seen in those days as a source

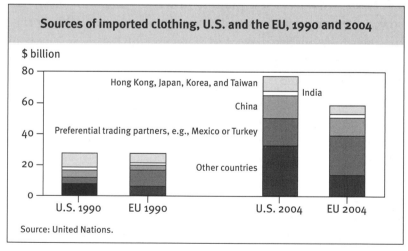

FIGURE 7.1. This chart shows the sources of clothing imports during the period of the U.S. quota system.

of low-cost apparel. Each country was free to decide how to distribute its quota, or *allocation*, which was issued according to fiber and garment type. A country's allocations were based on previous years' records of what it shipped in the past. Hong Kong, for example, had been a center of wool sweater manufacturing because many of the factories from Northern China had fled to the free market there at the time of the communist revolution in 1948. So Hong Kong had a substantial allocation of wool sweater quota despite its obvious absence of sheep. Fibers that were not significantly imported, such as linen and ramie, were excluded, as was silk. The exclusion of ramie led in short order to the development of ramie/cotton and other ramie or linen blends designed specifically to evade quota requirements (Rivoli, 2005).

The Textile and Apparel Industry Takes the Lead

This quota system was designed specifically for the textile and apparel industries despite the fact that trade deficits ran across many industries (Rushford, 2003). Japanese autos were beginning to make a significant impact on the U.S. market, for example. But apparel had long been a major industry in the United States, especially in the South, where there were many textile mills and factories, and in the New York City area, where a highly unionized workforce dominated a vast industry of manufacturers and small factories. San Francisco was also a significant apparel manufacturing center, with many large companies and a strong union presence. In 1972 and 1973, the dollar was under much pressure because of inflation connected to the Vietnam War. The Nixon administration took the dollar off the gold standard and let if float against other world currencies. It lost about 10 percent of its value immediately, making imports that much more expensive. But even that was not enough to stem the rising tide of apparel imports from Asia. Under intense pressure from apparel and textile states and the union, the quota system was adopted (Rushford, 2003).

The International Quota Trade

I started my first job in the apparel industry in January 1972. The company, Tami Sportswear, was a San Francisco-based designer, wholesaler, and manufacturer of medium- to low-priced women's sportswear. By 1972, the company was importing as much as two-thirds of its products, all knit tops, from Hong Kong and Taiwan. (There was no trade at that time between the United States and China.) Domestic production was done at an in-house factory of about 70 sewers and several large local shops. All the workers in the factory and the shops were union members. Tami also had a wholly owned Hong Kong subsidiary that purchased yarn in the open market and stored it in *godowns*, or public warehouses, in Hong Kong. In response to purchase orders issued at the home office in San Francisco, the yarn was sent to Hong Kong dyers and then to knitting factories. The finished products were usually aired-freighted to San Francisco to be included in coordinated customer orders that included sportswear made in San Francisco and nylon shirts purchased from Taiwan.

My tasks included the tracking of the Hong Kong inventory from purchases of raw material into finished goods, as well as the tracking of shipments from Hong Kong and Taiwan into San Francisco. I calculated the cost per unit of the styles and made endless worksheets, as there were no computers in those days, comparing the costs to the selling prices. That was a gross margin calculation, although I knew little about cost accounting at that time. The gross margins on the knits from Hong Kong, comparing the wholesale selling price to the landed cost including air freight, were about 65 percent on average. The margins on the nylon shirts from Taiwan were typically over 70 percent including air freight.

Quota never had an intrinsic cost. It was a term that denoted the license issued under bilateral agreements that accounted for the total amount of a particular type of garment or textile that was being shipped to the United States in any one year. The United States and its trading-partner country agreed to an amount of the category in

dozens or kilograms. The licenses giving the right to ship these products to the United States were granted to exporters from the foreign
government. The system was designed to create limits, not cost. From
the beginning, some countries saw the advantage of allowing the
quota to be bought and sold on the open market. This had the effect of
ensuring that the allocation would be used most efficiently, as only a
factory or exporting company with a profitable order would seek out
and buy quota. That would use up the quota or, at least, use it best.
Hong Kong, of course, started an open quota market immediately.
Brokers were called "farmers," and they did what any broker would
do: match buyer and seller at the best price. Prices for quota by category were listed daily in the newspaper just like the price of common
stock. Some factories that had received an initial large allocation of
quota based on their previous performance got out of the manufacturing business entirely; the cost of their continued allocation from
the Hong Kong government was zero, which left the entire selling
price as profit.

Other countries, such as Taiwan and Korea, both of which still had
command-type economies and military dictatorship governments,
made it a crime to sell or buy quota. Nonetheless, factories found a
way to trade under the table because one factory might have more
orders than its quota allocation permitted and needed to get more
quota to fill them, while another factory might not be doing as well
and have quota to sell. As a result, in every instance in both free and
controlled markets, quota came to have a cost. This was like an over-
ride on the cost of the garment, not unlike a "commission" that the
"mob," back in the United States, would impose on a manufacturer
to make sure the delivery truck wasn't hijacked. "It's a cost of doing
business."

When I started to do the cost accounting in 1973, I had to include
charges incurred for quota as a separate column. In Hong Kong, the
subsidiary went out and bought quota and charged the head office as
goods were shipped. The balance was held, just like yarn. In Taiwan,

the factory sent us debit notes, which were settled in Hong Kong using Hong Kong dollars so that the factory owner would not run afoul of Taiwanese law. I helped to work out a system with U.S. Customs so that duty would not be assessed on the value of the quota if we could show that the quota had been purchased by a third party. Did the cost of the quota slow down imports? Not for a minute. The margins were so high that the addition of this cost made little difference. We added 25 cents to our selling prices and forged ahead.

In the following decades, apparel manufacturing infrastructure was built up in many other countries, and therefore import capacity vastly increased (Burke, 2006). Quota was imposed on some of those countries, but not all—that depended on the desirability and suspected trade potential of the country. The U.S. government saw an opportunity to develop trade with some nations and gave these nations a "special introductory offer" (Marshall et al., 2005). Places like Mongolia, Cambodia, and Nepal became "quota havens." As exporters in Hong Kong and India did not have enough quota, they turned to these regions and quickly established factories and trading partners. The North American Free Trade Agreement (NAFTA) and the Caribbean Basin Initiative (CBI) exempted Mexico and some Caribbean countries from quota and in many cases duty as well. In effect, the textile and apparel industry became a useful tool in trade negotiations and broader foreign policy considerations.

The pretence that the quota system was designed to protect the domestic apparel manufacturing industry should have been dispelled decades ago. It was not operating to protect anything much in the United States, whatever its original intentions (Burke, 2006). It became a system of preferences so that the United States would have bargaining chips for whatever really mattered in trade. Because no other type of product had numerical limits included in world trade, it frequently became the only bargaining chip. But it did nothing to slow the ever-increasing flood of imports. The quota system helped to create an expanding global market for American and European designed clothes, as manufacturers and retailers scoured the world looking for the next best and cheapest source. It added cost to the consumer, but did nothing to slow the decline of domestic needle trade or textile jobs (U.S. Congress, 1987).

After Quota

When the quota system ended in 2005, the principal effect was to dislocate production in some less developed countries. For example, India had been farming out production to Bangladesh, Nepal, and Sri Lanka as Indian factories looked for ways to diminish or eliminate quota costs. In 2005, that production was brought back to India because it was far easier to manage and coordinate manufacturing in one place under one set of eyes. Those other countries, especially Bangladesh and Nepal, suffered significant economic losses as the Indian-owned factories closed, their garment manufacturing businesses could not sustain the changes, and the people, mostly women who had been working in the factories, suffered from a lack of employment. To a lesser extent the same thing happened with China as Chinese factories in Cambodia and Mongolia lost business. This was mitigated by the sudden unilateral imposition of safeguards, or *limits*, on Chinese exports of specific categories by the United States. But this has been a short-term issue based on the flood of Chinese production that was impacting other trading partners of the United States in the Caribbean and elsewhere. There is no question that China has greatly increased its share of apparel exports to the United States, and this has come almost exclusively at the expense of other countries such as Mexico, not U.S. producers (Knappe, 2003).

China was not part of the quota system when that system was implemented. When U.S. trade began with China, quota limits for that trade were established. Imports from China have grown rapidly, and China is now the largest single source of imported apparel (North Carolina and the Global Economy, 2004). China has a vast impact on the entire textile and apparel market throughout Asia and, increasingly, in other parts of the world as well.

Does the concept of sustainable fashion make any sense in this light? In most discussions of sustainable economies, there is an emphasis on conservation and "green" methodology. Apparel has come to be seen by the consumer as disposable because its relative cost has fallen dramatically over the past three decades. China has little incentive to participate in a scheme that would lower unit levels of production, and our own capacity as a society to impact the eco-friendliness of manufacturing has been severely limited both overseas and at home.

Sustainable China

As the largest and most efficient region where apparel is produced, China can offer us many lessons about manufacturing that can inform our approach toward sustainable fashion. When we think about manufacturing in terms of sustainability, the key concepts are *productivity*, *efficient use of resources*, and *eco-friendliness*.

Productivity

I went to China in 2002 to try to forge an alliance between an American company I was forming that would design and sell children's clothing, and a government agency in a part of Jiangsu province charged with coordinating the local economy for textiles and apparel. That negotiation was successful, and in the summer of 2002, we set up an office given to us by the agency. I began that summer to visit factories and textile mills in an effort to learn as much as I could about the capability and working methodology of Chinese factories. I had spent much of the prior 30 years in and around factories primarily in the Bay Area but also in Los Angeles. Chinese production on the surface was deceptively familiar because of the similar ethnicity of man-

FIGURE 7.2.
Map of Jiangsu
Province, where
Shanghai is
located. (Map
courtesy of
Cartographics,
Inc.)

agement and employees. This was despite the fact that the language used in Bay Area factories is universally Cantonese and hardly anyone in the part of China where I was could speak or understand a word of Cantonese.

The concept of productivity in making clothes relates to the output per worker hour, which in turn relates to the organization of the workplace and especially to the quality of the equipment being used. Why is productivity related to sustainability? As we have repeatedly seen with regard to fuel efficiency or organic farming, to name a couple of obvious examples, no significant shift in production can take place until the costs of the product are competitive. So organic produce need not be cheaper than produce grown with chemicals; it may even be more expensive. But the premium that the product can attract cannot be greater than the market will bear. This makes sense. Even in an environmentally conscious community like Berkeley, California, there is a limit on how much more you can charge for eco-friendly products. Productivity is a key element of sustainability precisely because the inefficient use of human labor is wasteful, not economically viable, and therefore not sustainable.

In 1999 I was executive director of an industry-sponsored nonprofit in San Francisco called Made by the Bay. I was approached by a top executive of one of the market's largest sellers of men's pants. He had an inside track on a contract with the U.S. Navy for "dress slacks," a part of the uniform. The catch was that the pants needed to be made in the United States because they were part of the uniform, but the company no longer had any facilities in the United States for manufacturing. I embarked on what widened to a national search, and the result was that it was not possible to do this production for the price that the Navy wanted to pay.

Why was it so difficult to find a suitable factory in the United States to make these pants? In the course of my search, I visited a factory in Los Angeles that made private-label men's wool slacks for Nordstrom, which was almost its exclusive customer. The factory had a highly trained workforce, a steady flow of work, and all the expensive equipment necessary to do the job. The owner explained to me that he had made the investment in the equipment as well as in workforce development because the ongoing contractual relationship with Nordstrom made this business profitable. He said that it would be crazy to purchase the type of equipment to do the waistband, pockets, and so forth without that long-term relationship in place because a manufacturer could never recover the cost of the equipment in a short period. A company would never, he said, speculate on buying the equipment, hoping that it could find more business later. The market was far too uncertain, and major customers had supply chains in place.

When I approached several Bay Area factories with the same proposition, I found that he was correct. I could get bids on the work, but the price per unit was far too high because the technical work, such as setting the pockets, was going to be done by machine operators, not with automated equipment. At U.S. labor prices, that added far too much to the cost. Why not buy the machinery? Because the contract was for only 180,000 pairs spread over two or three years. That was not nearly enough to justify the outlay for the equipment, which might have been $1 million. Through contacts in New York, I approached the Union of Needletrades, Industrial and Textile Employees (UNITE) to see if there was a factory in North Carolina or Tennessee that was capable of this job. I had no luck.

Most discussions of "cheap imports" start and end with a picture of low-paid foreign workers versus U.S. workers. However the problem is much more complicated than that. When I began to visit Chinese facilities for cut-and-sew, knitting, weaving, embroidery, printing, and so forth, I was struck by the high quality of the machinery in use as well as its ready availability. Chinese workers have an immense advantage because they are highly productive. They not only have a high output relative to their wages, which speaks for their work ethic, but more importantly, I think, the industry as a whole has a very high per-person, per-hour output due to the investment that has been made in modern, efficiently computer-driven equipment. The more work that

FIGURE 7.3. [LEFT] A small garment-sewing factory in Nantong city in China's Jiangsu province. (Photo courtesy of Paul Gill.) FIGURE 7.4. [ABOVE] A garment-cutting table in a large Nantong city factory in China's Jiangsu province. (Photo courtesy of Paul Gill.)

is done by machinery, the less dependent production is on low-cost labor to remain competitive. China has low-cost labor, to be sure, but it is not as low as that of some Southeast and South Asian countries or Africa. China's competitive advantage is its productivity. In a sense, and in my opinion, the 2005 controversy between the United States and China that resulted in the temporary imposition of safeguards is a complete red herring. There is virtually nothing that would induce an investor in the United States to buy the machinery and train the workers in an effort to become competitive with China. If it hadn't happened after 25 years of a full-blown quota system between the two countries, it is not likely to happen now. The issue was and remains the effect that the further lowering of Chinese prices will have on the competitiveness of Mexico and the Caribbean where U.S. textile interests are still at play, thanks to the fiber-forward rules in NAFTA and the Central American Free Trade Agreement (AFTA). Chinese apparel manufacturing is so much more competitive than other sources because of its advantage in productivity based largely on investments. Differing labor rates mean very little in situations where a garment takes 5 or 10 minutes to sew, which is typical for a T-shirt or other simple garments that flood the retail market (Knappe, 2003).

Efficient Use of Resources

All business management programs emphasize the benefits of "lean" manufacturing. That is to say, one should never have more money tied up in raw material and work in process than is absolutely necessary. This emphasis is very evident in retail inventory management as well. Most of the reasons for the popularity of this concept are obvious and are particularly important in the apparel industry. If you are making nails and you buy too much iron, your cash is idle when it could have been doing something else. But sooner or later, you will use the iron. When I started at Tami 35 years ago, we were buying our imported items six months in advance of our season, based purely on projections. Therefore, inevitably we were acquiring hundreds of thousands of unwanted units that needed to be sold off after the season to jobbers. All the way back up the line, we had ordered too much fabric, too much yarn, and too much dye; we had used too many boxes, too much fuel for transportation, and so on. Waste is inherently not sustainable, not only because it is damaging to the ecology but because it is ultimately not economical. The costs of waste, visible and invisible, inevitably get added to the product.

Western consumer economies, and especially the United States, are constructed around the presentation of as many immediate choices for the consumer as possible. When you go to the department store to buy a dress or a suit, you expect that they will have the color and size that you want. Nowadays stores try to manage their inventories in a "lean" manner by saying, "we can get it from another of our stores in a few days." But let's face it, that's a turnoff most of the time. You went shopping and want to come home with what you went to buy. Similarly, manufacturers want to buy fabric and trim that is in stock because it significantly shortens the production time and makes it possible to delay production choices (e.g., which styles to cut and how many) until the last possible moment. Retailers try to push the unsold inventory back to the manufacturers; they in turn try to push it back to the suppliers, which try to keep as little raw material as possible in a finished condition, adding little or no value to the raw material until absolutely necessary. Of course this effort to be lean inevitably lengthens the time necessary to fill an order when compared to a fully stocked shelf. Being lean and having happy customers at the same time is the trick. Retailers call this *partnering*, and manufacturers sweat daily trying to be good partners to them because what this means is that the bigger party is keen on transferring risk to the smaller one. Consultants call it supply chain management. Whatever you call it, eliminating waste, both of resources and money, is vital to any sustainable production.

Doing business in China is eye-opening in many ways. China is still an economy of scarcity, but it is also highly productive and technologically proficient; therefore, there is a de facto embracing of lean manufacturing without the consultants that add an extra layer to productivity elsewhere. Virtually nothing is in stock. Even the fast-food outlets such as McDonalds or KFC make the food to order. It is strange to encounter, but no manager will take the risk of taking the food out of the freezer until she or he knows it will be sold.

The enterprise with whom we have a partnership also deals in commercial and residential real estate. They decided to add a floor to the top of the building where our office is located. When the construction was finished, I went upstairs to look at it, as our office was moving up there, and found an odd-looking wooden floor down the length of the new hallway. This hallway had to be at least 200 feet long by 10 feet wide. What I discovered is that they had owned another building on the other side of town that was being torn down for an apartment building. In that building was a bowling alley. Our hallway was made entirely of bowling lanes. It is fairly attractive when cleaned but very slippery, especially when it has been raining and water is tracked on it. (They do not rent bowling shoes; you slide all by yourself.) Nothing is wasted in China. You constantly see people retrieving bricks and other building materials where there is something torn down for new construction, which is everywhere.

When it comes to manufacturing apparel, the same principles are involved. You do not buy trim except at a bazaar where you can find odds and ends of anything. You do not buy fabric. You do not buy shipping boxes. What you do is place an order for finished garments and provide complete specs including packing instructions. Everything is made to order. The production line is as efficient as possible. There is virtually no waste. There are, however, conditions and consequences to doing business this way:

- Your instructions must be complete and correct at the time you place the order.

- If your instructions are not complete, frequently the factory will not accept the order and you may lose your place in the production line. I have seen this happen, and it is not a pleasant experience.
- You cannot make changes. Once your instructions are delivered, that is it unless the factory has made the error. Even then, it is difficult to persuade those at the factory that it is, in fact, their error.
- Communication is vital with regard to instructions. It must be done in a standardized format, with every piece of information appearing in the same location for every item. The use of terms must be industry standard.

In other words, it is as unlike doing business with domestic contractors as you can possibly imagine. It is far more like working in an ISO environment than most apparel manufacturers have ever done, or needed to do.

This meeting of culture and production has lead to very efficient manufacturing. China, more than any other place, has embraced lean manufacturing in apparel. It is successful because the use of technology and the short supply lines (e.g., raw material factories to sewing factories) have combined so that time constraints are not an impediment. Typically, it only takes three or four weeks to assemble all the materials for a production run, and that means starting from fiber. Actual production time is another three or four weeks. Shipping time to the West Coast is 14 days. This means that China's products move from factory to port in 60 days or less.

Eco-Friendliness

China is terribly polluted. The values of a clean environment have taken a far backseat to short-term financial gain. The sky is gray on a nice day. The water is not potable even in luxury high rise hotels in Shanghai. The air quality is terrible. A friend of mine, living in China, wears a breathing apparatus to sleep because of apnea. The device includes a mask that has a changeable filter. The filter should last six months or more, but he must change it every two weeks because it turns black even when sleeping in an apartment with air conditioning.

Apparel manufacturing is no different. I have personally seen chemical dyes running in a rivulet along a street and directly into the Pearl River between Guangzhou and Hong Kong. Factory environments, while physically clean for the most part, are full of toxic chemicals that would be instant OSHA violations in the United States. There is nothing sustainable about garment manufacturing in China from a green perspective.

Unfortunately from what I have seen in India and elsewhere, this seems to be a general condition in less developed countries. A green environment is more costly in the short run. We demand it of ourselves, or at least we intend to. When our products are made out of our sight, we seem content to look at price and quality and ignore the "side effects" to the environment that may be included with the product itself. There is nothing sustainable about a dirty environment, and this principle applies to all types of industries operating around the world. Fashion is just one part of that puzzle. Can the developed world insist that China green itself if it wants to continue to export at these levels? That is a serious question that has not been addressed in manufacturing anywhere in the world. The Chinese environment is not sustainable regardless of its industry's quality of efficiency and productivity because that industry is a huge hazard to the health of the Chinese. The polluted air and water generated by the chemicals, dyes, and glues used in production are literally making people sick. One can assume that this will be addressed in the near future, but it is not likely to be the result of outside pressure (Knappe, 2003).

Conclusion

Despite its goals to sustain and protect domestic manufacturers from foreign competition, the quota system has not in any way reduced the runaway increases in import of apparel to the United States and the

European Union. Whatever trade disputes have arisen or may yet arise between the United States and Europe on the one hand and the United States and China on the other, China will be the leading source of U.S. apparel imports for as long as the emphasis on the textile and apparel industry makes sense for China.

As the leading source of the world's apparel, China is unparalleled in its productivity. This is primarily due to the development of China's highly technical industry. Chinese factories and workers hold a huge advantage over those in both the developed and low-paying countries. This is because China pays its workers relatively low wages compared to those in developed countries while possessing an infrastructure technically superior to those in other low-paying countries.

Moreover, China has a culture that emphasizes an efficient use of resources. This is evident in the organization of its textile and apparel industry. It is highly competitive because of the organizational struc-

FIGURE 7.5. This large garment manufacturing factory is located in Nantong city in the Jiangsu province of East Central China, on the Chang River, about 30 miles (50 km) from the East China Sea. The center of an important cotton-growing area, Nantong is still dependent upon the textile industry. (Photo courtesy of Paul Gill.)

tures used and because the industry can leverage its technical as well as human resources.

China has a long way to go before eco-consciousness can impact industry or day-to-day life. If sustaining life and sustaining the environment are priorities, we must seriously consider how to address our current production demands in China. The demand for a better life is overwhelming among the Chinese population. The easiest and most cost-effective, albeit short-sighted, way to achieve that life is to continue development in the same way that development has proceeded since the invention of the steam engine, and that is not eco-friendly. To advocate that China adopt a more costly process of development is unrealistic, at least in the short run. The entire notion of sustainability must take into account both this unequal development and the short-term costs associated with converting current industrial practices to more sustainable processes. No conversation that skips this issue can be seen as realistic.

References

Burke, K. (2006, July 27). Guest editorial. *Apparel Magazine*. Retrieved October 2006 from http://www.apparelmag.com/articles/feature052406.shtml

Knappe, M. (2003). Textile and clothing: What happens after 2005. *International Trade Forum*.

North Carolina and the Global Economy. (2004, Spring). Dimensions of globalization. Retrieved November 2006 from Duke University, Markets and Management Studies Program Web site, http://www.duke.edu/web/mms190/textiles/dimensions.html

Marshall, T., Iritani, E., & Dickerson, M. (2005, January 16). A world unravels, *Los Angeles Times*. Retrieved November 2006 from http://www.latimes.com/business/la-fi-quotaone16jan16,0,3076753.story

Rivoli, P. (2005). Tangled threads of protectionism—Part 1. Retrieved October 2006 from Yale Global Online Web site: http://yaleglobal.yale.edu/article

Rushford, G. (2003). The world's oldest infant industry, *The Yankee Trader*, Retrieved October 2006 from http://www.rushfordreport.com/2003/6_2003_Yankee_trader.htm

U.S. Congress. (1987, April). The U.S. textile and apparel industry, a revolution in progress. Special Report OTA-TET-332. Washington, D.C.: Government Printing Office.

TIMO RISSANEN is a fashion designer whose design practice is informed by inquisitive and innovative patternmaking and cutting. His current Ph.D. research, with strong practical focus, centers on unsustainable aspects of the fashion industry in which the fashion designer and patternmaker can directly affect change by rethinking their practices. He is a casual academic at the University of Technology, Sydney.

CHAPTER 8

Creating Fashion without the Creation of Fabric Waste

Timo Rissanen

With 10 to 20 percent of its fabric swept off the cutting-room floor, the fashion industry is leaving a significant ecological footprint. This waste could be dramatically reduced, however, with some creative design thinking. The "jigsaw puzzle" methodology challenges designers to team up with patternmakers and adopt a process that could result in 100 percent fabric use in the garments that the industry produces.

Patternmaking as Fashion Design

This chapter examines an aspect of clothing production that is often taken for granted and not regarded a problem: fabric waste. Arguably, the perception of fabric as disposable by many in the fashion industry should be questioned. To produce raw fiber and turn fiber into fabric consumes energy, chemicals, and water: fabric is precious. The wast-

ing of fabric occurs in garment manufacturing, but the power to eliminate the creation of fabric waste resides within fashion design and
patternmaking. To eliminate fabric waste, the garment pieces must
use up the entire length of the fabric, interlocking like the pieces of a
jigsaw puzzle. The combined expertise of the fashion designer and
patternmaker can achieve this. The jigsaw puzzle provides a useful
analogy to zero-fabric-waste fashion creation, although the two occur
in reverse. To complete a jigsaw puzzle, one begins with a jumble of
pieces and attempts to combine these into a unified whole. To create a
zero-fabric-waste garment, one attempts to create these interlocking
pieces within a two-dimensional whole and then cuts them out to
make a three-dimensional garment. The aim is to simultaneously
design (1) a set of garment pieces that take up a given length of fabric
in two dimensions like the pieces in a finished jigsaw puzzle and (2)
the garment in three dimensions. No fabric waste is then created
exclusive of the garment. Some fabric may be "wasted" within the
garment, but the potential benefits of that will be discussed further in
the chapter. A jigsaw puzzle garment is partly designed through the
making of its pattern. Fashion design and patternmaking are not hierarchically or otherwise distinct activities; patternmaking is part of the
design process.

Precious Fabric and Wasted Fabric

Why should we avoid wasting fabric? Fabrics are increasingly inexpensive, and the amount of waste may not seem worth worrying about. A
brief look at the two most commonly used fibers, cotton and polyester, reveals some cause for concern. As a natural fiber, cotton is easily mistaken for an environmentally friendly fiber. Cotton, however, is
a heavily sprayed crop; cotton growing takes up 2.4 percent of the
world's arable land, yet 24 percent of insecticides and 11 percent of
pesticides used globally in agriculture go toward cotton production
(Chapagain et al., 2005, p. 19). Cotton is also a "thirsty" fiber; both to

grow and to treat to achieve a finished cotton fabric from fiber. Cotton accounts for 2.6 percent of global water use (p. 31). The polyesters used in fashion come from a finite source, oil, and consume considerable energy to produce (Allwood, Laursen et al., 2006, pp. 13–14). Toxic additives accompany polyester, sometimes unnecessarily (McDonough & Braungart, 2002, pp. 37–38). At landfill, polyester breaks down slowly. On the other hand, polyester's resistance to physical degradation may be a great advantage. The polyester polymer can be recycled almost infinitely with no degradation to the quality of the fiber.

What happens to fabric waste? The dumping of textiles in landfill is problematic. Natural fibers will decompose but may release harmful chemicals and methane in the process; synthetics may take centuries to decompose. A large industry exists trading in scrap fabric (the real "rag trade") and thus keeps the waste from landfill. Fabric recycling, however, is a difficult issue. McDonough and Braungart (2002, pp. 56–59) use the term "downcycling" to describe the degradation in material quality through recycling. The quality of yarn spun from a natural fiber relies on the length of the fiber. Recycled natural fiber tends to be shorter than "virgin" fiber, and thus not suitable for all uses. A common product made from recycled textiles, often of mixed fibers, is the heavy-duty protective felt used by removalists, of limited usability in fashion, where its raw material came from.

Although only cotton and polyester are briefly covered here, one must remember that the production of any fiber and the manufacture of that fiber into fabric consume energy, raw materials, almost always water, and often chemical additives. Regardless of recyclability, cotton and polyester reveal that fabric arrives at the fashion designer with a significant ecological footprint acquired during its production. Yet fabric wastage for adult outerwear varies from 10 to 20 percent (Feyerabend, 2004, p. 4). Cooklin (1997, p. 9) estimates the average waste to be 15 percent of total fabric used, while Abernathy, Dunlop, et al.

(1999, p. 136) place the figure at around 10 percent for pants and jeans, but higher for blouses, jackets and underwear. According to Allwood, Laursen et al. (2006, p. 16) in the United Kingdom 1 million tonnes of clothing is consumed annually. With the wastage estimates, it is safe to say at least 100.000 tonnes of fabric is wasted to make the clothes consumed in the United Kingdom each year. The much higher global figure and the ecological footprint inherent in all fabrics should justify attempts to drastically reduce the amount of fabric wasted by the industry.

Fashion Creation Methods

To put jigsaw puzzle fashion design into context, a look at all fashion creation methods available to industry through existing technologies is necessary (see Figure 8.1). In fabric waste creation, three main cate-

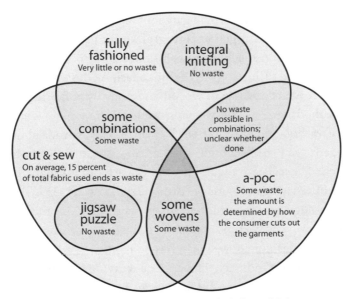

FIGURE 8.1. This illustration depicts fashion creation methods from a fabric waste perspective. Three broad fashion creation methods exist, but combinations of these are also possible. Jigsaw puzzle fashion design refers to cut-and-sew that wastes no fabric. (Illustration by Jenny Green from drawing by Timo Rissanen.)

gories emerge: *cut-and-sew*, of which jigsaw puzzle is a part; *fully fashioned*, which includes integral knitting; and *A-POC* (A Piece Of Cloth). The two most common methods of fashion creation in the industry are cut-and-sew and fully fashioned. An introduction into fabric construction is also necessary, as different fabric types have implications for the different fashion creation methods. Three broad categories exist for fabric construction: wovens, knits, and nonwovens. Wovens have yarns interlacing in two directions, warp and weft; knits are rows of looped yarns; and nonwovens are made directly from fiber without spinning it into yarn first, or may not consist of fiber at all (e.g., leather).

Fully Fashioned (Yarn + Knitting + Sewing = Garment) and Integral Knitting (Yarn + Knitting = Garment)

Fully fashioned in its true form eliminates yarn or fiber waste, and is commonly used in knits. The garment pieces are knitted individually and then sewed together. Integral knitting eliminates sewing from the process. A machine knits a finished garment (Black, 2002, p. 118). With the technology available to fashion design, a fully fashioned approach is possible in woven and nonwoven fabrics through craft methods (e.g., hand-weaving and -felting). Nonwoven sails made of carbon and aramid fiber by North Sails Nevada show that nonwovens can be adapted for an industrial fully fashioned approach. The sails are made into the exact required shape by specialized fiber-laying machinery (Brown, 2005, pp. 53, 55). To adapt this technology for the fashion industry seems likely as increasingly diverse nonwovens become available. Industrially available technology for fully fashioned weaving has not been developed for use within the fashion industry. The cost of weaving shapes other than long rectangular lengths of fabric may be prohibitive. A recent study predicts that most future development will take place in nonwoven and fully-fashioned knit applications (Allwood, Laursen, et al., 2006, pp. 25, 33).

A-POC (Yarn + Knitting or Weaving = Fabric, Followed
by Fabric + Cutting = Garment + Fabric Waste)

In the late 1990s, Issey Miyake and Dai Fujiwara launched A-POC (A Piece Of Cloth). In knits, a flat tube of fabric is knitted with the two sides of the tube joined in areas. The wearer buys a tube and, following the lines of the joins, cuts out finished garments (Kries & von Vegesack, 2001). A-POC is similar to integral knitting in that a machine produces a garment that requires no sewing, but the technologies used to produce each are different (Black, 2002, p. 118). How the wearer cuts out the pieces determines partly how much waste is created. An increasing number of woven A-POC garments have been developed; for example, *Caravan* and *Pain de Mie* from 2000. The latter, a dress or skirt and top depending on how it is cut, can be cut out as finished garments like the knits, while the *Caravan* jacket requires one row of sewing at the back after cutting (Kries & von Vegesack, 2001, p. 63). Considering the nonwoven fully fashioned sail technology, it seems possible to extend A-POC to nonwovens, too.

Cut-and-Sew (Fabric + Cutting + Sewing = Garment + Fabric
Waste) and Jigsaw Puzzle (Fabric + Cutting + Sewing = Garment)

Cut-and-sew is self-explanatory. Garment pieces are cut from fabric and sewed to make garments. Any type of fabric may be used. Conventional cut-and-sew wastes 10 to 20 percent of the total fabric used, while jigsaw puzzle refers to cut-and-sew that wastes none.

Unlike fully fashioned and A-POC, cut-and-sew and jigsaw puzzle require practically no reprogramming of machinery to create new garment styles and are suitable for all fabric types. Furthermore, cutting and sewing *woven* fabrics allows subtleties within a design that are arguably not possible through other methods. It is therefore likely that cutting and sewing will remain alongside emerging technologies.

Fashion Creation in Steps
The following sections describe the steps of fashion creation.

Fashion Design
Most fashion designers use sketching to develop ideas, from initial concept to a design that can be pattern-made and made into a sample garment. The benefits of sketching are many: It is fast, ideas become visible to the designer and others quickly, and various elements of design (e.g., silhouette, balance, and line) can be resolved before the costly patternmaking and construction processes.

Patternmaking
Patternmaking, or *pattern cutting*, is the making of a pattern for a garment. Usually a patternmaker does this, guided by the designer's sketch. Occasionally the fashion designer makes the pattern, and this chapter proposes through examples that patternmaking can be an effective design tool alongside sketching. Manual patternmaking using pens, scissors, paper and card is still common, although computerized approaches using increasingly sophisticated CAD/CAM software are on the rise.

Construction: Cutting and Sewing
Using the pattern, a toile is cut and sewed. The toile is a garment prototype in inexpensive fabric, to allow the design team to test fit and examine the design in three-dimensional form. Depending on the design and the amount of required alterations, more than one toile may be necessary before the pattern is made to the design team's satisfaction. A sample cutter then cuts a sample in the actual fabric, which a sample machinist sews.

Production: Grading, Making a Marker, Cutting and Sewing

Once the designer and patternmaker, and sometimes a buyer or a sales representative, approve the sample garment, the patternmaker or a grader grades the pattern into the required range of sizes. Grading may be done manually but is increasingly done digitally. A marker maker uses the graded pattern to create a marker. The marker is a cutting layout containing all the pieces of all the sizes to be cut for production. The cutter or an automated cutting system uses the marker as a guide to cut out the garment pieces in fabric. Production machinists, organized for maximum efficiency, make up the garments. Sewing may be segmented; for example, one machinist might only sew side seams while another works on cuffs. Finished garments are pressed, tagged, and shipped to retailers.

Frederick Winslow Taylor's *Principles of Scientific Management* (1911) and the two World Wars impacted the organization of clothing production. Since the early twentieth century, the steps in the process of garment making (from fashion design to production sewing) have been organized somewhat hierarchically. The specialization of each is the result of a search for better efficiencies. The benefits are many; as each role concentrates on fewer tasks, it is likely to result in a higher level of expertise in one area, and garment production also becomes faster. On the other hand, some consequences are problematic. The primary obstacle to fabric waste elimination is the increasing separation of fashion design and patternmaking, and perhaps cutting.

In current industry practice, the marker maker is responsible for efficient fabric usage. When creating the marker, the marker maker attempts to place all the garment pieces within the fabric as closely as possible. The motivation is economic; the tightest fit of the pattern pieces uses the least fabric per garment, thereby reducing production costs dramatically. Notably, it is economically affordable to waste 10 to 20 percent of the fabric, even if this is not ecologically sound. Even the latest computer software affords only mild increases in this efficiency, because it is bound by what has already been designed and pattern-made. The unpredictability of pattern shapes is the primary obstacle to eliminating fabric waste. Conventionally garments are not designed and pattern-made with the cutting layout (i.e., the marker) in mind. The amount of waste is determined by garment style (e.g., number and shapes of pattern pieces), the number of garment sizes and garments in one marker, and the marker maker's skill. A more efficient marker is usually achieved by mixing the pieces of several sizes in one marker or by cutting more than one of the same size in one marker.

Jigsaw Puzzle and Contemporary Fashion Design

To many fashion designers and patternmakers, designing and making clothes without wasting any fabric in the process may seem impossible or difficult beyond feasibility. Yet a careful look at fashion design literature and traditional forms of dress reveals many examples where fabric is treated as precious in the making of clothes, and very little or none is wasted. The sheer number of examples and the spread of these over centuries suggest that zero-fabric-waste fashion creation is not only possible but also feasible.

The study of this kind of fashion creation through literature is problematic. Often the text and visuals suggest, rather than state, that the garment's making does not waste fabric. The benefit of searching for such examples from literature is the relative speed with which this can be done, compared to, for example, searching through museum dress collections. It will be clearly stated where the zero-fabric-waste nature of a garment is conjecture on the author's part. Some examples waste fabric, but considerably less than the current industry average. Minor modifications to some garments would allow complete waste elimination; such examples will be noted in this chapter. Unfortunately, the literature is unclear on whether zero-fabric-waste fashion creation is different from other types of fashion creation and, if so, how. A detailed study of examples in literature begins to reveal some

common characteristics. Therefore, a thematic instead of a chrono-
logical approach seems appropriate.

The themes used here are *fabric, pattern design,* and *garment design.*
With fabric waste elimination as our focus, fabric has some specific
implications for design. Similarly, as the making of the garment pattern determines whether the making of the garment wastes fabric or
not, pattern design includes issues best addressed during patternmaking. Garment design refers to aspects that may be addressed prior to
commencing making a garment, and features that differ from more
conventional ways of designing. The themes may seem to contradict
an earlier statement that patternmaking is integral to fashion design, if
fabric waste is to be eliminated. The themes assist in building a new
understanding about zero-fabric-waste creation and should not be
considered exclusionary.

Fabric

In the most obvious examples of fabric waste elimination, fabric
equals garment, which is to say that the fabric is not cut into, thus
none is wasted. The himation, chiton, and peplos of ancient Greece,
and the sari of India are lengths of fabric with no cutting, worn
draped on the body. The sari yields several variations (Lynton, 1995,
pp. 14–16), as does ancient Greek dress (Rudofsky, 1947, p. 137). Different fabric lengths and widths allow further diversity.

In jigsaw puzzle, fabric width becomes a design consideration,
because the width determines how the pattern pieces may be config-
ured on a length of fabric. Fabric width is a major difference
between cut-and-sew and jigsaw puzzle fashion creation: Rarely
does one need to consider fabric width when designing a cut-and-
sew garment, while a jigsaw puzzle garment is fundamentally
informed by the width of its fabric. Perhaps the best-known garment
that wastes no fabric is the kimono of Japan. The narrow width of
the fabric used in the kimono determines its horizontal dimensions

(Tarrant, 1994, p. 36). Rather than make the kimono in a range of sizes, each is adjusted to the wearer by wrapping and tying on a belt (Van Assche, 2005, p. 7).

For Yeohlee Teng, a contemporary designer in New York, economical fabric use is integral to her work. In a 1998 jacket, fabric width determines the length of the sleeves, as these are cut in one and perpendicular to the body of the jacket (Major & Teng, 2003, p. 53). The pattern diagram lacks some pattern pieces such as facings, and the amount of waste is difficult to determine. In fact, most pattern diagrams of Teng's work have components missing. The purpose of the diagrams is probably to be broadly illustrative of garment cut, rather than to accurately reproduce the garment pattern.

For his final MA work in Textile Futures at Central Saint Martins in 2007, the Australian designer Mark Liu created a series of zero-fabric-waste garments using textile prints he designed. The dress in Figure 8.2, intricately cut from 10 pieces, wastes none of the fabric required to make it. The print is engineered to the fabric width. Both garment

FIGURE 8.2. Strapless dress by Mark Liu, 2007. Liu designed the garment pattern and the printed textile simultaneously. By cutting and sewing, the entire textile piece becomes the dress, with no fabric wasted. (Photograph by Mark Liu.)

cut and the print inform the detailed cutting; the print also prevents the cut edges from fraying.

Zandra Rhodes is an English designer whose fashion, like Liu's, is heavily influenced by her textile prints. Rhodes develops a print first, and this informs the garment shape (Rhodes & Knight, 1984, p. 9). A blouse from 1979 demonstrates this approach. The print pattern, Chinese Squares, is engineered to the fabric width. The garment is then developed according to the print; it uses the full fabric width with the possible exception of selvages (*Zandra Rhodes: A Lifelong Love Affair with Textiles*, 2005, pp. 34–36). The blouse does create some fabric waste, despite the sleeve and peplum pieces interlocking fully. For complete fabric waste elimination, the fabric selvages need to be incorporated into the garment somehow. Haute couture sewing, the most expensive level of hand finishing as demonstrated by Shaeffer (2001, p. 49) provides several examples. Selvage strips can be used internally to stabilize necklines, armholes, and other garment parts, and the technique is easily adapted to ready-to-wear. Selvage could also be left in the garment as an edge finish, such as a hem or facing edge.

A great variety of fusible interfacings are now available to support parts of a garment (e.g., the jacket front and shirt collar); printed glue bonds the interfacing to the garment fabric. Occasionally the main garment fabric may be used as a sew-in interfacing. For example, in the front neckline of the kimono, surplus fabric in the front neck is pleated inside the collar for support, rather than cut away (Dobson, 2004: 54). Often, fusible interfacings are not used with sheer fabrics; where added "body" is desired (e.g., the cuffs and collar), three or more layers of the garment fabric may be used. This could also make the eventual recycling of a garment easier, as the fiber content of the garment and its interfacing would be the same.

Pattern Design

In zero-fabric-waste garments, rectangular pattern shapes dominate because it often seems easier to achieve interlocking with these.

Bernard Rudofsky was an Austrian-American social historian and an ardent critic of contemporary clothing design and manufacture. Following the 1944–1945 exhibition and 1947 book *Are Clothes Modern?* (Rudofsky, 1947), Rudofsky incorporated some of his ideas into a range of clothing in 1950 (Bocco Guarneri, 2003, pp. 294–295). The garments in the collection, Bernardo Separates, were made in one size only from rectangular pieces of fabric. Fit was achieved with drawstrings or belts. The aim was a reduction in price through the minimization of sewing. Fabric was the main source of cost. While the pattern diagrams are too simplified to determine whether fabric was wasted, Rudofsky greatly admired fabric-as-garment in ancient Greek

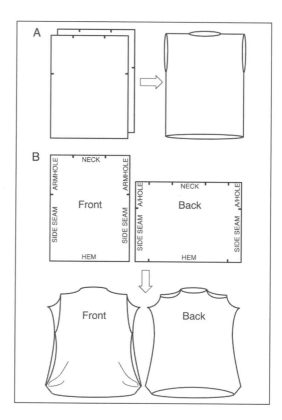

FIGURE 8.3. Two tops made of rectangles. Two identical rectangles may be made into a basic top with identical front and back (a); however, by offsetting one rectangle against the other, a completely different garment shape emerges (b). Varying the shape (e.g., by adding triangles), size, and number of pieces creates limitless potential of geometric fabric pieces for fashion design. (Illustration by Timo Rissanen.)

dress. The American fashion designer Claire McCardell was Rudof-sky's contemporary, and he included her work in *Are Clothes Modern?* (Rudofsky, 1947). The included garments were geometric in cut, not unlike the garments that Rudofsky created a few years later.

Initially rectangular pattern shapes may seem to only allow basic garment shapes. These shapes can, however, be offset in relation to one another to create three-dimensional rather than flat shapes. Max Tilke was a German ethnographer with an interest in dress from around the world. Whether his depictions of dress are accurate is open to question, but from a fabric waste point of view his work is undeniably interesting. In *Costume Patterns and Designs* (Tilke, 1956: Plate 89: Garments 6 & 7, 9 & 10), a pair of Chinese trousers is made from two rectangles. The offsetting of two rectangles against each other forces the trouser legs to hang "off-grain," on an angle. Figure 8.3a shows a top made from two identical rectangles, with holes left for the neck, arms, and body. Figure 8.3b is made from the same rectangles, with the back flipped to its side.

This offsetting forces the top into a three-dimensional form that will not sit flat and can be done asymmetrically. The two shapes do not have to be the same size or shape, and there can be more than two pieces. Even one rectangle may be folded back onto itself with openings left for the body. The possibilities for creating original forms using rectangular shapes are endless.

The Japanese designer Yoshiki Hishinuma has explored similar principles in garments made from equilateral triangles (Hishinuma, 1986, pp. 162–172). For example, he has created a pair of asymmetrical trousers from two triangles. While Hishinuma's garments do not seem to be designed with fabric waste as a consideration, it is possible to engineer the pieces of such a garment to interlock by splitting the equilateral triangle into two right triangles of equal size. These can then be flipped into interlocking rectangles (see Figure 8.4a).

Similarly, graduated fullness or flare can be achieved through the use of interlocking gores, as demonstrated in European gowns from

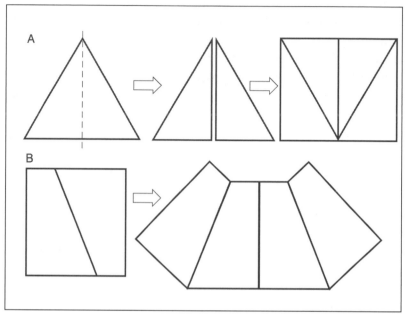

FIGURE 8.4. An equilateral triangle can be split into two right triangles, and pairs of right triangles can interlock within a larger rectangle (a). By splitting a rectangle with a diagonal line, two gores are created (b). Gores can be used to create graduated fullness in a garment.

the fourteenth to the eighteenth centuries (Arnold, 1977 [1966], p 3; Baumgarten et al., 1999, pp. 43–46; see Figure 8.4b). Rectangular gussets may be inserted into curved or straight slashes as an alternative to shaped seams to create three-dimensional forms. As the kimono demonstrates, folds may replace straight seams. In knits, even curved edges may be folded rather than cut. Rothstein describes a knitted jacket made of rectangles, where the curved neck and armhole are created through folding under rather than cutting fabric (1984, p. 17).

The 1979 Rhodes bodice and a 1982 hooded cape by Teng (Major & Teng, 2003, pp. 8, 155) show waste occurring from curved pattern edges. Minor modifications to the designs could eliminate most or all of this waste. The sleeve pieces of the Rhodes bodice are squares with a circular cutout in the middle. Straight slashes could replace the circles, and a slash could be offset against another, as described above. In Teng's cape, a more noticeable change would be required to eliminate waste: The cape hem and hood shape could interlock. The text describes the cape as cut "with no waste" (Major & Teng, 2003, p. 18), while the pattern diagram (155) shows some to occur. Achieving interlocking curves within the pattern to eliminate waste may be difficult, but it is possible; when designing curved pattern shapes, one needs to simultaneously determine how to use both sides of the curve.

Teng's cape suggests that larger pieces are plotted on a length of fabric first with smaller pieces slotted in where they fit. Therefore, the size of each pattern piece may be significant to the "order" in which a jigsaw puzzle pattern is conceived. It is unclear whether the number of pattern pieces in a garment is related to the ease of achieving the interlocking of the patterns. Thayaht, an Italian futurist, designed the "tuta" overalls in 1919; he would work for Madeleine Vionnet during the 1920s (Chenoune, 1993, pp. 140–142; Stern, 2004, p. 43). The tuta is composed of relatively few pieces; the entire body (e.g., front, back, and legs) is cut from one piece, with slashes for armholes. The pattern diagram (Stern, 2004) includes measurements, so the wasted fabric amount may be assessed accurately. The tuta does waste some fabric, but minor changes would allow full interlocking. For example, the four patch pockets could be redesigned to use up the waste.

In contrast to the tuta, a man's shirt from 1837 (Shep & Cariou, 1999, p. xxiv) has more pieces than most twenty-first-century equivalents. The shirt pieces interlock with no waste, but it is difficult to relate the diagram to the making instructions; the diagram includes 15 pieces (the main shirt body is not included in the diagram) while the instructions mention 19 pieces. Similar approaches to shirt making are the "square-cut" shirts from the Keystone Shirt System of 1895 (Shep & Cariou, 1999: 121, 123), and eighteenth-century shirts illustrated by Hart (1987, p. 153) and Baumgarten, Watson & Carr (1999, pp. 105–108).

Grading

Grading is the incremental change in pattern size to create a garment pattern in a range of sizes. The marker for each size is slightly different to the next, and jigsaw puzzle raises the question: Is grading the only way of producing a garment style in a range of sizes? The Rhodes bodice breaks some rules about grading in order to maintain the interlocking across a range of sizes. The square sleeve pieces with circular center cutouts do not grade, except for the two cutouts that attach to armholes. The vertical length of the largest-size bodice is the same as one size smaller, so that the pattern fits on the fabric width. The body and peplums are cut on the weft grain, perpendicular rather than parallel to selvage, to allow conventional horizontal grading. Baumgarten, Watson, & Carr (1999, p. 108) note that in the eighteenth century, shirt size was determined by fabric width, with different sizes cut according to the same pattern configuration. Using a wider fabric made a larger shirt. Weaving a range of fabric widths may be too expensive, but T-shirts without side seams cut from knitted tubes of various widths are common.

Large seam allowances may be regarded as waste. Cooklin (1997, p. 10) states that 5.5 percent of the total fabric in a garment is in the seam and hem allowances, and that the patternmaker is responsible for ensuring "that all these allowances are the practical minimum possible." Large seam allowances, however, can enable the repair or alteration of a garment. Tailored men's trousers often have wider seam allowance on the center back and inside leg seams, to accommodate future growth in the wearer.

A wider seam allowance is also useful if the fabric rips near a seam. The garment may be let out elsewhere, while the rip is concealed in another seam. Larger seam allowances could use some of the wasted fabric. To make sewing easier, the machinist may need a stitching template made from card. A template would be useful particularly with allowances that vary in width along the length of a seam, as conventionally the machinist uses the allowance as a visual guide for sewing.

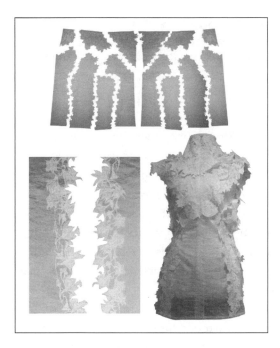

FIGURE 8.5. High-neck dress by Mark Liu, 2007. This dress is one of many where Liu has used seam allowances as a visual element on the outside of the garment. Hidden within the print is a line that guides the machinist during construction. Fabric that would normally be wasted between each garment piece is incorporated into the garment as a decorative element. (Photograph by Mark Liu.)

Mark Liu's garments not only utilize larger seam allowances of variable widths, but the seams become an aesthetic element as well. To make construction easier, in this dress Liu has incorporated a printed stitch line, hidden within the intricate print (see Figure 8.5).

Also on garment maintenance, a piece of fabric may be sold with a garment for the consumer to use in repair or for test laundering. The piece or pieces could be cut from a "gap" in the marker to use wasted fabric and can be any shape. This would not increase garment cost considerably.

Garment Design

Designing more than one style of garment simultaneously and cutting these from one length of fabric together can reduce the amount of fabric waste, although it does not necessarily do so. The mixing of jacket, trouser, and sometimes vest pieces on one length of fabric instead of cutting each separately is common tailors' practice (Cabrera & Flaherty Meyers, 1983, p. 57). Yeohlee Teng maximized fabric use on a 7-meter length by designing and cutting three different dresses from it simultaneously (Major & Teng, 2003, pp. 80–83).

To eliminate waste, the technical and visual elements of a garment need to be considered simultaneously; whether they should ever be *treated* separately is open to question. While considering the "look" of a garment, the designer also needs to understand its likely pattern and how the pattern pieces may interlock. The garment needs to be considered in two and three dimensions simultaneously, as seen in Mark Liu's approach. Using design practice as a research methodology, Katherine Townsend (2004) has explored this problem of the relationship between a two-dimensional textile print and three-dimensional garment form. Significantly, Townsend's research involves engineering the textile print to work within the flat shapes of the garment patterns as well as the three-dimensional garment. Similarly, the English designer Julian Roberts sometimes develops a garment pattern without an exact prediction of the garment itself. The garment form reveals itself once made (Quinn, 2002, pp. 89–91). If designers were open to some degree of trust in such unpredictability, the adoption of jigsaw puzzle could become easier. Jigsaw puzzle could not only eliminate waste but perhaps also offer new ways of practicing fashion design.

It may take longer to create a jigsaw puzzle garment than to create one through more conventional methods, particularly if a designer has not previously worked in such a way. Whether experience over time turns a designer into a jigsaw puzzle expert is subject to further research. For the time being, evidence shows that at the garment sampling stage more styles are created than are eventually taken to production. According to Waddell (2004, p. 40), "most design houses estimate at least 20 percent wastage at this stage"; the cull is due to limitations in technical or financial feasibility, or because of artistic reasons. The deleted sample garments represent a considerable amount of work by the design team, a cost to the company and a significant waste of physical resources. Would closer consultation with the sales department, combined with more effective market research and range planning, eliminate some of this waste? If design were subject to more effective research and planning, would more time become available for design?

Conclusion: The End of Fabric Waste

A goal may now be set: the fashion industry should aim for 100 percent of the fabric it uses to stay in the garments it produces. To eliminate fabric waste, the often hierarchically distinct areas of pattern-making and fashion design need to interact more closely. Sketching tends to dominate as the primary design tool, but to eliminate fabric waste, patternmaking needs to be integral to the design process, not a step following it. Sketching does have its unique advantages as a design tool, but sketching and patternmaking can and should work in tandem. If fashion designers were to address fabric waste, and evidence suggests they should, sketch-based designing could combine with pattern-based designing. How well current fashion design education encourages the latter kind of designing is a question for further research. Some of the initial difficulties of two-dimensional garment pattern design may be overcome by working through draping with fabric; the relationship between flat fabric pieces and three-dimensional form may then become easier to understand. Reflecting on the passion that the contemporary designers covered in this chapter have for textiles in fashion, perhaps "fabric-" or "textile-based designing" is more apt a term than pattern-based designing. Fabric is the backbone of fashion and fashion should respect it as such; fabric could positively inform and inspire fashion design in more ways than most current practice suggests.

Fabric waste elimination could foster more carefully considered design and making processes. To adopt more ecologically sustainable fashion creation practices, the industry needs to critically examine its present practices. Currently some of these practices may be taken for granted, such as fabric waste, grading, and the nature of fashion design itself. This is not a call for change for change's sake, but an acknowledgement that change may be justified. More importantly, this is an acknowledgement that change is possible.

When you next design or make a garment, examine the fabric. Try to see how the garment you want to create could use all of it. What is the relationship between the width of the fabric and the garment? If you have the pattern, see where the largest gaps or "waste" occur between the pieces. How can you adjust the design by incorporating these gaps into the garment? Remember, your creativity and openness to possibility are your greatest asset. Remember also that these can be your greatest limitations. Try to identify what learned rules guide your practice. One useful advantage of rules is that they can help us make sense of things. Once we have learned a rule, breaking it may take us forward. Be brave.

References

Abernathy, F. H., Dunlop, J. T., Hammond, J. H., & Weil, D. (1999). *A stitch in time. Lean retailing and the transformation of manufacturing: Lessons from the apparel and textile industries.* New York/Oxford: Oxford University Press.

Allwood, J., Laursen, S. E., Malvido de Rodríguez, C., & Bocken, N. (2006). *Well dressed? The present and future sustainability of clothing and textiles in the United Kingdom.* Cambridge: University of Cambridge Institute for Manufacturing.

Arnold, J. (1977/1966). *Patterns of fashion 2. Englishwomen's dresses and their construction c. 1860–1940.* London: Macmillan.

Baumgarten, L., Watson, J., & Carr, F. (1999). *Costume close-up. Clothing construction and pattern 1750–1790.* Williamsburg, VA/New York: The Colonial Williamsburg Foundation in association with Quite Specific Media Group, Ltd.

Black, S. (2002). *Knitwear in fashion.* London: Thames & Hudson.

Bocco Guarneri, A. (2003). *Bernard Rudofsky. A humane designer.* New York/Vienna: Springer-Verlag.

Brown, S. (2005). Textiles: Fiber, structure, and function. In M. McQuaid (Ed.), *Extreme textiles. Designing for high performance* (pp. 35–65). London: Thames & Hudson.

Cabrera, R., & Flaherty Meyers, P. (1983). *Classic tailoring techniques. A construction guide for men's wear.* New York: Fairchild Publications.

Chapagain, A. K., Hoekstra, A. Y., Savenije, H. H. G., & Gautam, R. (2005). The water footprint of cotton consumption. *Value of Water. Research Report Series No. 18.* Retrieved October 20, 2006, from http://www.waterfootprint.org

Chenoune, F. (1993). *A history of men's fashion.* Paris: Flammarion.

Cooklin, G. (1997). *Garment technology for fashion designers.* Oxford: Blackwell Science.

Dobson, J. (2004). *Making kimono and Japanese clothes.* London: B T Batsford.

Feyerabend, R. (2004). Textiles briefing paper. Retrieved February 5, 2007, from http://www.mrs-hampshire.org.uk/Workshop%204/Textiles.pdf

Hart, A. (1987). The clothing accounts of George Thomson 1738–48. In N. Rothstein (Ed.), *Barbara Johnson's album of fashions and fabrics* (pp. 149–153). London: Thames and Hudson.

Hishinuma, Y. (Ed.). (1986). *Clothes by Yoshiki Hishinuma.* Tokyo: Yobisha Co.

Kries, M., & von Vegesack, A. (2001). *A-POC making. Issey Miyake & Dai Fujiwara.* Berlin: Vitra Design Museum.

Lynton, L. (1995). *The sari: Styles, patterns, history, techniques.* London: Thames and Hudson.

Major, J. S., & Teng, Y. (Eds.). (2003). *Yeohlee: Work. Material architecture.* Mulgrave: Peleus Press.

McDonough, W., & Braungart, M. (2002). *Cradle to cradle. Remaking the way we make things.* New York: North Point Press.

Quinn, B. (2002). *Techno fashion.* Berg: Oxford & New York.

Rhodes, Z., & Knight, A. (1984). *The art of Zandra Rhodes.* London: Jonathan Cape.

Rothstein, N. (Ed.). (1984). *Four hundred years of fashion.* London: Victoria & Albert Museum.

Rudofsky, B. (1947). *Are clothes modern?* Chicago: Paul Theobald.

Shaeffer, C. B. (2001). *Couture sewing techniques.* Newtown: Taunton Press.

Shep, R. L., & Cariou, G. (1999). *Shirts and men's haberdashery: 1840s to 1920s.* Mendocino: R. L. Shep.

Stern, R. (2004). *Against fashion. Clothing as art, 1850–1930.* Cambridge & London: MIT Press.

Tarrant, N. (1994). *The development of costume*. London: Routledge.

Tilke, M. (1956). *Costume patterns and designs: A survey of costume patterns and designs of all periods and nations from antiquity to modern times*. London: A. Zwemmer Ltd.

Townsend, K. (2004). Transforming shape: Hybrid practice as group activity. *The Design Journal, 7*(2), 18–31.

Van Assche, A. (2005). Interweavings: Kimono past and present. In A. Van Assche (Ed.), *Fashioning kimono* (pp. 6–29). Milan: 5 Continents Editions srl.

Waddell, G. (2004). *How fashion works. Couture, ready-to-wear & mass production*. Oxford: Blackwell Science.

Zandra Rhodes: A lifelong love affair with textiles. (2005). [Exhibition catalogue]. Woodbridge, UK: Antique Collectors' Club.

JANA HAWLEY, PH.D. is professor and department head at Kansas State University. She has conducted research for nearly a decade on recycled clothing from a systems perspective that ranges from consumers' discard habits, to policy makers and international trade law, to charitable organizations, and finally to for-profit organizations that search for value-added opportunities for recycled clothing. Hawley believes that recycling clothing is just one of the fundamental solutions needed toward building a sustainable future.

CHAPTER 9

Economic Impact of Textile and Clothing Recycling

Jana Hawley

If most post-consumer waste is recyclable, why is such a high percentage of textiles and clothing products dumped into the landfill? To address this problem, we must first understand the economic impact of the textile recycling process. This chapter examines that process, its practitioners, its products, and the challenges it faces in the United States and throughout the world.

A Global System

Textile recycling is a fascinating story that few fully comprehend. In some parts of the world, it is part of an underground economy, so in many cases it is not even accounted for in national economy figures.

Trade laws prohibit the free flow of used textiles between some nations, citing health risks and negative impacts on fledgling industries as reasons for banning the trade. But no doubt, textile recycling has positive impact on many entities and contributes significantly to the social responsibility of contemporary culture, including the goodwill associated with environmentalism, charity, and disaster relief that also plays a significant economic role in the global marketplace.

Because textiles are nearly 100 percent recyclable, nothing in the textile and apparel pipeline should be sent to landfills. Rag traders have culled truckloads of used textiles and sorted them for a wide variety of markets. Grateful Dead T-shirts and Harley-Davidson jackets are sent to the Japanese vintage markets. Quality used clothing is sorted in El Paso and sent to developing markets in Central and South America where inexpensive used clothing is needed. Acrylic sweaters are baled in Brooklyn and sent to Italy to be garneted (i.e., the process where textile fabric is shredded back to the fiber stage) and spun into yarns for IKEA stadium blankets. Stained and torn T-shirts are cut into rags in Toronto and sold to furniture makers or machine shops. Old Indian saris are shredded and spun into hand-knitting yarns in Nepal. And mixed damaged clothes are ground into fiber and made into mats to line caskets in South Carolina. The textile recycling industry is a viable industry working diligently to keep waste out of landfills.

This chapter focuses on the economic impact of textile recycling. We begin with an overview of the recycling process, including issues of overconsumption and the resulting recycling processes that occur in the United States and throughout the world. Next, a micro-macro systems model depicts the global textiles recycling processes and its economic impact, particularly as it pertains to apparel waste, rather than manufacturing waste. Finally, we look at alternative options for recycling and future trends. My research is based on over seven years of qualitative data collection on apparel and other fashion products consumed and marketed throughout the United States and the world.

I have interviewed a myriad of participants along the pipeline of the recycling system both in the United States and globally. Perhaps one of the most interesting things I have learned is that textile and clothing recycling is both a small and grand phenomenon. Many of the rag dealers are small, family-owned businesses that work independently; yet they are tightly knit to a global network that move used clothing around the world through brokers and long-time associations that have taken generations to establish.

The Textile and Apparel Recycling Process: A Brief Overview

Fashion and Western lifestyle in general are significant contributors to landfill waste. Not only are products consumed at a high level, but Western goods are often overpackaged, contributing even more to the waste stream. As landfill scarcity continues to rise, the costs of dumping will also continue to increase. These escalating costs are of concern for businesses as they seek ways to reduce their overhead.

The Problem of Overconsumption

Fashion itself compounds the problem of overconsumption. Elizabeth Wilson calls fashion "dress in which the key feature is rapid and continual changes of style. Fashion . . . *is* change." (Wilson, 2003). But regardless of how dynamic fashion is or how economically viable the fashion industry is, (American) fashion is creating an overabundance of used clothing. Fashion marketers entice us to buy something new every season, sometimes with offerings that are truly new and exciting, but all too often the merchandise is simply a mere twist of last year's successful selling styles, offering the safe bet rather than taking a risk with the shareholders' expectations. Meanwhile, consumers satisfy their whims, often overburdening their closet space and probably their credit cards.

The result is a clothing accumulation that stems from planned obsolescence, the core of fashion. Thus, the essence of fashion fuels the momentum for change, which creates demand for ongoing replacement of products with something that is new and fresh. In addition, fashion has reached beyond apparel to the home furnishings industry. The result is fashionable goods contributing to consumption at a significantly higher level than need. Without the notion of fashion, the textile, apparel, and home furnishings industries would realize even more vulnerability in an environment that is already extremely competitive. Apparel and home furnishings companies in the United States today have continual fashion "seasons" that constantly capture consumer interest as these companies stimulate sales and profits.

Waste continues to accumulate as consumers continue to buy, which further compounds the problem of what to do with discarded waste of apparel and home textile products. Apparel in today's marketplace is different from that of several decades ago, not only in design but also in fiber content. When the twentieth century introduced synthetic fibers, textile recycling became more complex for two distinct reasons: (1) fiber strength increased, making it more difficult to shred or "open" the fibers, and (2) fiber blends made it more difficult to purify the sorting process. While for some textile recycling value-added processes concern for the fiber blend does not matter, for others, the fiber content is very important and sorting by blend is a tedious process that requires well-trained specialists.

Textile Recycling Statistics

The textile and apparel recycling effort is concerned with recycling, recyclability, and source reduction of both preconsumer and postconsumer waste. According to the Environmental Protection Agency, the per-capita daily disposal rate of solid waste in the United States is approximately 4.3 pounds, up from 2.7 pounds in 1960 (Environmental Protection Agency, n.d.). Although textiles seldom earn a category of their own in solid waste management data, the Fiber Economics

Bureau (2004) reported that the per-capita consumption of fiber in the United States is 83.9 pounds with over 40 pounds per capita being discarded per year. A recent report shows that China has surpassed the United States, making China the number one consumer of fiber in the world. As the Chinese market continues to prosper, it will continue to have the fastest-growing fiber consumption market for the next 10 years (Bharat Textile, 2004). Of course, as consumption increases, so will the increase of disposal. Thus, China will eventually become a significant contributor to the textile waste stream if plans are not implemented to salvage the waste from landfills.

It is well established that recycling is economically beneficial, yet much of the discarded clothing and textile waste in the United States fails to reach the recycling pipeline. The United States textile recycling industry annually salvages approximately 10 pounds per capita, or 2.5 billion pounds of postconsumer waste from the waste stream. According to Bernie Brill, executive director of Secondary Materials and Recycled Textiles (SMART), these pounds represent only about 30 percent of the total postconsumer annual textile waste (Brill, 2006). As an example, although there are several well-established uses for denim waste, the denim industry still deposits more than 70 million pounds of scrap denim in U.S. landfills annually (McCurry, 1996). In 2003, the Environmental Protection Agency (n.d.) noted that 4 million tons of textiles were going to the landfills each year. While this may not seem like a large amount, it does indeed seem so when one considers that nearly 100 percent of postconsumer waste is recyclable. Cognizant of this, the textile industry's current efforts, championed by the American Textile Manufacturer's Encouraging Environmental Excellence (E^3) program, focus on trying to increase recoverable textile waste that would otherwise end up in landfills. The EPA's 2006 analysis of municipal solid waste indicated that textile waste has a program potential of generating 1.6 million tons per year of additional textiles that are otherwise unclaimed (EPA, 2006).

The Textile Recycling Industry

Few people understand the textile recycling industry, its myriad participants, and wide variety of products made from reclaimed textile fiber. As one of the oldest and most established recycling industries in the world, the textile recycling industry reclaims used textile and apparel products and puts them to new and interesting uses. This "hidden" industry (Divita, 1996) consists of approximately 3,000 businesses that are able to divert over 1,250,000 tons of postconsumer textile waste annually. Furthermore, the textile recycling industry is able to process 93 percent of the waste without producing harmful by-products or new hazardous waste. The Council for Textile Recycling (1999) reports that nearly all after-use textile products can be reclaimed for a variety of markets that are already established (Stubin, July 17). The textile recycling industry partners with engineers, researchers, and industry leaders to search for new viable value-added products made from used textile fiber (personal communication with K. Stewart, October 22, 2006).

Textile recycling can be classified as either preconsumer or post-consumer waste. Preconsumer waste consists of by-product materials from the textile, fiber, and cotton industries that are remanufactured for the automotive, aeronautic, home building, furniture, mattress, coarse yarn, home furnishings, paper, apparel, and other industries.

Postconsumer waste is defined as any type of garment or household article made from manufactured textiles that the owner no longer needs and decides to discard. These articles are discarded either because they are worn out, are damaged, are outgrown, or have gone out of fashion. These textile products are sometimes given to charities and passed on to friends and family, but additionally are disposed of into the trash and end up in municipal landfills. Goodwill Industries is able to sell approximately 50 percent of the items it receives in their retail stores, with the remainder sold to used textile dealers and brokers. Figure 9.1 provides a schematic of options for postconsumer textiles.

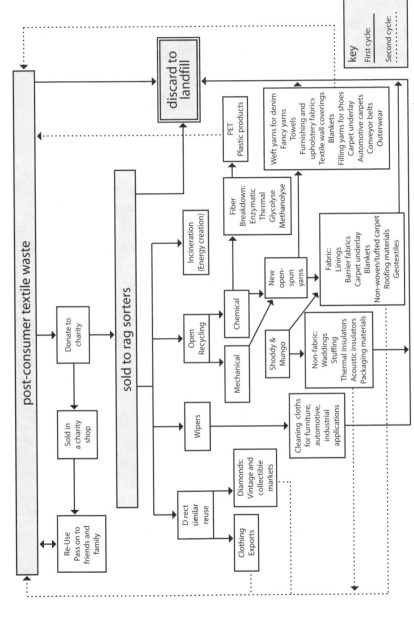

FIGURE 9.1. This schematic shows the multiple options for postconsumer textile products. (Model courtesy of Jana Hawley.)

The Textile Recycling Pipeline

Many essential participants take part in the textile recycling pipeline, including consumers, policy makers, solid-waste managers, not-for-profit agencies, and for-profit textile dealers (Hawley, 2000).

Getting Rid of It

Consumers could make a decision to part with their items by trying to sell them through a variety of channels that include garage sales, consignment shops, and online auctions. Items that do not sell could then be sent through the municipal recycling system, donated to a charitable organization, or thrown away. When consumers finally decide to donate them to a charitable organization, they have made the decision that someone in the world "needs" their clothing. For many Americans, this step makes them "feel good" about the donation they are making. For others, giving their things away is a difficult thing to do. One woman said that she would clean out her closets, carry her things in the trunk of her car for several months, and finally be able to drop the things off at Goodwill. The emotional tie that we have to *things* makes it difficult to discard, even at the end of their useful life (McCracken, 1991).

Another woman said that six months after her father died, she had sorted his things, put them in trash bags, taken them to Goodwill, and because Goodwill had so much excess inventory, she watched them put her father's things into a Dumpster without even looking in the bags. After sitting in her car crying for a while, she crawled into the Dumpster, retrieved her father's things, put them back in her car, and drove away.

Think about things in your own closet. Are there things that you haven't worn for more than three years? Try to analyze why. Are they a size you hope to wear again after you go on that diet? Is it something you simply paid too much for so how could you possibly *give* it away? Was it a gift from someone dear to you? But if it hasn't been worn for at least three years, isn't it time to give it to charity? As evidenced here, even after consumers make decisions about their things, they may or may not be able to part with them.

Municipal and Charitable Recycling Programs

Most municipalities do not offer convenient, or any, textile recycling options. Curbside pickup of textiles is problematic because when textiles get wet, problems of mold and mildew set in. Some cities have established textile recycling programs where textiles are collected at watertight collection sites. Denton, Texas, reported that when textile recycling was added to the municipal recycling mix, textiles subsidized the costs of the other recycling materials.

Charitable organizations are the primary option for most consumers when they decide to donate, or *recycle*, their clothing. Evidence reveals, however, that consumers will not donate clothing to charities if they feel the clothing is unwearable (e.g., out of fashion, stained, pilled, etc.). However, most charities cull the things they determine to be saleable at their resale shops and then bale the remainder, which they sell to rag dealers who will, in turn, further process the used clothing for further value-added markets (which will be discussed later in this chapter). It is important here for consumers to understand that all clothing and textile items are recyclable and should be sent into the recycling pipeline. If no municipal recycling option exists for textiles, then charitable organizations are the next best option. Charities are able to reap benefits for the clothing that is saleable in the retail stores and sell the rest of it to textile graders who in turn obtain their inventory to conduct their for-profit business. In other words, charities and textile graders are interrelated partners in the textile recycling pipeline.

Textile Graders

Each year, textile graders, also called *rag dealers*, *rag sorters*, or *rag graders*, acquire about 2.5 billion pounds of excess inventory from charitable organizations and municipal contracts. Clothes come in by the truckload and are off-loaded onto conveyor belts where they are sorted for a wide variety of markets ranging from vintage collectibles, exports to developing countries, wipers, and fiber for stuffing. Recycling International (2004) reported that only 40 percent of the clothes received by textile graders were saleable as clothing. Most textile graders are small, family-owned businesses that have been in operation for several generations (Allenbach, 1993; Shapiro & Sons, 1961). However, start-up entrepreneurs also have opened new rag dealer businesses because they perceive it as a low-cost, easily accessible form of entrepreneurship. What many of the start-ups fail to realize, however, is that this business is highly dependent on global contacts that take years of cultivating clients in overseas markets to sell their sorted goods. As one textile rag dealer told me, "I have spent as much as a year at a time away from my family while I developed and nurtured markets across Africa, Asia, and Latin America. Now that these business contacts have been established, I can pass the contacts on to my son, who will be taking over the business soon." Another rag dealer supported this notion when he said, "Establishing contacts in Africa is particularly difficult. But once those contacts are made, the bond between us has been very strong and full of respect." And an international broker from Europe said the following:

> Buying and selling in Africa is an underground business. The used-textile brokers in Africa are substantially wealthier than many of the citizens who are the consumers of the used clothing. They must hide their wealth in order to maintain credibility among the citizens. One of our buyers has a beautiful burled wood and gilded office that is [hidden away]. When we go to Africa to do business we have to be secretly escorted . . . to conduct our business.

Textile recycling companies are often located in large metropolitan areas because it is imperative to keep transportation costs to a minimum and the majority of inventory will come from the urban areas. Nousiainen & Talvenmaa-Kuusela (1994) reported that transportation and sorting costs were the decisive criteria for profitability for a textile sorting company. Depending on the current economic climate, primarily associated with materials availability, commodity pricing, fuel costs, and current value-added markets, for-profit rag-sorting companies can realize both success and hardship. Although the primary goal of these small businesses is to realize profits, most of the business owners are also committed to environmentalism and take pride in their contribution to waste reduction.

Once sorted, the goods are compressed into large bales, usually 600 to 1,000 pounds, wrapped, and warehoused until an order, often from a broker, is received. Several things are considered during sorting for this category: climate of the market, relationships between the exporters and importers, and trade laws for used apparel.

FIGURE 9.2. Used clothing is compressed into large bales, such as this one destined for India. A bale usually weighs 600 kg and is wrapped and stored in a warehouse until exported. (Photo courtesy of Jana Hawley.)

Grading Used Clothes: Recognizing Economic Opportunities

Textile graders sort for many categories, sometimes as many as 400. Rough sorts (i.e., pulling heavy coats, blankets, plastics, toys, shoes) from the conveyor belts occur first by new employees or employees that do not have the skills to recognize the finer categories. As the clothes move along the conveyor, the higher-skilled employees will sort for the more specific categories (e.g., particular brand names, acrylic or cashmere sweaters, collectible jeans, antique garments).

Vintage and Collectibles

Of all the categories that graders sort, the most lucrative is vintage collectibles. Many vintage or collectible items have global appeal, as evidenced by the movement of vintage goods from country to country. What might be considered ready for throw away in one country might be considered hip or cool in another. For example, American items are highly prized in Japanese markets, as I found when I was collecting data at one of the U.S. sites and saw five Japanese buyers rummaging through piles of used clothes to select what they wanted to buy. The owner of the business said that there are many days out of the month when Japanese buyers are in-house making their selections. Japan is the largest importer of used American collectibles and has proved to be very interested in Americana items such as authentic Harley-Davidson clothing, Grateful Dead T-shirts, and Coach handbags. After the September 11, 2001, terrorist tragedy, the secondhand signature red, white, and blue Tommy Hilfiger goods realized increased interest in some global markets. But perhaps the one item that has had consistent global interest is Levi's jeans, particularly certain older styles. One rag sorter found a pair of collectible Levi's and sold them on the Paris auction block for $18,000. Another rag sorter sold a collectible find for $11,000 to Levi Strauss & Co. A textile grader in the Midwest claimed that he found enough collectible blue jeans to "pay for my three kids' college education." However, it requires a special eye and the ability to forecast trends in order to find the high-value items in the huge piles of used textiles that rag sorters must sift through.

Products considered "vintage" collectibles include the following:

- Official Harley-Davidson clothing
- 1950s bowling shirts
- 1950s printed aprons
- Military issue leather bomber jackets
- Original Aran knit from Ireland, 100 percent wool
- Grateful Dead T-shirts, pre-1995 (death of Jerry Garcia)
- Vintage denim (Levi's, Lee, Wrangler)
- Vintage collegiate apparel
- Vintage movie apparel
- Hawaiian shirts
- Smoking jackets, pajamas, robes
- Vintage ties
- Vintage lingerie (slips, sleepwear)
- Vintage accessories (belt buckles, scarves, sunglasses)
- Bell bottoms
- Swimwear

The collectible category accounts for approximately one to two percent of the total volume of goods that enter the textile recycling stream, yet this category also accounts for the largest profit center for most textile recycling companies. The manager of the collectible division of a recycling company told me that "when you find the [really good things], they are still diamonds in the rough, but once they are cleaned, pressed, and packaged, they are worth a lot in the marketplace." As a result, many people get into the vintage clothing business, as evidenced by the tremendous number of hits received when "vintage clothing stores" ($n > 9,000,000$) is used as a search string in Google. J. Usatch, a recycling company owner and industry proponent, warned, however, that many people can find and sell vintage collectibles, but it is "the companies that are able to sell the not-so-good qualities to secondary markets [at a profit]" (Recycling International, February 20, 2006, p. 95) that distinguish themselves from the others as successful textile graders.

The word *vintage* is really a misnomer; *collectible* might be more accurate. Items that qualify for collectible status include couture clothing and accessories, Americana items such as Levi's, uniforms such as those worn by Girl and Boy Scouts of America, particular branded items such as Izod, vintage items identified as collectible trends such as old Harley-Davidson T-shirts or 1960s bowling shirts, luxury fibers (e.g., cashmere and camel hair), and antique items, which by the strictest definition means over 100 years old but with regard to clothing usually means 1920s or earlier. Customers for collectibles range from well-known designers, eccentric college students, or wealthy celebrities. Retail boutiques featuring vintage clothing can be found in trendy SoHo or Beverly Hills, and the Internet offers a plethora of vintage options.

Vintage shop owners or Internet sellers are often members of the National Association of Resale and Thrift Shops (NART). This Chicago-based association was established in 1984 and has more than 1,000 members. It serves thrift, resale, and consignment shops and promotes public education about the vintage shop industry. TRAID (Textiles Recycling for Aid and Development) is a charity organization that finances itself through the sale of quality secondhand clothing.

Wipers

Another important sorting category for graders is wipers. The wiper market comes from clothing that has seen the end of its useful life as such and may be turned into wiping or polishing rags for industrial use. White T-shirts, sweatshirts, and polo shirts are a primary source for this category because the cotton fiber makes good polishing cloths and absorbent rags. Bags of rags can be found at retail stores such as AutoZone or in Wal-Mart's automotive department. But in some cases, some synthetic fiber, particularly olefin because of its excellent wicking and oleophilic properties, is used where oily spills need to be cleaned up. An industry insider revealed that he sells reclaimed olefin from the sorting process to the oil-refining industry to be used in combinations with hydrophobic fibers as stuffing for "snakes" in ocean oil spill cleanups. Another rag sorter said that he sells rags to washing machine manufacturers for use-testing of machines.

Wipers maintain a fairly stable market over time, yet processing wipers may not be cost-effective. It requires labor to cut the neckband and sleeves from shirts, and also often requires laundering. Both of these add costs to the processing and may not make this category cost-effective, even though the market demand remains stable.

Twenty-Nine Percent Conversion to New Products

Converting used materials to new products is an important category for growth. Companies are partnering with engineers, researchers, and industry leaders to determine value-added products where recycled textiles and apparel can be used. When fiber is cut, shredded, carded, or otherwise machined back to the fiber stage, it is referred to as *shoddy*. Shoddy can be reengineered into value-added products such as stuffing, automotive components, carpet underlays, casket lining, building materials (e.g., insulation and roofing felt), and low-end blankets. The majority of this category consists of stained, torn, or otherwise unmarketable garments. A textile grader from the Midwest, however, was sorting for 100 percent cotton sweaters because he was selling shredded cotton fiber to mix with sand for use in "Punch-n-Kick" bags made by one of the world's largest sporting manufacture companies. Another informant reports that reclaimed fibers are being used in the production of U.S. currency.

A vast number of products are made from reprocessed fiber. Much of this fiber is respun into new yarns or manufactured into woven, knitted, or nonwoven fabrications such as garment linings, household items, furniture upholstery, insulation materials, automobile sound absorption materials, automobile carpeting, and toys (Querci, 2000). New yarn producers like those in Prato, Italy, that reduce cashmere sweaters to fiber, spin new yarns and produce cashmere blankets for the luxury market. The blanket manufacturers in Prato also make acrylic stadium blankets for IKEA from acrylic sweaters that are reclaimed from all over the world (see Figure 9.3).

Converting fiber into value-added products is a process that represents an economic and environmental saving of valuable fiber that would otherwise be lost to the landfill. The most unusable and damaged of postconsumer textiles often have the highest level of specifications forced upon it by the end-use industries (e.g., building, auto, aeronautics, sporting equipment, construction materials, and defense).

The other category for conversion to new products is the actual redesign of used clothing. Current fashion trends are reflected by a team of young designers who use and customize secondhand clothes for a chain of specialty vintage clothing stores in the United Kingdom. Its offerings include "cheap, chic, and occasional designer surprises" (Ojumo, 2002; Packer, 2002). As another example, a young designer in Dallas, Texas, creates new from the old and sells wholesale to various trendy stores such as Urban Outfitters. This concept is common among boutiques with a youth-oriented target market.

Household Textiles

In general, household textiles do not play a significant role in the used textile market; however, in Europe, bed feathers continue to capture a significant price in the used textile markets. Feather beds have been commonly used in many European homes for years, and they continue to command a good price on the used market for export to developing markets.

FIGURE 9.3. Used acrylic fiber sweaters are sorted by color before being shredded apart; then, their reclaimed fiber is woven into a new acrylic blanket. (Photo courtesy of Jana Hawley.)

Landfill and Incineration for Energy

For some reclaimed fiber, no viable value-added market has been established, so the used goods must be sent to the landfill. Rag sorters work hard to avoid this for both environmental and economic reasons because the average cost to dump in the landfill in the United States is $70 per ton for textile-sorting companies (Brill, 2006). Still the average American throws away about 68 pounds of clothing and textiles a year (http://www.textilerecycle.org).

The incineration of reclaimed fiber for energy production may be another solution to keep textiles out of the landfill. In the United States, early testing reveals that emissions of incinerated used fibers are more than satisfactory, but the process of feeding the boiler systems in many North American power plants is not feasible (Weide, 2004). The incineration of used textiles as an alternative fuel source is more commonly done in Europe than in the United States because European fuel costs have historically been much higher than those in the United States. More research is needed for used textiles to become a viable choice, both economically and environmentally, as an alternative fuel source. As fashion retailers continue to stimulate retail sales and consumers continue to overload closets, however, burning used clothing might become a very viable economic option.

Export of Used Clothing

On many street corners throughout the developing world, racks of Western clothing are being sold. I have seen for myself such racks in Taiwan, Thailand, India, Greece, and Mexico (see Figures 9.4 and 9.5). The secondhand exports markets compose the largest volume, or roughly 48 percent, of used clothing (Stubin, May 21); most of these goods are shipped to developing countries or used for disaster relief.

Most used clothing from the United States goes to Africa or South and Central America, but markets also exist in parts of Asia, such as India and Pakistan. Most European exports go to either Eastern Europe

FIGURE 9.4. In an open market-place, such as this one in India, Western clothing is highly valued. Entrepreneurs earn a living selling this used clothing, or mitumba. (Photo courtesy of Jana Hawley.)

or Northern Africa. It has been reported that "used apparel serves as the largest export from the United States based on volume" (Industry insider, 2004). The United States exports $61.7 million in sales to Africa. One of its primary export sites is Uganda, where a Ugandan woman can purchase a designer T-shirt for $1.20 (Packer, 2002). However, in January of 2005, the East African countries of Tanzania, Uganda, and Kenya imposed upwards of 300 percent import tax increases on used clothing in attempts to shut down the used-clothing imports, citing protectionist measures for their fledgling textile industries. It can be argued, however, that imports of new clothing dumped from China impose more threat on the local textile industries than do secondhand clothing from Europe and the United States (Usatch, 2005). These increased taxes gave rise to protests from millions of small businesses who survive by selling used clothing. The protests eventually forced authorities to pay attention, and in early 2006 the tax increases were reversed.

Western clothing is a highly valued commodity and perhaps serves as the only source of affordable clothing in many developing countries where levels of income are so low that food and clean water are the primary concern. Some have argued that the export of clothing to these nations has threatened the traditional dress for many indigenous cultures and at the same time may threaten the fledgling textile and apparel industries of those countries. While this is certainly a sensitive issue that needs consideration, it is also the case that export of wearable, climate-appropriate, and affordable clothing to developing countries is a valuable commodity for most of the population in less-privileged areas of the world. It not only provides affordable clothing but also opportunity for micro-enterprise development of used-clothing stalls throughout the developing world.

Not all used clothing is exported to poorer countries. One textile

FIGURE 9.5. This young Indian child wears mitumba, or used Western attire, instead of her native clothing. (Photo courtesy of Jana Hawley.)

grader shared that he has a new market in the United Arab Emirates, one of the richest countries in the world. Used clothes in the United Arab Emirates are not intended for the local population but, instead, for the immigrant labor from Bangladesh, Pakistan, and Indonesia because labor jobs do not allow the workers enough discretionary income to purchase the designer labels that are offered in the local shops.

In recent years, rag graders have noted that Africans desire higher quality and more fashion-forward styles. As J. Usatch noted, "Today, selling used clothes to Africa is almost like running a boutique" (Recycling International, May 2, 2006, p. 123). In the past, bales sold to African countries were not graded according to particular style or brand, but today's shipments must be carefully sorted to meet the ever-increasing savvy African consumer demands. This adds value to the bale, which can demand a higher price but also requires higher processing costs.

Used clothes arrive in Africa on ships in 600- to 1,000-pound bales and are then opened and sold to brokers and small retailers throughout Africa. In 2003, Tanzania imported more than $94 million dollars of U.S. clothing worn by all social classes (e.g., rich, educated, poor, children, clergy, politicians, old, and young). They call it *mitumba*, a Swahili word that means bale or bundle. When people put on mitumba, you can't tell the rich from the poor.

Because of trade laws, much of mitumba is smuggled through the black markets from Burundi, Zambia, and the Democratic Republic of Congo. When it arrives in Tanzania, it looks like a plastic bundle the size of a refrigerator. Djibril Duany, the local dealer, cuts open the plastic wrap he bought for about $90 and digs through it to see what great pieces it contains. In it he finds a Cher Farewell Tour T-shirt, a Chicago Bulls jersey, several men's suits, two track suits, and his prize, a Samuel Eto'o jersey. He is thrilled. According to Duany (2006), most mitumba is imported by charitable organizations and intended for the poor, aged, and ill. However, businesspeople can acquire a license to sell mitumba if they pay all pertinent taxes to the government.

Mitumba is often divided based on quality and type. A high demand is placed on shirts, trousers, suits, T-shirts, jackets, and athletic wear. Used suits are of particular value, especially when compared to new suits at substantial prices in boutiques. Prices vary depending on the target market. For rich markets, mitumba can be relatively high.

As mitumba has become commonplace, notions of Western fashion have also become more understood. At one time Tanzanians were draped in colorful colors and patterns of local industry, but today's Tanzanian manufacturers cannot produce clothing at a cost lower than secondhand clothing. Therefore, mitumba serves an important role to fill the gap. Mitumba is also an important price point for the country's poor. Small entrepreneurs earn a living from selling used clothing in the marketplace. Finally, used clothing provides income in the form of taxes to the Tanzanian government.

However, there is a negative side to mitumba. Some argue that used-clothing imports have slowed the growth of the fledgling textile manufacturing industry. Used-clothing options are very cheap compared to the handmade cotton goods produced by artisans and the cotton farmers in the area. Others have argued that used clothing contains health risks that could spread skin diseases. And finally, some exporters are shipping clothing that is beyond wearable condition, therefore making Tanzania a dumping ground. Used clothing has been shipped to Africa for years; standards may need to be established where quality goods are shipped so that nothing is left for the dumping ground (Duany, 2006).

Even though Africa remains the strongest export area for U.S. exports of used clothing, it is not a consistent market and is impacted by the calendar and other market forces. For example, November is one of the best months of the year for exports to Africa because many people return to their villages with gifts of clothing for their relatives.

Used-clothing markets can also be impacted by natural disasters such as Hurricanes Katrina and Rita or the 2004 Indian Ocean tsunami. In the case of the U.S. hurricanes, Americans often donated their clothing to the hurricane relief projects rather than through their normal channels of donation, thus changing the supply to rag graders. When the flow of supply changes as dramatically as it did in the case of Hurricane Katrina, it impacts both rag graders and charitable organizations such as Goodwill and The Salvation Army. The truth is, relief agencies often dread the influx of used clothing that inevitably follows a disaster because it requires valuable and scarce resources (e.g., time, money, and personnel to sort, clean, and distribute it). Often there is so much donated that it requires locating warehouse space to be able to manage the huge volume of clothing that is donated. In addition, volunteers or relief workers are diverted from other, more critical recovery activities. It would be better for Americans to continue to donate through their normal charitable channels so that the charitable organizations and rag graders (i.e., the experts) can grade and sort the clothing and ship the appropriate donations to the disaster area as needed.

Conclusion: Future Trends and Directions

We cannot conclude the discussion of the economic impact of textile recycling without also discussing the global nature of the phenomenon. As consumers in developing countries begin to gain access to discretionary goods and disposable income, the plethora of used textiles in the marketplace will grow as well. Currently, much of today's market for used clothing is located in the poorest parts of the world. As these countries develop, the desire for used clothing in these poor nations will diminish and be replaced with desire for new goods. At present, these developing countries provide markets where industrialized nations can transform their excessive consumption into useful export.

As landfill space continues to become scare and costs continue to escalate, so will concerns for environmentalism. Consumers must be provided with easy and informed choices for discarding their used clothing. Policy makers must provide a political environment that allows for the free flow of goods and the easy disposal of recyclable materials.

As environmental concerns continue to rise, consumers must continue to shift their attitude toward the use of recycled goods in the marketplace and embrace recycled goods. Citizens should lobby their municipalities to add textiles to their recycling options. When we consider the complexity of the textile recycling system and the importance of cooperation among the players, we then understand both the environmental and economic importance of textile recycling. To recycle successfully, everyone must embrace the system and not just make an occasional charitable donation. Meanwhile, arbiters must continue to develop new value-added markets and market the after-use possibilities so that the system functions at full capacity and with commitment from all.

References

Bharat Textile. (2004). World's biggest fiber consumer: China. Retrieved November 25, 2004, from http://bharattextile.com

Brill, B., executive director, Secondary Materials and Recycled Textiles. (2006, June). Personal communication.

Council for Textile Recycling. (1999). Retrieved from http://textilerecycle.org

Divita, L. (1996). Missouri manufacturers' interest in textile recycling. Unpublished master's thesis, University of Missouri, Columbia.

Duany, D., local dealer, United Republic of Tanzania. (2006, July). Personal communication.

Secondary Materials and Recycled Textile Association Council for Textile Recycling fact sheet (1999). Retrieved June 7, 2007, from http://textilerecycle.org

Environmental Protection Agency. (n.d.). Recycled textiles. Retrieved September 28, 2003, from http://www.epa.gov

Environmental Protection Agency (2006, February 10). Source reduction program potential manual: A planning tool (text version). EPA 530-R-97-002. Clothing and footwear reuse. Retrieved November 20, 2006, from http://www.epa.gov/epaoswer/non-hw/reduce/source5.txt

Estur, G. and Becerra, C. A. (2003). Developments in world fibre consumption pattern: An overview of 1996 and 2000 FAO/ICAC world fibre consumption survey. Retrieved from International Cotton Advisory Committee Web site: http://www.icac.org/icac/cotton_info/speeches/estur/2003/fiber_cons_pattern.pdf

Fiber Economics Bureau (2004). Retrieved from http://www.fibersource.com/feb/feb1.htm

Hammer, M. (1993). Home environment. Institute of food and agricultural sciences. University of Florida, Gainesville.

Hawley, J. M. (2000). Textile recycling as a system: A micro/macro analysis. *Journal of Family and Consumer Sciences, 93*(5), 35–40.

Industry insider, wiper market. (2004, May 10). Personal communication.

McCracken, G. (1991). *Culture and consumption.* Bloomington: Indiana University Press.

McCurry, J. W. (1996). Blue jean remnants keep homes warm. *Textile World,* 84–85.

Moore, M. T. (2006, October 24). When disaster strikes, Americans clean out their closets. *USA Today,* p 1.

Nousiainen, P. & Talvenmaa-Kuusela, P. (1994, September 27). Solid Textile waste recycling. Paper presented at the Globalization–Technological, Economic, and Environmental Imperatives. 75th World Conference of Textile Institute, Atlanta, Georgia.

Querci. (2000, July 22). Personal communication.

Recycling International market analysis. (2006, October 2). Contented in the comfort zone. Retrieved November 20, 2006 from http://www.recyclinginternational.com/markets/textiles.aspx

Recycling International market analysis. (2006, May 2). Spring collections boost supply. Retrieved November 20, 2006 from http://www.recyclinginternational.com/markets/textiles.aspx

Recycling International market analysis. (2006, February 20). Winter weather impacts on supplies. Retrieved November 20, 2006 from http://www.recyclinginternational.com/markets/textiles.aspx

Recycling International market analysis. (2004, October 4). Germany pleads for recycling levy on clothing. Retrieved November 20, 2006 from http://www.recycling-international.com/markets/textiles.aspx

Stewart, K. (2006). Personal communication, October 22, 2006.

Stubin, E., owner, TransAmerica. (2001). Personal communication, May 21, 2001.

Stubin, E., owner, TransAmerica. (2001). Personal communication, July 17, 2001.

Usatch, J., recycling company owner (2005). Personal communication, February 10.

Usatch, J. (2006, February 20). *Recycling international,* p. 95.

Weide. (2004, March 20). Personal communication.

Wilson, E. (2003). Adorned in Dreams. Camden, New Jersey: Rutgers University Press.

VAN DYK LEWIS, PH.D., is a fashion design professor at Cornell University. He uses ethnography as the catalyst for research and the formation of textual and visual commentaries. His focus considers the dynamic intersections that propel fashion toward new definitions; these concern the globalization of fashion and imbalances between the fashion industry, the product, and the self.

CHAPTER 10

Developing Strategies for a Typology of Sustainable Fashion Design

Van Dyk Lewis

The success of the fashion industry has caused consumers to endorse mass addictive consumption. This chapter centers upon the industry's lethargy in developing clear principles for self-management of sustainable practice. But it also explores creative new strategies, analogous to those of the 1960s when the democratization of fashion became a reality that could reverse the effects of clothing production and consumption on our planet.

Taking a Hard Look at the Fashion Industry

"Save the planet, kill yourself."

This rather eccentric statement serves to introduce a discussion about the viability of mass fashion production and consumption in an increasingly uncertain world. This slogan of radical environmentalism may be adversarial, but it shocks thinkers, policy makers, designers, and consumers, at least to some extent, into reevaluating many of the fashion industry's most important and difficult issues.

Whether or not our collective lack of foresight has sealed the planet's fate, it remains of paramount importance to question the meaning of fashion and how it affects our lifestyles. As one of the largest industries in the world, one that continues to grow and pollute the planet at a tremendous rate, fashion is entwined in the establishment of cultural and economic progress and is synonymous with change, innovation and revolution.[1]

Fashion is also synonymous with narratives of exploitation. Numerous examples of underage and generally exploited workers from the developing world are recorded in the news media and entered into the annals of dire business practice. That a sewing machinist in the developing world may be paid 70 times less than her counterpart in the United States has enormous relevance to the project of sustainability; this disparity demonstrates why clothing production in the United States has all but ceased. The growth of "fast fashion" (i.e., low-cost, fashion-forward clothes) has generated a new breed of fashion shopper; she is young and takes fashion clues from high-profile celebrities. The fast fashion shopper updates her wardrobe constantly and frequents stores such as Topshop, H&M, and Zara.

The contention exists that the oversupply of garments is inextricably connected to the contamination of the environment (Chen & Lewis, 2006). This state prompts the necessity for a review of fashion's efficacy as being socially and culturally innovative and capable of reflexivity. Principally such a review must be undertaken by designers of clothes and the manipulators of fashion such as stylists, photographers, and fashion editors. However, the most important group in such a review is the consumer. Consumers are capable of instigating new definitions of fashion and leading in its reterritorialization.

As a popular ideology, fashion is led by mass industry; as expressive

FIGURE 10.1. The growth of "fast fashion" (i.e., low-cost, fashion-forward clothes) has generated a new breed of fashion shopper; she is young and takes fashion clues from high-profile celebrities. (Courtesy of Fairchild Publications, Inc.)

form, it is significantly contributed to by individual wearers. Since the current mood of fashion moves toward the valorization of handmade garments, individuals have deployed personalized fashions as intervention strategies that bring the wearer into disrepute with mass-produced fashion. The consequence is that ideology and expressive forms of fashion are now imploding. Tropes of fashion such as glamour (i.e., sensual pleasure), sophistication, irony, and exclusivity are fixed essences that become points of departure for those operating a sustainable fashion practice. In exploring the viability of these tropes within a sustainable fashion, it becomes clear that such ethereal tropes are incompatible in a system that regards object narrative and counter-hegemonic practice, if not defiance and subversion, as the *new glamour*.

Exclusivity is used as a marketing strategy to create and increase the demand of garments and, therefore, is contradictory to the sustainable project.² So what remains of fashion? Design ideas are stimulated by irony and ingenuity; these, I suggest, are the catalysts of a new scheme of democratic participation in the process of design. Sustainable fashion design is an oxymoron; it is made so because of vacuous attempts to circumvent the core problems of sustainable production for unaccountable and equally uncontrolled consumption. It seems that mass fashion's take on sustainability is reduced to a semantic ensemble rather than convictions made tangible through a rational examination of how fashion might serve the physical world. In this transaction, sustainability has become misrepresented by *organic cotton* and *hemp,* materials that have become distinguished by a consciousness that is reminiscent of a naïve, pure, and natural world. This mishandling of sustainability and the installation of garments made from organic material is, as a trope, similar to avant-garde fashion's abstraction and misuse of Jacques Derrida's deconstruction into a theme that has informed creative practice. The suggestion is that sustainability has the opportunity to critique fashion in the same way that Derrida's deconstruction of linguistics introduced ways to analyze text by providing alternative interpretations and opening up creative potentials.

The Circuitry of Fashion Objects

As a prime strategy, the ability of fashion to transform bodies, objects, behaviors, and events into scenarios that benefit sustainable practice remains undeveloped. Governments and major infrastructural planners are beginning to make some limited engagement with the dilemma of sustainability. This is done from the narrow confine and safety of shielding the political and commercial status quo from the acknowledgment that consumption behaviors must undergo a significant review. Such a review should be meticulously understood if the luxury of overconsumption is to be preserved. Resistance to a review of fashion calls into question an economic system's potential to be moral.

Peter Koslowski, who writes about the philosophy of management and organization, argues that capitalism as utopia, or *true capitalism*, cannot suffice because the economic theory of production, exchange, and coordination must neglect social action and political integration, which are the guiding values of freedom and efficiency of coordination (Koslowski, 2002). Koslowski's thinking is similar to the deficient perception of consumption within economics that hampered an early understanding of capitalism. The renowned sociologist and economist Thorstein Veblen's work on consumption, notably in *The Theory of the Leisure Class* (1899), did much to stimulate discussion about consumption. However, during the early part of the last century, conventional economics did not explain what was called "hedonistic theory"; in fact, economic behavioral studies were spread across the social sciences. Within contemporary economics, the fickleness of personal consumption has become highly influential and serves as an index to inform markets about price changes, inflation, and other variables. Fashioned objects (i.e., those that reflect taste) are capable of stimulating increases and decreases in consumption and occupy a frontier's space in the partnership of social and economic activities. Therefore, it is accurate to say that fashioned objects convey status and validate human progress through time. The cultural capital between fashion as objet d'art and the workings of nature remain purely symbolic; terms such as "organic" and "sustainable" are not adequately defined for fashion's new tasks. Without destination or knowledge of what the journey toward sustainable practice might mean, a general definition of sustainable fashion design remains imprecise and without origin.

Associative Neglect

The Chartered Society of Designers (2006), a London-based professional design association, comments on the British government's 2006 commissioned report, *The Stern Review Report on the Economics of Climate Change*:

> If Stern is taken seriously then designers will see new opportunities for their services. They will need to adopt a business language in order for design to become embedded in the range of business strategies and to take a seat in the boardroom, and they will enter new overseas markets which need to invest in products that allow them to trade in carbon emissions.

The prospect that sustainability might become the catalyst for more than design may provide a link between a respite in feverish manufacture and the trend-driven consumption cycle. Although the *Stern Review Report on the Economics of Climate Change* (2006) does not mention the fashion industry directly, the labyrinthine global production and retail of fashion garments is one of a number of global manufacturing and consumption operations that require the implementation of sustainable strategies. In implementing sustainable policies, the fashion industry has been lethargic.[3] Sustainability in fashion has a protracted history; many of the fashion industry's efforts to introduce sustainable fashions have been superficial and of little effectual consequence. Certainly the various international fashion trade associations (e.g., the Chambre Syndicale de la Haute Couture Parisienne, Council of Fashion Designers of America, and the British Fashion Council) have not promoted the debate of sustainable futures. To the detriment of the "superior" end of the fashion industry and its self-defining mantra of leading the zeitgeist, the affiliates of these associations have largely disregarded the wider issues of sustainable design practice. A kind of *easy* sustainable fashion practice has arisen; this centers upon the use of organic cotton as the obligatory fabric to demonstrate an acknowledgement of the importance of sustainable design practice. Currently no examples exist of leading fashion companies committing to a universal sustainable doctrine to their practice; instead, the tropes of exclusivity, glamour, luxury, irony, and superlative design technique remain the core attributes.[4]

The idea of multipartite, human-centered sustainability is based upon a proposal by the Sustainable Development Department of the Food and Agriculture Organization of the United Nations (2001). The practice is distant from the scope of the fashion industry's perspective; nevertheless, a broad worldview places sustainability as one among many activities that indicate a consensus for a reappraisal of what cost societies are willing to forfeit and whether individual consumers are willing to pay the "real" cost for manufactured goods.[5] Multipartite sustainability is a change strategy that argues for an inclusive sustainability composed of fair-trade initiatives, anti-racist initiatives, support for diversity, and support for civil and human rights.[6] Borrowing from the idea of multipartite sustainability, from here on I will refer to *design sustainability* as distinguishing fashion products that are designed, manufactured, and retailed globally. Practices in design sustainability are not naturally rooted within the fashion industry; therefore, design sustainable fashion companies tend to fall short of an absolutist ideal. I refer to fashion's new task: the creation of a universal, joined-up structure that has genuine ethical integrity. Such a company does not yet exist, and there are no signs that fashion commerce will be able to make this enormous leap. Design sustainability is a proposal that asks companies to consider the ecology of all components that contribute to the production and consumption of fashion.

Implementing Sustainable Management

Sustainable fashion products represent a new attitude and a fundamental departure from the references and cycles elucidated by Roland Barthes in his meta investigation *The Fashion System* (1967) and Gilles Lipovetsky's (1994) work on fashion democratization. In a very fundamental way, designers of fashion garments now have the opportunity to configure and reestablish a system based upon post-humanist value sets.[7] Sustainable fashion design offers an opportunity to displace current fashion industry value sets for values that place emphasis upon considerations of how garments are made, and what impact the existing fashion system has upon the Earth and people. The success of design, and especially design benefited by technology, has "obscure[d] the extent to which mass production technology under 'free market' conditions necessarily entailed the transformation and displacement of traditional aesthetic criteria" (Hebdige, 1989).

Ultimately, the mission of sustainable fashion design is contradictory to personal constructions of fashion and industrially produced fashion garments and images. The former, which is phenomenological fashion (e.g., the activity of dressing up and acting out roles), extends the need for social and psychological growth. Accumulations of fashion garments are an absolute reckoning that demonstrates societies' "social form."

Georg Simmel (1972), the German sociologist who wrote on social differentiation and money and published the small but important paper "Fashion" in *The American Journal of Sociology*, calls fashion a social form, a certain dynamic, arising from a set of social facts. The idiosyncratic nature of these social facts is the basis for fashion's dialectic and the dialectic that we encounter in these evolutionary stages that tracks fashion now and into the future. The first dialectics of personal fashion and industrial fashion are not only opposite but are reactionary, as is fashion design that explodes from the confines of opposition to pit the rights and needs of the individual in the form of post-humanist sustainability against an industrial version of sustainability.

Progression toward sustainability in fashion design is manifest in the evolution of fashion articulated in both design and character. Further, the design of clothes affirms the evolution of humankind and demonstrates fashion's conductivity as social and political product capable of initiating alluring debates, if not change in industrial capitalism and, therefore, mass social behavior. During the last 250 years, distinction between commerce and culture has been eroded to a point where all creative action has become a profit center. For the maximization of profit, high-consumption capitalism has required attenuated designs, scenarios, and services. These are relatively ensured because taste and demand are conferred through the industry of design managers, forecasters, legislators, merchandisers, advertisers, writers, and journalists who script what fashions will exist. All forms of commodity aesthetics are sanctified by fashion; clothing, architecture, car design, city planning, white goods, personal technology, and even thinking are fashioned as constructs of *taste*.

The first tentative steps on the path to sustainable design reveal how sustainable practices are engaged within the profit-led mechanism; questions of motive must be scrutinized, as might queries concerning integrity. No distinguished fashion brands exist that have maintained sustainable practice from the conception of their enterprise. Neither have any distinguished fashion companies begun to develop a discourse where sustainable design is at the forefront of their company policy.[8, 9] The lackluster development of sustainable practice, let alone sustainable design, is similar to the introduction of design management. According to design manager Maristela Da Silva (1999), design management evolved because of experience and because general management teams began to understand that, when used in all departments of the company design, provides strategic advantage. Similar to design management, sustainable design practice does not reveal its benefits until the design cycle is completed; we will not understand the impact of sustainable fashion practice until sustainable fashion has a firm foothold and has transformed the designer, retailer, and consumer triangle. Like design management, sustainability in fashion must integrate fully into the corporate structure.

The following observations from design management may provide clues to the implementation of sustainable design:

- All levels and departments of the organization must understand and commit to sustainability practice.
- Sustainability must be coordinated throughout the companies' structure and products.
- Conditions of implementation must always sustain the survival of the business.
- Sustainable profits, or *benefits*, must equal financial profits payable to company stakeholders and beyond.
- Sustainable initiatives must be regularly reexamined as part of a rolling program.

If sustainability is to become essential to the operation of fashion design industries and therefore society, an expansive, totalizing, and inclusive form of sustainability must be avowed. The reasoning is as follows; when sustainability is framed in the arena of fashion, it becomes part of a popular synthetic culture that is adroit to change and uncovering new tendencies. In strategizing sustainable fashion practice to include all employees, consumers, and the leadership of design companies, an inclusive policy must be adoptable.

No matter how inclusive policies for sustainability might be, individuals involved in design, retail, and consumption pose insightful questions about possible dichotomies. An example is the relationship between the consumer and the garment machinist, both of whom share much through the creation of fashion garments; both reconfigure their bodies by means of the operation of exchange. Buying clothes and making clothes shapes and reshapes the body, its social status, and its potential for and of the stringency of work and the exultation of self. Manufacture and consumption are political acts; deciding to manufacture or consume sustainable products becomes an opportunity to verify modernity's delinquencies. In committing to the terms of sustainability's insertion in culture, manufacturers and consumers have recognized some contrariness. This applies to contiguous concepts such as ethical manufacturing and ethical trading, recycling and remaking, and the maintenance of fashion distinction and profit. Design is capable of contributing to the resolution of social problems and may impact the transformation of every aspect of life. Victor Papanek (1971), the designer and educator whose life's work focused upon social and ecological responsibility, wrote that "design is basic to all human activities"; therefore, we might all hold the keys to solving some of the problems that confront us. Consider a manual windup computer made for use in the developing world,[10] or the research from The Helen Hamlyn Research Centre on aging at the Royal College of Art, or the performance clothing company Patagonia that intends to produce all of its clothing from materials that have been or can be recycled by 2010 (Tran, 2006); they all demonstrate how functional design advances social life and separates design from the sexy patina that has distinguished it since the optimism of the Reagan and Thatcher years. Design may improve function. Yet the essence of fashion design is inescapably idealist. The finest of examples that are supposed to be visually enhanced through wear and tear (e.g., denim jeans or polo shirts), accomplish excursions toward utopian themes where life is improved either temporarily or permanently through the resolve of emotional and physical inconsistencies. Fashion has a further response as a contrivance of beauty and personality. It is a promise of free and unhindered passage, transforming fashion wearers into exquisite dissenting objects. Sustainable fashion garments are redeemed when they possess contradictions of fashion meaning and the prowess of being meaningful. It is not that garments are expected to expose equivalencies; seductive tropes of fashion garments such as desire and glamour tend to be aesthetically innate, whereas sustainable features are profoundly constructed and tend not to represent beauty. This amalgamation of characteristics encapsulates how fashion garments transgress mainstream fashion's Fordian production for the stylistic nonrepeatability of a Xuly Bët dress and fabric abstracted in the recycling. It is important to remember that the character of sustainable fashion goes beyond the material object to a process of devel-

FIGURE 10.2. Xuly Bët integrates new garments with secondhand garments. (Photo by Fashion-Stock.com.)

opment that helps to define the very nature of the fashion garment in its campaigning role against resource depletion.

Globalize It

As Earth tailspins toward possible environmental catastrophe, the thoughts and speculations of inventor, architect, engineer, cosmologist, and most importantly, conceiver of "Spaceship Earth," Buckminster Fuller (1963) and later the insight of how systems would make paradigm shifts, have further been articulated by Fritjof Capra (1984). Capra, the physicist and systems theorist who founded the Center for Ecoliteracy in Berkeley, California, comments that the application of these became the endeavor of various subcultural groups such as the New Agers, Travelers, and Neo-Hippies.

I want to go back to the rather stringent yet prophetic thinker Thomas Malthus (1798, 1999), the eighteenth-century theoretician of the political economy whose thoughts on population control are now thought to be somewhat problematic but do serve as a transcendental template in determining problems with fashion sustainability. Malthus's general thesis offered ideas about population growth and imbalances with food supplies. Malthus's idea that populations increase geometrically and that food supplies may increase arithmetically have some relevance to sustainability.[11]

Much of these ideas are reflected in the difficulties that much of the developing world presently experiences in the cultivation of food for its own consumption. The subsistence level on which countries such as Lesotho, Haiti, Rwanda, Bangladesh, Myanmar, Sierra Leone, and Burkina Faso are constrained to survive parallels the developed world's populations, plentiful foods, and manufactured objects that define its success. If for a moment we substitute food for manufactured objects (e.g., clothes), populations and objects would share geometric increases because the cycle of manufactured goods are less likely to suffer from catastrophes such as war, disease, and famine, which Malthus mentions as factors that may affect the production of food. Annually, governments publish figures for their gross national production; such figures are used to formulate comparison with previous year's productivity and to make projections for future planning. Retail figures have become an instant indicator of how well the economy is doing. Retailers are particularly adept at speculating and reporting actual retail figures. Retail figures are believed to be an assured method of assessing recent and present market confidence. Indeed, the greater the demand for manufactured goods, the more we assume the economy is in favorable shape. If all things were equal, this thinking would be correct; however, as Malthus cautioned, things are never equal.

Recycled, recut, do-it-yourself, and exchanged products may hinder account of the true level of activity, creative or otherwise. Some sustainable production levels may circumvent a number of textile and apparel production stages. It is accepted by most governments, media, and commercial enterprises that we live in a global village. In fact, we live in a world were the dominating ideology, capitalism, has mannered all aspirations, events, structures, and cultural and creative outcomes of society.

Since the European enlightenment during the eighteenth century and the advent of feudalism's metathesis capitalism, any potential to question the political basis of capitalism has failed. The common logic that governs capitalism is not escapable; this is because capitalism pursues a mono-focal viewpoint held by various chiefdoms that rise out of capitalist behaviors. Such behaviors are monolithic yet desirable, particularly if humankind is to realize constant improvements to material lifestyle. Fashion is a superlative indicator of capitalist activity. Indeed, any perusal of popular print media shows that fashion in its widest sense is elegantly positioned to straddle resonant beliefs and disparate geographic territories. Furthermore, fashion's networks are ordered in the reality of the everyday and in the dream of utopia, internally and externally, locally and globally.

Immanuel Wallerstein (1999), the sociologist and ardent critic of globalization, astutely notes that globalization is not new; globalization, according to Wallerstein, has its basis in the exploration of other cultures for the purpose of trade. We know that amongst the items traded during the last 500 years, cultural exchange, information, ideas, talent, and people have superseded designed material objects, although as a culture, we are more accommodating of the foreign object and less so to the foreigner. The original scope and principle of globalization has only recently altered (e.g., trade tariffs), and even though the numbers of items traded and the countries involved in globalization have increased, well over 55 percent of the world's population lives an urban existence (United Nations Educational, Scientifica, and Cultural Organization, or UNESCO). To thrive, fashion needs the urban environment; therefore, in terms of maximization the job of colonialism (i.e., capitalism's concomitant) is half done. Both fashion and colonialism attempt to inflict their colors and brands upon the world map. There are strong nonacademic arguments why and how fashion and colonialism have "civilized" the rest of the world with a distinctly "better" way of doing things. The problem with colonialism is methodology; it is limited and reductive, and it hinders the creativity of the subjugated. The problem with fashion is that it organizes the passing of time, hence its link to death (Leopardi, 1824/2004). However, both take our world forward, although the directions may be debatable.[12]

The fashion industry seems to be trapped in the uncertainty of development and a lack of methodological purpose. It is not that the fashion industry does not recognize that fashion change and sociological change are entangled; the issue is one of incompatibility and faux equilibrium between consumer demand and political and institutional values and beliefs. Fashion evolves through dissonance, an opposition to seemingly permanent and stable conditions. Bridging the gap between material fashions, dissonance allows role-play to take place. If products are to be continually renewed, the fashion industry needs dissonance. Using fashion image and objects, the fashion industry attempts to (re)interpret culture and provide a vigilant speculation of what tendencies the public might need. The fashion industry consists of all manner of companies that include designer companies; however, these do not act as a self supporting-system. Designer companies that operate at the very sharp end of the innovation curve do so in the glare of speculation and without support of bourgeois ideals of less innovative companies that must, in an absolutist sense, adopt the practice.

Advocates

In his book *Al Muqaddimah: The Introduction to History* (1967), the great fourteenth-century Arab scholar Ibn Khaldun sets up the opposition of nomads and those settled in urban locales. In the twenty-first century, the ideologically peripheral have become the nomads, sampling different regimes while maintaining their post-humanistic position that provides support of human ecology. Nomads challenge fashion's core tropes and determinations of the larger culture's use and abuse the world's resources. It is perhaps a truism that any demonstrative sustainable practice is something of *evangelical* protest, but for those who wish to know, the sustainable garment asks questions about everyone involved in the design and production and wearing process. Change within fashion is presided over by fashion's mercantile groups who collaborate in the development of style tendencies. Generally, fashion change ignores its esoteric character that is determined by a need to react to culture's significant incidences, such as human and civil rights, ecology, and discrimination. The constraint upon this action is that fashion is delimited by a need to produce items and consequences that are profitable. Where fashion includes social issues in its repertoire, it does so in temporary and superficial ways. The lack of depth or joined-up sustainable practice afforded by the world's leading fashion designers is evidenced in the "Do the (RED) thing" initiative to eliminate AIDS in Africa, partnered by Gap, Converse, and Emporio Armani. Do the (RED) thing" is not strategized with broad programs of recycled products, optimization of waste, or careful selection of promotion images that include others and do not offend (also see Chapter 2). Eclipsed by a quest to produce more products mitigated by biannual fashion presentations and multi-lined branding, more objects, not less, have become the mantra of modernity; fashion continues to ignore the questions raised by advocates of deep sustainability. In understanding the problem as one of insecurity, it is peculiar that fashion does not revel in this circumstance; after all, fashion is skilled in the illusion of uncertainty and organized to resist truths about the struggle of human existence and development.[13]

Utopian Dreamers

Piercing the future with the fervor of a utopian faction motivated not for profit but for the grand gesture, groups such as Yomango and Serpica Naro, to be discussed below, ask questions about the fashion disconnect with individualism. Their attempts at utopianism, despite being only gestures, provide useful experiments into alternative consumptive practices and stimulate the debate of dissonant actions.

Just as postmodernity questioned and inevitably altered taste, advocates of new ways of practicing design, production, and consumption are compelled to question concepts of consumption that situate the manufactured object into obscurity. The assertion that fashion, once imbued in garments, possesses magical qualities is no longer plausible. Concept now drives change; the prominence of taste, mode, and, indeed, trend are underrepresented by the "epiphany" of concept, which is the consequence of unearthing issues of deep sustainability.

Yomango

Yomango means, in Spanish slang, "I steal." Less a collection than an attitude, Yomango ignores constrictions of the legal and illegal. Living free and not paying, Yomango hacks into the false security of fashion distribution, retail, and media; it does this by eroding the accumulation of garments existing in stores. Through attempts to subvert the traditional retail moment by replacing the purchase of garments with "free" clothes purloined from stores, clothes become the device that represents the confrontation of unequal compensation, an inadequate portrayal of culture.

Yomango's intervention makes a significant modification to the sociology of consumption. Instead of obsessing about the act of purchase, the act of using and reusing garments provides a conspicuous attempt to disrupt the fashion system and transfer potency to the individual.

What's Mine Is Yours

Other more passive but nonetheless potent advocates have launched initiatives to distribute, at no cost, clothes for reuse. One idea is that garments are placed in a public place to be taken at will, worn, then returned for a new wearer to adopt. The only rule is that the adopter must leave his or her garment before taking the found garment. The whatsmineisyours.com Web site operates in a similar way. The goal of Anti-Apathy, the London-based collective, is to promote awareness and action for positive social change by illuminating the politics and economics behind consumption. Fashions, along with food, are targets of its focus. Its work includes the Fashion Addict Experiment, in which 12 individuals were asked to forgo their usual fashion shopping for new clothes; instead, the subjects were tasked to seek out recycled, reconditioned, organic, or nonsweatshop garments. Another project, Worn Again, created training shoes from recycled quilts and prison blankets.

Serpica Naro

Similar to Linux (i.e., the computing operating system that offers free software and nonexistent intellectual property rights), Serpica Naro uses an open source method to extend the sharing of clothing. Bringing openness to the fashion system, it invites new ways of thinking about creativity, sustainability, and authenticity around the demand of fashion garments. This is an exciting idea; it provides respite from the leader-follower dichotomy that has subdued expression and possibility. The new perspective ushers in a creative process that cannot be planned or controlled. The future of design might be produced by a 12-year-old from Colombo, Sri Lanka, her 10 friends will see her work on MySpace.com. The 12-year-old's designs will inspire individuals outside her circle. One might be a professional designer working in Paris who copies the designs for a collection. In moving toward a reevaluation of fashion, we enter a situation where

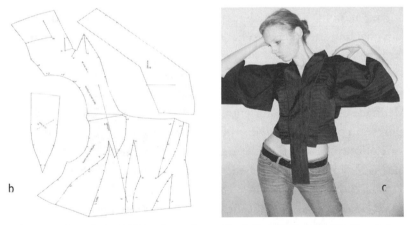

FIGURE 10.3. The Web site SHOWstudio.com has archived slopers by important fashion designers, encouraging the public to make clothes and send in pictures of themselves wearing clothes made using the garment slopers offered on their site. This screenshot (a), for example, shares an Alexander McQueen pattern (b) and a photo of a model showing the finished garment (c). (Courtesy of SHOWstudio.com.)

production patterns by professionals and amateurs are freely available to share.

Similarly, SHOWstudio.com, a fashion culture Web site, has archived slopers by important fashion designers Alexander McQueen, John Galliano, Junya Watanabe, and Yohji Yamamoto, thereby encouraging the public to make clothes and send in pictures of themselves wearing clothes made using the garment slopers offered on the site. This implies two things: The most suitable infrastructure for sharing fashion designs exist over net-based time and space; and, after the amateur has been involved in the design process, brand, and professional design can remain inviolate.

[RE_TALL]iation

Empowerment is the feature of a series of workshops titled RE_TALL]iation by the Swedish artist Otto von Busch. With participants ranging from Norwegian fashion designers to art collectives to shoe manufacturers, von Busch's ideas concern simple alterations to original designs. The initial purpose of the design is rerouted, therefore enabling the wearer to have extended the use and enjoyment of the garment.

Von Bush's project explored alternative paths and mechanisms of fashion creation, production, and distribution. Conducted at the Merimetsa Rehabilitation Centre in Estonia, the project produced garments in collaboration with the patients. Every garment bears two inscriptions: the visual signature of the maker and the experience of the maker, invisible and etched into the production of the garment.

The clothes were sold at a local shop. These examples of what is called "slow design" significantly contrast with mainstream fashion's attempts at sustainable design. Slow design's reevaluation of manufacture offers less literal design specifications than those of mass manufacture. Furthermore, slow design dislodges the notion of any central ownership of design. The concept of slow design allows us to glimpse what could be possible if sustainability were a total and encircling action.

Creating Process and Praxis Models

Using pressure groups and artists as the solution for excellent process and praxis is problematic, if only for the incompleteness of their practice. Process refers to design development and praxis, the distinctiveness of the fashion industry in relation to other design fields and society. Generally, the dialectic concludes that fashion and fashion garments are not considered vital or significant to political and social life. This position can also be viewed as commentary about the training of fashion designers and the position of fashion within the academy. This view is based on its underevaluation of fashion, a reliance upon surface, visual stimulation and simulation, and a prudent use of ethical causes and underdeveloped thinking about the natural or organic as placatory to profits. If fashion is to achieve its purpose as articulator of agendas for the creation and use of garments that improve our existence, it must refashion itself from the ground up. The foundation for fashion design must be [re]valued for its conscience and opportunities.

A proposal of a new self-awareness has been at the basis of architectural practice. Architects are all too aware of the importance of their profession, claiming that buildings are often substantial economic, cultural, and social investments, and pointing out that individuals occasionally die during construction. Clearly, fashion is not yet able to apply methods that are rigorous and valid in any part of its predesign, design, and development processes. Fashion design's new territory is impressed over the old principles that upheld fashion as a feminine field and against masculine fields of technology and science. Currently, fashion design lacks the rigor of a professional discipline. Fashion design must affect methods that are rigorous, valid, and intended in the technocratic sense and also in terms a humanistic, universalistic perspective.

The phenomenological structure and operation of fashion design has applications to a number of situations. It is undoubted that the role of the fashion designer has become somewhat eclipsed by three R's of sustainability: reduce, reuse, and restyle. These have had effect on design development. For influential designers the three R's have become additional design resources, even though the effect has been to increasingly articulate retrospection as fashion. The requirement for subsistence and enunciation of the fashion design role will require the designer to act as a processor of phenomena. In fact, fashion designers do not produce fashion; fashion is an unmanageable article, and therefore one deduces that fashion is constructed by people wearing the clothes, who may, in fact, be the constructors of design policy. This goes further than the current process model, which seats the fashion designer as limited to a process where the governing factors are trend forecasting, merchandising reports, trade shows, and filtered highlights from the latest art exhibition, pop bands, and other descriptors of the zeitgeist. This methodology is insufficient and is not reflective of our images and the issues that frame them. It is undeniable that the issues fashion might affect are immense; making sense of such issues requires a discussion of profound depth. This postulation provides the opportunity to investigate and expand upon the nature of fashion's theory and praxis model.

Sustainable Design Strategies for Fashion

If we accept that the design process employs cognition and intuitive sense, we must accept without exemplary theoretical components that the design process remains incomplete. The proposition of using theory to interrupt the flow of intuition and intellect fuels the creative process by adding to the nonchartable unpredictably of the creative act. In its focus, theory is absorbed with the qualitative nature of behavior; behavior may be universal as developed in concepts like modernism, postmodernism, deconstructionism, or in close focus of theories like symbolism interaction, adoption theory, or object theory.

Sustainable design is not a creative decision; rather, it is privileged by what model of the world society accepts. In one position are romantics favoring revivalism, utopianism, and supporting continuity; in the other position are industrial representations favoring mass consumption and industrialized complexity. Indeed, the role of creating and styling fashion products is now divided between technically led products and artistically led products. This divide continues and is made significant through the elaboration of fashion object versus apparel object; each requires quite different design approaches, although to some degree they remain interchangeable. This is because objects are never neutral; affixed ideologies are always provisional.

The Future of Sustainable Fashion

Certainly, the fashion industry, including consumers of fashion, must make an evolutionary step to react favorably in support of fashion's subjective character. This might indicate that fashion develops slow design as part of a mixed strategy consisting of pragmatic structural and behavioral proceedings. Slow design must use design and post-design, as shown in Otto von Busch's work and to some extent in Issey Miyake's A-POC line, a methodology that allows new purpose to be generated and new experiences formed.[14] Potentially, slow design poses the methodological revolution for fashion design practice; it supports the reduction of resources in industry, trade, and the environment. Slow design is the mind-set that decelerates the increased velocity of design, production, and consumption. Faced with fast fashion, the imposition of designers producing multiple lines, and the expansion of mainstream fashion into sites such as Iceland, the Far East, Turkey, and New Zealand has formed a surplus of designers, clothes, and ideas. Juilet Schor (1999) reminds us that consumer culture has dumbed down culture and has yielded few true human satisfactions. Yet fashion situated within apparel continues to benefit consumers beyond a purely material standpoint. When slow design is added as a precept to fashion, fashion's metabolism for function, theme, quality, profit, space, and image might be likened to an expansion of concept rather than a reduction of the medium. Slow design probes the specifics of traditional or accepted design process. Its basic tenets include the following:

- Clothes design is for people and their dreams and their situations.
- Clothes designs must be created locally and shared globally.
- Individuals must negotiate visual values such as glamour and quality.
- Clothes designers must design for society's good as well as for corporate profit.
- Design must be positioned centrally in economic and business models.
- Clothes design management processes must build in regenerative benefits for people and the environment.

Although her proposition is contradictory, the California-based designer Linda Loudermilk has launched her line "Luxury Eco" with the ambition to "give eco glamour legs, a fabulous look and a slammin' attitude that stops traffic and shouts the message: eco can be edgy, loud, fun, playful, feminine (or not) and hyper-cool. All created by meticulously researched sustainable business practices and fair labor standards" (Loudermilk, n.d.).

Slow design in fashion is not an attempt to bypass fashion; rather, it is a critique of fashion that seeks to uphold the essence of fashion. "Fashion" might not even be the correct term to use when referring to the creation of this new form. As the Loudermilk example shows, sustainable fashion is oxymoronic and is therefore an unsafe position. The idea that fashion might be disbanded or slowed down is not mentioned.

Other than using "sustainable fabrics" and being "fair" to workers,

FIGURE 10.4. Although her proposition is contradictory, the California-based designer Linda Loudermilk aims to blend fashion with sustainable design, production, and business practices through her Luxury Eco line. (Courtesy of Fairchild Publications, Inc.)

sustainable fashion designers are reluctant to pose profound questions about the fashion system or its motives as an alternative system. Distinguishing clothing from fashion, slowness from speed, and the textured from the streamlined will allow us to appreciate the experience of wearing clothes and affixing personal rather than mass characterizations of fashion. The materials that haute couture garments are made from comprehensively outlast the preeminence of the garments styling. Ready-to-wear garments are similar to couture, though the sheer numbers of ready-to-wear sales are many times more calamitous to quality of life on this planet.

However, ready-to-wear garments are more harmonious than couture, because fashion and design are more harmonious when fabrics are less exclusive. Where fashion and design are osmotic, design and material become close to equilibrium and a state of design veracity.

Yet slow design goes further; it charges designers to think about the materials and design as simple statements that are not concerned with the transient fragility of garments. Garments formed using slow design relinquish much of the character that is present in garments that are deemed fashionable. Fashion, and therefore the role of the fashion designer as well, is contrary to the edict of slow design. Traditionally, designers are charged to coordinate the trends and themes of the everyday and transform these into profits. The designer is something of an authoritarian figure, abiding by the principles of the capitalistic apparatus; in contrast, the designer of slow fashion has to resolve his or her findings with both consumers and the larger audience. If slow design is to disconnect from the mainstream fashion, it must not mirror or even abstract mainstream fashion but confirm an autonomous system. The question of how sustainable design might disconnect from mainstream fashion is exceedingly difficult to navigate. The very poorest boundaries of both sustainable design and mainstream design will continue to interfere and interface with each other until sustainable fashion is able to create boundaries demarcated by infrastructures, praxis, and the ideologies that set the two apart.

Conclusion

Our present is occupied with agendas that are unavoidable. In many ways we are living our future in the present; the luxury of excess that we have enjoyed was sequestrated from the future. The quest for sustainable practice has been characterized by our excessive indulgences and delusional planning that has framed the evolution of fashion in its broadest sense. The impediment of design is to improve, and objects that improve upon the last set of objects punctuate progress toward a utopian and therefore unattainable state; such is the progress of humankind. This is the paradox of sustainable fashion design. Fashion's scorn for itself is uncovered in its haste to discard objects for new and improved versions. The quandary is of description and categoriza-tion of objects and the structure they subsist in. If consumer practice is to become more ecologically responsible, concepts of fashion are less likely to fit. How far are we from fully adopting a benign form of clothing that disregards the function and aesthetics of fashion for sus-tainability?

In French fashion, *récupération* has become a long-lasting trend; designers Xuly Bët and Martin Margiela integrated new garments with secondhand garments while becoming one of the most aesthetic and ideologically important fashion brands. In effect, these designers have jammed the fashion system and have opened a fissure pertinent of our precarious existence.

The sustainable age is a time to react with innovation, to do empirical and theoretical work that will nourish creativity. If this work is not done, we stand the risk of becoming confined in prac-tices that we know well but recognize as oppositional. The answer may be to collapse the dialectic by melding sustainability and fashion as a political rather than a commercial maneuver that strategizes caring about everything. The immediate choice for the fashion industry and consumers is to decide whether the existing fashion system is retained.

Endnotes

1. CIRFS: International Rayon and Synthetic Fibers Committee.
2. Famously the Swedish "fast fashion" giant H&M has successfully launched a number of *exclusive* fashion collections designed by guest "celebrity" designers, including Stella McCartney and Karl Lagerfeld, and Viktor & Rolf.
3. Clothing is the nomenclature for functional garments as opposed to aesthetic and emotional garments that tend to be defined as being fashion(able). The clothing sector that has led developments in sustainability, in particular the Cali-fornia-based outdoor clothing company Patagonia, has taken a lead in recycling. Famously Patagonia has recycled plastic drinking bottles into fleece garments;

this contrasts with fashion companies that have ventured beyond recycling used garments or using organic cotton.

4. The term "leading fashion companies" refers to, and is distinct from, fashion houses based in New York, Paris, or Milan that feature regularly in the editorial and advertising pages of leading fashion magazines.

5. The true cost of apparel is offset by globalization and technology. Giant factories in Thailand, China, and Vietnam, holding up to 25,000 workers and technological advances in production, have conspired to undercut the basic salary of the American worker by almost 80 percent.

6. Triangular sustainability also refers to institutional, economic, and ecological sustainable practices.

7. Post-humanism refers to the philosophical position that humans are not above nature and therefore do not possess any rights of providence over nature. See *Giles Deleuze & Felix Guattari, Anti-Oedipus: Capitalism and Schizophrenia.* Viking: New York, 1977.

8. In 2000 Levi's publicized its Engineered Jeans as featuring "organic cut," yet the garment label did not mention the use of organic cotton. Californian designer Linda Loudermilk's Luxury Eco label is an example of a company coming to terms with opposing concepts and their incompatibility, rather than mounting an effusive discourse of new design opportunities.

9. There is little integrity in companies that do not employ systemic and joined-up ethical and therefore sustainable practice. See Nick Buckley's "Why I'll Never Buy a Pair of Levi's Again," *The Mail on Sunday,* November 27, 1994, pp. 37–38.

10. In 2005 "Green Machine" was showcased for the first time by MIT's Nicholas Negroponte at the United Nation's Internet summit in Tunis. At $100, the laptop, which was due in production within a year, is powered with a wind-up crank, has very low power consumption, and will let children interact with each other while learning.

11. Malthus's idea that populations increase geometrically (1, 2, 4, 8, 10, 20, 40) while food supplies increase arithmetically (1, 2, 3, 4, 5, 6, 7, 8, 9) have some relevance to sustainability. Not forsaking built-in supply-and-demand controls of the marketplace, the production of manufactured goods are also produced arithmetically. Growth in fashion and clothing garments could be planned to shadow

population growth. Production planning has been a feature of the quota system that regulates the importation of garments that have been manufactured off-shore. Oversupply in the market results in the downward pricing and upward demand of garments.

12. See Giacomo Leopardi, "The Dialogue of Fashion and Death from the Moral Essays" (1824). Fashion and Death are in conversation with each other at a funeral. Fashion reminds Death that they are sisters, daughters of Decay. Fashion comments, "I was saying that our common nature and custom is continually to change the world people to put up every day with a thousand difficulties and a thousand discomforts."

13. The extreme precariousness of our times is outlined by AIDS, war, and poverty; sustainability provides a method of counteracting the uncertainties of modern living.

14. A-POC is a conceptual line of clothes made by the Japanese clothes designer Issey Miyake. A-POC is an acronym for "a piece of cloth." In the store, the customer cuts his or her sweater, dress, skirt, or sleeves to the length he or she desires. The roll of knit is made on a computerized industrial knitting machine; however, the actual process remains proprietary.

References

Barthes, R. (1983). *The fashion system*. Ward, M., & Howard, R. (Trans.) New York: Hill.

Fuller, B. (1963). *Operating manual for spaceship earth*. New York: E.P. Dutton & Co.

Brenton, A. (1960). *Nadja*. (Trans.) Richard Howard. New York: Grove.

Capra, F. (1984). *The turning point: science, society, and the rising culture*. Capra, F., & Pauli, G. (Eds.). New York: Bantam Books.

Chartered Society of Designers. (2006). Stern words: Chartered Society of Designers responds to the Stern Review Report on the Economics of Climate Change. *FX: The Business of Design*. Retrieved July 12, 2007, from http://www.fxmagazine.co.uk/story.asp?storycode=915

Ecological tax reform. (1995). *Steering Business toward Sustainability* (pp. 108–24). Tokyo: United Nations University.

Chen, C., and Lewis, V. D. (2006). The life of a piece of cloth: Developing garment into a sustainable service system. *International Journal of Environmental, Cultural, Economic and Social Sustainability, 2,* 197–208.

Da Silva Graciete, M. (1999). Design management for the textile industry, presented at The European Academy of Design in Design Cultures, Sheffield Hallam University.

Derrida, J. (1976). *Of grammatology.* Gayatri, C. S. (Trans.). Baltimore: John Hopkins University Press.

Koslowski, P. (2002). Ethics in capitalism. In *Ethics and the Future of Capitalism.* Gasparski, Z. (Ed.; pp. 42–67). Piscataway, NJ: Transaction Publishers.

Hebdige, D. (1989). *Hiding in the light: on images and things.* London: Routledge.

Jacobs, P. M. (1994). Xuly Bët: A brother from the "mother" turns fashion inside out. In *Essence Magazine 26.*

Khald n, I. (1967). *The muqaddimah: An introduction to history.* Rosenthal F. (Trans.) Dawood, N. J. (Ed.). Princeton University Press. (Abridged).

Kruglanski, A. (2005). Precarity explained to kids (a medley): Cut, paste, and articulated (somewhat). In *The Journal of Aesthetics & Protest, 1*(4), 103–117 .

Leopardi, G. (1824/2004). The dialogue of fashion and death. Purdy, D. L. (Ed.) In *The rise of fashion: a reader.* University of Minnesota Press.

Lipovesky, G. (1994). *The empire of fashion: dressing modern democracy.* Princeton, NJ: Princeton University Press.

Loudermilk, L. (n.d.). Mission statement. Retrieved from http://www.lindaloudermilk.com/

Malthus, T., (1789/1999). First essay on population. Gilbert, G. (Ed.). Oxford: Oxford University Press.

Papanek, V. (1971). *Design for the real world: Human ecology and social change.* New York: Pantheon Books.

Ross, A. (1997). *No sweat: fashion, free trade and the rights of garment workers.* New York: Verso.

Schor, J. (1999.) *The overspent American: Why we want what we don't need.* New York: Harper Perennial.

Simmel, G. (1972). *Georg Simmel on individuality and social forms.* (Heritage of Sociology Series). Donald N. L. (Ed.), Chicago: University of Chicago Press.

Stern, N. (2006, October 30). The Stern review report on the economics of climate change. London: United Kingdom Treasury.

Sustainable Development Department Food and Agriculture Organization of the United Nations. (2001, June). World Summit on Sustainable Development, Johannesburg 2002.

Veblen, T. (1899). *The theory of the leisure class: An economic study of institutions.* New York: The Macmillan Company.

Wallerstein, I. (1999). Globalization or the age of transition? A long-term view of the trajectory of the world-system. Retrieved from http://www.binghamton.edu /fbc/iwtrajws.htm

Williams, C. (2000, February 6). These old denims? In real life. In *The Independent on Sunday.* London, p. 1.

Martex Fiber Southern Corp,
Eco2Cotton™ by Jimtex Yarns™, In2Green™
Interview by Connie Ulasewicz, April 2007

Section 2 was introduced with the idea that there are many ways to think about how fashion is produced and the impact of production and related economic processes on sustainability. The following questions were posed:

- Fashion goods are consumable, thus waste seems inevitable—or is it?
- Are there processes we can develop and implement that can reduce or eliminate the consequences of overconsumption?
- How can we overhaul our way of making more to sell more in order to keep the economic engine behind fashion functioning?

It is time to approach production and economic processes from a different angle, adjusting not just the ways of doing but also our ways of thinking. As Section 2 highlighted, the linear concept of beginning to end leaves many issues unsolved. From beginning to beginning is a more sustainable model, and there is a company championing this model. Martex Fiber Southern Corporation, (www.martexfiber. com) founded in 1974, is a leading U.S.-based manufacturer of recycled industrial textile waste products. Using Martex's recycled and pre-dyed fiber, Jimtex Yarns (www.jimtexyarns.com), founded in 1997, produces high quality, extremely economical cotton-blended, open-end yarns. Eco2Cotton™ (www.eco2cotton.com), launched in 2006, is a brand name for the yarns and woven and knitted products produced from Jimtex Yarns that are available for purchase by apparel companies and others seeking to produce and promote environmentally responsible products. The figure on page 265 displays the five-

(Courtesy of Martex Fiber.)

step process used within and between Martex Fiber's waste collection, Martex Fiber products and the Eco2Cotton™ by Jimtex Yarns.

Steps 1 and 2: Textile Waste Collection and Pre-Consumer Cuttings

Martex Fiber offers a waste removal collection service to its customers. Textile waste (e.g., seamer waste, table cuttings, and other remnants) are collected from mills and manufacturing facilities after the cut-and-sew process.

Step 3: Reprocessed Fiber

Preconsumer cuttings are sorted by grade and color. Martex Fiber processing equipment is then used to actually break down the fabrics and yarns into reprocessed fiber. Baled fiber is created and is sold for use in a variety of consumer markets, including mattresses and futons, undercarpet pads, component parts for automotive (e.g., sound insulation), and fill products for a variety of home furnishings.

Step 4: Regenerated Yarns

Using the recycled fiber, regenerated yarns are spun at Jimtex Yarns. Because the yarn originates from recycled, and in this case never before used, colored cotton apparel cuttings, the resulting yarn may have hints of several colors, but no new cotton dyeing is required. In the spinning process, the cotton fiber is blended with fibers, such as acrylic, polyester, and now even recycled polyester, to help with strength and to tweak the color. These regenerated, or "second-generation," yarns are appropriate for many knitting and weaving applications.

Step 5: Woven and Knit Products

Using regenerated fibers and yarns, the Eco2Cotton™ brand is positioned to highlight the eco characteristics of the yarns for a wide variety of finished products, including blankets, socks, T-shirts, and sweaters. The Eco2Cotton™ brand seeks to generate awareness at the consumer level regarding the economic and ecological savings its recycled products offer.

The following interview provides a closer look at the practices of this company. I am grateful for the time and information shared with me from Harry Matusow, president of Jimtex Yarns; Stefanie Zeldin, director of corporate marketing, Martex Fiber Southern Corp: and Lori Slater, design and production manager, In2green™.

How Is Your Company Involved in Sustainable Business Practices?
"We see our role as an innovator, seeking and finding new materials to convert into useful fiber grades, which often can replace or supplement staple fibers. We reprocess over 110 million pounds of textile waste a year," stated Matusow. His company, Martex Fiber Southern Corp., located in Spartanburg, South Carolina, has pioneered the introduction of an array of products and services, including innova-

tions in textile waste removal, baling, processing, transportation, and the development of a variety of textile waste by-products, such as battings and fillings for blankets or pillows. Martex collects textile waste, the excess from the sewing and cutting operations, which would normally be sent to landfill or incinerated, and extends the life cycle of these products.

As the textile and apparel manufacturers moved out of the United States, Martex Fiber needed to ensure it had enough waste material to maintain its business objectives. In 2004, a strategic partnership was developed with INVEX, a collector of textile waste with operations in Honduras and El Salvador. Jimtex Yarns is the only U.S. manufacturer of recycled yarns, made from materials generated from Martex Fiber in South Carolina and the Honduras operation. "Our process actually eliminates the growing and dyeing of cotton," said Zeldin. "If more companies made products from recycled materials, we would all feel better about our impact on the carbon footprint and wastewater management. For example, we can take green-colored T- shirt cuttings, sort and process them, and then spin them into green yarn. In doing this, we are offering a product that is far more ecological and economical that producing yarn and dyeing it.

We continue to strive to find new ways to 'upcycle' waste into nice and nicer end products and have virtually no waste from our operations."

What Is the Most Innovative Aspect of Your Company?
"I think the most romantic aspect of our business is the new product lines of Eco2Cotton™. The end consumer can buy, use, or wear the products and feel good because the products are ecologically responsible," said Matusow. The concept of beginning to beginning is a fundamental part of the Eco2Cotton™ business model. Zeldin explained, "While organic cotton production benefits from low pesticide utilization, it still requires large quantities of water and energy in the grow-

ing phase, and most end products will be dyed and wet finished with the resulting added cost to the product and the environment. Our cotton requires no new water to grow, no fertilizers, no insecticides, no dyes, and produces no waste."

Slater explained that when marketing the products, the hand feel and quality is what upscale stores are looking for. "Second-generation cotton actually feels softer after washing and makes environmental sense. We design it into products that make good fashion sense, which results in a greater value to the consumer."

What Is the Most Challenging Aspect of Your Business?
The two challenges expressed by Zeldin are diverse, inspirational, and in line with the vision of a sustainable future. First, Zeldin explains, "there is not yet a clear method of certification for what is sustainable. Consumers get confused with the terms organic, recycled, and sustainable. We need to better communicate that we are doing a good thing." As the apparel market recognizes the trend and demand for environmental responsibility, the Eco2Cotton™ brand will support apparel companies it serves by using hangtags, brochures, and possibly in-store displays to educate consumers on the benefits of recycled fiber.

A second challenge Slater expresses is, "keeping up with the requests." As more companies and consumers are looking for greener alternatives, value-added recycled products are in hot demand. Also, as businesses strive to understand and adapt their practices to become sustainable, they grasp at how to best use their resources to give the consumer something that will have a lasting benefit for the environment."

I believe that Martex Fiber Southern Corporation is a leader and will continue to innovate as they expand with their Eco2 products. Their sustainable strategy, informed by their desire to decrease the carbon footprint of their processes of production, is a beautiful example of the change required to make our fashion industry sustainable.

SECTION 3

The Environment, the Planet,
and the Materials Used in Fashion Making

INTRODUCTION

Clearly the time is now to implement strategies that generate environmental improvements for the planet. There is no need to explain this point here. Instead, the chapters in this section look at what is unique about fashion and the everyday components we take for granted. It is the hidden things that may have the most chance for the largest impact. Consumers are aware that hybrid cars are the choice for environmentally responsible transportation, but are they aware that the basic fibers that make up their clothing can also be part of meaningful and significant environmental change?

As you make choices regarding design approaches or sourcing decisions relative to fabrics, design approaches, and production techniques, how important is your awareness of current and future carbon footprints? We have heard over and over that the apparel industry is too large to turn around, that the sustainable segment doesn't have enough consumer acceptance around it to drive change, but how real and embedded are these excuses? We have also heard that the consumer is reluctant to pay the higher price for environmentally conscious fashion, or at least not enough of them are on board to drive change. Any business change may result in initial cost increases, but does the price need to be higher in the long run? Many companies have found that there are great savings over time when implementing decisions that assist the environmental goals. A follow-up question to consider is, what are the costs involved with *not* making a commitment to sustainability and lowering environmental impact?

We start the exploration of environmental situations and solutions by looking at how artists have addressed these challenges. In Chapter 11, Julia Schwartz and Gyöngy Laky open our eyes to the value of one-of-a-kind creative exploration through wearable art. Their unique perspective challenges us to separate ourselves from the over-production that the fashion industry helped to create in order to fully engage in the development of a more sustainable model. By posing examples, they generate ideas that designers and producers of fashion apparel can use as a springboard while creatively exploring sustainable solutions.

Taking us back to the fiber basics, in Chapter 12, Belinda Orzada and Mary Ann Moore evaluate the consequences and environmental concerns involved in the processes used to turn raw fiber into finished fabric. The environmental impact of all stages of textile processing from washing to dyeing and finishing are discussed. Worldwide, there are several proactive programs from industry and government that review and provide the textile industry with recommendations for meeting environmental regulations. The chapter contains a wealth of information to assist designers and manufacturers as they make critical sustainable fiber and yarn choices.

To further this understanding, Gail Baugh, in Chapter 13, explores new possibilities available to the fashion industry as we consider how to resolve the issue of sustainable fiber supply by using emerging fiber innovations. Environmentally responsible fiber choices are not limited to natural or organically grown fibers; they can also include fibers manufactured from renewable raw materials. Fiber choices are expanding, and this discussion provides a clear description and analysis of how best to understand their design potential and role in sustainable product development.

In Chapter 14, Shona Quinn introduces new methodologies for environmental and sustainable sourcing of textiles and apparel products. She explains how established sustainable apparel companies proactively reduce risk by encouraging suppliers to look at the entire system of activities and resources linked to their business, including but not limited to management, processes, raw materials, and community. She takes us through the key components to environmental stewardship and shares new models of sustainable sourcing.

Leaving us on a note of possibility, Wendyrosie Scott introduces several new directions that designers are investigating through the reuse and redesign of fashion products. With a glimpse into festivals and the world of vintage, Chapter 15 ends and begins our journey. Inspired by an awareness of how old becomes new again, we are encouraged to bring sustainable fashion into the realm of excitement and possibility.

Why Now?

- Customers are curious about how things are made. What kinds of pesticides and thus fossil fuels were used in the growing or manufacturing of the fiber? How much water did it take to produce the clothing?
- We all live on one planet and share the same air and water, yet environmental protection regulations and enforcement vary from country to country. There are no global standards.
- Recycled clothing no longer carries the stigma of being somebody else's old, used stuff.
- Textile technology has advanced, and factories can weave soft and supple fabrics from bamboo, hemp, seaweed, and other sturdy, renewable plants.
- It's fashionable.

JULIA SCHWARTZ is a freelance writer and designer based in San Francisco. After graduating from the design program at the University of California, Davis, she began selling her work under the moniker CHEESECREAM. Schwartz makes bags and custom garments from reclaimed fabric, using hand embroidery and classic finishing techniques to give each piece a unique, handmade quality. She draws inspiration for her embroidery patterns from scientific imagery, maps and diagrams, and historical textiles. See www.juliaschwartz.com

GYÖNGY LAKY is a San Francisco artist and professor emerita at the University of California, Davis. Her sculptures, temporary site-specific outdoor works, language sculptures, and vessels—composed principally of orchard debris, park trimmings, and street tree pruning—often reference environmental issues and sustainability. In addition, her activist art interests also address social justice and, more recently, antiwar sentiments. Her work appears in museum permanent collections in the United States and Europe. The Smithsonian Institution houses a collection of her personal papers, photographs, and documents at the Archives of American Art. See www.gyongylaky.com

CHAPTER II

Exploration of Materials and Concepts:
An Inspirational Overview

Julia Schwartz and Gyöngy Laky

The wearable art movement of the 1970s sparked an ongoing dialogue between the art world and the fashion industry that brings together the body, sculpture, and social issues in the context of fashion. How is art-to-wear addressing social and ecological issues? How can ideas from the art world encourage new ways of thinking in the industry? Is it possible for fashion to be both innovative and responsible? This chapter highlights the work of artists and designers employing methodologies and concepts drawn from diverse, nontraditional sources. From grapefruit peel sculptures to kitschy shoes with a feminist slant, the featured work guides an inquiry into the emotional and physical significance of clothing in daily life. In looking at the underlying themes of these pieces, designers may be inspired to shift fashion toward a more sustainable future through both material and concept.

The Wearable Art Movement: An Overview

The San Francisco Bay Area served as the epicenter of the wearable art revolution during the late 1960s and early 1970s, as it teemed with young artists bent on expressing their individuality via clothing. The term *wearable art* is commonly interchanged with *art-to-wear*, *artwear*, and *art couture*. Melissa Leventon, author and curator of the exhibit "Art to Wear: Fashion and Anti Fashion,"[1] defines wearable art as "an art of materials and processes whose creators are passionate about making art with textiles . . . artwear can be said to exist at the intersection between art, craft, and fashion. It is all three, but is owned wholly by none of them" (2005, p. 12). Wearable art found a home in museums, in galleries, and on runways.[2]

As many young people mobilized over political issues such as the Vietnam War, free speech, civil rights, and feminist concerns, the movement solidified. The Bay Area counterculture listened to icons such as Mario Savio and Timothy Leary as they made national headlines, adding to the dissemination of Bay Area styles to a wider audience. The hippie culture of the late 1960s and early 1970s asserted a growing concern for the environment, impacting clothing and methods of adornment. Touting individuality and liberty, hippies turned away from marketers, instead focusing on personalizing fashion through handcrafted embellishments. People became participants in hippie subculture by actively rethinking their wardrobes.

Interest in embroidery, patchwork, and dyeing grew along with the hippie culture, fueling the wearable art movement's creative vocabulary. During this time, artists began to look at techniques and traditions that had fallen by the wayside during the technological advances in fiber science of the mid-twentieth century. Fiber artists turned away from synthetic fabrics, instead choosing cotton and wool, which could be dyed with organic materials. The general backlash against industrial production led to a resurgence of interest in many technical aspects of textile art, from hand dyeing to weaving and crocheting. The movement has been described as "the uncompromisingly high standards of workmanship and an insistence on the primacy of the fabrics that were to be created or embellished" (Constantine and Reuter, 1997, pp. 37–38). The San Francisco Bay Area's numerous textile programs helped foster and maintain this quality of craftsmanship. The region's diverse residents brought textiles of the Pacific Rim into museums and galleries for the first time,[3] nurturing an environment for multiculturalism. The exhibits and ethnic textiles became increasingly popular, and a growing interest in styles from around the globe helped engage a wider scope of people into the possibilities of fashion. This foray into the creative art of clothing may have ushered in the current trend of self-composed fashion, as consumers are no longer restricted to the head-to-toe designer look. Instead, fashion magazines encouraged mixing designer looks to achieve a personal style that expresses individual preferences. The prominence of fashion auteurs like Dior and Chanel was being challenged.

Corporate brands like Levi Strauss embraced the trend. In 1974, the famous denim company held a competition in which contestants were asked to send photos of their customized Levi's jeans and jackets. The national contest collected almost 10,000 slide entries, indicating the influence of the wearable art movement on pop culture. The winning garments were displayed in design and craft museums around the country in a traveling exhibition (Leventon, pp. 28 30). In this way, the wearable art movement trickled up from pop culture into the museums.

Wearable art that evolved from the initial flowering of the 1970s has earned textile art a spot in museums and craft galleries around the world, yet it remains marginalized, an awkward stepchild among these venues. Nevertheless, art-to-wear and related textile sculptures serve as important visual mediators for artists' philosophies on fashion, identity, and lifestyle. They serve designers with tools for creative thinking and serve the art world with a continuing conversation about the individual's experience in society.

Assessing the Creative Process

The creative work described in this chapter can be broken down into five areas of consideration: assessing material options, material sourcing, alternative concepts for production, conveying a message, and impacts and implications. The following sections in this chapter highlight the individual methodologies and concerns of textile artists within these aspects of production.

In looking for raw materials, one can make conscious choices for a more environmentally sound and sustainable focus within the fashion industry. Designers face a myriad of options for textiles but largely pass over the alternative resources that many art-to-wear practitioners embrace. The following section takes a closer look at artists who have reassessed the potential of their materials and methods in addressing environmental issues and social concerns.

Where does a product end its useful life? Is there a way to extend the life of objects that have lost their intrinsic or popular values or have been worn out? Is there a way to preplan an extension to the life cycle of clothing? The term *life cycle* is often used when describing the stages of plants and animals, but its theoretical basis, that a being or an object follows a chartable path of growth and decline that ultimately results in death, can be applied to nonliving consumables and objects too. By looking at an inanimate item as a living entity, from its creation to productive use to a final destination, designers can identify areas where change is possible and important. Furthermore, authors William McDonough and Michael Braungart suggest the "cycle" is not even an accurate model; rather, they suggest that products be assessed as part of a continual loop where components are reformed into new products rather than simply "dying" (2002, pp.27–28). Similarly, how can designers predict future uses for a product before it is put into production? How can we expand on the new trend toward a more responsible and sustainable industry?[4]

Material Options

The following artists draw materials from highly nontraditional sources. They serve as examples for what is possible when thinking outside normal parameters.

The Artist in Residence Program at Sanitary Fill Company in San Francisco has hosted over 58 artists since its inception in 1990. Artists specializing in diverse mediums, ranging from textile art to photography to metal sculpture, come together to glean materials and inspiration from a massive and ever-growing collection of discarded items. It is a veritable treasure trove to those who are accepted into the program; artists are given free reign over the dump's raw materials, and a fully equipped studio space aids in turning the junk into something worthy of a new life. The three-month program ends with an on-site public reception. All works, including the wearable art of Daphne Ruff and Estelle Akamine, are posted on the Sanitary Fill Company's Web site for archival purposes, and large pieces are displayed in an extensive sculpture garden (Norcal, 2006). The Sanitary Fill Company proudly displays work made in the program, as it informs the public about the amount of usable goods and raw materials that are discarded each year. A clever quote painted on the side of a truck for The Body Shop reads: "Think before you throw. There's no such place as *away!*" And indeed, the recycling center is the sad "away" location that society would rather ignore. In taking a trip to the dump, one realizes the direct impact humans have on the environment. According to the Environmental Protection Agency, rubber, leather, and textiles comprised 7 percent of goods discarded in landfills in 2003 (EPA, 2003).

Each of the artists in the San Francisco residency program has come away with a better understanding of the life cycle and the importance of reuse and innovative thinking.

Estelle Akamine participated in the Sanitary Fill Company's artist-in-residence program in 1993. Her outstanding craftsmanship and innovative use of materials for costume is apparent in the series of garments she made during the program. Akamine wove such ubiquitous materials as computer tape, shredded paper, and plastic bags into wearable art. Several of the garments she created were worn to the 1993 Black and White Ball, an annual formal event in San Francisco.

Akamine later approached corporations in San Francisco and collected waste material from their facilities; she then created a series of wearable art pieces based on each company (including The Sharper Image, among others). The garments were displayed in a parade down Market Street (Sorenson, 1996).[5] While Akamine's work remains strongly rooted in the wearable art genre, designers can draw

FIGURE 11.1. "Typewriter Ribbon Dress" by Estelle Akamine, 1993. Estelle Akamine created this garment as a part of her artist residency at the NorCal Sanitary Fill Company. (Photo by Judy Reed.)

FIGURE 11.2. NorCal Site, 1993. Though it may be dirty work, scavenging used materials can prove rewarding. Recycling plants, neighborhood swap meets, and thrift stores can yield an array of materials unavailable in typical stores. (Photo by Estelle Akamine.)

on her methodology as inspiration for sustainable fashions. She acquired raw materials by approaching established companies, and in taking their waste products for her creative purposes, she reduced their impact on the environment. Though Akamine chose ubiquitous office materials, her artful arrangement made them into something new, something unusual to adorn the body. Her work's underlying statement about industrial and office waste give the playful styles a dimension of meaning beyond clothing's normal boundaries. While designers tend to focus on the fashion industry for information about appropriate materials and interesting silhouettes, fashion artists like Akamine look everywhere. One-of-a-kind wearable art has the advantage of using odd and discarded materials, but larger manufacturers could take this same approach if raw scrap materials were consistently made available in the public forum.

Chakaia Booker's raw material falls on the far end of the spectrum:

For over a decade, she has been creating large-scale art pieces and garments out of used rubber tires. She takes a material that has seemingly outlived its use and reshapes it into a new form. Booker leaves textured and worn treads visible to indicate the material's industrial origin, but the sculptures and clothing she creates hardly resemble the stacks of tires at the dump. Instead, her large-scale sculptural forms echo a strong and sophisticated presence with subtle references to African tribal culture. Booker creates garments that echo her other works, turning her body into a moving sculpture.[6] Wall hangings like "It's So Hard to Be Green" (2000) transform a heap of tires into a dense, writhing textile form, alluding to yarns and snakelike forms in varying shades of charcoal, brown, and black (Glueck, 2006).

Booker's interest in harvesting tires formed out of a concern for the environment. From wall pieces and large freestanding sculptures to wearable art, Booker has honed her skills with a material guaranteed to stand the test of time. Since tires are so widely consumed and discarded, their presence in landfills is a constantly growing problem. As Matthew Guy Nichols noted: "Booker's often ominous rubber sculptures speak to the problematic persistence of industrial waste" (2004). Pieces like "(Wrench)(Wench)"—in which a sensual curve covered in strips of tire connect two wrench ends—juxtapose masculine and feminine imagery. The frilled curve is reminiscent of hair or a feather boa, and it seems to dance between the stoic ends of the wrench. When Booker clothes herself in tire materials, she presents a similar balance of playful and fierce imagery, utilizing long strands and small clippings of rubber pieced together in elaborate garments and accessories. She had been exploring reused materials for garments for many years. Early experiments in recycling and piecework resulted in "Remnant" (1991), a yellow vest covered in dried orange peels.

Similarly, fiber artist Jan Hopkins works with dried organic materials such as citrus peel, cantaloupe rind, kelp, and seedpods to give her sculptures a distinct texture and symbolic meaning (artist statement). Her work entitled "Dressed to the Nines"(2005) exemplifies a clever use of natural materials in artwork (see Figure 11.3). Hopkins uses grapefruit peel as a quilter might use fabric or leather: After drying and preparation is complete, the skins are delicately patchworked together into a three-dimensional form with waxed linen thread. The empty freestanding garment structures made with fruit peels gain an added level of meaning from the skin's immediately recognizable texture, which references its original function as a skin, a protective layer, and an organic vessel, and makes Hopkins' sculptures come alive with the richness of memory and association. Her work references both body forms and the garments that cover them. A grapefruit peel's dimpled texture, though tough and dry, is reminiscent of human pores and wrinkles.

Hopkins gleans materials that have seemingly outlived their main purpose (e.g., protecting the seeds of a grapefruit) for a second life in a new context. What can nature's bounty provide for a designer who looks beyond the obvious? Harvesting materials outside of the main-

FIGURE 11.3. "Dressed to the Nines," by Jan Hopkins, 2005, constructed with grapefruit peel, waxed linen, yellow cedar bark, and paper. Jan Hopkins's approach to materials and texture may provide inspiration for a reevaluation of fashion textiles. How can we glean more from the renewable resources in our midst? (Photo by Ken Rowe; courtesy of Mobilia Gallery.)

stream concept of natural materials may provide new opportunities for texture, color, and meaning in fashion. The mass market may never see a grapefruit peel garment, but visions such as these may suggest to designers that they can find alternative materials to accent and add value to clothing or accessories.

Material Sourcing

Given the inspiration for using alternative raw materials, where can designers go to find resources for larger-scale projects? There is a need to devise a new methodology for gathering and charting resources, a concise online database that operates on a national scale to connect designers with locally available materials.

Many waste exchange programs already exist on a local scale, but they cater to construction markets. Plastics, metal scraps, excess paint, and wood are traded for fair prices through these databases, which aim to reduce the dumping of useful materials in landfills. Though some include sections for textiles, it can be cumbersome to navigate through the other materials to find the desired sources.

Some communities have a physical site for connecting artists with scrap materials. San Francisco's Scroungers' Center for Reusable Art Parts (SCRAP) is hailed as a premier destination for students, teachers, artists, and designers in the San Francisco Bay Area and beyond.[7] Visitors find donated paper, textile, glass, and metal, as well as assorted miscellany. Partially used bolts of fabric and a thoughtfully organized scrap textile area compose over a third of the space; bins of buttons, buckles, D-rings, and metal scraps are displayed near a bookcase full of discontinued greeting cards and envelopes. Office supplies from defunct companies fill another aisle, and the far end of the warehouse is filled with shelves stocked with unused scientific jars and micropipettor tips, tile samples, and large pieces of glass and metal. It is a remarkable community "store" that fosters a creative spirit while providing a venue for used or remainder materials and postconsumer products with leftover potential. But where can a designer go to find 500 yards of remnant ribbon for a larger project?

Freecycle.org is an outstanding Web site that could serve as a model regarding the future transfer of scrap materials for fashion purposes. The group provides a forum for the free transfer of used materials and goods among community members, in the manner of a virtual flea market. As a national Web site, it helps visitors quickly find a local "freecycle" group to join. The Web site promotes trading used goods instead of sending them to the dump, and members can join local groups for information on events and available items.[8] For example, on a given day the group may receive postings for available scrap material or requests for old knit garments. The freecycle network trades everything from furniture to mix tapes, but a fashion-based subset of the organization could spark opportunities within the textile industry.

The Waste Exchange, a New Zealand-based recycling program, is a similar online database for finding and connecting used materials with the public.[9] Though the program operates on a local scale, again catering mostly to plastics and construction supplies, it serves as another excellent model for future online resource lists because it gives detailed descriptions of available materials, including their location, availability, and future availability. Some materials are continually available, while others are only listed for a short time. In the fashion industry, perennially available materials might include industrial cuttings, while goods such as damaged and outdated fabric might be available for a limited time. If scrap textiles and overstocked notions could be charted in a similar method, limited-run designers could take advantage of high-quality and surprisingly novel materials that might otherwise end up in a landfill. While vintage fabric dealers already exist on a small scale, new sites catering specifically to fabrics and the fashion industry are needed to fuel the current interest in alternative and environmentally friendly resources.

Of course, the repurposing of these new materials in the fashion industry will direct a reevaluation of handling and compiling the raw goods. Considerations would then include laying out scraps of material for cutting, negotiating around worn or damaged areas of fabric, and patching pieces efficiently. Small-scale designers may benefit the most from the influx of quality scrap materials, as they do not use the same cutting and layout methods employed in factories.[10]

Concepts for Production

From architecture to fashion, artist and designer Andrea Zittel has produced numerous products relating to human comfort and safety. Each project blurs the line between art and design, raising the question: Is it feasible to live in a piece of conceptual art?

Zittel creates objects with the aid of thorough scientific observation and charting systems. Upon a friend's request for help in reshaping his environment, Zittel completed a lengthy assessment and set out a plan of action far beyond the client's initial goals. The ultimate success of the experiment, informed by detailed mapping of the subject's eating, sleeping, and work habits, led Zittel to form A-Z Enterprises, a conceptual art and design project. She made a logo to garner attention from busy contractors and businesspeople, setting the wheels of a faux-company in action (Connelly, 2000, para. 2).

Zittel has made numerous experimental living structures, but her functional clothing series, A-Z Uniforms, best exemplifies the reevaluation methods she promotes. In the early 1990s, she began making herself seasonal garments, to be worn constantly for six months.[11]

In 2004, a collection of the A-Z Uniforms were assembled for a show at the Andrea Rosen Gallery in New York. Gathered together, the exhibition raised questions concerning simplicity, identity, public perception, and the human connection to material things. Zittel is interested in simplifying garments to a most basic form but maintaining sophisticated styling. Her trials have led to an extraordinary collection of styles and silhouettes over the years. Each phase in Zittel's A-Z

Uniforms has a quirky playfulness—the garments she wears are engaging and colorful, rather than stern or ascetic as one might infer from her reductionist tendencies. She began by making aprons from rectangles of fabric, tying the simple patchwork pieces around her body with adjustable straps. She then moved to crocheted dresses, as they are constructed from a single strand that forms a three-dimensional piece that looped by means of fingers or hooks. For example, she made a red cap-sleeved dress with contrasting crochet stitches—it is a lovely summertime garment with a sleek silhouette. Her most recent line of garments utilizes felting techniques. These pieces are seamless and loosely fitting, but adjustable to the needs of the wearer via oversize safety pins (Regen Projects press release, 2002). She created a backless cream and mustard yellow tank top, which is held together in the back with one large pin. Its variegated color and stiff shape of the garment hearkens back to primitive clothing made from animal hides.

The work has been related to Bauhaus and De Stijl sensibilities, and indeed her ingenious simplification and modular architecture can parallel works by renowned designers like Gerrit Rietveld (Connelly, 2000, para. 5). However, Zittel's projects reflect a theme of charm and fantasy as well. They maintain a human touch and a sarcastic wink despite a pared-down style rooted in scientific methodology and interpretation.

At the end of each season the garments are well worn, indicating their constant presence over a period of time in Zittel's life (Regen, 2006).[12] Each garment gains an inherent personal meaning, as she remembers all of the daily events and projects connected with the time she wore the piece. The creation of each garment became a ritual representing the anticipation, expectations, and excitement for the future, as well as the physical act of making a symbol that would come to define her.

Zittel's work has inspired collectors to commission garments for their own seasonal clothing experiments. One client signed a contract, promising to wear his uniform, a lightweight wool suit, for the entire six-month duration. He had the uniform remade for several subsequent winter seasons, indicating a level of success in his own journey for identity and simplicity within corporate life.[13]

The A-Z Uniforms highlight a human desire for identity while also questioning the idea that variety is what sets a person apart. The uniforms turn into a symbol of identity; for example, Zittel could be easily recognized as the woman in the red crocheted dress. She stood apart from others because, for several months at a time, she always looked the same. Zittel asserts that the uniform frees people from the everyday stress of dressing. It becomes a visual marker of recognition and familiarity—after all, we always know what to look for in the "Where's Waldo?" books, and Charlie Brown would not be so charmingly recognizable without his yellow and black zigzag shirt. It seems that social taboos against wearing a garment multiple days in a row are outdated, considering technological advances and modern personal hygiene habits.[14] Zittel's projects encourage an examination and assessment of everyday objects, forcing viewers to question how they define themselves.

Perhaps not everyone is ready to toss out all but the essentials of a whole wardrobe, but embracing the theme of a pared-down lifestyle is something to seriously contemplate.

Designer Christina Kim exemplifies the luxurious side of a pared-down lifestyle with Dosa, her Los Angeles-based clothing label. Kim's richly embroidered and hand-painted garments have drawn throngs of admirers by focusing on material, craft, and tradition, aspects that make a garment special. She employs artisans around the world to create garments with traditional techniques such as shibori and metal ribbon embroidery. Aggressive marketing is less important to the brand; instead, customers help spread the brand's fame by word-of-mouth. Dosa's grassroots marketing also helps it remain on an even keel; other trendy brands may come and go, but her quiet style has been successful for over 20 years.

Dosa's philosophy encourages the selection of a few special garments over a closet full of unsatisfying pieces (Song, 2003). How can designers stress the importance of quality and creativity to shoppers, and how can consumers make informed decisions? How can designers inform and empower those shoppers?

Planned obsolescence has plagued consumers for over a century, forcing a continual cycle of purchasing new goods and dumping obsolete models. The short life cycles of things we buy and use, especially clothing and electronics, is entirely controlled by marketers and business leaders, and has dangerous implications for the environment. Planned obsolescence leaves consumers with the short end of the stick; they are enticed with reasonable prices and are drawn into a continual cycle of purchasing and replacement of outdated and quickly worn out goods. The influx of low-cost, low-quality goods flooding the market is possibly dumbing down the consumer.

Paradoxically, society does benefit from the continual revision of what we buy and use. Goods are refined, rethought, and remade in increasingly efficient ways and innovative materials. What comes with the process of constantly creating fresh objects and materials, curiously, is a great deal of invention, alteration, innovation, and problem solving with the potential of enhancing product lines and generating an increasingly better world. Therefore, the paradox of the "new, new thing" both helps and hinders.

Conveying a Message

Deeply engrained gender roles persist because society does not challenge them enough, but wearable art pieces like Gaza Bowen's are able to subtly raise awareness of feminist issues. Upon first viewing, Bowen's dainty handmade shoes seem sugary sweet and innocent, but under a playful composition of kitchen sponges and Brillo pads lies a biting message about female stereotypes and gender roles. Bowen began making art shoes in 1985, using household objects commonly associated with housewives (Waters, 1997, para. 2). Bowen was classically trained in the art of shoemaking, and each piece she made was constructed as carefully as any functional shoe. She crafted Tuff Scuffs (1990) from plastic bottles, cleaning brushes, and multicolored scrubbers; an accompanying backdrop sells the product with phrases like "dance your way to a cleaner house!" and "never scrub floors on hands and knees again!" (see Figure 11.4). The familiar selling points of durability and efficiency push the viewer to assume the role of consumer, to engage with the product and desire it for its abilities. But the underlying message (i.e., a female shoe for a female task) leaves viewers questioning a woman's role in the household. Should these shoes be marketed only to women? Why are gender roles perpetuated in mass marketing? Would men be likely to don these shoes and dance their way to a cleaner house? Bowen's shoes engage a dialogue between

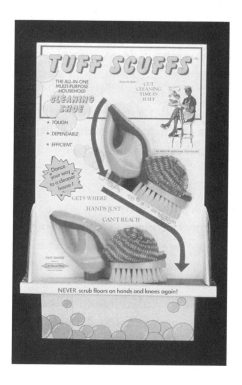

FIGURE 11.4. "Tuff Scuffs" by Gaza Bowen, 1990, constructed with plastic bottles, cleaning brushes, and plastic scrubbers. Gaza Bowen's wry feminist take on shoes, complete with packaging that encourages customers to "dance your way to a cleaner house."

marketers and consumers, suggesting a second look beyond the hype and excitement surrounding products.

Louise Bourgeois has also embraced the use of recycled textiles in her recent sculptures. She cut apart old sweaters and stitched them into three-dimensional forms, crafting eerie, featureless bodies laden with patches and scarlike seams. A review in *Fiberarts Magazine* noted that she "uses fabric as if it were a gauze bandage over bleeding wounds or guillotined heads with hollow eyes" (Sonnenberg, 2006, p.38). The mild color palette of soft pinks, purples, and taupes represents a distinct feminine voice, while the forms depict issues including relationships, pain, and loss. Bourgeois' sculptures, though abstracted to anonymity, relay human emotions with a painful immediacy. Her use of personally significant garments, cut apart and stitched back together, signify a method of recapturing and reassessing old emotional wounds.

Jean Shin's art focuses on the social and personal value of clothing. Rather than celebrating fashion in all its glory, Shin takes a closer look at the discarded belongings that surround everyday life. In "Alterations," she collected waste scraps from altered pants (see Figure 11.5). The cuffs, stiffened with wax for stability, are set on the floor in an organic arrangement reminiscent of a topographical map or an urban skyline. The varying colors of denim and twill cuffs suggest personalities and individual preferences, while the differing cuff heights indicate the physical discrepancies in the human body. Each pair of cuffs represents a person, and the collective display of their discards connects them as members of a community (Scheinman, 2005, pp. 20–21).

Shin's work with discarded clothing materials emphasizes the accruement of waste in modern life. The broken umbrellas, discarded clothing, and old reading glasses that are destined for the trash heap gain a new life when grouped into larger compositions under Shin's creative vision (Harris, 2004, para. 4). Her pieces quietly tell a story of individuals and the things they discard, of an anonymous life that has

FIGURE 11.5. "Alterations" by Jean Shin, constructed with pant scraps and wax. Jean Shin's work with discarded and deconstructed textiles evokes the human and personal aspects of modern urban life. (Collection of Peter Norton. Photo by Jean Shin.)

been lived. Shin's textile works serve as monuments to urban life and give the viewer a sense of humanity's ever-growing scale.

In 2004, Shin created a site-specific work entitled "Project 81" for the New York Museum of Modern Art's temporary location in Queens. She gathered an item of clothing from each museum employee, then deconstructed the garments by cutting away all of the seams. The resulting flat pieces were starched and arranged on two walls, fit closely next to each other like space-saving cutting patterns (Scheinman, 2005, p. 20). The long strips of seams and waistbands were displayed along the ceiling, creating a mass of hanging loops reminiscent of threads and yarns. Shin's work highlighted the people behind the art museum's glossy fame. Surprisingly, their clothes were nondescript, filling up one entire wall with neutral tones. It seems ironic to see such plain clothing in an environment that emphasizes form, color, and creative thinking. Regardless, Shin's interpretation of the garments turns them into a work of art. It presumably led the museum staff to see themselves in a different light as a group, and also as individual members of the community.

Fashion designer Hussein Chalayan continues a commentary on social issues. His discourse takes place on the runway in haute couture collections. In his autumn / winter 2000 collection, Chalayan fused furniture and fashion into a series of multifunctional objects. His most widely known piece from that year was a circular table made of concentric rings of wood; a model stepped into the center of the table and drew up two straps, which brought the centermost ring to her waist and formed a large bell skirt around her. The collapsible skirt/table, an entirely conceptual piece, suggests the possibility of one object serving two purposes.

The 2002 collection "After Words" included two chair/dress prototypes; one lightweight chair folded down into a briefcase shape, while the larger, padded style collapsed to a suitcase size. Models wearing undergarments removed the chair slipcovers, which they donned as dresses, and folded up the chairs while on stage (Reisman, para. 5). Chalayan's dress/slipcovers looked innovative on their own, and they fit the models perfectly; it is remarkable that no aesthetic sacrifices were made to achieve the two functions. The performance's stark simplicity gave each garment a meaning beyond typical runway display, engaging the viewer to consider clothing's function in a larger context.

Chalayan's work had a personal meaning as well. A native of Cyprus, his country is one divided by ethnic groups and aggression. His family watched refugees leave their possessions behind as they fled for safer territory. Later, the stress of war and the loss of civilians in Kosovo deeply affected Chalayan, and the simultaneous suffering and innovation of refugees in their temporary homes motivated "After Words" (Quinn, 2002, para. 4).

An earlier group of avant-garde artists known as the Gutai Art Association (Gutai Bijutsu Kyokai) commented on the condition of society after World War II. This group formed in Japan during the mid-1950s as the citizens of a postwar nation sought to redefine their position in the world. Members of this group aimed to create an art form that did not rely on the traditions, techniques, or materials commonly utilized for art (SAST Report, 2002, para. 1).

Atsuko Tanaka's "Electric Dress of 1956" was one of the Gutai group's most well-known works. Tanaka created a full-body garment from dozens of painted neon and tungsten lightbulbs, which formed a sort of pyramidal cocoon. The lights, hooked up to a circuit board and plugged into a wall socket, flashed on and off in succession every 2.5 minutes. Tanaka's dress was first shown as a performance piece; works like hers influenced the performance art, or "Happenings," staged by U.S. artists in the late 1950s (SAST Report, 2002, para. 1).

Tanaka created the garment to reflect the spirit of the modern Japanese cities, bursting with light and sound, texture and color. The flashing neon lights contrasted greatly with the tempo of old-world Japan, and Tanaka sought to embody this new urban energy. Japan's new city landscapes exemplified the desire for change and reinvention; after the destruction and suffering of World War II; technology and renewed urban areas represented a promise of the future.

What can a designer draw from a tangle of blinking lights? Most importantly, the "Electric Dress of 1956" links the human body with technology and the environment (Stevens, 2004). As the physical embodiment of a city's lightscape, Tanaka prods the viewer to explore what really defines a city, its people or its environment? Furthermore, where does the human body end and the sculpture begin? Wearable art often challenges this concept of boundaries, and Tanaka's piece implies that the human form is an integral and indivisible part of the sculpture's structure and meaning. Her work suggests that, similarly, fashion should act not only as a means of warmth and protection but should also provide a means for discourse in society.

Tanaka's dress also implies the potential danger of technology when donned as clothing. She noted concerns about the electric current and the possibility of shock, relating her experience to the frightening moments before institutional electrocution (Tiampo, 2005). Tanaka's personal concerns can be related to the technology and materials that surround us every day. How can one know what is safe? What happens to clothing as it is worn? Are synthetic dyes, which contain toxic chemicals, safe to wear? Professor Gang Sun at the University of California, Davis, suggests that molecules of dye off-shed and have the potential to engage with the pores of the skin. Studies linking cell phones to cancers have become part of the public conversation, but research on textiles and synthetic dyes is not widely known.

William McDonough and Michael Braungart highlight this issue in their 2002 book *Cradle to Cradle: Remaking the Way We Make Things*. During a collaborative project, they were challenged to create a compostable textile for DesignTex.[15] As they put it, "the team decided to make a fabric that would be safe enough to eat: it would not harm people who breathed it in, and it would not harm natural systems after its disposal" (pp. 106–107). During the process, McDonough and Braungart charted fibers, dyes, and processing chemicals to determine the best approach for the fabric's production. Working with a Swiss textile mill, they conceived a method that produced no toxins in the effluent, or *wastewater*, making it safe enough to reuse as influent, or *input water* (pp.108–109). This project exemplifies the holistic perspective needed to achieve truly sustainable systems. McDonough and Braungart successfully created a product for mass production in a factory without compromising their ecological concerns. Their success relied on detailed research of materials, pollutants, and factory outputs. By making conscious choices about dyes and fibers, the team was able to create a system that makes the factory run more efficiently.

Conclusion: Impacts and Implications
Wearable art creates a connection between fashion and art: It holds substance and messages within a decidedly wearable fashion format.

It turns heads and sparks conversations about identity, visibility, and fashion, both in and out of the museum. But what can art-to-wear contribute to the market? How do one-of-a-kind pieces relate to industry? Unique materials, fine craftsmanship, and an emphasis on the personal touch have guided the work of the practicing fiber artists noted above. In a touch of irony, designers may have to divorce themselves from the mass production that the fashion industry helped to create in order to participate in the future market. What are the implications of specialized handmade garments on an ever-expanding industry? Such materials would oblige the designer to either adapt mass production to work more wisely, or to force a reversion to smaller and more personalized production. By thinking of the entire life cycle of garments, from considering alternative materials to understanding clothing's final destination, designers stand to make a significant change in the way the garment industry operates.

Endnotes

1. The exhibit "Artwear: Fashion and Anti-Fashion" was displayed at the Legion of Honor in San Francisco, California, from May 14 to October 30, 2005. Curator Melissa Leventon wrote the accompanying catalog, which serves as an excellent resource for the history of the wearable art movement and its continuing legacy.

2. In 2006, Marna Clark coordinated a series of wearable art trunk shows in fine art galleries, aiming to bring more attention to local designers of art couture.

3. Chere Mah curated the first exhibition of Chinese textiles in California since the 1940s at Fiberworks in Berkeley.

4. Designers like Eileen Fisher are actively working toward sustainable products and methods of production; see http://www.eileenfisher.com.

5. This project was made possible with a grant from the San Francisco Arts Commission, which was awarded to Akamine in 1994.

6. Booker's garments can be seen in photographs on her Web site, http://www.chakaiabooker.com

7. http://www.scrap-sf.org, 834 Toland Street, San Francisco, California 94124.

8. http://www.freecycle.org

9. http://www.nothrow.co.nz

10. Designer Ellen Hauptli makes garments from scrap material, patching them into jackets, vests, and shirts; see http://www.ellenhauptli.com.

11. Later garments were designed for three- to four-month periods.

12. *Art21*, PBS, Spring 2002 television show, Episode 4 of 4: consumption (watched on DVD October 5, 2006).

13. All of Zittel's garments, including the commissioned pieces, can be seen on her Web site, http://www.zittel.org.

14. As recently as the mid-twentieth century, many people seldom took full baths.

15. DesignTex is a subsidiary of Steelcase, a furniture manufacturer.

References

Connelly, J. (2000, Summer). Andrea Zittel. *Surface Magazine*, 88–91.

EPA (2003). Municipal solid waste in the United States: 2003 Facts and Figures.

Glueck, Grace (2006, March 16). Art in review: Chakaia Booker. *New York Times*, p. E37.

Harris, Susan (2004, October). Jean Shin at Fredrieke Taylor. *Art in America*.

Hopkins, Jan. (n.d.) Artist statement from Mobilia Gallery Web site, http://www.mobilia-gallery.com/artist_detail.php?art_id=42

Leventon, M. (2005). *Artwear: fashion and anti-fashion*. New York: Thames and Hudson.

McDonough, W., and Braugart, M. (2002). *Cradle to cradle: Remaking the way we make things*. New York: North Point Press, a division of Farrar, Straus and Giroux.

Nichols, Matthew Guy. (2004, June–July). Chakaia Booker: Material matters [Electronic version]. *Art in America*.

Norcal Waste Systems. (n.d.) SF Recycling Artist in Residence Program. Retrieved October 10, 2006, from www.sfrecycling.com/AIR/aboutus.htm

Quinn, Bradley (2002). A Note: Hussein Chalayan, fashion and technology. *Fashion Theory*, 6(4), 359–368.

Regen Projects. (2002). Information retrieved November 11, 2006, from the Regen Projects Web site at www.regenprojects.com/exhibitions/2002-12-andrea-zittel/pressrelease

Reisman, Jessica. Hussein Chalayan. *Fashion Encyclopedia*. Retrieved November 10, 2006, from http://www.fashionencyclopedia.com/Bo-Ch?Chalayan-Hussein. html

SAST Report (2002). Atsuko Tanaka [Online edition]. http://www.geocities.com/ sastreport/tanaka.html

Scheinman, Pamela. (2005, April–May). Jean Shin: Playing with space and time. *Fiberarts*, pp. 20–21.

Sonnenberg, Rhonda. (2006, September–October). Louise Bourgeois: Stitching salvation. *Fiberarts, 33*(2), 36–39.

Sorensen, Annelise. (1996, September). Trash Culture. SF Live. Retrieved November 14, 2006 from MetroActive Newspaper Web site, www.metroactive.com /papers/sfmetro/09.96/garbage-96-9.html

Stevens, Mark (2004, October 4). Everything is illuminated, *New York* magazine..[Electronic version]. Retrieved November 10, 2006, from http://newyorkmetro.com/ nymetro/arts/art/reviews/9937/

Tiampo, Ming, ed. (2005). Electrifying Art: Atsuko Tanaka 1954–1968. New York: Grey Art Gallery, New York University, and Vancouver, B.C.: The Morris and Helen Belkin Art Gallery, University of British Columbia.

Waters, Christina (1997, May 8–14). Footloose at last. Metro Santa Cruz. [Electronic version]. Retrieved from Metro Active Web site at www.metroactive. com/papers/cruz/05.08.97/shoes-9719.html

In 2000, news of Kosovan civil war and genocide filled headlines and the US deployed troops to help peace efforts.

BELINDA T. ORZADA, PH.D. is an associate professor of Apparel Design in the Fashion and Apparel Studies Department at the University of Delaware. Her research bridges apparel design and textiles through environmental, economic, and social sustainability directions. Currently, she is focused on using natural dyes as design inspiration for original apparel designs.

MARY ANN MOORE, PH.D. is the associate dean of research and graduate studies in the College of Human Sciences and is a professor in the Department of Textiles and Consumer Sciences at Florida State University. In her research she has concentrated on textile product development, product performance, and textile industry issues. She is a member of the American Association of Textile Chemists and Colorists, the International Textile and Apparel Association, and Educators for Socially Responsible Apparel Business. She was awarded a University Teaching Award and University Teaching Incentive Program by Florida State University.

CHAPTER 12

Environmental Impact of Textile Production

Belinda Orzada and Mary Ann Moore

What effects does textile production have on the environment? The textile industry may be addressing issues of pollution caused by the "processing" of its products, mostly in response to direct pressures from environmental legislation, but few in the industry truly consider the degradation to the environment suffered by air, wind, water, and other pollutants. To seriously address this problem, designers and manufacturers must first understand and critically evaluate the processes used to grow or manufacture fibers and yarns, including the dyeing and processing of the fibers into fabrics.

Taking a Closer Look

In this chapter we will scrutinize the methods used to produce textiles. First, we will examine the industry from a historical perspective; then we will critically evaluate areas of environmental concern in the processes used to turn raw fiber into finished fabric. Finally, we will look at positive steps taken by government and industry to address environmental concerns and develop more sustainable and environmentally responsible textile products and processes. These include efforts of the Environmental Protection Agency with clean air and clean water laws; recycling of materials; the Oeko-Tex standards that verify that textile products are safe for humans; and the importance of the ISO 14000 on environmental management standards.

Historical Overview

Water is a powerful tool for spurring economic development. The growth of eighteenth-century industry along New England's rivers took advantage of the available waterpower to produce textile goods, but caused problems for farmers in the region by damming the rivers and flooding farmlands (Steinberg, 1991). Additionally, mills built in wetland areas caused environmental damage to sensitive areas.

By the nineteenth century, advances in technology brought Sir Richard Arkwright's water frame for spinning to the cotton mills of New England. With this and other technological advances came numerous "large, integrated textile factories with substantial demands for energy" (Steinberg, 1991, p.114). Industrialization had a significant effect on the environment in New England, including the river ecology, the natural flow of streams, and migrating fish species. The textile industry used water for power, as well as various washing, dyeing, and finishing processes. Water law in the region developed to suit the needs of the industrial economy (Steinberg, 1991).

In the nineteenth century, most pollution from dyeing and printing textiles was organic, using natural dyes. However, mordants were

FIGURE 12.1. Textile mills, like this one in New England, was built nearby water, the main source of power for the mill. (Courtesy Library of Congress.)

required to "fix" the color. Mordants are largely inorganic chemicals that are less easily tolerated in a river system and included sulfuric acid, muriatic acid, lime, and arsenate of soda. Since only a small amount of dye was actually absorbed by the fabric, a large amount of dye entered the river as waste, which caused the water to discolor (Steinberg, 1991).

Life Cycle Assessment of a Fiber Product

All manufacturing has an effect on the environment. Production of consumer goods requires raw materials, energy, equipment, and labor. As materials and processes for a textile product are selected during design and product development, the environmental impact of that textile is determined. Based on these decisions, the manufacturing process, usage, maintenance, and disposal of a textile product may have a range of environmental impacts from minimal to severe.

Design of textile and apparel products for a sustainable future depends on an understanding of the relationship between fiber, yarn, and fabric. A holistic, integrated approach to design and manufacture of products is necessary (Heely & Press, 1997).

An assessment of the environmental and economic impact of a product during its entire life is necessary to ensure sustainable development. Life cycle assessment involves (1) determining the product life cycle, (2) assessing resource inputs and waste outputs during each life cycle stage, (3) calculating the environmental impacts, and (4) identifying options that will reduce the total environmental impact of the product over its entire life cycle. BASF, the world's leading chemical company, uses eco-efficiency as a strategic tool to assess the environmental and economic impact of its products and processes. Using a software program, the company is able to input data, then evaluate various scenarios utilizing different production methods, or raw materials (Wall-Markowski, Kircherer, and Wittlinger, 2005).

Environmental Effects of Textile Production Processes

Designers need to be aware of the environmental effects of the various processes involved in developing a fiber into a textile product. Several stages in the fiber-to-fabric process are environmentally problematic. Fiber production, dyeing, finishing and other wet processes, drying, and shipping all impact air, water, and land quality. Throughout the textile manufacturing process, there are basic production needs which utilize energy, produce noise, and often heat and by-products. The discussion in this chapter will lead the reader to informed decisions about the environmental impact of his or her textile choices.

Fiber Production

Fibers provide the initial source for textile products. Cotton, flax, silk, and wool are the most commonly used natural fibers in apparel. These are fibers found in nature and are classified as either cellulosic or protein. Manufactured fibers are substances chemically created to have qualities useful to textiles. They are either synthetic or formed by regenerating or modifying a natural source.

Each fiber has its own inherent environmental weaknesses. Cotton requires heavy usage of insecticides to control boll weevils and other pests. When the fiber is mature, defoliants, sprayed from low-flying airplanes, cause the leaves of the cotton plant to fall. This step significantly reduces the amount of trash content and the cleaning needs of the fiber; however, the chemicals used cause air and water pollution. One fiber, cuprammonium rayon, has not been manufactured in the United States since 1975 because it requires dissolving cellulose in a copper ammonium solution before fiber extrusion into a waterbath; the wastewater from the cuprammonium process contaminates the water. Copper and other chemicals must be removed for the water to meet U.S. standards for clean water, which is an expensive process (Collier & Tortora, 2001). This fiber is still manufactured in Japan, Italy, and Germany. In Japan, a recovery system developed for copper has a 99.9 percent recovery rate (Kamide & Nishiyama, 2001). Synthetic fibers have petroleum as their source of raw material and are neither biodegradable nor renewable. Polyester production, for example, requires nonrenewable resources, such as fossil raw materials, which uses on the average 63 percent higher energy consumption than the production of cotton per 1 kg fiber. Water use in polyester production, however, is less than 0.1 percent of the amount of water required to grow cotton (Kalliala & Nousiainen, 1999).

Washing of Fibers

The chemicals used to clean raw fiber can be extensive and may include toxic, corrosive, or biologically modifying reagents. Environmentalists have been concerned about the impact of fiber cleaning processes for years. However, the need to remove impurities from virtually every fiber produced makes cleaning unavoidable. Not cleaning the fibers would result in products that consumers would not find acceptable (Slater, 2005).

Fibers, especially natural fibers, require cleaning prior to spinning into yarns. Initial washing is accomplished with water or detergent. Wastewater from washing natural fibers may contain pesticides or other contaminants (IFC, 2006). Scouring provides fibers with an in-depth cleaning to remove persistent dirt from cotton, de-gum silk, or remove dirt and grease from wool. In scouring, sodium hydroxide, an alkali, is most often used to supplement the cleaning process. This chemical has major disadvantages in use including damage to the fibers and environmental contamination (Slater, 2005).

Bleaching is used when further cleaning is necessary. In bleaching, an oxidizing or reducing agent destroys the molecular bonds of the pigmentation in the colored or off-white fibers. Chlorine, the traditional bleaching agent, damages protein fibers and is a major cause of environmental harm, producing dangerous by-products during oxidation reactions (Slater, 2005). Alternatives to chlorine bleaching have been developed. Hydrogen peroxide was the first successful substitute for chlorine. Unfortunately, it is very unstable, and its effectiveness as an oxidizing agent can be lost before the bleaching process is completed. Other bleach substitutes for cleaning fibers include peracetic acid, which gives improved whiteness and less loss of tensile strength compared to hydrogen peroxide, ozone bleaching, and carbonizing for wool fabrics (Slater, 2005). More recently, the addition of enzymes to enhance the effectiveness of scouring operations while minimizing the environmental load has been explored.

Dyeing and Finishing

The greatest environmental problems in textile processing occur during dyeing and finishing. These processes require using chemicals and large quantities of water. Excess dye not exhausted onto fibers is often discharged into waterways. Residuals from preparation and finishing can also be found in industrial effluents. In addition, heat causes the vaporization of organic compounds used in finishes such as durable press or coating of fabrics. These organic compounds are carried off as airborne gases and must be controlled to reduce air pollution (Slater, 2005).

Finishes

Fabric aesthetics and functional characteristics may be changed or enhanced through the application of finishes. Finishing is a basic step in processing fabrics for consumer use. Almost all fabrics used in consumer products have received one or more finishing treatments. Fin-

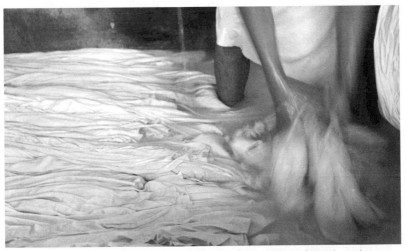

FIGURE 12.2. This worker is washing and bleaching textiles in a factory. (Photo by Andy Nelson/The Christian Science Monitor via Getty Images.)

ishes are applied to fabrics either by mechanical or chemical means. Historically, finishing required the fabric to be saturated in a water-bath before and during the process. Concerns for water and energy usage spurred the development of other techniques.

Mechanical finishes are those applied using a mechanical action accompanied by the use of heat and moisture. Many finishes in this category affect the surface characteristics of the fabric. Chemical finishes use chemical substances to produce the desired end product. Many of these are functional finishes designed to enhance the performance of a fabric. Finishes that create designs on fabrics are chemical finishes applied in a method similar to printing. Sulfuric acid, phenol, and sodium hydroxide are some of the chemicals used in these aesthetic finishes (Collier & Tortora, 2001).

Methods of textile finishing have been improved through several directions. First, low-wet pickup finishing techniques use less water than traditional finish application methods, thus reducing drying costs as well as water usage. One of these, foam finishing, involves applying finishing chemicals in a foam form. In foams, as much as 95 percent of the water previously needed to apply finishes is replaced by air (Greenwood & Holme, 2003). Operations such as scouring and bleaching may be combined to save energy and water (IFC, 2006). For many finishes, alternative, less-environmentally sensitive chemicals are substituted.

Wastewater recycling and the recovery and reuse of alkalis, dyes, or other chemicals are contemporary methods for pollution prevention and control. Mercerization, for example, is a chemical finish in which cotton reacts with caustic soda (NaOH), causing the fibers to swell and change in structure. This process improves dimensional stability, tensile strength, and dye affinity, among other properties (Vigo, 1994); however, the fibers must be neutralized with acid then rinsed several times. The wastewater from this process is strongly alkaline (IFC, 2006), but the alkali may be recovered and reused.

Many of these waste treatment methods involve the use of filters or membranes. Successful filtration involves the correct technological choices of filter and well-designed treatment system (Gale & Bide, 2000). Enzymes have been used to decolorize dyes. In addition, membrane systems are widely used in industrial filtration and separation processes for purification and recycling in water treatment. In the textile industry, membrane systems are used to recycle synthetic warp sizing and the water used in the desizing process, recycle dyehouse effluent water, recycle wool scouring liquor, water softening, and many other processes (Greaves, 2003).

Coloration

Pollution caused by dyeing and printing processes is a major concern in the textile industry. The majority of compounds used for applying color are highly carcinogenic or otherwise toxic. Particularly problematic are the original synthetic dyestuffs developed in the nineteenth and twentieth centuries (Slater, 2005).

Natural Dyes

Natural dyes come from a variety of plant, animal, and, to a lesser extent, mineral sources. Prior to the discovery in 1856 of synthetic dyes by William Perkin, an 18-year-old inventor, only dyes from natural sources were available for the coloration of textiles. Health and environmental concerns about synthetic dyes, however, have led to renewed consumer interest in purchasing products dyed with natural dyes (Collier & Tortora, 2001).

The use of natural dyes is often advocated as a means of reducing environmental damage. In some instances, natural dyes can provide benefits such as lowered energy and water consumption, reduced allergenic effects, and easier biodegradability. However, dye lot consistency is low, fabrics are not as colorfast as with synthetic dyes, and color variation may be so great that re-dyeing is needed (Slater, 2005).

Natural dyes are being used in modern mills to color fabrics (Collier & Tortora, 2001). A concern is whether these renewable resources can be produced in great enough quantities to sustain commercial production. Historically, sources of some natural dyes were depleted, and therefore, the use of them was banned (e.g., brazilwood in the 1800s). Development of commercially marketable natural dyes is ongoing in the Philippines (Fresco, 2004). Research objectives at University of Leeds include developing a range of natural and environmentally safe textile dyes, investigating environmentally friendly extraction and concentration processes, and developing coloration processes using natural dyes to obtain high color depth and high fastness on natural fibers (Blackburn, 2004).

Synthetic Dyes

The development of synthetic dyes provided a broader range of color possibilities and dyes that were more colorfast and less expensive than natural dyes. Recent research on synthetic dyes has focused on developing dyeing techniques with lower planetary loading that can provide appreciable long-term savings of water, dyestuff, energy, and waste treatment costs. One theme of current research seeks a crucial change in dye chemistry due to the harmful effects of certain dyestuffs, while a second approach has found that plasma treatments can accelerate dyeing, increase brightness, and improve color penetration and fastness (Slater, 2005).

Types of Synthetic Dyes

Acid and cationic, or *basic*, dyes are applied to fabric directly and provide a wide range of colors, but colorfastness is often a problem. Low colorfastness can result in bleeding, fading, and early pollution. Many of these dyes are carcinogenic or otherwise toxic. Substantive direct dyeing increases fastness, thus reduces waste (Slater, 2005).

Azoic dyes, or *azo dyes*, generally need low temperatures for which energy is expended. Azo dyes are versatile dyes, constituting 60 to 70 percent of the world dyestuff market. However, toxic chemicals are used for their production, and they contain carcinogenic compounds (Slater, 2005) that appear as the dyes break down or decompose.

Certain dyes depend on an auxiliary compound, or *mordant*, to provide color fastness. Mordants are usually heavy metals (e.g., chromium) that can cause serious environmental problems once the excess reagent is discarded (Slater, 2005). Gale and Bide reported in 2000 that chrome dyes were used for approximately 30 percent of wool dyeing, despite the environmental problems, because for dark colors they provide the most level, fast color and are the least expensive method. Metal-free alternatives are being explored. Reactive dyes are one option for substitute dyes (IFC, 2006).

Disperse dyes are used to color synthetic fibers. This type of dye is insoluble in water, but soluble within the fibers, so the excess dye is less difficult to extract once the dyeing process is complete. Sulphur dyes, also insoluble in water, can similarly be removed from waste liquors slightly more easily than most other types. Thus, both of these dyes provide a means of reducing pollution (Slater, 2005).

Vat dyes are insoluble in water as well. These dyes require oxygen to develop their color. Through a chemical reduction process, vat dyes are converted to a soluble form. The fabric absorbs the dye, which then must be reoxidized to its insoluble form to reveal the color. Because vat dyes are more difficult to control, there is an increased chance of rejection of the dyed goods (Slater, 2005). The reducing agent normally used for vat dyes is sodium dithionite. This chemical is not very stable to air or heat, so an excess of it is needed to ensure good color. Additionally, and most significantly, the sodium dithionite oxidizes into sodium sulphate, sulphate ions, and thiosulphate ions, which are all toxic substances (Bozic & Kokol, in press). These dyes are no longer produced in the United States due to environmental concerns (Collier & Tortora, 2001).

Reactive dyes have replaced direct and vat dyes in many applications. They provide bright colors and exceptional wash-fastness (Skelly, 2003). Reactive dye wastewater contains a high level of color and dissolved solids such as salt and some heavy metals. These characteristics make reactive dye baths strong candidates for recycling (Perkins, 2003), since "the percentage of dye lost in the effluent may be as high as 50 percent for reactive dyes" (Skelly, 2003, p. 185). Adoption of low-salt dyeing techniques is also recommended for these dyes (IFC, 2006).

In solution dyeing, pigment is dispersed in the fiber solution, prior to extrusion. Thus, the color is developed because the dyestuff is soluble in the synthetic fiber (Collier & Tortora, 2001). Solution dyeing is extremely fast to laundering and is possibly the most easily prevented from polluting the water supply (Slater, 2005).

Printing

Printing involves application of dyestuffs to selected areas of a fabric. To control the placement of the design, a thickener is used to prevent the color from straying outside the desired area. The thickener, a substance such as starch, gum, or resin that increases the viscosity of the coloring agent, is combined with the dye to form a printing paste. However, thickeners cause water pollution when excess amounts are discarded after completion of the printing process (Slater, 2005). Environmental problems associated with printing are related to water pollution and health hazards from the print and resist pastes, and with the organic solvents used with pigments. Each component presents environmental risks after the excess is discarded (Slater, 2005).

Direct methods of textile printing create a colored design by applying a coloring agent directly to the fabric surface. Pressure is used to force the dye paste into the fabric. For resist printing, a protective coating is applied on the fabric surface to prevent the dye from penetrating the design area. Discharge printing is essentially the reverse of resist printing. First, the fabric is piece-dyed; then a discharge paste is applied to selected areas to remove the color. This creates a pattern of white on a colored background.

In heat-transfer printing, dye is first printed on a sheet of paper and then transferred to the fabric. The paper and fabric are placed in close contact and with the application of heat, and vaporization of the solid dye occurs across to the fabric. Liquids and printing pastes are not necessary for this printing technique. Thus, the washing, steaming, or drying steps in conventional dyeing are omitted. Ecological harm is reduced, but not eliminated, because the need for special paper, a separate printing stage when applying dye to it, along with the disposal of the paper, reduce these advantages considerably (Slater, 2005).

Digital printing deposits dye on the surface of the fabric, while with screen-printing, the dye penetrates the fabric. Conventional printing systems waste a large quantity of dye and fabric. They require colors to be mixed and applied to the print roller or tray. Test samples must be printed on the fabric to ensure the dye goes onto the fabric correctly at the necessary speeds. After printing, surplus dyestuff is dumped, with resulting implications for effluent and cost. Compared to conventional printing methods, there are several environmental benefits of digital printing. Digital printing methods are cleaner than conventional printing methods used in applying color to textiles. The fixation rate is higher for digital printing, usually above 90 percent, compared to reactive dyes, which have a fixation rate of 65 to 70 percent. For digital printing, the amount of dye applied to the fabric is precisely controlled. Additionally, for digital printing, there are no thickeners or carriers that must be washed off later as waste (Tyler, 2005).

Pollution Aspects of Dyeing
The textile industry is currently focusing on both reducing the effluent emerging from its dye houses and on developing less harmful dyes, with limited success in each of these areas. Today's dyeing methods

meet environmental regulations but have room for improvement. New dye machines developed have "reduced cost, energy use, and environmental impact." (Slater, 2005, p. 191). Dyebath reuse is an effective technique for minimizing the environmental impact of dyeing; however, it has not yet been widely adopted. The two methods for dyebath reuse differ due to the type of dye being used. In the first method, the amount of dye used is measured and replenished for the next dye session. This is successful for dyes that have a high exhaustion, those that are not affected chemically during the dye process, and when auxiliaries are not either absorbed by the fiber or consumed in the dye process. This recycling technique has been successfully used in acid dyebaths for nylon hosiery and for carpet dyeing. The second dyebath recycling method, developed for use with reactive dyes, requires a color removal treatment for the exhausted dyebath. The remaining dyebath receives fresh dye and any auxiliaries necessary (Easton, 2003).

Colorants are developed to be fast, resist degradation, and thus are difficult to break down in a conventional treatment plant. Coloration of discharged treatment water can occur for very small concentrations of residual dye. Decolorization may not be the best solution, however, as many colorants have low toxicity as integral compounds but have the potential to become toxic during breakdown depending on their chemical structure (Buschle-Diller, 2006). "However, in regard to a brighter horizon for textile coloration, the knowledge of the ecological and toxicological effects of dyes and their residues should be considered for the design and synthesis of more biodegradable, benign structures for future applications" (Buschle-Diller, 2006, p.102).

Drying
Cleaned fibers must be dried to prepare them for the next production stage. During drying, large quantities of energy are used and impuri-

ties are often produced that are discharged into the air or water, including vaporized solvents, small quantities of decomposed reagents, and excess waste detergent and its by-products. Additionally, heat from the drying process must be dissipated into the environment, either inside or outside the plant, which consequently wastes heat energy and can contaminate the area with the previously mentioned impurities (Slater, 2005).

Further, almost all fabrics undergoing a finishing stage need to be dried at least once during manufacture. Conventional fabric drying systems (e.g., thermal drying using hot rollers or hot air) have different environmental problems, although one shared by all is energy use. As with fiber drying, much of the heat escapes to the surrounding environment and may also cause decomposition and emission of toxic materials from any chemical reagents remaining on the fabric (Slater, 2005). Radio frequency waves and microwaves are options for fabric drying. For these methods, only the fabric, and not the equipment, is heated. Faster drying and lower energy consumption are advantages of this type of drying system (Collier & Tortora, 2001).

Government and Industry Initiatives

In the United States, the Environmental Protection Agency (EPA) monitors federal regulations from several Acts of Congress that directly influence the environmental impact of the textile complex. These include the Clean Air, Clean Water, and Resource Conservation and Recover acts. Worldwide, there are several proactive programs from industry and government that provide the textile industry with voluntary standards, recommendations, and solutions for meeting environmental regulations. One of these programs, ISO 14000, will be discussed. Another program, called Encouraging Environmental Excellence, was eliminated, although two prominent national textile industry groups are considering reestablishing it. Their reason for reviving the program will follow.

Environmental Protection Agency

The Environmental Protection Agency (EPA) was fashioned "to protect human health and the nation's environment." Since its creation in 1970, this agency has been influential in implementing protection to achieve clean air and water, and reduce solid waste. There are many areas of sustainable fashion that are regulated by the EPA through several laws. For example, the dry cleaning solvent perchloroethylene (perc) is regulated by EPA through laws including the Clean Air, the Clean Water, and the Resource Conservation and Recovery Acts (U.S. Environmental Protection Agency, n.d.). Because of these acts of the EPA and other federal regulations, the dry-cleaning industry has reduced the use of perc by 75 to 80 percent over the past decades (North Carolina Department of Environment and Natural Resources, 2001). The state of California, through the South Coast Air Quality Management District, was instrumental in the passage of legislation that will eliminate the use of perc by 2020 (Eckman, 2004, p. 9).

Clean Air Act

The 1990 Clean Air Act (CAA) is a federal law that authorizes the EPA to establish restrictions on how much of a pollutant can be in the air in order to guarantee that all Americans have similar environmental and essential health protections. States are responsible for developing implementation plans that describe the regulations necessary to clean up polluted areas. Each state can set limits that exceed those established by the EPA.

To comply with the Clean Air Act, local industry and business must be aware of air pollutants that can impact air quality. An example of this is the impact of insect- as well as drought-resistant varieties of cotton on air quality. These varieties require less plowing and disturbing of the soil, resulting in the reduction of CO^2 emissions. "These practices, as adopted in the United States from 1996 to 2004, have reduced CO^2 emissions by an amount equivalent to removing over 27,000 cars from the road" (Cotton Incorporated, 2006).

Clean Water Act

The Federal Water Pollution Control Act Amendments of 1972 are the result of increasing public recognition and concern for controlling water pollution. In 1977, this act was amended and is now universally recognized as the Clean Water Act (CWA). The Clean Water Act provided the EPA with the "authority to set water quality standards for all contaminants in surface waters." Under the provisions of the CWA, it is illegal for anyone to discharge any pollutant into navigable waters without a permit.

Large amounts of water and a wide variety of chemicals are used by the textile industry for fiber and fabric wet processing. There are measures being taken to reduce pollutants in the wastewater. "Once all possible measures are taken to reduce pollutants in the effluent, there remains the problem of dealing with the wastewater that remains. There are a variety of systems available. One approach is to minimize the cost of treating effluent by chemically reducing the waste so that few pounds of biosolids are produced." (Sharma, 2005, p.10). Ciba Special Chemicals Water and Paper Treatment, for example, works with textile plants on reducing their total process costs for wastewater treatment facilities by providing technical service and chemicals as well as chemical application equipment. Using both microfiltration and nanofiltration has resulted in reduced effluent waste and also recovering most of the wastewater. "Today's textile industry manufacturers are motivated to limit their waste not just by a concern for the environment, but by a very real concern for their bottom line. As water and energy costs go up, and limits on pollution increase, every drop that runs down the drain means a drop in profits as well" (Thiry, July 2005, p.11).

Resource Conservation and Recovery Act

The Resource Conservation and Recovery Act (RCRA) was endorsed by Congress in 1976 and modified in 1984. Its primary goal is to protect humans and the environment from the potential dangers of waste disposal. RCRA gave the EPA the authority to control hazardous waste from the "cradle to grave." Textile manufacturing processes often include the use of hazardous chemicals necessary to provide the desired aesthetic and functional characteristics. Disposal of chemical wastes from textile processes such as bleaching and mercerizing or solvents from equipment servicing are regulated by the RCRA (U.S. Environmental Protection Agency, n.d.). The disposal of solid waste is also regulated by the EPA, and recycling is one recommended management practice to reduce the solid waste stream. (International Finance Corporation, 2006; U.S. Environmental Protection Agency, n.d.).

Municipal solid waste (MSW), normally referred to as trash or garbage, is made up of common items such as product packaging, clothing, and plastic drink bottles. "In 2005, U.S. residents, businesses, and institutions produced more than 245 million tons of MSW, which

FIGURE 12.3. Municipal solid waste (MSW) is typical waste generated from residential and nonindustrial commercial sources. Unless recovered or reused, MSW goes to municipal landfill sites.

FIGURE 12.4. The International Organization for Standardization (ISO) is the principal developer of global standards with 157 member countries standing behind one national standard. Interests of manufacturers, consumers, and governments in international standards development are all represented by the ISO. (Logo courtesy of ISO.)

is approximately 4.5 pounds of waste per person per day" (Thiry, April 2006, p. 27). Of the 245 million tons of waste, rubber, leather, and textiles make up 7.3 percent of the total. Recycling is a management practice that can prevent materials from being added to solid waste. Recycling not only makes sense from an environmental standpoint but also makes good financial sense. A national goal for the EPA is to annually recycle 35 percent of the MSW generated. "Recycling, which includes composting, diverted over 72 million tons of material away from landfills and incinerators in 2003, up from 34 million tons in 1990, doubling in just 10 years" (Thiry, April 2006 p. 27).

ISO 14000

The International Organization for Standardization (ISO) is a nongovernmental worldwide body established in 1947 to promote the development of international standards in order to assist global trade of goods and services based upon global acceptance of criteria. Today ISO is the principal developer of global standards, and there are 157 member countries, with one national standard institute for them all. Interests of manufacturers, consumers, and government in international standards development are represented by the ISO. The 14000 standards are broadly utilized and address environmental management standards on an international level; this benefits the environment (air, land, and water) and manufacturers conducting business in the global marketplace. Companies that implement the ISO 14000 management systems become more aware of environmental issues with their corporate decision making. These standards have essential social importance in making the production and distribution of both products and services cleaner and better for the environment. Labeling and life cycle assessment are some of the sustainable issues addressed by the ISO 14000 standards. "The ISO 14000 management system registration may become the primary requirement for doing business in many regions or industries" (http://www.iso.org).

Encouraging Environmental Excellence

The Encouraging Environmental Excellence (E3) program was established in 1992 to help textile companies promote environmental awareness and to implement environmental policies. Participation in the E3 program promoted and broadened the awareness of the efforts being taken by the U.S. textile industry to be environmentally responsible. It allowed textile companies to meet the federal regulations being placed on them in a cost-effective manner and also improve air, water, and land quality (American Textile Manufacturers Institute, America's Textiles: Encouraging Environmental Excellence Guidebook, 1995). Unfortunately, the E3 program was eliminated when the American Textile Manufacturers Institute was dismantled in 2004 (http://www.textileworld.com/News). However, two leading national textile industry groups, National Textile Association (NTA) and National Council of Textile Organization (NCTO), have revived the old E3 program. According to Poole (2006), director of Regulatory and Technical Affairs for the National Textile Association, reinstatement of the program is now under review by the textile industry. Poole also stated the textile industry would continue to build on the enormous progress made since inception of the E3 program in achieving and maintaining environmental excellence within the U.S. textile industry, one of the most environmentally sensitive manufacturing industries in the world (Poole, 2006). Some of the benefits to textile firms that were certified by the E3 program that also serve as the goals for reviving the program, include the following:

• Establishing a voluntary minimum standard for process and performance
• Developing advertising and promotional material responding to the powerful impact environmental concerns have on consumer purchases
• Generating environmental investment opportunities that will be cost effective
• Improving air, water, and land quality

Moore, Money, and Orzada (1999) surveyed the textile firms that were certified by the E3 program and found that certified E3 firms had a good environmental record and were being environmentally responsible. All of the firms had an environmental policy in place, while a majority followed written specifications that exceeded national governmental regulations. The respondents report many environmentally responsible practices including reuse and recycling programs, reusing and recycling water, using less toxic chemicals in the finishing process, reducing water level use, and reducing the discharge volume. The firms also reported control of overall liquor flow and optimizing levels of dye fixation. Half of the respondents used environmentally friendly packaging methods and reused fabric beams, thread cones, plastic warps, and other items.

Oeko-Tex Association
Once the General Agreement on Tariffs and Trade (GATT) expired, remaining quotas on textile imports were lifted by the World Trade

Organization (WTO). Therefore, there has been an increase in the volume of textile and apparel imports into the United States particularly from China (National Council of Textile Organization, n.d.). With this increase of textile product imports, the International Oeko Association in Switzerland provides designers, product developers, retailers, and consumers with global information on textile products that include which products are environmentally friendly and free of unsafe substances. Certificates are granted by the association to manufacturers for environmentally preferable products according to two standards; the Oeko-Tex 100 and 1000 standards. Manufacturers attach certifications labels on these products at the retail level for consumers. The Okeo-Tex Standards 100 was introduced to the textile and apparel industries in 1992 and tests for harmful substances in textile raw materials as well as intermediate and end products at all stages of production. This standard is based upon current legislation and tests for harmful substances including those banned and controlled by law, substances that are harmful but not banned or controlled by law, and preventive measures to safeguard health of consumers who use the products. Oeko-Tex Standard 1000 cover environmentally friendly production procedures and disposal aspects of textile products. Products can only be certified for the Oeko-Tex Standard 1000 that have been granted the Standard 100 certification, the ISO-standard 14000 series, or the European Union's environmental management certification system (EMAS, for Eco-Management and Audit Scheme).

The advantage of these certifications is that the Oeko-Tex Association monitors all national regulations and revises the standards as new regulations are developed; therefore, these standard are important to all companies involved in global trade since all relevant international governmental regulations would have been met. Since the textile complex is global, it is important for the certification to be global. The globally accepted Oeko-Standard certification system "has established itself in the textile chain as a firm benchmark for textiles that aren't harmful to health and the environment" (Textile World Special Report, July 2005).

American Apparel and Footwear Association

The American Apparel and Footwear Association (AAFA), the U.S. trade organization for the apparel and footwear industries, established the Social Responsibility Committee that examines corporate issues on global social responsibility that impact the apparel and footwear industries. An Environmental Task Force (ETF) was established by the committee to identify environmental best practices. According to Chair of the Environmental Task Force John Eapen, vice president of environmental, health, and safety at American & Efird, "the Environmental Task Force has taken a strong and visible role in educating the industry on restricted substance lists and chemical management systems and in providing information on best practices. For companies interested in environmental sustainability, it is a critically important forum. It is the group's responsibility to ensure that member companies are apprised of environmental legislative and regulatory developments that could impact their global operations and to educate policymakers on the group's efforts to be responsible environmental stewards and minimize pollution" (http://www.apparelandfootwear.org).

Conclusion

Designers and product developers need to be aware of environmental effects in the processing of textiles and should consider the impact their decisions have on the environment. These are complex decisions, as all stages of textile processing greatly impact the environment. Some choices are more environmentally responsible than others, and the entire product life cycle should be considered during product development.

Both government and industry initiatives are addressing the impact of textile manufacturing on the environment. The U.S. government has implemented legislation that influences the environmental impact of the textile industry. The textile industry has developed voluntary programs and implemented environmental policies that encourage sustainable practices. It is imperative, however, that government and industry work together to ensure the development of environmentally sustainable textile products and processes.

References

American Apparel and Footwear Association. Retrieved November 10, 2006, from http://www.apparelandfootwear.org

American Apparel and Footwear Association. (n.d.). Retrieved June 19, 2007, and November 27, 2006, from http://www.apparelandfootwear.org

American Apparel and Footwear Association. (n.d.). Social Responsibility. Retrieved November 22, 2006 from http://www.apparelandfootwear.org/Legislative-TradeNews/SocialResponsibility.asp

American & Efird, Inc. (1997). Environmental policy. Retrieved November 7, 2006, from http://www.amefird.com/env_policy.htm

American Fiber Manufacturers Association. (n.d.). Retrieved October 18, 2006, from http://www.fibersource.com/f_tutor/fib-env.htm

American Textile Manufacturers Institute, America's Textiles: Encouraging Environmental Excellence Guidebook. (1995).

Blackburn, R. S. (2004). Natural Dyes: Opportunities for a greener textile and coloration industry. Retrieved November 12, 2006, from http://www.chemsoc.org/pdf/gcn/richardblackburn2004.ppt

Bozic, M. & Kokol, V. (in press). Ecological alternatives to the reduction and oxidation processes in dyeing with vat and sulphur dyes. *Dyes and Pigments* doi:10.1016/j.dyepig.2006.05.041

Buschle-Diller, G. (2006). Recycling and re-use of textile chemicals. In Y. Wang (Ed.), *Recycling in Textiles* (pp. 95–113). Cambridge, UK: Woodhead Publishing Ltd.

Collier, B. J., & Tortora, P. G. (2001). *Understanding Textiles*, (6th ed.). Upper Saddle River, NJ: Prentice Hall.

Cotton Incorporated (2006). U.S. Cotton and the environment: A proven track record. Retrieved November 10, 2006, from http://www.cottoninc.com/sustainability

Easton, J. R. (2003). General considerations in reuse of water: Reuse from coloration processes. In J. K. Skelly (Ed.), *Water recycling in textile wet processing* (pp. 3–15). Society of Dyers and Colourists.

Eckman, A. I. (2004). The dirt on drycleaning: Health risks bring new methods to the forefront. *AATCC Review, 4*(3), pp. 9–11.

Fox, A., & Moore, M. A. (2006). Effects of laundering on environmentally improved and classic denim fabrics. *Journal of Testing and Evaluation, 34*(3), pp.181–186.

Fresco, M. C. (2004). Common tropical plants yield new natural dyes. Retrieved Januar 10, 2007, from Science and Development Network Web site: http://www.scidev.net/News/index.cfm?fuseaction=readNews&itemid=1697&language=1

Gale, M. E., & Bide, M. (2000). Environmental update: Textiles and the environment from AATCC. *Textile Chemist and Colorist, 32*(8), pp. 75–78.

Greaves, R. (2003). Membrane systems. In J. K. Skelly (Ed.), *Water recycling in textile wet processing* (pp. 53–70). Society of Dyers and Colourists.

Gulich, B. (2006). Development of products made from reclaimed fibres. In Y. Wang (Ed.), *Recycling in Textiles* (pp. 25–37). Cambridge, UK: Woodhead Publishing Ltd.

International Finance Corporation. (2006). *Environmental, Health, and Safety Guidelines for Textile Manufacturing.* Retrieved December 2006 from http://www.ifc.org/ifcext/enviro.nsf/Content/EnvironmentalGuidelines

International Standards Organization (2006). Retrieved November 1, 2006, from http://www.iso.org/iso/en/aboutiso/introduction/index.html

ISO 14000. (n.d.). Retrieved from http://iso.org/iso/iso_catalogue/management_standards/iso_9000_iso14000

Kalliala, E. M., & Nousiainen, P. (1999). Life cycle assessment environmental profile of cotton and polyester-cotton fabrics. *AUTEX Research Journal, 1*(1).

Kamide, K., & Nishiyama, K. (2001). Cuprammonium processes. In C. Woodings (Ed.), *Regenerated Cellulose Fibres* (pp. 88–155). Cambridge, UK: Woodhead Publishing Ltd.

Milliken & Company. (n.d.). Retrieved November 7, 2006, from http://www.milliken.com/hr/wwwmlkn.nsf/sweb?OpenFrameSet

Moore, M. A., Money, A., and Orzada, B. (1999). An examination of environmental aware in the textile industry. *Textile Chemist and Colorist, 31*(4), 27–31.

National Council of Textile Organization. (n.d.) Retrieved from http://www.ncto.org.

National Textile Association. (n.d.) Retrieved November 6, 2006, and November 22, 2006, from http://www.nationaltextile.org

North Carolina Department of Environment and Natural Resources (2001). Alternatives to the Predominant Dry Cleaning Processes, North Carolina Department of Environment and Natural Resources Study Group Report to fulfill request by the North Carolina legislature, October 2001. Retrieved October 10, 2006, from http://www.ncdsca.org/dc_critcom.htm

Oeko-Tex (2007). Oeko-Tex Standard 100 Certification. Retrieved April 10, 2007, http://www.oeko-tex.com/OekoTex100_PUBLIC/content4.asp?area=hauptmenue&site=zertifizierung&cls=02

Perkins, W.S. (2003). Chemical oxidation and electrochemical systems. In J. K. Skelly (Ed.), *Water recycling in textile wet processing* (pp. 83–97). Bradford, UK: Society of Dyers and Colourists.

Poole, H. (2006). Personal communication.

Sharma, H. S. (2005). Textile biotechnology in Europe: Microbiological degradation of wastewater dyes. *AATCC Review, 5*(11), 45–48.

Skelly, J. K. (2003). UK experience in municipal treatment of industrial wastewater containing dyehouse effluent. In J. K. Skelly (Ed.), *Water recycling in textile wet processing* (pp. 181–195). Bradford, UK: Society of Dyers and Colourists.

Slater, K. (2003). *Environmental impact of textiles: Production, processes and protection.* Cambridge, UK: Woodhead Publishing Ltd.

Steinberg, T. (1991). *Nature Incorporated: Industrialization and the waters of New England.* New York: Cambridge University Press.

Textile Institute. (2005). Recycling: The next challenge for the textile industry. *Textiles the quarterly magazine of the textile institute, 33*(2), 13–15.

Textile World. (n.d.). Retrieved June 5, 2007 from http://www.textileworld.com/News

Thiry, M. (2006, April). 2006 NTC Forum. *AATCC Review, 6*(3), pp. 27–28.

Thiry, M. (2005, July). Sending profits down the drain. *AATCC Review, 5*(7), pp. 8–11.

Thiry, M. (2005, March). Every shirt has a story: The marketing and certification of sustainable textiles. *AATCC Review, 5*(3), pp. 7–12.

Tyler, D. J. (2005). Textile digital printing technologies. *Textile Progress, 37(4).*

Wall-Markowski, C. A., Kicherer, A., & Wittlinger, R. (2005). Eco-efficiency: inside BASF and beyond. *Management of Environmental Quality: An International Journal*, 16(2), 153–159.

Wellman, Inc. (n.d.). Retrieved November 29, 2006, from http://www.wellmaninc.com/Fibers/FAQs/F_FAQs.asp

Wellman, Inc. (n.d.). Fibers. Retrieved November 28, 2006, from http://www.wellmaninc.com/Fibers/F_Home.asp

U.S. Environmental Protection Agency. (n.d.). Retrieved November 22, 2006, and October 18, 2006, from http://www.epa.gov

Van Ravenswaay, E. O., and Blend, J. (1997). Using ecolabeling to encourage adoption of innovative environment technologies in agriculture. Flexible Incentives to Promote the Adoption of Environmental Technologies in Agriculture, June 8–10, 1997, Gainesville, FL.

Wall-Markowski, C. A., Kicherer, A., & Wittlinger, R. (2005). Eco-efficiency: inside BASF and beyond. *Management of Environmental Quality: An International Journal*, 16(2), 153–159.

Woodruff, F. A. (2003). Coating, laminating, bonding, flocking, and prepregging. In D. Heywood (Ed.), *Textile Finishing*. Bradford, UK: Society of Dyers and Colourists.

GAIL BAUGH has extensive fashion industry experience, particularly in global product sourcing for large
retail chain stores and for NI-Teijin Shoji (USA), Inc.
Experienced in retail buying, production management, and product development, Gail is currently
teaching textiles and merchandising at San Francisco
State University and the Fashion Institute of Design
and Merchandising. "It is my mission," she says, "to
raise awareness and empower the fashion industry to
change the way fashion apparel is designed and produced using creativity and restoration."

CHAPTER 13

Fibers: Clean and Green Fiber Options

Gail Baugh

Fiber is the basic building block of textiles, so understanding the
pros and cons involved in choosing a fiber is the first step to creating sustainable fabrics. Environmentally responsible fiber choices are
not limited to natural or organically grown fibers; they can also
include fibers manufactured from renewable raw materials such as
corn, soy, bamboo, and even chicken feathers. This chapter focuses on
fibers and their fabrics, sizing up their design potential and role in sustainable product development.

Taking the First Step
The fashion industry is at a crossroad as it considers how to use
emerging fiber innovations and resolve the issue of consistent, cost-
effective fiber supply, while reconciling environmental issues and

alternative fiber resources. With fiber as the basic building block of the fashion industry, it seems appropriate that "clean and green" fiber production is a first step in creating responsible fashion apparel.

Until recently, consideration of fiber content in fashion apparel was important only if the target market placed value on certain fibers, such as silk fiber content for designer clothing. Otherwise, aesthetic choices, such as color and texture, were the primary criteria in fabric selection. This chapter questions and explores the fashion industry's use of fiber, its current practices and future choices. Topics include the following:

- The perception that natural fiber (e.g., silk, cotton, and wool) is of high value and quality. Is this a true statement?
- A review of available fiber choices today. Should fashion business leaders stay on their current course?
- The future of fiber. What are the emerging fiber developments that may play a key role in sustaining future fashion business and supplement, or perhaps replace, current fiber choices?

The fashion industry clings to historical fiber preferences, some based solely on recent use, while the needs of a clean environment and "green" textile production methods are forcing different choices on their target markets. Most designers choose fabrics based on aesthetic considerations, not positive environmental choices. The issue of "clean and green" is then left to the production teams to source and implement, often separate from the designers' initial aesthetic decisions. Now is the time to ask the decision makers in the fashion industry (e.g., designers, merchandisers, and leaders of corporations) to reconsider their fiber selections, first for their easily renewable sources and minimal negative impact on the environment and second for their aesthetic and performance values. The fashion industry is embarking on a new era in textiles and awareness of new fibers. Future development will encourage new fashion ideas and a new generation of designers and companies to use these new fibers in their collections and assortments. New fiber ideas are emerging more frequently now, as the demand for more "clean and green" fiber increases.

This chapter offers a glimpse of what is coming, and it is hoped that this information will encourage decision makers in the fashion industry to seek out new fibers, challenge suppliers to produce fabrics using these fibers, and therefore change the supply chain from one of creativity and waste to that of creativity and renewal.

Is Natural Fiber of Better Quality and Higher Value Than Manufactured Fiber?

What do the terms "pure cotton" and "fine wool" mean? The haute couture and other better fashion designers continue to use exclusive fabrics composed of expensive, difficult-to-produce fibers and yarns, most of which use wool and silk as well as cotton and linen fibers. For example, the Coco Chanel suit, reinvented by Karl Lagerfeld for Chanel, continued to use the wool fabrics inspired by original fabrics from the early twentieth century. New fabric choices were used to re-create the texture and hand of other original suits, and so buyers placed a higher value on a suit produced in the original wool fiber content than one produced in a wool/acrylic blend. But if a fiber occurs in nature, such as the wool fiber in Chanel's example, is it always the best choice for high-fashion products?

Historic Reference

In the past two generations, the fashion industry has promoted the concept that natural fiber (i.e., fiber produced by plants and animals) is superior to manufactured fiber (e.g., rayon or polyester). Natural-fiber marketing associations have formed alliances with designers, manufacturers, and retailers and for many years promoted their fiber. Meanwhile, manufactured fiber mills imitated natural fiber, reinforcing the perception that natural fiber was superior.

Further emphasizing the use of natural fiber, the hippies of the 1960s and 1970s embraced cotton and wool fiber as a way to reject "establishment values" of that time. Widely popular polyester, nylon, and acrylic fabrics of the late 1950s and early 1960s, used by their parents, were rejected by young hippies, who wore cotton T-shirts and jeans to set themselves apart from the older generation. This perception that natural fibers were superior because of their natural "roots" has led to an increased demand for cotton fiber, in particular, at all price levels. In addition, the popularity of American-style T-shirts and jeans has increased the global demand for cotton fiber.

Today, most designers and merchandisers continue to promote wool, silk, and cotton fabrics as "pure refinement" (i.e., high quality) because these are the fiber choices of the haute couture and other leading designers and retailers. The fashion industry has shown little interest and devoted little time to weigh the pluses and minuses of using these natural fibers instead of other fiber alternatives.

The designer's priority has been to select fashionable colors and textures in textiles. The priority for fashion manufacturers and retailers has been to have the desired natural fiber available on demand globally, at appropriate prices, to offer timely product at competitive prices.

Now is the time to add fiber choice to the early decision-making process because it is clear, as mentioned in the previous chapter, that fiber choice has a significant impact on a clean environment. And, since the fashion business is global, fiber choice can have a positive influence worldwide. Broadening fiber choice beyond accepted perceptions of high-quality cotton, wool, and silk is a first step in calling attention to the fashion business's role in making responsible fashion decisions.

What Are the Familiar Fiber Choices in the Industry Now?

Designers and merchandisers, when visiting the textile shows in Paris, Milan, New York, Hong Kong, Hamburg, and Shanghai, continue to focus on the familiar fiber choices (divided into natural fiber and man-ufactured fiber content and the assorted blends), choosing new textures and colors to reflect the new fashion trends. Below are the familiar groups of fiber that are most often offered to fashion designers at these shows. Again, it is usual to discuss color and texture and much less usual to discuss fiber content unless the fiber choice has a specific characteristic that is a desired feature, such as the soft sheen of a silk/wool blend satin fabric.

Choice 1: Natural Fiber

Most designers will select varieties of linen, cotton, wool, or silk fiber, grown or raised in conventional agricultural methods for the highest yield. Synthetic chemical fertilizers and pesticides are used to improve the quality of the fiber and generate consistent and predictable fiber quantities. As the chart in Table 13.1 shows, there are other fibers that are commonly used in apparel, and they are listed there as well.

TABLE 13.1 Naturally Occurring Fiber

Raw Material Source	Renew-able	Water Use/ Acre	Pesticides/ Chemicals	Recyclable/ Biodegradable	Comments
Plant Fibers					
Cotton*	Yes	High usage	Yes	N/A / Yes	Most cotton production grown this way.
Chemical-free cotton	Yes	High usage	No	N/A / Yes	Alternative to nonfood crop.
Organic cotton	Yes	High usage	No	N/A / Yes	Grown to USDA organic food standards.
Flax* (becomes linen)	Yes	Less than cotton	N/A	N/A / Yes	Flax is more pest-resistant and requires less water than cotton.
Jute	Yes	Less than cotton	Resistant to most pests/diseases	N/A / Yes	Easily grown crop.
Ramie*	Yes	Less than cotton	Resistant to most pests/diseases	N/A / Yes	Easily grown crop.
Hemp	Yes	Less than cotton	Resistant to most pests/diseases	N/A / Yes	Easily grown crop. Must have permit to grow in the United States.
Animal Fibers					
Hair fiber*	Yes	Dependent on animal	Yes	N/A / Yes	Domestic animals are dipped in chemicals to remove pests/dirt. Shearing methods designed for mass production. Not humane treatment.
"Organic" hair fiber (sheep only)	Yes	N/A	Nontoxic	N/A / Yes	Toxic chemical dipping is eliminated and replaced with nontoxic methods. Shearing methods are humane and monitored by PETA. Note: Not the USDA guideline definition of "organic."
Silk	Yes	N/A	N/A	N/A / Yes	Requires steam/water during the fiber reclamation from the cocoons. Very labor-intensive production process.

Note: Recycling fiber dependent on finishing/other issues.
*Commonly used natural fiber today.

Choice 2: Organic Natural Fiber

Textile mills are now promoting organically grown fiber products to designers expanding beyond the aging hippie demographic. Giorgio Armani is now selecting organically grown fiber for his collections, following the lead of other smaller designers, such as Stella McCartney.

The word "organic" is somewhat misleading in describing textile production. It refers to standards defined by the USDA Organic Foods Production Act, passed by Congress in 1990, which provides strict guidelines for the production and certification of organic food (Sustainable Table, n.d.). Therefore, the costly adherence to these USDA production standards requires time to provide soil that is defined as organic, and farming methods to meet the federal organic farming standards.

So far, organically grown cotton is the only plant fiber that has met the USDA organic standard. Though many apparel companies attempt to use organic cotton fiber, it is clear that the cost and available quantity cannot meet the production requirements. For example, Dockers, a division of Levi Strauss, supports organic cotton fiber production, but the high cost and limited production prevent the company from adopting this fiber for all its products. Wool, unless produced to the USDA organic standard, is also not considered "organic." (See Choice 3 below for an explanation.)

Choice 3: Chemical-Free Fiber

Since organic fiber is not food, the question arises if it is necessary to produce "organic" fiber (i.e., fiber produced to the standards of food) or to simply grow fiber without the use of harmful chemicals used in fertilizers and pesticides. As noted by the specific USDA's requirements in using the term "organic," there are costly and time-consuming procedures that must be followed to meet that labeling standard. Unlike the organic standard, producing chemical-free fiber can be done immediately and without time required to certify the soil as organic before planting. Twenty-five percent of all pesticides used in the United States are applied to the cotton crop (Allen, 2007). Chemical-free cotton fiber is available now, as is chemical-free linen and wool fiber, but the effort to market fiber produced without chemicals is not widely known nor marketed well by textile mills or fiber marketing associations, such as the Cotton Inc. or the Wool Bureau. These fiber associations should brand and promote chemical-free cotton and wool. The removal of the harmful chemicals used in natural fiber production is a big first step for fiber producers and for providing an alternative to the more costly and less available organically grown cotton fiber.

Some wool producers are marketing their fiber as "organic," but the wool is actually produced using humane methods, such as eliminating harmful chemicals in the dipping process and administering a sensitive shearing process. Wool labeled "organic" may not meet the USDA organic standard, but it may actually be chemical-free or reduced-chemical fiber (National Organic Program, 2003).

Choice 4: Manufactured Fiber

Manufactured fiber, produced from a variety of raw materials, has been avoided by most high-priced designers, especially since the 1960s. Viscose and lyocell rayons, polyester, nylon, acrylic, and spandex were not promoted as status fibers. Therefore, chemical fiber companies such as Dupont Chemical (producers of Dacron® polyester, Lycra® spandex, and others) or Teijin, Ltd. (producer of Capilene® polyester fiber and others) have sought mass-market production quantities, targeting moderate-priced retailers and manufacturers. The need and desire for more affordable prices and care-free apparel have become priorities among consumers, so these low-cost, low-maintenance fibers are continuously in demand. Manufactured fiber was developed to imitate the more expensive and higher maintenance fibers used for the haute couture and other designers, so the merchan-

TABLE 13.2 Current Manufactured Fibers

Fiber	Hand	Luster	Drape	Resiliency	Abrasion Resistance	UV Resistant	Anti-Bacterial	Wicking	Absorbency	Quick Dry	Machine Washable	Dyeability	Color-Fastness	Heat Sensitive	Thermo-Plastic	Comments
Regenerated-Cellulosic (Plant Raw Material)																
Acetate	Fair	Good	Fair	Fair	Poor	No	No	No	Good	Good	No	Excellent	Fair	Yes	Yes	Easily melts
Viscose rayon	Excellent	Good	Excellent	Fair	Poor	Yes	No	No	Good	Good	No	Excellent	Fair	Yes	No	
Lyocell rayon	Excellent	Poor	Excellent	Good	Fair	Yes	No	No	Good	Good	Yes	Excellent	Good	Yes	No	
Oil-Based (Petroleum Raw Material)																
Nylon	Fair	Good	Fair	Very good	Excellent	Poor	No	No	No	Very good	Yes	Fair	Fair	Yes	Yes	Very strong fiber
Polyester	Good	Good	Good	Excellent	Very good	Yes	No	No*	No*	Very good	Yes	Fair	Good	Yes	Yes	*Can be changed to have wicking/absorbent features
Acrylic	Good	Good	Good	Very good	Fair	Yes	No	No	No	Very good	Yes	Fair	Good	Yes	Yes	Very heat-sensitive fiber
Olefin	Fair	Good	Good	Excellent	Excellent	Yes	No	Yes	No	Very good	Yes	Good	Excellent	Yes	Yes	Very durable fiber
Spandex	Fair	Very good	Fair	Excellent	Fair	No	No	No	No	Very good	Yes	Poor	Poor	Yes	Yes	Heat-sensitive

disers and retail buyers continued to value natural fiber more than the imitating manufactured fiber.

Manufactured fiber is divided into two main categories:.

1. *Fiber produced using plant-based raw material.* Viscose, HWM and lyocell rayons and acetate fiber are produced using this raw material. Historically, acetate and rayon were extremely toxic to produce. Because of the toxic waste generated during fiber production, which has often ended with toxic wastewater, these fibers are less available now. Lyocell rayon is the first fiber that uses trees grown for fiber production; it uses a closed, recycled production system (i.e., it uses the same chemicals again in further Lyocell production) that keeps the toxic chemicals out of the water supply. Tencel®, by Leizing Fiber, is an example of this lyocell fiber.

2. *Fiber produced using petroleum-based raw material.* Nylon, polyester, olefin, acrylic, and spandex are the "big five" manufactured fibers that are very important to fabric production. Polyester is second only to cotton fiber in usage. Chemical fiber companies, especially DuPont in inventing nylon fiber, used petroleum, a plentiful raw material at the time, as the basis for new fiber development. A seemingly unlimited oil supply meant unlimited fiber production to meet the textile needs of the U.S. economy. The textile industry continues to diversify these fibers to enhance fabric performance.

Should the Fashion Industry Stay with the Current Available Choices?

As with haute couture, other designers and merchandisers continue to select fabrics produced from the available fiber choices. Are these choices most appropriate today? There are obvious changes in the world market that are challenging the way fiber is perceived and selected for use:

1. *The popularity of "clean and green" fiber and textile production.* The environmental impact of fiber and textile production are more visual now. The fashion industry acknowledges the pollution created in both natural fiber and manufactured fiber production. With designers Giorgio Armani and Stella McCartney making organic fiber choices, leadership is emerging in a fashion industry that needs to rethink the perceived social and market value of natural fiber.

2. *The reduction of the global oil supply, which produces the key component of polyester, nylon, acrylic, olefin, and spandex.* How will the fiber suppliers react to the shrinking raw material supply?

3. *The pressure of increasing fiber production to meet the apparel needs of an increasing global population.* This pressure has challenged fiber producers to consider alternative raw material resources. With the oil supply shrinking for fiber production, easily renewable resources are becoming a priority.

The consuming public has placed increasing pressure on the fashion industry to take responsibility for wasteful consumption of raw materials and pollution created in fiber production. Past choices are being questioned, and designers and merchandisers are considering the three points listed above. The next section introduces new or less-used fibers that expand the fashion industry's fiber options and question current fiber choices.

The Future Choice of Fiber for the Fashion Industry

What will fashion be like in a post-cotton and post-polyester world? How can the fashion industry manage without these two popular fibers? Adding more fiber choices is gaining momentum as pressure for a clean environment and alternative raw materials challenge current fiber choices. Choosing between a natural or manufactured fiber is no longer simple. Natural fiber, perceived as an "eco" and "pure"

fiber, is often being produced with very toxic chemicals, and manufactured fiber, perceived as "unnatural" and "polluting," can be produced
with minimal toxic process.

Emerging Choices

Today, the usual fiber choices used in fashion are being reviewed, both
for natural and manufactured fiber. Organic fiber, seen as one possible
solution to solve the chemical pollutants used on cotton fiber, cannot
fulfill the demand for fiber due to cost and the slow production cycle.
The fiber industry is experimenting with a variety of new ideas to minimize the negative environmental impact and expand raw material
fiber sources. These new ideas may be ways to supplement the current
fiber supply, either by blending with the new fibers or replacing the
currently available fibers altogether. The industry is increasingly turning its attention to fiber sources that are both *easily renewable* and have
fewer toxins in the production process. Described below are naturally
occurring fiber and new manufactured fiber that address both issues.

Naturally Occurring Fiber

Cotton fiber now represents nearly 40 percent of the globally available fiber. Designers and merchandisers have little to no experience
with alternative fibers for cotton. However, there are several fibers
that provide similar characteristics to cotton. It's important to note
that these naturally occurring fibers are not produced in enough
quantities to replace all cotton fiber production, but there is enough
production to offer alternative choices. It is important for fashion
industry decision makers to know the alternatives to cotton fiber, as
cotton production comes under increased scrutiny as a high-main-
tenance crop, questioning its use of toxic chemicals and substantial
use of water. Below is a review of fibers that are gaining more
recognition as viable options to replace or supplement cotton fiber.

It is also very important to note that textile finishing techniques have greatly improved the hand and dyeability of these alternative fibers, making them more desirable fabrics for fashion. The development of nanofinishing (i.e., tiny particles that are applied to a fiber, yarn, or fabric) has imparted a beautiful, soft hand and new functional finishes never possible before for these fibers. Now these improved finishing techniques on hemp and ramie, which have a very coarse hand, can gain a pleasant touch that is very important for consumer acceptance.

Hemp

Hemp is naturally pest- and mildew-resistant, is easy to grow in many climates, requires less water per acre than cotton, and is a cousin of the marijuana plant. The U.S. federal government prohibits the production of hemp, but court challenges could change the status quo soon. There are laws in numerous states that allow hemp production. Other countries grow hemp without restriction, and hemp fabric and garments can be imported into the United States. Having almost all the same characteristics as cotton fiber, hemp fabric is no longer a material to be associated with aging hippies. Fabric-finishing techniques have greatly improved, resulting in a final fabric product that is nearly the same as cotton. Hemp's obvious advantage is that it can supplement or replace cotton as a fiber source, if it were more available worldwide. Recognizing the need for inexpensive, naturally occurring fiber that is easily grown without chemicals and without excessive use of water is an important step in adding this cottonlike fiber choice.

Ramie

Ramie is a stem fiber like flax; it is very resistant to mildew, is very absorbent, is quick-drying, and has good strength. Grown easily in many countries, ramie is often used as a flax substitute for lower-priced linen-like fabrics or blended with cotton for a similar effect. Production and use of ramie fiber could be expanded, particularly with improved finishing technology.

TABLE 13.3 Alternative Plant Fibers Compared to Flax and Cotton

Fiber Name	Absorbency	Abrasion Resistance	Machine Washable	Wet Strength	Drape	Hand	Comments
Compare to flax (linen) and	Excellent	Excellent	Yes	Excellent	Fair	Fair	New finishing techniques are improving the
to cotton	Very good	Very good	Yes	Very good	Good	Good	drape/hand.
Jute	Excellent	Excellent	Yes	Excellent	Fair	Fair	" "
Ramie	Excellent	Excellent	Yes	Very good	Fair	Fair	" "
Hemp	Excellent	Excellent	Yes	Excellent	Fair	Fair	" "

Note: Cotton replaced flax (linen) from the 1940s as the fiber of choice in the United States.

Jute

Jute is also a stem fiber like flax, but it is shorter than flax and is very coarse. It is very resistant to mildew, bacteria, and insects. Jute has good strength and fair abrasion resistance, so its main use is for bagging, backing for fashion accessories and furniture, and cording. With better finishing technology, jute's production and use could also be expanded.

New Developments in Manufactured Fiber

Manufactured fiber creates strands, or *polymers*, from a chemical fiber "soup" developed by chemical fiber companies, such as DuPont or Toray. Many chemical fiber companies worldwide have been working

FIGURE 13.1. Ramie grows as a flowering plant to heights of 1 to 2.5 meters and can be harvested up to 6 times a year. When broken down, the stalk of the vegetable can be used as fiber. (Photo by John Dominis/Time Life Pictures/Getty Images.)

on alternative raw material sources for new fiber manufacturing, and these new fibers are beginning to emerge in the marketplace. These new fibers can be divided into three groups: those manufactured from easily renewable, cellulose-based raw materials; those recycled from fiber material; and those produced from other waste products.

Easily Renewable Raw Materials for Manufactured Fiber

Chemical fiber companies, such as DuPont with its Dacron® polyester or Teijin Chemical, realized that oil-based fibers, such as polyester and nylon, could not expand in production to meet the future fiber needs. As global oil production continues to decrease and become more costly, the amount of oil devoted to fiber production will continue to decrease in the coming years. At the same time, regenerated cellulosic fiber, like rayon and acetate, sometimes uses wood that is not easily

TABLE 13.4 New Manufactured Fibers Compared to Petroleum-Based Fiber

Manufactured Fibers

Raw Material Source	Renewable	Pesticides/Toxic Chemicals	Fibers	Production Method	Recyclable/ Biodegradable	Comments
Oil-Related			**Petroleum-Based**			
Petroleum-based	No	No/Toxic chemicals at raw material production stage	Polyester, acrylic, olefin, spandex, nylon	Toxic by-products. Some may enter water supply.	No/No	Production methods haven't considered closed cycle procedures, but new ideas are being considered. We like these fibers for their ability to be manipulated at the fiber level for performance.

Regenerated Cellulose Raw Material Source	Renewable	Pesticides/Toxic Chemicals in Fiber Production	Fibers Cellulose-Based	Production Method	Recyclable/ Biodegradable	Comments
Plant pulp and other wood by-products	Yes	N/A	Acetate, rayon, viscose rayon, cupramonium rayon	Toxic production and by-products into water system	N/A/Yes	Some production methods are now banned due to toxic production methods and waste material.
Plant pulp	Yes	N/A	Lyocell (specific wood crop)	Closed cycle	N/A/Yes	Trees grown especially for lyocell production. Fiber production chemicals do not enter the water supply. They are recycled into the production process immediately. Minerals absorbed into skin. Seacell® produced in Germany.
Plant pulp + kelp extract	Yes	N/A	Lyocell w/ special mineral features	Closed cycle	N/A/Yes	
Corn	Yes	Synthetic fertilizers/ pesticides in crops	PLA fiber	Closed cycle	N/A/Yes	Corn is already grown for food, energy, and now fiber. Yet to be determined if pesticides and other chemicals are being controlled on nonfood corn crops.
Kenaf	Yes	No	PLA fiber	N/A	N/A/Yes	Crop is now being planted for automobile interior fabrics by Toray for Toyota and others.
Bamboo	Yes (several crops per year)	No	A type of rayon	Closed cycle or toxic production	N/A/Yes	This raw material is a type of grass that can be harvested several times in a year. Produces a very soft, absorbent, and quick-drying fiber. Naturally antibacterial feature.
Soy (tofu by-products)	Yes	N/A	Soy (tofu by-products)	Closed cycle	N/A/Yes	Fiber seems to have a beneficial character by providing amino acids on the surface of the fiber to be absorbed into the skin.

TABLE 13.5 Comparison of New Manufactured Fibers to Cotton

Fiber	Hand	Luster	Drape	Resiliency	Abrasion Resistance	UV Resistance	Anti-Bacterial	Wicking	Absorbency	Quick Dry	Machine Washable	Dyeability	Color-Fastness	Heat Sensitive	Thermo-Plastic	Comments
Regenerated Cellulosic																
Lyocell Rayon Tencel®	Excellent	Poor	Excellent	Good	Fair	Yes	No	No	Good	Good	Yes	Excellent	Good	Yes	No	
PLA (fiber made from corn, sugar beets, cane sugar, etc) Ingeo® by INVISTA/Cargill Ecodea® by Toray Lactron® by Kanebo	Fair	Poor	Fair	Good	Poor	Excellent	No	Very good	Fair	Very good	Yes	Excellent	Good	Yes	Yes	Accepts from disperse dyes, heat transfers possible. Yarns/fabric look/feel like cotton. Very lightweight fiber. Test for heat-set pleating.
Bamboo China Bambro Textile Co.	Excellent	Fair	Excellent	Very good	Good	Very good	Excellent	No	Excellent	Very good	Yes	Excellent	Very good	N/A	No	Excellent characteristics for hospitals, underwear, bath towels.
Compare to Cotton	Fair	Poor	Fair	Poor to fair	Excellent	Poor to fair	No	No	Excellent	Poor	Yes	Good	Good	No	No	
Regenerated Plant Protein																
Soy Swicofil, Jiangin Jinda Textile Co., Ltd.	Excellent	Excellent	Excellent	Very good	Fair	Very good	No	No	Excellent	Very good	Yes	Excellent	Very good	Poor to fair	No	Cashmere substitute. Amino acids in the fiber, which may be absorbed into the skin—a beneficial health feature.
Compare to Wool	Good	Good	Good	Very good	Good	Very good	No	Good	Excellent	Fair	No	Very good	Very good	Good	No	

renewed, requiring many years before the wood can be harvested. Finding alternative, easily renewable raw material resources to replace oil and wood subsequently occupied fiber research. Now there are several raw material resources that have successfully been used in creating new fiber that may provide alternative choices to the oil-based (e.g., polyester) and wood-based (e.g., rayon) fibers with which we are so familiar.

These new fibers, using easily renewable raw materials, seem to offer an alternative to existing manufactured fiber and perhaps another option instead of natural, and especially cotton, fiber. It should be noted that many of these new fiber developments are designed to fulfill a performance function rather than to simply imitate nature.

The most significant research has been to use existing crops, such as corn, to create fiber. Using a method similar to that in the creation of rayon from wood, INVISTA and Cargill, a chemical fiber company and agribusiness giant, have teamed up to find other cellulose plant materials that can be used to create regenerated, cellulosic manufactured fiber. These fibers are produced by dissolving plant material into a chemical solution that is then formed into long fiber strands. Corn was one of the first new materials that was successfully developed into a new fiber. A new generic fiber group was formed, PLA (i.e., polylactic acid), that described the basic chemical compound of the new fiber polymer. Some of the new, easily renewable, plant-based materials manufactured into textile fiber include the following.

Corn

Trade name fibers of corn (fiber group PLA) include Ingeo®, Sorona®, Lactron®, and Claretta®. This fiber is very resilient and absorbent. Abrasion resistance is similar to cotton. It seems to also have good wicking ability and thermal insulation, similar to wool. It is also thermoplastic, which means heat-setting may be possible. It also has a soft hand and good drape (Dugan, 2000). Some consider PLA a good combination of polyester and cotton in one fiber. Again, when growing corn for non-food uses, chemical use may be uncontrolled. This point should be reviewed in more detail. Also, competition for corn as an energy source (i.e., ethanol) may make corn less available for fiber production.

Bamboo

This very fast-growing grass can be cut and grown repeatedly in one year. Bamboo is pest-resistant and easy to grow in many climates. As an agricultural crop, bamboo is not grown in the United States. It is primarily grown in Asia, particularly China. Its fiber has a lustrous, soft hand and many of the desirable cotton characteristics of strength and absorbency, but it is faster-drying than cotton. It is also more easily dyed, producing beautiful colors not possible in cotton. Bamboo fiber is already in use for terry-cloth towels and bed linens. Its natural antimicrobial characteristics and faster drying ability make it a wonderful choice over cotton, especially for interior design use (Bambro Tex, 2003).

FIGURE 13.2. Bamboo is actually a generic plant name; there are hundreds of varieties of bamboo grown for a variety of end uses. (Courtesy Library of Congress.)

Kenaf

This stem fiber gained acceptance as a substitute for jute during the 1940s after hemp crops were banned in the United States. Kenaf has much of the same resistance to insects and mildew as ramie and hemp (ApparelSearch, 2007). Recently, Toyota, Ford Europe, and others have been experimenting with kenaf-based manufactured fiber as an alternative to nylon, polyester, and olefin fiber in automobile upholstery and other surfaces in the car interior. In 2003, Toray announced production of a PLA fiber using kenaf as a raw material for certain textiles used by Toyota (Toray Group, 2003). Watch the development of kenaf fiber closely, as it could be useful in replacing or supplementing nylon or polyester oil-based fibers in interior, recreational, and industrial products.

FIGURE 13.3. Kenaf is a baste fiber that has great environmental advantages for paper production. (Photo by David Nance/Courtesy USDA.)

Agricultural Waste

Not yet in mass production, there is an effort to create a regenerated cellulosic fiber from leftover grain crops such as rice stalks. More on these new ideas will follow in this chapter.

Protein Material

Protein material, either plant-based or animal-based, has also become a viable renewable raw material. The process to create fiber is similar to regenerating cellulosic fiber, meaning that protein material is added to a chemical solution, to begin the development of the polymers or strands. So far, three protein raw materials have been used to manufacture fiber.

FIGURE 13.4. Rice stalks, considered a type of agricultural waste, are being converted to fiber in Japan. (Photo by SUKREE SUKPLANG/Reuters/Landov.)

Soy

Though a plant, soy is protein. Using the by-products of tofu production as the raw material source, a Chinese scientist, Mr. Guanqi Li, succeeded in creating soy fiber. The resultant fiber is extremely soft and has been useful as a cashmere or rayon substitute (Harvest SPF Textile Co., 2003). Nearly all research on this fiber source is being conducted in Japan and China, though the United States is one of the major soybean producers.

Cow's Milk

Similar to soy, cow's milk fiber produces a very soft hand, yet seems to be a weak fiber and easily wrinkles. The soft hand makes for a very appealing product, but more research is necessary to confirm the fibers viability for apparel products. This fiber is being produced in several countries worldwide, but only in small test quantities (Swicofil, n.d.).

Chicken Feathers

The keratin in feathers can be regenerated into polymers (i.e., fiber strands). It is too early to know how this new fiber source can be used in production (Comis, 1998).

Waste Material to Create Fiber

Studying the use of waste as raw material for fiber production is a new idea. Rice stalks, feathers, and other waste products could find new life in fiber form. As competition from energy and food producers for other crops (e.g., corn) put pressure on fiber resources, the creation of fiber from waste material is generating more interest.

Recycling Fiber Material

Recycling fiber from apparel or other fiber-based textiles has a long history. Wool products, for example, have been recycled into a fabric called "melton" wool. The U.S. Navy peacoat is traditionally produced from recycled wool, which has a very thick, felted texture, making it an ideal fabric to protect against cold, wet ocean climates.

Oil, primarily produced for energy use, is now considered a nonrenewable fiber resource. The cost of oil-based fiber production will continue to escalate as the amount of available oil decreases. But the need to reclaim fiber of limited production, such as oil-based fiber (e.g., polyester, nylon, acrylic, olefin, and spandex), makes the idea of recycling more motivating. There are efforts underway to discover ways to recycle these fibers. Patagonia, the outdoor apparel company well known for its environmentally sensitive fabric selections, and Teijin Mill in Japan have introduced a new recycling program for Capilene® polyester. The two companies are working together to encourage the consumer to return the Capilene® garments to Patagonia and then shipping them to Japan for recycling into new polyester fiber and fabrics. According to Teijin's ECO-CIRCLE, the recycled polyester fiber is almost indistinguishable from new "virgin" polyester, but the recycled polyester requires 70 percent less energy to produce than new polyester.

The fiber recycling concept of oil-based fibers is just beginning, and it is an important step to conserve the amount of these fibers currently available worldwide.

Recycling today's manufactured fibers is complicated, particularly since many fabrics are often blended fiber content and use chemical finishing that may not be possible to separate from the fiber. It is now possible to extract polyester fiber from a blended fabric. Teijin Mill has invented such a recycling process. Research is ongoing to perfect recycling manufactured fiber.

Other fabrics, especially those that cannot be recycled into fiber, must end up in the landfill. Therefore, the idea of biodegrading, or breaking down into simple, organic compounds, is now another consideration if recycling fiber is not possible. Most of the new manufactured fibers discussed above are biodegradable. Those fibers that are not biodegradable should be recycled into new fiber, like the recycling effort with Capilene® polyester.

The designer and the merchandiser should be aware of the progress that is being made in creating fiber from materials that have less impact on the environment in production and also are easily renewable, biodegradable, and perhaps recyclable back into fiber. There are now options from the beginning of textile production, and it is important for designers and merchandisers to discuss them with suppliers.

The Brave New World: Fibers by Design

With the invention of polyester microfibers back in the early 1980s, fiber production crossed the line of simply imitating nature and moved

FIGURE 13.5. The size and shape of the holes on the head of the spinneret determine the dimensions of synthetic fibers like polyester. (Courtesy Fairchild Publications, Inc.)

on to manipulating fiber for specific functions. Manufactured fiber today is created for specific products, such as Nike's fabrics that wick moisture away from the body, dry fast, kill bacteria, and are colorfast.

Though polyester microfiber was originally intended to imitate silk, the process of creating microfiber opened the way to manipulating the fiber-making process and created classes of manufactured fiber that go beyond imitating nature. Fibers are being created that fulfill the expectations of performance-based athletic and other functional apparel. By changing the fiber structure, particularly polyester, it has become possible to create manufactured fibers that can:

- *Wick moisture away from the body without absorbing moisture into the fiber*. This means that fabrics can keep the body warm and dry without extra weight in extreme weather conditions and help prevent muscle injury during and after athletic performance.
- *Absorb water into the fiber*. Polyester fibers are hydrophobic, or *non-water-absorbent*, but new fibers have been developed that actually absorb moisture, while still retaining many of the positive characteristics of the original fiber.
- *Resist static electricity*. Adding certain chemicals to the pre-fiber solution, fibers that are usually poorly resistant to generating static electricity can become highly resistant.
- *Resist oil absorption*. Normally oleophyllic, fibers have been developed to resist oil absorption and to prevent unsightly oil stains from body oils and other environmental circumstances.

Today, fiber and textile producers design their products to the lifestyles of consumers who demand convenience, comfort, and fit: very light-weight, warm and dry or cool and dry, wrinkle-resistant, quick-drying, and colorfast. Designers and merchandisers are now able to specify how they want the fabric to look and function, and textile mills can design the fabrics using fibers and yarns to fulfill their customers' expectations. Nike's Dri-Fit™, a fabric trade name owned by

Nike, satisfies athletes' needs for comfort during action and cool-down, as well as their interest in having a good fit during and after activity.

Designing fibers to meet function mostly uses manufactured fiber, and as noted in discussing the expanding choice of manufactured fiber in the coming years, it will prove worthwhile to stay informed of these newly emerging fibers. It is also important to remember that many of the enhancements that can be added to an existing fiber, both natural and manufactured, will further expand the fiber functions.

One of the more interesting developments in textiles is the use of nanotechnology. In the case of fiber production, the use of tiny molecules at the fiber level (i.e., nano) has eliminated some of the negative aspects of the usual chemical finishing process on textiles. By reducing the molecular size of a functional (e.g., antibacterial or water-resistant) finish, it has become possible to make this finish undetectable by hand, yet the performance is very good to superior and the life of the finish very durable. Yet to be understood are potential negative aspects of nanofinishing, such as the environmental impact of extremely small molecules absorbed into the skin, added to the wastewater, or released into the soil. These very important issues are yet to be clear. In the meantime, fiber producers are using the nano-finishes with very positive results.

The Categories of Fiber by Design

We can now divide these "fibers by design" into several categories. As of this writing, new developments are being created, so the following introduction to this new fiber world is a partial list.

Pre-Fiber and Fiber Enhancements

As mentioned in discussing petroleum-based fibers that are not resistant to static electricity (e.g., polyester), it is possible to introduce new function chemical structures at the fiber solution level before the extrusion into fiber or to existing fiber. By adding performance function before the fiber is extruded or to existing fiber, more traditional (i.e., often more toxic) fabric finishing methods are avoided. The resultant fiber has a highly durable extra fiber property that is highly resistant to static electricity; highly resistant to bacteria, in some cases destroying bacteria; and water-resistant.

Intelligent Fiber

Using new chemical components, manufactured fiber can respond to temperature changes by expanding or shrinking in length and diameter. The result will be fabrics that can keep us warm or cool as the air temperature changes (Agrawal, 2005).

Fiber Morphology

This development of changing the physical structure of textile fibers is opening a new world of fibers and textiles, for not only apparel, but for power and light generation, as well as digital transport of data. We are just beginning to see the possibilities of these new uses for fibers, some of which are further described below.

Carbon Nanofiber Nanotubes

This microscopic fiber construction allows for heated or cool air, moisture, light, or electric charge to move along inside a mass of fiber for various purposes (Singh, 2004). Beginning with optic fiber in the 1960s, the idea of fiber as transport has gained momentum. There is research going on now to consider how to create electronic products that don't depend on specific wiring for power. For example, carbon fiber nanotubes may find uses in creating conductive surfaces, replacing traditional yarns or wire. By using the concept of microscopic hollow fiber tubes as the transporter, research is ongoing to create new classes of fiber and the resultant textiles for heating, cooling, light, energy, and digital transport (Kem, 2003). Georgia Institute of Technology is one of many research labs that are working on this important new textile development (Toon, 2004). There is discussion about using carbon fiber to create antigravitational features. The impact of textiles that generate power or light, provide communication, defy gravity, or provide heating and cooling can be enormous.

Composite Fiber

Enhanced fiber, created from existing manufactured fiber or natural fiber through a variety of methods and composites include the following:

Nanocomposite fiber. Used to create bioactive fabrics that will "regenerate or replenish chemical coatings and chemically active components" (National Textile Center Report, 2000).

Layered fiber. Each layer is positioned for a different purpose, and the final fiber combines several features in one fiber. These fibers are designed for specific functions. The interior core is the base fiber and the outer layer is functional (e.g., water-resistant, antimicrobial, antistatic, heat-retaining, cooling.) While much of the applications are on fabric finishing, there is ongoing research at the fiber level as well (U.S. Patent 4756958).

Bicomponent fiber. Created by splitting fibers to contain more than one type of fiber. In a split fiber, chemists can place PLA (e.g., corn) and polyester, for example, within a single fiber structure, thereby combining the benefits of both fibers.

Encapsulating Fiber

By enclosing, or *encapsulating*, fibers within a fabric, it is possible to extend performance enhancement. EPIC (Encapsulated Protection Inside Clothing) by Nextec Applications, Inc. provides fabrics that breathe but are highly wind- and water-resistant. This new field of encapsulating fiber is just beginning, and further developments will emerge to enhance existing fiber with addition performance properties (Anderson, 2006).

Ultralight Fiber

There is a continuing effort to create fiber that has a very low specific gravity yet maintains all expected fiber properties (Toon, 2004). The U.S. military, for example, has focused on creating an ultralight Army uniform and gear. Fabric has played an important role in reducing the weight of the uniform, and efforts are ongoing to lighten fabric weight even further. The early polyester and later nylon microfibers introduced us to lightweight yet functional products. However, by comparison, these early developments will seem heavy as these new fibers become more available and we understand how to use them. For example, corn-based PLA fiber has a much lighter weight than polyester (Dugan, 2000).

Genetically Engineered Fiber

This fiber is a combination of naturally occurring sources that amount to a new raw material fiber source. For example, goat's milk, enhanced with a spider gene, has created a new, very strong yet lightweight fiber. This new fiber shows promise to replace Kevlar®, a very strong yet heavy fiber used in bulletproof and fire-resistant garments, but more time is needed to develop more reliable production methods (BBC News, 2000).

Medically Enhanced Fiber

Manufactured fiber, such as lyocell rayon fiber, is produced carrying seaweed minerals along its surface to provide for absorption of those minerals through the skin. Cornell University has developed clothing for thymic cancer patients to wear that encourages absorption of needed minerals via clothing produced from specially manufactured fiber (Foundation for Thymic Cancer Research, n.d.). We are just beginning to realize the scope of medical applications using fiber as the carrier of health benefits and for tissue engineering (Cohen, 2003).

Conclusion: What Are the Fashion Industry's Next Steps?

In presenting how fiber choice is expanding and changing fabrics, designers and merchandisers must make it their priority to ask several important questions when sourcing fabrics. Is natural fiber important? If so, can chemical-free fiber, as opposed to organically grown fiber, be used or perhaps a less-known natural fiber? What are the new manufactured fibers? What are their positive features and drawbacks? How can the use of these newly enhanced fibers add value to products? How can companies be encouraged to recycle fiber?

Could the textile and fashion industry market a globally recognized logo that communicates "good fiber choice for the environment" similar to the internationally recognized care symbols required on all apparel? As the fashion industry is globally sourced, produced, and

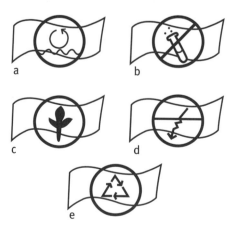

FIGURE 13.6. Graphic symbols, functioning like current international care symbols, could be developed to represent (a) closed-cycle fiber production; (b) toxic chemical-free fiber production; (c) organically grown fiber; (d) biodegradable fiber; (e) recyclable fiber, fabrics, and garments. (Illustrations by Kristina Berberich-O'Toole from symbols courtesy of Mark Baugh-Sasaki.)

sold, international symbols that are recognized throughout the world would be of great help in promoting positive fiber choices by suppliers, designers, merchandisers, and consumers. The standards must be developed to include the following: organically grown fiber, chemical-free fiber, closed-cycle production fiber, biodegradable fiber, and recyclable fiber (see Figures 13.6).

Ongoing fiber research has acknowledged the need to change the way fiber is produced. Apparel fabrics have moved from simple protection and adornment uses of fiber into a world of fiber manipulation for both aesthetic and performance designs, with an enhanced definition of body adornment. Fiber is again the engine for change in textile production. From the new fiber information provided in this chapter, it is obvious that the fashion industry has many options from which to choose. The fashion industry, previously focused on pure aesthetics, must develop a new standard in defining fashion with an environmental sensitivity and an artistic balance.

References

Abel, T., Cohen, J. I., Escalera, J., Engel, R., Filshtinskaya, M., Fincher R., Melkonian, A., & Melkonian, K. (2003). New trends in biotextiles: The challenge of tissue engineering. *Journal of Apparel, Textile, and Management, 3*(2). Retrieved Feb. 18, 2007, from http://www.tx.ncsu.edu/jtatm/volume3issue2/vo3_issue2_abstracts.htm

Agrawal, A. K., Jassal, M., Save, N. S., Periyasamy, S., Ghosh, A. K., Ramasubramani, K. R. T., Vishnoi, A., Palanikkumaran, M., & Gupta, K. K. (2005). Environmentally responsive smart textiles—II. Retrieved February 18, 2007 from http://www.expresstextile.com/20050515/hiperformance01s.html

Allen, W. (2004). Cotton subsidies and cotton problems. Retrieved March 26, 2007, from Organic Consumers Association Web site from http://www.organicconsumers.org/clothes/224subsidies.cfm

Anderson, K. (2006). Innovate or disintegrate: the latest in textile finishes. Retrieved February 18, 2007, from http://www.techexchange.com/thelibrary/innovateor.html

ApparelSearch description of kenaf fiber. (2007). Retrieved February 18, 2007, from the Apparel Search Company's Web site: www.apparelsearch.com/kenaf_description.htm

Bambro Tex's description of bamboo fiber patented manufacture and fiber characteristics. (2003). Retrieved February 18, 2007, from http://www.bambrotex.com/second/bamboocenter_nab.htm

BBC News. (2000). GM goat spins web-based future. Retrieved February 18, 2007, from http://news.bbc.co.uk

Comis, D. (1998). Chicken feathers: Eco-friendly "plastics" of the twenty-first century? Retrieved February 18, 2007, from the United States Department of Agriculture Web site: www.ars.usda.gov/is/pr/1998/980209.htm

Dugan, J. S. (2000). Novel properties of PLA fibers. Retrieved February 18, 2007, from Fiber Innovation Technology, Inc. Web site at www.fitfibers.com/publications.htm

Foundation for Thymic Cancer Research. (n.d.). Protective clothing initiative. Retrieved February 18, 2007, from http://www.thymic.org/clothing/initiative.htm

Harvest SPF Textile Co., Ltd. (2003). Soybean protein fiber description and history. Retrieved March 26, 2007, from www.spftex.com

Kem, Y. K., & Lewis, A. F. (2003). Concepts for energy-interactive textiles. Retrieved March 26, 2007, from Materials Research Society Web site at www.mrs.org/s_mrs/sec_subscribe.asp?DID=168004&CID=2985&SID-1&VID=113&R

National Organic Program's Labeling Packaged Products table. (2003). Retrieved March 26, 2007, from United States Department of Agriculture Web site at http://www.ams.usda.gov/nop/ProdHandlers/LabelTable.htm

National Textile Center Report, Project #M00-D08. (2000). Nano-composite fibers. Retrieved February 18, 2007, from http://www.ntcresearch.org/pdf-rpts/AnRp00/m00-d03.pdf

Singh, K. V., et al. (2004). *Applications and future applications of nanotechnology in textiles.* Retrieved March 26, 2007, from www.utexas.edu/centers/nfic/fc/files/nanocot.pdf

Sustainable Table's definition of organically grown crops and certified organic labeling. (n.d.). Retrieved March 26, 2007, from http://www.sustainabletable.org/issues/organic/

Swicofil AG Textile Services milk fiber characteristics. (n.d.). Retrieved February 18, 2007, from www.swicofil.com/products/212milk_fiber_casein.html

Toon, J., & Kumar, S. (2004). New class of fibers: composites made with carbon nanotubes offer improved mechanical & electrical properties. Retrieved February 18, 2007, from Georgia Research Tech News, Georgia Institute of Technology Web site at http://gtresearchnews.gatech.edu/newsrelease/nanofibers.htm

Toray Group press release. (2003). Toray starts production of automobile upholstery material. Retrieved February 18, 2007, from the Toray Group Web site at http://www.toray.com/news/fiber/nr030513.html

United States Patent 4756958. (n.d.). Fiber with reversible enhanced thermal storage properties and fabrics made therefrom. Retrieved March 26, 2007, from http://www.freepatentsonline.com/4756958.html

SHONA BARTON QUINN is an apparel industry executive currently serving as the sustainability specialist at Eileen Fisher. She authored and teaches *International Corporate Responsibility* at the Fashion Institute of Technology in New York City; this chapter examines how ethical, social, and environmental issues are addressed by multinational corporations. Ms. Quinn holds a master's degree in Industrial Ecology from the Yale School of Forestry.

CHAPTER 14

Environmental Stewardship and Sustainable Sourcing

Shona Quinn

With so many options, how does a fashion executive choose? From fiber to fabric to garment, this chapter focuses on new methods of sourcing, such as bioregionalism and "supply chain cities." By incorporating sustainable sourcing practices into the business plan, a "holistic" strategy emerges that capitalizes on cross-functional product teams, supply chain relationships, strategic location, fiber choice assessment, and cost analysis.

"You must be the change you want to see in the world."—Mahatma Gandhi

Connecting Sustainability and Sourcing

It's fashion week in New York. Design students love it. They dress models backstage and look for famous people. Meanwhile, designers and CEOs cross their fingers and hope that buyers and writers like the show. Much inspires these shows; even planet Earth is a source of inspiration. But the link between fashion and Mother Nature typically stops on the runway. Sustainable sourcing strives to take nature-inspired design all the way up, down, and across the supply chain to justly link sustainability to brand identity.

"But," one may say, "sourcing is complicated enough without sustainability." That response is a fair one. Sourcing managers have to contend with price, quality, time, vendor relations, and regional issues. Yet incorporating environmental issues into these criteria may simplify sourcing strategies while adding value to the brand. Fashion executives who want to incorporate sustainability into their decision making must fully understand what products are made of and how they are processed. One might start by asking two questions:

1. Can the company continue making clothing following a traditional unsustainable model *forever?*
2. Will the company *always* have unlimited access to materials, energy, and water?

The answer to the questions will likely be no. Zero emissions, zero waste, and sustainable product development is a tall challenge. It's important to have goals, but very difficult to create a product that has no negative impact on the Earth. Without an end and with ever-increasing possibilities, sustainable sourcing is a journey toward innovative ways of making, using, and recycling clothing. It is complex, detail-oriented, never-ending work that can add value and improve business metrics if applied correctly.

Viewing Business Strategy Holistically

Over the last decade the apparel industry has gone through a transformation in its business strategy. Large retailers are in a race to the bottom, competing over who can sell the most units at the lowest price.

While lowering prices may drive revenue and appeal to a larger customer base, it may also be undermining labor and environmental standards farther up the supply chain. Sustainable sourcing requires a shift in strategy. It's not about getting the lowest-priced garments on the selling floor faster, but about how retailers can increase profits through smarter strategies. Inditex, a large fashion conglomerate and owner of Zara, offers a business strategy that should be applied to sustainable business management. By concentrating on its customer and supply chain relationships, Inditex is raking in profits. It offers fewer units at higher margins, focusing on getting the right product on the floor at the right time (Ferdows, Lewis & Machuca, 2004).

Legitimate sustainable business managers understand the impor-

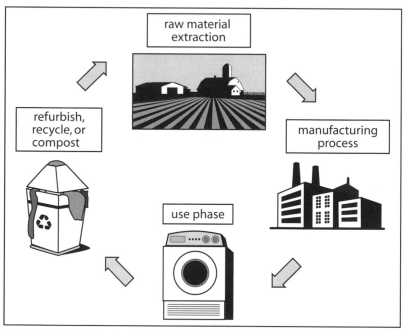

FIGURE 14.1. This drawing depicts the simple life cycle of a clothing product. (Drawing adapted from T. E. Graedel & B. R. Allenby (2003). *Industrial Ecology*. Upper Saddle River, NJ: Prentice Hall.)

tance of the *what* and *how* of sourcing as opposed to *more* and *cheaper*. Additionally, a sustainability executive is not only aware of the customer's needs and the supplier's capabilities, but also views a garment in holistic terms, considering all aspects of its life cycle. This includes: raw material extraction, manufacturing process, consumer use and reuse, and recyclability or compostabilty. Each stage of the life cycle will have environmental, social, and economical impacts, such as the availability of raw materials, energy use, water use, labor practices, and waste (Figure 14.1).

Why Sustainable Sourcing Matters

The emergence of sustainability within the fashion industry has happened for many reasons, which include labor rights, media attention, legal risk mitigation, government regulations, Internet transparency, and societal pressures (Esty & Winston, 2006). This section considers the role these issues play in the development of sustainable sourcing in the fashion industries.

Stepping on the Shoulders of Social Responsibility

In the early 1980s many U.S. retailers and brand labels began shifting their production to developing countries to take advantage of lower labor costs. Unfortunately, most of these companies were unaware or uninterested in the environment in which their goods were produced. Labor advocacy groups began researching and publicizing the exploitation of factory workers and pinned responsibility on brands like Nike and Wal-Mart's Kathy Lee. Hastily, legal departments at apparel companies created codes of conduct to protect themselves from the liabilities associated with labor rights violations within their supply chain. Additionally, brands invested in factory audits to protect their corporate reputation. The focus on labor issues also brought increased awareness to and aided the growth of sustainable initiatives.

As social audits become more common, leading apparel companies are beginning to review the risks associated with environmental issues. Established sustainable apparel companies proactively reduce risk by encouraging suppliers to look at the entire system of activities and resources linked to their business, including but not limited to management, processes, raw materials, and community. This holistic approach better enables factories to manage both social and environmental compliance issues and run more efficiently. H&M recently added environmental questions to its auditor's checklist, a form containing over 300 points for factory visits. The audit allows H&M to specify its position to suppliers on behavior with regard to the environment and human rights (Hennes & Mauritz, 2007). Nike has created a six-step selection process for adding new factories to its sourcing base, referred to as New Source Approval Process (NSAP). NSAP is intended to help Nike build supply chain partnerships with well-managed factories and reduce the risk of adding any inefficient or unethi-

FIGURE 14.2. Established in 1947 in Sweden, H&M now has an international presence, with fashion goods delivered daily to stores. (Photo by Erin Fitzsimmons.)

cal partners. Nike's NSAP steps include a factory profile; quality inspections; environmental, safety, and health inspections; labor inspections, third-party labor audits; review for the need of new factories; and approval by Nike's compliance department (Nike, 2004). While labor disputes and proactive corporate programs have helped to highlight environmental issues, governmental regulations are also creating work in corporate law departments.

Mitigating Risk and Regulatory Barriers by Being Proactive

Governments at all levels, particularly in Japan, Germany, and the Nordic countries, are beginning to incorporate sustainability into new regulations. If a company's sourcing department does not follow developing policies, it may lose business in the regulated region when products don't conform to the law. For example, the European Union's Registration, Evaluation, and Authorization of Chemicals (REACH) policy has a goal "to protect human health and the environment through the better and earlier identification of the properties of chemical substances." (European Commission's Environment Directorate-General, 2006). Apparel companies must understand which chemicals are health risks and find alternatives for textile processing.

Local, state, and federal governments are also concerned about climate change and are creating policies to restrict how much carbon dioxide a company can emit. Watching this trend offers companies a telescope into the future. Within the United States, 14 states representing approximately one-half of the U.S. population and energy consumption have climate change policies in place (Environmental Protection Agency, 2006). Therefore, one may predict that U.S. federal policy is down the road and proactive companies should measure and reduce CO_2 emissions today.

Governments and international health organizations also warn society about the possible outbreak of infectious diseases. The potential of a disease spreading regionally or worldwide could drastically reduce or stop the flow of internationally traded goods. For example, if Avian Flu overwhelmed regions of Asia, sourcing mangers would need to consider two questions:

1. Will importing countries ban goods from the infected region?
2. Will there be supply-side constraints due to a health crisis in the exporting country? (Langton, 2006)

If an outbreak occurs, how will companies continue to deliver products? One option companies are considering is to produce a portion of goods within the same region as the customer, thereby allowing the flow of goods and reduction of economic losses. Yet by far the largest incentive for corporations to embrace sustainability is that it builds trust within society.

Building Societal Trust

Environmental scientist Janine Banyus states, "The Earth is ringing—ringing off the hook" to let us know about the destruction humankind has caused it. An increase in hurricanes due to climate change, ozone depletion, raw material depletion, droughts, water pollution, and air pollution are just a few of the weekly media topics. The Earth is "ringing off the hook," yet we watch. For Banyus, it is important for humans to realize that we are not the owners of Earth but its "keystone species." People are the cornerstone of survival and must take responsibility to protect and sustain life on Earth (Banyus, 2005). As consumers and producers, businesses must take accountability by understanding their role in conserving resources. By embracing sustainability, corporations build trust within society, which includes their customers, suppliers, and employees.

Communication through the Internet has changed the playing field. Traditionally, companies had control of their message. Today they do not. The Internet offers a broader scope of information to

FIGURE 14.3. Few companies are fully aware of their carbon emissions, but full disclosure is essential if greenhouse emissions are to be constrained. (Photo by Paul Ellis/AFP/Getty Images.)

society, both good and bad. Media has helped put environmental issues on center stage. Brands can only overcome negative attacks by being honest and sincere about their interests in contributing to society. By taking care of reputational capital, a company creates a motivating work environment, a loyal supply chain, and a trusting name. The first sections of this chapter have covered what sustainable sourcing is and why it has emerged within the fashion industry. The next section reviews key components of environmental stewardship and sourcing.

Key Components to Environmental Stewardship and Sourcing

An executive's decision on where to produce clothing is based on several key criteria: creation of highly functional product teams, construction of supply chain relationships, production in a strategic location, assessment of fiber choice, and analysis of costs. This section shows how each of these criteria can be incorporated into sustainable sourcing practices.

Understanding the Depth of Commitment

Sustainability starts with a company's commitment to the issue. Once the commitment is made, staff must be educated about sustainability and its link to corporate growth. Although staff members may understand there are some environmental impacts linked to the fashion business, they may not tie it directly to their jobs. Developing a training program will give staff a clear understanding of the components of sustainability and how they can contribute to a greener supply chain. The next step, create a sustainability policy that takes a systemic approach to business and product development. This can be done by reviewing all aspects of the life cycle of the company's environmental footprint, including the life cycle of its products.

When taking a holistic approach to sustainability and corporate development, people from various parts within the organization and its network of stakeholders should be considered. One of the most important parts is the designer. Engaging the designer allows a company to filter out many of the toxic compounds that might be used in the product and incorporate greener substitutes that will become part of the product at the point of product creation. There are many issues to consider when creating a garment, such as corporate image, consumer needs, price, quality, and innovation. Layering on environmental aspects may overwhelm a designer unless a thoughtful approach is taken. Because designers are often detached from the environmental impacts of a product, it will be important to create a cross-disciplinary team that includes experts from other product stages to tackle these challenges. Sustainable sourcing requires a more thorough knowledge of the supply chain, thus educating designers will be an important aspect of its success (Lofthouse, 2000).

Cross-functional sustainability teams may have two or three lay-ers: the core team, the extended team, and the external stakeholders. The core team includes a sourcing executive, a manufacturing engi-neer, a designer, and an environmental expert. It's important that the core team includes an environmental expert to solve up front issues related to new product development. The extended team may include a market researcher, a legal counselor, a logistics manager, a sales manager, and the suppliers. Chemical supply companies will play an important role within the extended team by offering new green chemistry alternatives to the core team and ultimately to the dye and finishing houses with the supply chain. External stakeholders may include nonprofit groups, government agencies, trade associa-tions, and local communities. Fostering collaboration among indus-try businesses through external stakeholders, such as trade associa-

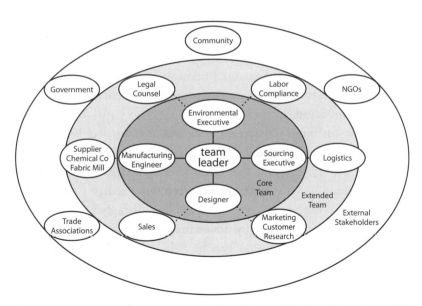

FIGURE 14.4. A structure of a cross-functional sustainability team. (Adapted from T.E. Graedel and B.R. Allenby, Industrial Ecology, NJ: Pearson Education, 2003.)

tions and nonprofit groups, has allowed companies to share results of factory assessments, reducing the number of audits per factory, making both the supplier's and buyer's job easier. Figure 14.4 is an illustration of structure of a cross-functional sustainability team. Nordstrom's product development group, for example, has recently created an environmental specialist position to work within this type of framework.

The links among cross-functional teams can be demonstrated through the most common design elements. For example, connections among chemical companies, designers, and dye houses will be one of the new dynamics to choosing color; this connection will allow the designer to evaluate color choices not only on aesthetics but also with respect to environmental impacts. As part of creating a sustainable supply chain, the core team should assess their current business relations, product categories, and marketing strategies by asking the following questions:

1. Rank current suppliers by importance and identify potentially "green" suppliers.
2. Rank fabrications based on importance and sustainable traits. Then brainstorm on how to incorporate eco-characteristics into each fabrication.
3. Review customer satisfaction polls and SKU, or *stock keeping unit*, counts. If the company can satisfy customer demand making fewer quality garments that sell with a higher margin than many styles with the same functionality but a lower margin, the company will succeed in generating equivalent or higher profits using less material. Additionally, there may be a market segment the company is missing that can be filled through eco-innovative products.

The core team should then consider these questions when reviewing the sustainability of its supply chain:

1. Is this the right product for our customer?
2. Where are the raw materials for the product coming from?
3. If it is a natural or regenerated fiber, is the supplier using sustainable practices to produce and extract the raw material?
4. If it is a synthetic fiber, what percentage of the raw material is made of high-quality recycled content?
5. Does the supplier have a successful management system (e.g., the International Organization for Standardizations environmental management standards—ISO14001) in place with an appointed compliance manager?
6. What is the energy source used for spinning, knitting, and weaving the fabric?
7. How energy-efficient is the machinery used in the production process?
8. Are green chemistry concepts being used to pretreat, dye, and finish the fabric?
9. Is the dye house investing in closed-loop water systems?
10. How many miles does the fiber travel throughout its life cycle (i.e., from raw material extraction to production process to retailer to consumer)?
11. What mode of transportation is being used?
12. Can the same high-quality garment be produced with less material?
13. What percentage of fabric waste is produced in the cutting phase?
14. Are workers rights respected? (See International Labour Organization's Web site for example of standards: www.ilo.org/public/english/standards/norm.)
15. Can this product be returned to the retailer, refurbished, recycled, or composted by the consumer?

This series of questions should spur some ideas within the sustainability team, allowing the company to consider which strategy it will take to develop a sustainable sourcing policy. The questions will also allow the team to contemplate alternative strategies for sourcing, such as location and product miles. The next part of this section addresses location through the possibilities for supply chain cities and "local for local" products.

New Models for Sourcing

Towns across the world have historically been built around industry, and the apparel trade was a key driver of this movement. Mill towns were developed around factories producing textile products. Today, sustainability managers embrace the advantages of local industry, referring to them as supply chain cities and bioregionalism. Alternatives to current decisions regarding where apparel is manufactured are discussed below.

Supply Chain Cities

The "supply chain city" was the brainchild of Henry Tan, CEO of Luen Thai, a vertically integrated apparel company, and Chris Chan, a vice president with the Liz Claiborne company in Asia. The "city" was conceived to support everything from design concept to fabric development to finished products, giving buyers a total supply chain solution. One big advantage of having many processes within one area is a highly organized vertical operation that reduces the turn time of product development from 1 year to 12 weeks. The first Luen Thai supply chain city is located in Dongguan, approximately 30 minutes from Hong Kong (Luen Thai, n.d.).

Burlington Worldwide Apparel refers to their "supply chain city" as a full-service production location. Burlington launched a joint venture with Phong Phu, a state-owned apparel business in Vietnam. (Burlington Industries, 2006). India refers to this close grouping of industrial facilities as "clusters." Tirupur, located in Southern India, is referred to as a "cluster" but offers the same opportunity as a supply chain city.

Because of the vertical platform used by supply chain cities, the opportunity to incorporate sustainability into processes exists at both the facility level and the municipal level. By using "eco-industrial parks" as a template, waste is sent back "upstream," solar panels create energy, water is recycled, and transportation emissions are reduced when suppliers are located in close proximity to one another. Thus, the supply chain city reduces the garment turn time and develops the product using sustainable business practices. This business concept has a better chance of gaining acceptance when governments at the local and national level support such initiatives by offering incentives, eco-tax rebates, training, and technical assistance to "supply chain cities" that create sustainable products.

Bioregionalism

Another alternative to a global supply chain is making clothing closer to the market. This is referred to as bioregionalism. Bioregionalists develop products through the local population within a naturally defined region using local renewable materials and waste reduction strategies (Desai, P.. & Riddlestone S., 2002). Bioregionalism maintains that the homogeneous consumer culture has lost its understanding of its dependency on the natural world. Supporting local economies results in reduction in various business and environmental costs, such as transportation costs, carbon dioxide emissions, infrastructure costs due to reduced truck-to-port miles and sea or air miles, and financing costs due to lower insurance and warehousing requirements.

Bioregionalists seek to minimize "product miles," a relatively new idea in the debate about sustainability. Typically, product miles are defined as the distance it takes for a product to get from the field to the end consumer. By reducing transport miles, greenhouse gas emissions linked to transport can be reduced. Additionally, reducing product miles may also reduce the time between producing a product and selling it, thereby improving a garment's chance of success in the trend-oriented fashion industry.

The University of Cambridge recently released a report comparing three different scenarios for apparel production:

1. Production would be moved from China closer to the UK market, thereby reducing product miles and greenhouse gas emissions.
2. Production would be moved closer to the market, and high technology knitting equipment would be used to reduce the labor cost increase caused by relocating production from China to the United Kingdom.
3. Production would be moved closer to the market, high technology knitting equipment would be used to knit equipment, helping to eliminate production steps, and recycled material would be taken advantage of as a raw material resource.

The researchers discovered that each of these scenarios reduced overall global environmental impacts. But the first scenario of simply shifting production closer to the market did not yield much environmental benefit and the environmental impact in the United Kingdom actually increased because of increased production within that region. Additionally, each scenario has a negative social impact on sewing operators in China. If production is moved from China to the United Kingdom, Chinese sewers would be out of work. The third scenario, moving production using high-tech knitting equipment and using recycled material, had the lowest global environmental impact because the local industry is using recycled fiber instead of extracting and transporting new fiber (Allwood, J., Laursen, S., et al, 2006).

Although the scenarios were developed for the United Kingdom, one might consider a scenario for the United States using Mexico as a local source for production. For example, cotton grown in Texas would be transported by train to Mexico for the production of fabric and garments, then finished apparel would be transported back to the United States for sale. Yet in order for this scenario to be considered a "low-carbon" alternative, logistics managers would need to assess emissions of the mode of transportation selected (from the United States to Mexico and Mexico to the United States). If goods were shipped by train, carbon dioxide emissions would be low. If goods were trucked, carbon dioxide emissions may be just as high as goods transported by boat from Asia (Hopkins, Allen, & Brown, 1994). Therefore, it is important for companies to review their logistics systems to fully understand the environmental benefit of regional production.

Bioregional concepts may become an attractive strategy for company's to reduce miles, if governments move in the direction of creating a green tax on air or road miles (Harvey, 2006). Currently, EU leadership is debating this type of policy to reduce global warming trends. The Bioregional Development Group, a nonprofit organization in the United Kingdom, did a feasibility study on growing, processing, and making hemp apparel within the United Kingdom. Hemp was chosen because it can grow in the United Kingdom's climate without much water and no pesticides. Although this was only done on a small scale, bioregionalists believe local communities all over the world can take advantage of this concept (Blackburn, K., Brighton, J., James, I., Riddlestone, S., & Scott, E., 2004).

Location, Emissions, Efficiencies, and Alternatives

When brand labels went to China to produce clothing, factories offered garments at a lower price. But most Chinese factories are powered by coal, which has many environmental and health issues associated with it. Burning coal produces greenhouse gas emissions, air pollutants, and acid rain, and contributes to respiratory disease in humans (U.S. Energy Information Administration, 1997). Some groups have linked climate change to human rights by asking, "Isn't it the right of all the world's citizens to breathe clean air?" Many Chinese factories are not energy-efficient, emitting more carbon dioxide than necessary. Additionally, due to the increase in production of goods in China, energy demand exceeds domestic supply and China imports coal, overextending an already compromised distribution system (U.S. Energy Information Administration, 1997).

Sourcing managers of multinational corporations should consider supporting several options:

1. Identify greenhouse gas sources within their supply chain, collect data, and develop goals for reduction of these pollutants.
2. Support local Chinese government officials and suppliers in the creation of energy-efficient systems. Most local government officials in China are evaluated on economic productivity, and local officials and suppliers may be receptive to reducing costs through energy efficiencies. The challenge may be the initial upfront costs of such technologies, and allocating the subsequent cost savings to alternative energy sources.
3. Support the development of alternative energy sources within the supply chain, such as on-site solar panels, fuel cells, geothermal systems, or windmills.
4. Move a portion of production closer to its destination market using locally sourced recycled material and technologically advanced equipment.

Mapping Regions to Mitigate Risk

Water, one of the global economies most vital resources is at risk, especially in developing countries. In general, there are three sectors in the apparel industry that use large amounts of water: agriculture, the dyeing and finishing plant, and consumer care. As with energy consumption, consumer care has the largest water use and can best be mitigated through care label instructions and educational initiatives targeted toward changing consumer behavior. Large corporations interested in a long-term supply of raw materials can assess drought risk to cotton fields, for example, using new GPS mapping technology. Simply by overlaying a global cotton production map over a drought map will allow companies to see where the "hot spots" are and prevent a future risk in the deficiency of raw materials.

Here are a few questions one might consider:

1. In what region of the world is the firm's cotton grown?
2. Is the region at risk of drought and water scarcity?
3. Are the cotton plants rain-fed or irrigated?
4. If irrigation is used, is it done efficiently (e.g., drip irrigation)?

Building Supply Chain Relationships

Beyond deciding where to source raw material or produce garments, fashion executives need to motivate current and potential suppliers on the importance of incorporating sustainability into their management plans. Influencing suppliers to create a sustainable supply chain will take commitment from both buyers and sellers. There must be a high level of communication, trust, and genuine interest in rewarding suppliers that develop sustainable initiatives. Initially, preferred suppliers may be seen as falling into two categories: those that are technologically innovative and most able to adapt to changing conditions and those that are valued based on trust and economic interests.

The apparel industry does not have a good track record of building long-term relationships within the supply chain. Factories and textile regions go out of fashion as quickly as the latest skirt length. Suppliers believe for good reason that buyers see low cost as a priority over building deeper, long-term relationships. But as Liker and Choi (2004) point out, well-run companies focus on supply chain relations because they may achieve results that go beyond just lowering costs, such as quicker turns and innovative products that produce higher margins.

When companies build stronger ties within their supply chain, factories better understand how the company works and can make an educated guess on the direction the company might take in the future. This allows the supplier to work on innovative products with a clearer understanding of the customer's direction (Liker & Choi, 2004). Contradictory to this, if the relationship is superficial, it will only lead to temporary improvement. A supplier may try to be compliant with a company's code of conduct, but if there is no real commitment to managerial change from the supplier level, the effort will dissipate or worse, lead to cover-up (Hurst, Murdoch, & Gould, 2005).

Consider the case of Toyota Motor Corporation and why auto part suppliers like working with them. Toyota takes the time to understand the hurdles its suppliers may face and helps to remove them. Toyota is known to commit its own "intellectual capital" for up to two years to address its supplier's challenges. By making this type of commitment to the relationship, the supplier gains respect and insight into the buyer's business interests. It shows that change is about business opportunity for all parties, not just compliance with customers' demands (Liker & Choi, 2004). Suppliers may need training or technical assistance, but only through a review of the supplier's management processes will an outsider understand its needs. It may be revealed that a buyer's habits of constant price pressure, noncommittal policy, incessant requests for shorter order cycles, and frequent changes in orders need to be relayed to corporate executives as a serious business disadvantage for both parties (Bremer, 2005). To elevate this, companies can review their design calendars, allowing for a longer lead time for core items. Therefore, instead of taking 6 to 12 months to produce basic items, a time frame may be adjusted to 18 months, allowing the supply chain enough time to allocate its resources and production line.

Coordination throughout the supply chain is a key component for all companies, but for sustainable sourcing, it is crucial. Many brands only have a direct connection to the apparel manufacturer. A sustainable company will have contact with each link in the supply chain. Therefore, when a company can reduce its supplier base and build

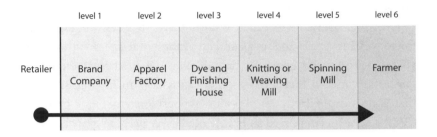

FIGURE 14.5. Instead of independent transactions at each level, partners are part of a coordinated complex supply chain. (Illustration by Jenny Green from sketch courtesy of Shona Quinn.)

long-term relationships, it will more readily lead the coordination effort. A clear communication channel must then be established and each member's interests incorporated into the business strategy. The approach converts the supply chain into a "knowledge chain" and holistic business system. The result will be a prevalence of best practices and supplier innovation within the chain. Eventually, the brand will give responsibility for leadership in sustainable practices back to chain members (Goldbach, 2002). Figure 14.5 demonstrates the various levels of a supply chain relationship. It is important for retailers to go beyond the first relationship and deeper into the supply chain to understand where environmental impacts are occurring. Eventually independent transactions become a part of a highly coordinated supply chain (Goldbach, 2002).

Fiber Sourcing Options

Knowing the *where* and *who* of sustainable sourcing is important, but one also needs to consider the materials being sourced. Choosing fabric has many environmental aspects attached to it. Unfortunately, most designers have little understanding of the environmental impact of fabrics, and current information about eco-fibers is limited. But rather than choosing one fiber over another, companies should seek improvement in both synthetic and natural fiber production.

Growing natural fibers can be environmentally intensive, especially for cotton. Incorporating social and environmental issues within natural fiber production generally proceeds in one of three scenarios: a fair-trade standard that focuses on social issues, an organic standard that addresses environmental issues, or best management practices (BMP, a concept supported and promoted by WWF, the global conservation organization) that focuses on a hybrid of economical and environmental aspects specific to a particular country or region. A company may hope to capture all three aspects of sustainability (i.e., social, environmental, and economic) with one standard, but each system has specific strengths.

Many cotton farmers in developing countries receive a low price for cotton. The fair-trade standard aims to make sure farmers are paid a fair wage. While fair trade also has an environmental component, it focuses on the well-being of the farmer. Alternatively, organic farming and BMP farming promote ecologically sound growing methods and the use of advanced irrigation technology, increasing the efficiency of water utilization (Clay, 2004). Still, organic and BMP differ as well. Organic production focuses on the avoidance of synthetic chemicals and genetically modified organisms. BMP encourages the reduction of chemical use but may not ban it. In Pakistan the Pakistan Sustainable Cotton Initiative (PSCI) aims at developing and promoting best management practices for sustainable cotton production that includes the development of best water practices and the reduction in applications of pesticides and fertilizers. Additionally, BMP tends to be neutral regarding genetically engineered crops. For example, if a chemical company develops a seed considered "drought-tolerant," it may be acceptable for production under BMP guidelines. It is important to a sourcing manager to review all these options and decide which standard makes sense for their business.

A New Resource: Recycling Synthetic Polymers

As mentioned earlier, waste can be recycled into new products. Governments may be the initiators of this "new" resource. The EU introduced regulations for producers, known as Extended Producer Responsibility (EPR), requiring producers to take back goods from consumers after their useful life is over. Although many companies see this as simply another forced policy initiative, it is intended to act as a market incentive that will encourage companies to find innovative ways to create new products from old materials (Mayers, France & Cowell, 2005). U.S. residents are the largest consumers of products and, therefore, the largest producers of waste. But most U.S. companies do not view waste as a resource for new raw materials. Teijen and Toray, two Japanese polyester and nylon textile producers, have found a profitable way to recycle material and produce new material. However, it's important to note that when using recycled content in new products, one must be aware of the quality and source of the recycled material. Companies do not want products that contain harmful toxins. For the textile industry there are opportunities to create technologically advanced recycling plants that classify waste, identify fibers, and test for hazardous compounds. This may, however, prove more achievable for EU companies than for those in the United States because the EU has a stronger textile processing industry within its region that may be able to take advantage of recycled fibers. Bar code or radio frequency identification (RFID) tags, containing information about where the garment came from and its physical and chemical characteristics, could also aid in the end-of-life stage. Besides helping corporate buyers trace their products or use as a marketing tool, these tags could identify fibers and garments, sorting and recycling them based on quality or fiber content (IIED, 2002).

Reducing the Multiplication Effect by Analyzing Costs

"How much will it cost?" is an important question, yet many fashion executives spend little time researching the answer. Direct costs, which include materials and labor, have always been the focus of cost-ing. Indirect costs (i.e., everything but materials, labor, and trim) are less understood and therefore sometimes missed. David Birnbaum, author and apparel industry consultant, created a flowchart showing 101 steps needed to produce a style and says that only 15 percent of these steps are direct cost. The other 85 percent are indirect costs, such as the employment of designers, sales staff, and Web site devel-opers (Birnbaum, 2000). Birnbaum points out the importance of find-ing the critical cost drivers of a business by looking beyond how much fabric costs and what sewers make.

Some companies interested in analyzing indirect costs, employ Activity-Based Costing (ABC), an accounting method that helps man-agers identify what elements of their business are contributing to their expenses. ABC helps identify and assign costs to products and then allows the company to make an informed strategic decision about how to proceed. (Goldbach, 2001) For sustainable sourcing, this not only entails looking at the companies costs but at the entire supply chain, pinpointing critical cost drivers, and using specific accounting measures to analyze the problem.

For example, currently the retail price of organic apparel is higher than conventional apparel. One main reason is that organic cotton farmers are paid more for their product than conventional cotton farmers. The higher premium is much deserved because organic farming is far more labor-intensive than conventional farming, but this cost is multiplied at each stage of production and ends up creating a large gap between the retail prices of organic versus conventional apparel, referred to as the "multiplication effect." By looking at the entire chain, a sourcing manager can identify this magnification of raw material costs and reduce the inflated price (Brooks, Davidson, & Palamides, 1993).

Following are a few costs that should be reviewed:

- Switching costs at the spinning mill.
- Green chemicals and dyestuff.

- Certification and tracking material flow.
- Regional energy costs.
- Material waste.
- Time. The learning curve of sustainable sourcing should be included as a cost. Employees and suppliers will be learning new processes and spending time developing a coordinated supply chain. This will include both technical training and managing a variety of supply chain relationships (Goldbach, 2001).

Conclusion

On a daily basis, the fashion industry interprets society's interests concerning clothing. One of those interests is the environment. Leading companies need to consider how their products will represent this societal issue, whether by changing a store lightbulb or creating sustainable products. For some companies, it will mean equipping their

FIGURE 14.6. Women modeling dresses by From Somewhere, a design house that creates garments out of scraps from the factory floor. (Courtesy Fairchild Publications, Inc.)

staff with a new set of skills based on an understanding of sustainability, why it's important, and how to implement responsible sourcing practices.

Sustainable sourcing takes many players within the supply chain, each bringing his or her own expertise to the team. Companies will benefit by taking advantage of these collaborative efforts. But in the end, what matters most is what speaks to you as a fashion executive and human being. What is your truth? The Dakota Indians used the saying, "We will be known forever by the tracks we leave." Although not all the answers to sustainable development are available to us, we have many options. Let's get started.

References

Allwood, J., Laursen, S., Malvido, de Rodriguez, C., & Bocken, N. (2006). Well dressed? The present and future sustainability of clothing and textiles in the United Kingdom. Cambridge, UK: University of Cambridge Institute for Manufacturing.

Banyus, J., (2005). What life knows: New ideas from biology that could change the world. Bioneers 2005 Conference. San Rafael, California.

Birnbaum, D. (2000). *Birnbaum's global guide to winning the great garment war.* Hong Kong: Third Horizon Press, Ltd.

Birnbaum, D. (2003). 101 steps to producing a style: flow chart. Retrieved November 1, 2006, from www.fashiondex.com/globalguide/index.html

Blackburn, K., Brighton, J., James, I., Riddlestone, S., & Scott, E. (2004, November). Feasibility of hemp textile production in the UK. Retrieved November 21, 2006, from Bioregional Development Group Web site at http://www.bioregional.com/programme_projects/pap_fibres_prog/hemp%20textiles/hemp_hpg.htm

Bowen, B. (2001). Chapter 2: Let's go fair. *Fair trade yearbook 2001.* Retrieved November 06, 2006, from European Fair Trade Association Web site at http://www.european-fair-trade-association.org/Efta/Doc/yb01-en.pdf

Bremer, J. (2005, June 21). *Kenan institute initiatives in china.* American Apparel and Footwear Association Annual Meeting, New York.

Brooks, P., Davidson, L., & Palamides, J. (1993, February). Environmental compliance: You better know your abcs. *Occupational Hazards*, 123.

Burlington Industries. (2006, June 6). *International Textile Group's Burlington World-Wide to Build Manufacturing Complex in Vietnam*. Retrieved November 01, 2006, from International Textile Group Web site at http://www.burlington.com/news/

Clay, J. (2004). *World agriculture and the environment: A commodity-by-commodity guide to impacts and practices*. Washington D.C.: Island Press.

Desai, P., & Riddlestone S. (2002). *Bioregional solutions: For living on one planet*. London: Green Books.

Environmental Protection Agency, (n.d.). Clean energy-environment partnership program. Retrieved December 10, 2006, from Environmental Protection Agency Web site at http://www.epa.gov/cleanenergy/stateandlocal/partnership.htm

Esty, D., & Winston, A. (2006). *Green to gold*. New Haven: Yale University Press.

European Commission's Environment Directorate-General. (2006). Registration, evaluation, and authorization of chemicals (REACH) regulations. Retrieved November 15, 2006, from European Commission Web site at http://ec.europa.eu/environment/chemicals/reach/reach_intro.htm

Ferdows, K., Lewis, M., & Machuca, J. (2004, November, 1). Rapid-fire fulfillment. *Harvard Business Review*, p. 4.

Goldbach, M. (2001). *Managing the costs of greening: A supply chain perspective*. Proceedings of the 2001 Business Strategy and Environment Conference, September 10–11, 2001, Leeds, UK, 109–118.

Goldbach, M., (2002). *A conceptual framework for green supply relationships: The example of green cotton chains*. Conference Proceedings of the International Expert Workshop, May 16–17, 2002, Fontainebleau, France.

Graedel, T. E. & Allenby B. R. (2003). *Industrial ecology*. Upper Saddle River, NJ: Prentice Hall.

Harvey, F. (2006, December 6). Lose-lose: The penalties of action alone stall collective effort on climate change. *Financial Times*, 13.

H & M, A. B. (2007). *Supply Chain Monitoring*. Retrieved January 15, 2007, from http://www.hm.com/corporateresponsibility/supplychainworkingconditions/supplychainmonitoring/factoryaudits_monotoringarticle2.nhtml

Hopkins, L., Allen, D., & Brown, M., (1994). Quantifying and reducing environmental impacts resulting from transportation of a manufactured garment. *Pollution Prevention Review* 4(4): 491–500.

Hurst, R., Murdoch, H., & Gould, D. (2005). *Changing over time: Tackling supply chain labour issues through business practice.* Retrieved December 10, 2006, from http://www.impacttlimited.com/site/casestudy_item.asp?CS_ID=9

Langton, D. (2006). *Avian flu pandemic: Potential impact of trade disruptions* Congressional Research Service Report for Congress, Library of Congress. Retrieved October 30, 2006, from U.S. Department of State Web site: http://fpc.state.gov/documents/organization/68827.pdf

Laursen S., Hansen, J., Bagh, J., Jensen, O., & Werther, I. (1997).

Environmental assessment of textiles, Ministry of Environment and Energy, Danish Environmental Protection Agency. Retrieved November 11, 2006, from http://www2.mst.dk/Udgiv/publications/1997/87-7810-838-1/pdf/87-7810-838-1.pdf

Liker, J., & Choi, T. (2004). Building deeper supplier relationships. *Harvard Business Review.*

Lofthouse, V.A., & Bhamra, T. A. (2000). Ecodesign integration: Putting the "co" into ecodesign. In Scrivener, S. A. R., Ball, L. J. & Woodcock, A. (Eds), *Collaborative design* (pp. 163–172). London: Springer-Verlag.

Luen Thai Holding Limited. (n.d.). *Supply chain cities.* Retrieved November 25, 2006, from http://www.luenthai.com/supplychain.htm

Mayers, C., France, C., & Cowell, S. (2005). Extended producer responsibility for waste electronics. *Journal of Industrial Ecology, 9,* 169–189.

Nike's corporate responsibility report. (2004). Retrieved on January 15, 2007, from http://www.nike.com/nikebiz/nikebiz.jhtml?page=29&item=fy04

Organization for Economic Co-operation and Development. (2004). *The development dimension of trade and environment: Case studies on environmental requirements and market access.* Paris: OECD Publications. Retrieved October 24, 2006, from http://www.oecd.org/dataoecd/23/15/25497999.pdf

PCI Membrane Systems, Division of Aquious. (2000). *Wool dyer T Forsell slashes water bills by 75%.* Retrieved October 10, 2006, from http://www.pcimem.com/dsp_press.cfm?PressID=18

U.S. Energy Information Administration. (October). *China's energy demand now exceeds domestic supply.* Retrieved October 16, 2006, from http://www.eia.doe.gov/emeu/cabs/china/part2.html

WENDYROSIE SCOTT is a freelance broadcast journalist, writer, lecturer, and consultant based in London. Specializing in culture and lifestyle, she has been involved in this area in the wider arena for over two decades. Acting as an anthropologist and cultural advisor, current collaborations have focused upon native fashion design and styling. A recent residence in San Francisco enabled her love of festivals, alongside her appreciation for organic and eco design, to be explored in both architecture and fashion. Present involvements include design trend prediction.

CHAPTER 15

Recycle and Reuse as Design Potential

Wendyrosie Scott

Old is becoming new again on many levels of fashion. An increasing appreciation for vintage style is driving consumers not only to thrift stores and nostalgic festivals but to high-street shops like Liberty and Marks and Spencer; moreover, this drive is creating new outlets such as high-end secondhand stores, finder services that comb the globe via the Internet, brand-new wares fashioned to look old, and styles of the future where parts and pieces of cast-off garments find clever homes in restyled, recycled clothing.

A Green Renaissance

Mention the word "fashion" and pretty much no matter where you are or whom you are with, there will be a response, even if it's to negate or provocate. Fashion is deeply embedded in our cultural notions of self and expression, style and taste, leisure and pleasure, protection and liberation, flamboyance and annoyance. Like it or not, it brings in big business, is all-pervasive, and is subliminally encoded into our lifestyle. For some, fashion is a philosophy. From the ridiculous to the divine, it is hard to evade. Personally, it is a subject I have always loved and been involved with in one realm or another. It enthuses and captivates me, while equally being something that perversely brings to me a sense of shame. Like the dichotomy of being a vegetarian butcher, I am ill at ease with it all. By its very nature, fashion is fickle, frivolous, essentially superficial, and often nonsensical. So, to be predominantly working in an area that to all intents and purposes is pompous and superfluous, sometimes makes me feel like I should conduct my work behind closed doors and with a minder, or bouncer, on guard.

That said, having had plenty of opportunities to struggle and then placate myself with this dilemma, it was with pleasure that I agreed to do this chapter in a book that clearly has a conscience as well as a love of fashion. Sustainability as a concept is currently at the core of the fashion industry. Yet the very premise of fashion dictates that in order to keep ahead, one must frequently purchase the latest trends, thus constantly fuel the consumption of clothing and continue the circle of fashion fads. Therefore, by exploring the realm of recycled design, one can conclude that "the new black is green."

This is an exciting and poignant time in fashion, and having closely watched it develop over the course of many years, I can easily conclude that a definite new movement is dawning; and just like the Renaissance within the history of art, a period like this one for the fashion world only occurs when there is receptivity toward it. Hence, we now have a chance to welcome in change both in consumer consciousness and demand. This movement may not be major, but it is impacting upon society enough to cause serious ripples, if not quite waves, in the turbulent sea of fashion. A number of key players, such as Katherine Hamnett, Bora Aksu, and Rebecca Earley, whether established or more recent, are at the helm ready to steer us through. For some of the many designers in this field, it has been a somewhat difficult journey, but essentially all were optimistic. This is not a self-righteous rant or a platform for ethical companies; the designers included in this chapter were chosen as much because their designs exude style, whether the cost is pennies or megabucks, as for their contribution and innovative stance in trying to forge forward in an industry frequently fraught with hypocrisy and hierarchy. By looking beyond the merely superficial to the more practical and achievable alternatives, we find that new threads emerge.

Conscious Couture

Throughout this research, it became apparent that many of the designed clothes in question could be considered *couture* items, in that these are individually created, using key skills. Therefore, whether vintage, refashioned, restyled, or recycled, their current form and status quantifies them as couture, although perhaps not as the highly crafted *haute* couture. Haute couture is more often associated with the international fashion world, which is financially, socially, and creatively exclusive and resides in an area of the fashion business that is diminishing yearly. What might replace this diminishing area? The evidence is certainly looking positively sustainable. It will be interesting, therefore, to follow what could be referred to as the new allure of conscious couture.

Vintage

Vintage is in vogue, in every sense of the word. It can currently be seen in numerous publications, is stocked in high-street stores, and is worn at the best fashionista events and award ceremonies. Designers and copyists, not for the first time, are copying vintage looks in their contemporary styles. Nevertheless, there is no replacing the real deal, and today more than ever, owning and wearing vintage is desirable and sought after by everyone from Kate Moss to Cate Blanchett. It has achieved an acceptance unheard of as recently as five years ago; then, it was more associated with notions of poverty-stricken students, and its general image was seen as more "mothball" than à la mode. Yet currently it's *the* fashion pièce de résistance, or it could be said that it's all about the vintage advantage. Certainly in terms of ethical and environmental fashion, you can't get any greener.

Katherine Hamnett, a key designer in the 1980s who is notorious for being personally and creatively political and progressive, has remained steadfast in her devotion to a broad sense of sustainable fashion. Anyone involved in fashion over the last two decades is aware of her, not least because as far back as 1989 she launched her own investigation into the impact of clothing and the textile industry on the environment. She wholly supports the validity of recycled fashion at a time when designers are surely threatened by its very nature. As Hamnett states, "Vintage really is the key word in fashion at the moment, recycled clothing ticks all the boxes, [and] it conserves energy and cuts landfill."

But what *is* vintage? Basically, I remember it as secondhand clothes, or *antique* if you wanted to attribute it to a more exclusive and elevated realm. *Vintage* covers the period 1910 to 1960, while 1960 to 1980 is regarded as *retro*. Any preceding period is classified as antique. But establishing exactly what vintage actually is proved difficult. Many shops also did not know, and so they classified garments approximately five years or over as vintage.

Many vintage garments sold today remain well preserved, and not all have been previously worn. Established designer vintage fetches prices in quadruple figures, especially the more pristine conditioned and classical designs. In London, prices in pounds, ranged from single to four-figure sums. The businesses that sell them have a new attitude, have a greater insight, and are fast emerging as a force to be reckoned with in the heady, glitzy world of "worn before." I therefore wanted

FIGURE 15.1. Sporting twenty-first-century vintage style, model Jay wears a new vintage 1970s San Franciscan original silk poncho coupled with recycled wool and silk scarf from Liberty Store and vintage Chanel dress in silk and wool, circa 1940s. (Photo by Wendyrosie Scott.)

to bring a new spin to the mix and explore alternative notions of vintage. Let's begin with festivals, because it is there where a new generation of style-conscious consumers reign.

The Jewel at the Festival

More usually held outdoors in a series of temporary constructions, festivals essentially remain true to their founding nature in that they are gatherings of like-minded souls intent on being entertained but also enlightened. And, it is usually a two-way process of teaching and learning, a shared responsibility more in tune with a philosophical approach and lifestyle choice reminiscent of the 1960s and 1970s. But before it all seems too starry-eyed, presently companies with an emphasis on profit making have monopolized and thus "unpurified" the festival that once was. Nevertheless, the festivalgoers continue to make these events hotbeds of creativity and talent, and with a new generation, in part more suitably shrewd and astute and therefore attuned to practices concerning issues such as recycled and ethical fashion. Festivals serve as pointers of heritage, networking havens, celebrations, and unavoidably, indeed unashamedly, opportunities to launch ideas, not all of which work outside of this arena. Notably, festivals act as receptive and active entities where experimentation, in all its glory, flourishes. Cue the cutting-edge creatives and misfits. All are welcome here. Fashion knows no bounds, *especially* at the festival.

The focus of the festival has grown from music and ambience to encompass fashion and style, and the hefty theatricality that goes with them. So within the context of old becoming new again, recycling and refashioning is presently at the forefront of what was previously only a small movement within a certain subsection of underground society, amongst a conscious and already converted few. Beginning with the likes of the Big Green gathering, or "BGG" as it's commonly called, and Glastonbury, where Lost Vagueness, the foremost production company whose performance concept was established here, recycling clothes was essentially a conscious and communal practice or ideal, not the focus of revelry. But the festival scene proved a perfect fit. No need to extol the positive aspects of actively seeking out and wearing recycled garments as everyday wear here; that would be like preaching to the converted. Such events have always been consistently radical and philosophically progressive, as has the fashion sported.

In terms of UK fashion, the festival has sparked a revival where dressing up and putting effort, humor, and thought into an outfit is de rigueur. Here is a new and creative clothing outlet where ingenuity and decadence meld together and collude to compose an entirely unique new look that's outlandish, individual, and imbued with the cult of cutting-edge fashion. Poignantly, festivals encompass the core elements of sustainable style; vintage, recycled, and refashioned designs result in multifaceted implications for the future of fashion. In fact, trend-forecasting companies dispatch trend spotters to detect the next trend, most notably at Bestival. Thus, styles and notions borne out of the festival entity impact upon mainstream design, where, of course, the current fashion is for vintage, which I believe was conceived here at the humble festival.

Vintage clothing was in part borne out of economic necessity alongside a desire to create a socially and environmentally friendly look. For some years now, themed events, particularly burlesque, at festivals and events such as Lost Vagueness in the United Kingdom and Burning Man in the United States, encouraged the art of adornment. These events initially emerged to create a new dimension in the performance arena and to pull in paying attendees; inadvertently, they helped spark the notion that secondhand fashion was hot. The anarchic progressive always finds ways forward, and Lost Vagueness led the way, facilitating a kind of leisure-pleasure phenomenon, where dressing up thrives in the playground that is the festival. In this contemporary escapist environment, retro is the real thing and living the lifestyle means more than just dressing the part. Elements of a dress code have emerged that act as signifiers. Some garments are associated with certain life choices and may act as indicators of a chosen way of living, more usually nonconformist and essentially bohemian.

Colorful, individual, flamboyant, and symbolic, clothes in this arena have enabled a cultural climate of choice to be donned, whether for the weekend or beyond. For instance, a chosen era, such as the 1920s, could be specifically adopted where not only the clothing style was sported but essentially the attitude of that period of time, including social and political approaches. This is no easy feat given that events are often held in environments such as an inaccessible field, where dressing up takes extra effort. That people, mostly from the city, take the trouble to select, purchase, and assemble an entire look and bring it to obscure, countryside locations is wonderful enough, but to then take what can be an expensive, exquisite, finely detailed, and original outfit made of delicate material means that at times the resultant assemblage are ephemeral. Transporting these looks to the festivals, often in these muddied, weatherworn, isolated, and some-what primitive areas where the walk to the large tent housing the event means rough underfoot conditions can prove quite hazardous for those wearing heels! Without adequate lighting to lead the way, and further challenged, for some, by the inevitable consumption of alcohol, stylish vintage dishevelment reigns supreme.

An environment where fertile minds and anarchic activism is not only hedonistic but also visibly productive. It establishes eye-catching theatrical, surreal, otherworldly, and wild capsule collections salvaged from obscure sources and clothes swaps. Many participants are professional performing artists immersed in their work. Their minds are bold and inquisitive. Converged, they create an alchemical appearance that is ironically spawned by some, possibly as a response to an oral chemical experiment. Notably, such uninhibited creativity formulates an unforgettable image that fans the flames of a new movement. Inevitably and with greater frequency, all this attracts precious and positive media coverage, for such is the cauldron of creativity, over-flowing with its many bright minds, so stylistically futuristic in their endeavors to really put on a show. The results are often startling and provocative given that they come mostly from making use of available and limited materials. This utilization of the secondhand and vintage move these products into the mainstream. Customization and incor-poration of homemade crafts is just one example.

There is also a marked change in the attitudes of a new generation of consumers. "Over the years and especially since the 1980s, con-sumers have been making an ever-increasing impact on the way gov-ernments and companies behave in all parts of the world" (Ethical Marketing Group, 2005).

I have personally conducted random interviews at all of these festi-vals, interviewing people for years on these subjects in my role as a radio journalist. I took polls over a period of nine months, from March to November 2006, at various fests with a random selection of usually about 20 people informally discussing the subject. Almost 100 percent of those approached were positive about purchasing second-hand clothes. Only 3 percent had any reservations, which mostly consisted of the notion that secondhand equaled soiled. While this may not be a representative sample, the festival attendance in the United Kingdom has seen a marked rise in visitors annually (British Arts Festival Association, 2002), and these festivals are significant across a range of generations. Additionally, vendors also utilize recycled and refashioned goods brought back from developing countries, where designs are then adapted in high-street stores.

The popularity of vintage rose further when it was adopted by the likes of Victoria Beckham shopping at Oxfam, a leading UK charity selling secondhand clothes. "Beckham's visit to Oxfam saw a 70 percent rise in donations to the store and a threefold rise in people shopping for secondhand glamour. Oxfam sells £22 million worth of clothes yearly," according to *New Consumer* magazine, which calls this phenomenon as the "celeb effect."

The Bestival Festival

Alongside great music, Bestival typifies the very pleasure we can get from clothes and the consequential transformational effect they play as part of the festival experience. Ingenuity and good-humored revelry combine to create a mishmash of fashion faux pas, as well as stylized new looks. The flamboyant flapper (Constantino, 1991) converging with the space age chic of Miyake (Watson, 2002) influenced high-street copies and customized cutoffs. Or the men living out their cowboy fantasy, sporting the full regalia. Bestival has astutely incorporated these elements into their event. As Bestival Press Manager Clare Woodcock explains, "Bestival always encourages lots of dressing up. We find it really lets people lose their inhibitions and let loose for a weekend. We always stage a fancy dress parade on the Saturday, usually with a theme such as 'cowboys and Indians' one year and then 'circus' another. But generally people tend to dress up all weekend in all sorts. There is a 'dressing up box' on-site and a few other stalls that hire out various different costumes. Lots of vintage stuff included." Dipping into the "dressing up box" and becoming whomever one wants to be for however long clearly is a great idea and success. Bestival's popularity is testament to that. When I asked as part of the overall fest polls I carried out if folks were apprehensive about wearing essentially secondhand clothes, they said this did not really enter into the equation. It was much more about "getting into character" and also a great chance to try a new look.

Lost Vagueness

Lost Vagueness Productions is a performance production company that runs its own festival while residing within Bestival. Renowned for its decadence, hedonism, and costumery policy, it demands dressing

FIGURE 15.2. These Lost Vagueness revelers exemplify the festival's spirit of self-styled expression and indulgence. The female dancer wears a vintage 1980s broderie anglais top, an embroidered corset, and a cotton-and-silk mix skirt. The male dancer wears a woolen kilt and a linen jacket. (Photo by Shelly Graham.)

up. Entry is at the discretion of its "style masters." These are usually the minders or bouncers working at the door. Style masters have often been involved, albeit remotely, in the field of fashion, or as long-term members of the company. This in itself attracts crowds eager to be accepted and so dress outlandishly. For the most part, it is a casino with several stages showing performers in old vaudevillian style, and in anything regarded as decadent. Emphasis is upon burlesque-themed performers, and anything from the Prohibition era has been an overwhelming success and imitated by many. Success has consistently grown via publicity coverage on both TV and radio. In 2003 the demand to enter the Lost Vagueness tent was so overwhelming, the area had to be closed, and then in 2004 when Kate Moss and Pete Doherty visited again, the place was overwhelmed with people trying to gain entry.

Goodwood Vintage Revival Festival

With its emphasis on "old style," or more traditional classic glamour, the Goodwood Festival has gone a long way to whet the mainstream appetite for vintage. Holding clothing at its core, this motoring event ensures that its participants adhere to the rule of sporting the correct attire. A wondrous mix of styles posing as next season's trends parade the grounds that, when coupled with the vintage cars at this infamous racing track, creates a time warp unlike any other. Exhilarating, authentic, and unmissable, Goodwood actively encourages those attending to buy recycled goods. Press Manager Janet Bradley explains, "We actively encourage dressing up to help attendees feel more involved. It isn't difficult to dress appropriately, i.e. sports jacket with tie or cravat, flannel trousers and trilby for men, with a touch of Brylcreem of course. A waisted dress, big skirt, or tweedy suit for women, complete with twin set and pearls, seamed stockings, lipstick, and eyeliner. Many charity shops will supply the basics at little cost. Then our shows and the 'vintage revival' market also give you a further chance to buy. If you are exhibiting your product, it must be classical, pre-1966 in style and based on the fashions and trends of motoring or aviation of the time, including automobile, memorabilia, aeronautical, art, publications, vintage clothes, and accessories together with an authentic vehicle. Restoration services for vintage are welcome."

High-Street Vintage

Vintage looks and trends have now spread to the high street, introducing themselves to a new audience. Iconic stores such as Liberty have their own vintage concession and mostly present the classics (e.g., Dior, Ossie Clark, and Celia Birtwell); these reside next to contemporary cutting-edge designs, which are essentially exclusive. Notably, other established stores, such as Selfridges and Jaegar, are clearly informed and influenced by past styles that have been incorporated accordingly into contemporary designs, yet it is essentially Liberty that presents authentic vintage as high art to the discerning customer. Sadly, vintage has not sold as successfully as might have been predicted. The diehard notion that "secondhand equals soiled" appears to be the major obstacle. Yet this store remains eager to ensure that the vintage area does not become a "museum section."

In terms of streetwear, the largest and main Topshop chain store, its London outlet, has introduced a vintage "corner" concession. Interestingly, many customers have not been aware that these were secondhand goods and even when informed were not phased or discouraged from buying. This suggests that the store location was apt despite the relatively high prices; a shrewd marketing campaign also helped sell these secondhand goods most notably in their peek-a-boo range. Notably one of the United Kingdom's most established stores, Marks and Spencer, a quintessentially traditional British store, introduced a range of brand-new products wholly influenced by past styles. The focus of its autumn magazine was labeled "A fine vintage." How wonderful, if idealistic, to think that perhaps someday this would be necessary, due to all vintage clothes having been purchased. Still, it's worth noting that the allure of authentic vintage is what is driving this market upward.

Palette Store: Future Vintage?

Being a confessed shopaholic (the antithesis of this chapter; I am trying to mend my ways and wares), it was with awe that I returned from living amidst the wonder of San Franciscan thrift to find a beguiling vintage diamond of a shop right on my doorstep in London. Palette is a jewel of a capsule that holds within it a sparkling taste of the States buffed with the smoothness of Europe, and polished off to make it glitter with style.

By providing a service that oozes old-school attitude toward glam

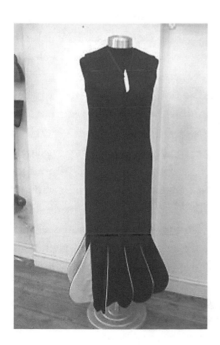

FIGURE 15.3. This black Pierre Cardin dress, circa 1969, seen here in Palette Store window in Islington, London, was since sold to a private buyer for collection in a museum. This dress of crimplene jersey fabric, from Cardin's 1968–1969 collection, emulates a rocket. The idea of ultramodern, genderless space uniform was a look favored by Cardin and Courrèges, although many design houses played with space-travel themes throughout the sixties. (Photo by Mark Ellis.)

garb, it is a joy. Mixing garments of the past with those of the present, it is the kind of shop where its demure size is not reflective of its professional and massive attitude. Such is the quality and authenticity of its contents that I find I ask myself if I am correctly attired before entering. The atmosphere is of elegance and a knowing reassurance of its wares, which hopefully will not become self-aggrandizing. *It is, after all, only fashion*, I say to myself, as though to shake away the haze of the evocative and decadent bygone age that is conjured upon entry. Here, there is none of that mustiness that for some still signifies secondhand. It is pure pleasure to shop in the most exquisite and modern of surrounds, but it's really all about the clothes, which speak for themselves. The clothes say things like, "I'm the most chic piece you'll ever see," and "I've lived a manicured life of leisure, parties, and glam gossip. In fact, despite my price tag and the fact that you absolutely don't need me, well, you just know I could be so good for you! Especially for that 'special do' (i.e., anytime). So *this* is what it's all about, this new vintage scene, *ahhhhh*, just as you dreamed it! Vive la vintage."

In all seriousness, because there is definite seriousness to Palette, it is inspirational to discover such a place where everything has clearly been carefully sourced and is absolutely modern looking. The "it's a lifestyle" approach is evident, and it is a cool response to the formerly stuffy associations of outdated secondhand goods. This store is the missing link between high-street shops, festivals and thrift vintage. It really is in a league of its own in being the crème de la crème of clothing, whether used or unused vintage, and it fully captures contemporary style by always being informed of current looks whilst actively seeking sources from unique and diverse arenas, which in no small part is due to Ellis's unique approach and passion. Whist it is self-aware and celebrates the art of dressing up, festival style, it is unlikely that anyone is buying a piece from here would want to risk ruining it in the festival environment. This is dressing up for grown-ups, and with a price tag to match. Yet as couture, it is wholly affordable and incomparable, yet equally unique.

Clothing rails are displayed in blocks of color with stunning collections of mint-condition vintage and contemporary designer lines, including shoes and handbags. These rails are furnished with 1920s to 1990s collectibles that include interior design goods covered in vintage textiles or reclaimed materials. So when seriously missing the States and yearning to express your love of U.S. vintage, you can rest assured that founder Mark Ellis will come to the rescue. According to its statement to the media (Palette, n.d.), "Palette differs from other vintage stores because it stocks some of the most important American designers from the 1950–1970s, ranging from impeccable dresses by Halston, Pauline Trigere, Ann Fogarty, Lilli Ann, Lilly Pulitzer, Vera, Norman Norell, to many exclusive pieces by Koos Van Den Akker, the King of Boho, and master of fabric collage in the Seventies."

The store doesn't necessarily adhere to fashion trends but tends to stock the season's colors and fabrics. It is an education to see how perceptive the store is in knowing the seasons big vintage labels: Halston, Biba, Ossie Clark, Jean Varon, Janice Wainwright, Missoni, Diane von Furstenberg (1970s), Koos Van Den Akker, Pucci (1960–1970s), Maud Frizon, Frank Usher (1950–1970s), Marimekko (1960–1970s), Jean Muir (1970s), Emilio Pucci (1960–1970s), and Gucci (1970s), as well as modern vintage luminaries Comme des Garçons, Betsey Johnson (punk label), and Moschino. Evidently versed in fashion history, the shop and its contents is an education in itself, and clearly provides a forum for "contemporizing" vintage in an updated environment.

Vintage has become for some, a successful specialist business, particularly online. But the experience of seeing a piece firsthand cannot be replaced. The quality at Palette remains superior to any other vintage store and is comparable in price. As Ellis says, "This fashion is sustainable, as well as recyclable because many of my customers want ageless, collectible pieces that are a talking point. There is kudos in going to a party and being able to sport a vintage designer label garment from 15 years ago. No one else is likely to be wearing it." Running a small enterprise can be hard, but with his genuine affection of clothes and commitment to the shop, Ellis's business acumen is acute. "I have to be robust, hand pick the pieces in store, and reinvent my proposition. Mixing the old with the new in design and interiors enables a lifestyle concept to prevail, and my customers like where the shop is situated. It's not high street. It's ever so slightly off and a little tucked away. They like it being their secret."

Vintage Finder Service

As well as being a treasure trove of resource and recycled, Palette shrewdly provides a new and unique vintage finder service. Customers request the look they require, and Ellis searches the globe to find the perfect, vintage outfit or item for that special event, holiday, or every day. Name your dream look along with your size, coloring, and budget, and with a little help from his 50 vintage suppliers across Paris, London, and the United States, what you are looking for will be found. Having himself been featured in *Vogue*, Ellis says, "It is like having 30 years of *Vogue* not only come to life, but at your own personal disposal. The evidence is undeniable. The service allows shoppers to see photographs of their prospective purchase via e-mail before buying it in person or by post and is available to customers across the United Kingdom. If the customer comes into the shop to buy the look, Ellis will also style the customer. A theme is requested, and Ellis obtains each specific piece in accordance with the style required, via his many sources if it is not already at hand in store. Who could ask for more?

By continually keeping abreast of fashion trends and incorporating other associated services, smaller specialist stores such as these will contain sustainable fashion that also sustains the stores.

Recycled and/or Redesigned

Creating something new from something old seems to be a logical solution in making fashion more sustainable. Because this is a relatively new field, precisely what it entails is still being uncovered. Yet an exhibition organized by the British Crafts Council called "Well Fashioned: Eco Style in the U.K." addressed the role of the recyclable. According to the council, the exhibition was "the first survey of the U.K.'s blossoming eco-fashion industry," and it "introduced the U.K.'s hottest designers who are making clothes that don't cost the Earth." It was a modest yet distinctive display that drew attention to a range of "green" fashion materials and techniques. Some outfits used fabrics like hemp, bamboo, and biodegradable and recycled plastics. But in terms of purely recycled fashion, one company was especially progressive: Junky.

Junky Styling: The Shop, the Production, the Concept

Once you view the upside-down shirts fitting parts they wouldn't normally embrace and skirts caressing the neck in their new form as a jacket, you know you have entered the topsy-turvy world that is Junky. These clothes bring a smile and a sense of stylish fun with a chic twist that commands attention. A fusion of vintage castoffs transformed into contemporary classics reflects the company's interest in popular culture and love of clothes and the people who wear them; this enabled the business to evolve into a small empire in the East End of London. Founded in 1997 by Annika Sanders and Kerry Seager, Junky is driven by the possibilities of the recyclable. Having traveled to areas like San Francisco and Tokyo and observed the resourcefulness of people in Vietnam and Thailand, on returning to London, Sanders and Seager were inspired to recycle clothes for themselves. Taking old men's suits bought from secondhand shops and turning them into experimental pinstripe and tweed creations to wear to London clubs in the early 1990s, Sanders and Seager were quickly commissioned to make outfits for friends, which led to a stall in Kensington Market. Junky very quickly outgrew the market stall and acquired a boutique in London's Brick Lane. This boutique remains the hub of Junky today. Housing the industrial design studio, this is where customers are actively encouraged to "participate" by bringing their old, worn-out clothes for Wardrobe Surgery; thus, customers are involved in the redesigning and recycling process. Junky has since secured stockists nationally and internationally. Its simple but effective concept is creative, innovative, educational, functional, and inclusive. Everything produced is recycled from quality secondhand clothing and deconstructed, recut, and completely transformed into a new product that belies the former identity of the raw material. All garments are made in-house or carefully outsourced locally. All products stocked in the Junky store are recycled, fair trade, and made from organic or ethically produced materials. Talking to Kerry and employee Kurt, it is obvious people here are happy in their work; this is reflected in their attitude to customers and in their approach to design. A can-do attitude has helped the business grow and built a talented team. "Off the Peg" original designs and "Made to Order" premium services are offered, plus collaboration projects with other designers. These are certainly attractive and achievable examples of what can be done to try and change entrenched old ideas and replace them with new, refreshing fashion designs.

As Kerry pointed out, "Junky doesn't conform to fashion trends because they want to promote timeless original designs and offer a repair service to customers." This has helped some garments last more than five years of extensive wear. The individual is the focus at Junky, as they ensure no two garments are the same; they can be cut from the same pattern, but the raw materials will always be different. Junky hopes to inspire all their customers to look at their discarded clothes, and other discarded items, with fresh eyes and a resourceful frame of mind. The future, therefore, is a busy one, with more international stockists planned, further London shows, and a pair of books being launched called "deconstruct-reconstruct," which include step-by-step, easy-to-execute designs for anyone to try at home. Furthermore, exciting collaborations are planned with high-profile designers in footwear and sportswear. Junky's success is surely testament to the potential of the recyclable.

TRAID

TRAID (Textile Recycling for Aid and International Development) is a UK charitable company launched in 1999 that continues to grow while remaining at the forefront of fashion via ingenuity and sharp redesigned garments and customized vintage. With its unique link between recycling and fashion retail, TRAID continues to raise money to fund international projects while helping promote recycling and waste reduction in the United Kingdom. Through its strong branding and bright, clean-looking stores with color-coded rails, it has gained a reputation for being innovative and edgy, appealing to a predominantly young, fashionable, and environmentally conscious audience. More than any other organization, its unique status and signature skills transform secondhand garments into futuristic forms of clothing, ensuring they remain one step ahead. Most noticeable when wandering about its accessible stores are their accessible prices. The clothing here is affordable to all, and that means for even the homeless and otherwise underprivileged. Through its price ranging, TRAID tries to ensure that there is something for everyone throughout its range of styles.

Media coordinator Kelly O'Connor Kay indicated how TRAID continues to produce street-style clothes by using "customizers," skilled workers who reconstruct donated materials to make new (i.e., recycled) garments. In so doing, TRAID actively strives to reduce waste that goes into landfill and encourages recycling in the United Kingdom. According to Kay, "Our network of 800 conveniently placed textile banks in communities across the United Kingdom makes the recycling of textiles easy and accessible. TRAID works with local councils, helping to reduce waste by paying for, installing, maintaining, and promoting textile-recycling banks to the local community. We also run a schools education program to encourage young people to recycle. Additionally we recycle 94 percent of all donations and collect nearly 2,500 tons of textiles per annum. Textiles are either brought to a central warehouse where they are sorted according to quality and style to be sold in shops, or sold in bulk through commercial dealers."

Such innovation and forethought means that they are looking to expand, and they have a list of well-known designers waiting to work with them. TRAID's recent fashion show invited designers to refashion an outfit from recycled items. The result was topical, innovative, and impressive, with some of the finest designs coming from the likes of top creatives Bora Aksu, Betty Jackson, and Weardowney.

TRAID Remade is the company's recycled clothing initiative, where designers create unique garments by customizing and reconstructing secondhand clothes and vintage fabrics that have been donated to the charity. Set up in 2000 as a direct response to the abundance of waste created by the fashion industry, it provides an ethical alternative to fashion on the high street. From recycling banks to the catwalk, TRAID Remade has transformed the image of secondhand clothing. As Kay explains, "The re-made clothes are dynamic and fresh. One of the most exciting aspects of working with donated materials is that designers have to be creative and reactive to each individual garment that is given to them or hunt to find appropriate material to suit their design. The results are as varied as the materials received. The nature of donated materials is that there is no control over what is donated, so instead designers must find ways of utilizing what is available. An alternative way of working is both necessary and encouraged to make the TRAID Remade clothing range individual and unique. The scope for experimentation and innovation is immense, which is what makes the job attractive and forever challenging for designers."

The creation of the TRAID Remade range is developed using a variety of techniques. Many are traditional craft techniques but used to create very contemporary clothing. Often a garment starts at the pattern-cutting stage, where either a length of vintage fabric is cut to the designer's requirements or a garment is taken apart, recut, and reconstructed to make something completely new. Sections of vintage fabrics are used to create appliqués on structured and modern shapes. The juxtaposition of these elements gives the garment its character. Graphics and printing techniques are endless in their possibilities and are used in striking contrast with the traditional floral of vintage fabrics. TRAID Remade collections offer a wide range of styles, from hard-edge images made from leather appliqués on distressed T-shirts to intricate crochet features.

Of course, doing anything about creating something new from something old and not including one of the most influential designers within that realm would be folly. Red or Dead company founder and personal design favorite Wayne Hemmingway, breath of fresh air in stale post punk 1980s and 1990s. Red or Dead's clothes were imbued with humor and kitsch, fueled by thrift and born out of financial necessity. Tamsin Kingswell (1998) explained how pop culture and fashion were inextricably linked and helped make the company the success it was before being sold at a profit and all the while extolling the virtues of recyclable goods during the 1980s when it was all about labels and constant consumption. Hemmingway remains in demand as a design consultant and has also helped promote TRAID.

Estethica at the British Fashion Council (BFC)
The thrilling thing about fashion is that, like art, its constituent components may not be easily classified or quantified. In fact, anything goes. Conceived of creativity, energy, and experimentation, it remains nevertheless an area ultimately "driven by the dollar." Perhaps this explains why many companies are employing people to assist with their transition to becoming environmentally friendly. Potentially, "going green" equates to bringing in gold. So, is it about jumping on the ethical bandwagon? It was therefore with initial skepticism that I greeted the new BFC Estethica stand. While there is a definite new attitude and evident awareness, both in business and from the public toward fashion consciousness, *why* is this emerging? The consumer desire is "green," and it speaks volumes. So, as this chapter is about focusing on the positive side of this new avenue, it is surely a fortunate

thing that there are several companies emerging and joining the sustainable front. Overall, the exposure that designers and exhibitors get at BFC is global and has an impact in areas that are directly related to fashion in many arenas. The fact that it has been adopted by the BFC helps denote its significance and growing acceptance in the fashion industry. Although impartial and independent, the BFC remains a powerful organization within the greater fashion industry and, as such, yields major influence in its ability to support designers and project concepts such as Estethica.

Deborah Milner's Ecoture

I wanted to end this chapter on a high note with high couture that has arisen out of an ethos and style that appears to encompass all the aspects under discussion except perhaps being financially beyond the majority of consumers' reach. It makes no illusion otherwise. Deborah Milner's Ecoture is ethical, sustainable, and wearable. It incorporates recycled old-stock tie fabric and is ultimately unique. It remains, at heart, clothing that highlights Brazil's Yawanawa tribe, a people whose traditions and lifestyle are rapidly changing, if not disappearing altogether. In a visual modern-day dialogue, it narrates a fashion tale more in tune with the natural world. These are captivating stories depicted in divine design. Certain dresses have been executed to incorporate artistic practices currently becoming defunct. Milner has also teamed up with Aveda, manufacturers of the popular skincare products. She and Aveda both have a long-standing and active interest in the environment and in producing sustainable products; together, they are endeavoring to raise the fashion industry's conscience as to what can be achieved. Ecoture translates Aveda's socially responsible business partnerships into Milner's high fashion to arrive upon a high couture that is guaranteed to be recyclable because it is so collectible. It is composed of materials and craftsmanship that render it desirable and exquisitely beautiful, both in aesthetics and application. To see a

Debra Milner design is to see a sincerely beguiling work of art. This is vintage of the future.

The Yawanawa dress, for example, depicts the native Brazilian tribe and is a mixed media mélange that is part art, part fashion, part photography, and part anthropology (see Figure 15.4). It communicates on a new level—viscerally, literally, and visually. It tells its own story, statically and almost frozen in time; like a record of an already fast disappearing environment, its poignancy poses the question, how will this way of life be in the not-too-distant future? It could be said that it's crass to address this subject matter in such a way; yet it is often from beauty that we are moved and enthused, and there is surely nothing more beautiful than nature itself. Milner's designs are also inspired by the ecology of the Amazon and its people, as is also shown in the Rousseau dress (see Figure 15.5). Wholly created from recycled material of old tie stock, a jungle scene is hand sewn using a mixture of appliqué and reverse appliqué. The unusual white wedding dress design is made from recycled plastic bags and recycled netting underskirt then furnished with crystals.

Milner explains, "With the benefit of so many years in the fashion industry, I have been able to put together an experienced and committed team, including Karen Spurgin, who is responsible for co-coordinating textile research; Penny Walsh, an expert on natural dyes; and Sally Payne, couture pattern maker. We have approached a different aspect of eco-clothing with each of the dresses. This is essentially an experimental research collection to try and see what is viable within their financial budget too. We have used a combination of organic and fair-trade fabrics. These include handwoven fabric by Women Weavers; a fair-trade weaving collective based in India, and recycled fabrics such as "end-of-line" tie fabrics donated by Mantero, an Italian fabric manufacturers with a good environmental record. Fabrics have been hand dyed using natural dyes.

Notably the recycled elements within the designs surely indicate that there is waste from various industry sources, including high-end

FIGURE 15.4. Materials for Debra Milner's Yawanawa dress, silk duchess and recycled old stock tie fabric, were donated by Mantero textiles in Italy. For this dress, silk threads were hand-dyed using natural dyes. Palm leaves from the Jardim botanical gardens in Rio de Janeiro in Brazil inspired this dress, which was created in conjunction with the Aveda Corporation. (Photo by Manuel Rason.)

FIGURE 15.5. Silk fabric for Debra Milner's Rousseau dress was donated by Mantero textiles in Italy from old stock tie fabrics. The jungle scene was hand-sewn using a mixture of appliqué and reverse appliqué and backed on a mixture of silk organza from Women Weave Company and Italian "super organza." Inspiration came from the layering of leaf shapes in the Brazilian Rain Forest and was interpreted as a Henri Rousseau painting. It was created in conjunction with the Aveda Corporation. (Photo by Manuel Rason.)

and thus exclusive, which can be utilized fully to create stunning designs, sustainably sourced and ecologically sound. Whether this could be an enduring source is unpredictable. Milner concedes that the work is challenging, but she is determined to encourage more environmentally friendly and socially responsible business practices within the fashion industry. This is a result of her work so far; she is in consultation with a variety of companies, all of which surely amounts to a promising arena full of possibility.

Conclusion

Consumer demands have changed. Attitudes toward what are basically sencondhand garments have contributed to their becoming sought after, as opposed to throwaway items, particularly when they are fashionable, comfortable, affordable, and generally in good condition. Previously, certain members of the fashion fraternity adopted a haughty haute couture stance and frosty approach toward recycled garments, but like so much in fashion, this has come full circle to a more conscious awareness, and a trend toward vintage. This is surely a step in the right direction, whether in vintage Manolos or eco shoes with a safe and pure conscience from McCartney. It doesn't have to be perfect. We are only human, after all. I'm as partial to a bit of bling as anyone. But in order to try and be sustainable, we need to consume less and appreciate more. Surely then, by cherishing what we have, we can create a new branch of fashion, one where the trend is to repair, rework, redesign, and rewind. By taking a step back and reviewing, we can move forward with a greater understanding and awareness. From small shoots, blossoms emerge. It is therefore essential that smaller businesses be encouraged and sustained. Whether working independently or in conjunction with larger companies and the fashion industry as a whole, such unison is surely progressive. Fashion and its future course is a fascinating, perplexing, enlightening, and ultimately optimistic area full of potential and positivity. Realistically, we compose one body that, in fashion, often surrenders to the imposed perimeters placed upon it at every avenue. Will things ever really change then? Fashion trends play a major role but are not always easy to predict. Still, there are ways of influencing fashion to highlight certain styles. But clothes are about people, and people can be very unpredictable. What is apparent is that by utilizing what we have already as best we can, it is possible that the past can be the new future.

References

Palette media information. (n.d.). Retrieved July 10, 2007, from http://www.palette-london.com/

British Arts Festivals Association press release. (2002, March). *New research shows that festivals mean business.* London: BAFA.

Bestival Festival. (2006, September). *Despatch their coolhunters to Bestival for latest trends and fashion mix styles/materials.* Retrieved from http://www.trendhunter.com/

British Fashion Council. (2006, September). Estethica. London fashion week exhibition and discussion with press department.

Easier Lifestyle. (2006, November 16). Victoria Beckham starts Oxfam trend. Easier Lifestyle. Retrieved 2006 from http://www.easier.com/view/Lifestyle/Fashion/Trends/article-83917.html

Ethical Marketing Group. (2005). *The Good Shopping Guide.* (2005). London: Ethical Marketing Group.

Constantino, M. (1991). *Fashions of a decade: The 1930s.* London: B. T. Batsford Ltd.

Hamnett, K. (2006, September). Personal interview.

Goodwood press information. (n.d.). The revival policy for dress. Retrieved from http://www.goodwood.co.uk.

Jenkyn-Jones, S. (2005). *Fashion Design.* London: Laurence King Publishing.

Kingswell, T. (1998). *Red or dead: The good, the bad and the ugly.* London: Thames & Hudson.

Lawrence, E. (2007, May). Time Out Pullout Guide. *Time Out* magazine, London..

Liberty of London. (2006, August). Personal interview with press department and customer relations at vintage concession.

MacKrell, A. (1979). *An illustrated history of fashion*. London: Quite Specific Media Group.

Marks & Spencer's Magazine. (2006, September). *The "vintage" look collection*. London: Marks & Spencer.

Milner, D. (2006). Aveda press release on Ecoture range. London.

O'Connor Kay, K. (2006). Press and Communications Interview for TRAID.

Palmer, A., & Clark, H. (2005). *Old clothes, new look*. London: Berg.

Early, R. (2006, March). *Well fashioned: Towards our eco fashion future*. Retrieved from Crafts Council Web site: http://www.craftscouncil.org.uk/wellfashioned/noflash/essayp2.html

Watson, L. (2002). *Vogue twentieth century fashion: 100 years of style by decade and designer*. London: Carlton Books.

Woodcock, C. (2006, September) Personal interview with press manager, Bestival.

Junky Styling (n.d.) Press information and interviews with employees.

Brooklyn Industries
Interview by Janet Hethorn, May 2007

Many ideas were expressed in this section that address the need to find more environmentally sustainable ways to develop fabrics and clothing. Beginning with inspiration and strategies from the wearable art movement through the impact and opportunities occurring within textile and fiber development, challenges and options were presented. Then guidance was provided in the form of sustainable sourcing suggestions and models. Completing the section, we were inspired by the many examples of design explorations with a focus on recycle and reuse from vintage to haute couture.

One company that provides us with an insight into how it has worked through many of these options is Brooklyn Industries. What began in 1998 as a way to make a living through the creative efforts of two artists, Lexy Funk and Vahap Avsar, is now a business involved in design, production, and retail offerings. There are seven Brooklyn Industries retail locations in New York City, and all of them are in corner locations within distinct New York neighborhoods. Its motto, "Live, Work, Create" illustrates its commitment to enhance the world around them. It has explored sustainability, in its many facets, through its interactions with artists and consumers as well as its product development processes and retail environments.

I had the privilege of interviewing Lexy Funk, president of Brooklyn Industries, in order to find out more about its explorations and practices. Following are her comments and my elaborations.

How Is Your Company Involved in Sustainable Practices?

"We started the company with a recycled product: cut-up billboards," Funk explains. Funk and Avsar's first product was a messenger bag. They rented an old factory in Brooklyn and began manufacturing from discarded vinyl billboards. Now they create garment designs from organic cotton, Ingeo™ fabric, and applications on garments, using leftover materials from the production of other garments. "We create simple bodies that you can add something to, applications that are decorative, a bird, or an animal, or some funky design, or a star, and it seems it's suited to a casual garment," she says. The company has an in-house sewing team that actually does this. Its graphic designer will come up with the idea for the kind of cutout, whether the designer thinks that crowns are interesting or favors handmade water tower applications, and then the work is done right in the design studio. "We couldn't do that anywhere else," states Funk. "Even with the billboards, you couldn't apply mass manufacturing. We would cut out old billboards—certain sections were interesting, others weren't. It's a manual process, as you have to handpick." Their best efforts with sus-

(Photograph by Joe Leonard.)

tainability, she explains, are with fabric, and the company orders goods from producers that use environmentally friendly practices such as nonchemical, natural inks, and organic cotton, because recycling is quite difficult at the garment level. "It would be very challenging to ask them [other producers] to do recycled or reused, as there is not enough control. It's always going to be a selective market, recycling."

Brooklyn Industries provides a lifetime guarantee on all its bags. "We tell our customer that you shouldn't throw away your bag. We can actually fix it for you, free of charge," Funk says.

"Everybody would always buy organic if they could, if the pricing was similar and the design was good. We are just testing it now. We're not a very large company. We buy grey goods already in the market and are limited to what the market is already doing in terms of fabric," Funk explains. They have begun developing T-shirts from Ingeo™ fabric.

"Ingeo is incredible, but very expensive," Funk says. If the pricing was within what our customer was interested in, [we could do more]." I ask why the T-shirts made of Ingeo™ were so expensive and she explains, "If the grey goods were in the United States, it would be much easier to do at a reasonable cost," she clarifies. "Since requirements for fabric purchase are often five to ten thousand meters, we have to rely on mills that have already produced it and can sell smaller lots. Our other idea recently is to partner with other designers who have already investigated this and are using it." Funk aptly informs me, "In production, it's often a numbers game. What I am able to do, what I can afford to do, underlies what I *can* do."

How Do You Make Choices about Sustainable Action?

As they learned from their original business practice, sustainability is also cost-effective. "We could only build a greener store when we had a bit better cash flow," Funk explains. "A lot of sustainable practices come out of not having any other options. We developed a brilliant product (i.e., the messenger bag) but didn't have to pay for the bill-

(Photograph by Joe Leonard.)

boards. Labor was expensive, but the fabric was free. We got it from an erector, and he wanted us to donate to a local Catholic charity. In exchange, we got the billboards. We got more than we could ever possibly use. You could never make enough bags to recycle all of them. Our first sustainable practice was because it was a cool idea, but also it was because it was free."

One of Brooklyn Industries' guiding principles is about community citizenship. Its mission is to "contribute positively to the communities around our stores and to the world. Operate with honesty, integrity, and responsibility." It has demonstrated this through its selection of studio and retail locations, as well as through its business practices and interactions with consumers. Funk explains, "We are a part of revitalizing neighborhoods, going into neighborhoods that are up and coming." She further elaborates, "We only went where we could afford it and where our customer is. As the neighborhoods mature and become less edgy, it's going to get more expensive. As we grow, we have been part of a revitalization in Brooklyn neighborhoods."

"The negative side is eventual gentrification," says Funk. "This can be negative and positive. There are some pretty crime-ridden areas, not a lot of economic development. But the buildings are already there. Even through your choice of real estate, you can be a part of making something very positive, not a new shopping mall. It's a place that you're making vital. People are walking by and walking in. All our locations are very subway accessible. It makes it interesting, also more accountable. People will tell you what they like and what they don't like. It's nice. You get immediate feedback. We can produce a more sustainable item if our customer likes it and buys it. It's almost like the consumer can vote."

The company also has a unique philosophy about consumption and product longevity. Funk explains, "We are also about not overconsuming. We're selling clothes, a consumptive act, but the idea that you don't have to throw anything away is really a third-world concept. My partner [Avasar] came from Turkey, a huge culture of repair. His father had repair shops, repairing umbrellas, stoves, refrigerators, bicycles, basic mechanical objects. My partner came to the business with that mind-set. We could build a business out of nothing, free fabric, and could go into neighborhoods with our nonconsumerist approach." She recommends, "Be mindful of what you are producing and mindful of how you are using your resources. Turn the paper to the other side."

What Is Your Most Innovative Action or Aspect?

"Our design," Funk answered immediately. "We are perpetually creative and artistic." A look through its Web site, www. brooklynindustries.com, shows its passion for artist collaboration. One of its guiding principles about design is "create the most innovative and artistic designs for everyday living." Funk backs this up by stating, "We approach our design much quirkier than others and add a lot of interesting twists. The way we run the company is creative and artistic. We come up with the best business practices through innovative, artistic, and local collaboration."

What Is the Most Challenging?

In answer to the question, Funk simply states, "The pricing question and the availability of fabric."

What Are the Possibilities for Sustainable Futures?
New Directions?

Clearly this area is something that the people behind Brooklyn Industries have given a lot of thought to. After several years of growing a company with an artistic commitment that spills out to the community, and exploring and implementing any sustainable practice that makes sense, with the development and repair of products and throughout the interior of their new Chelsea store, Funk knowingly answers, "To think about the life cycle of the product, where it's made, how it's shipped to you, how it's bought, and what happens at the end of it. Being responsible for the entire process. It's a whole new way of looking at the product, and also requires thinking of new ways of engaging with the consumer. I think that it's going to be more relevant and more interesting and it's very pertinent. If the consumer starts to get engaged in that thought process, as a business, you will be able to make different decisions because it won't just be about price. Because the U.S. clothing market is so indexed to cheap suppliers of clothing, people don't want to pay a lot of money. If the processes change, they may be more willing to pay more. Markets or consumers have to change. Unless the consumer wants it, it's not going to happen."

Somehow, I believe that Brooklyn Industries will continue to innovate and lead in this effort. Their grassroots strategy, informed by necessity and opportunity, and embedded in the creative process, is at the core of driving this change.

INDEX